REBEL RULERS

REBEL RULERS

Insurgent Governance and
Civilian Life during War

Zachariah Cherian Mampilly

CORNELL UNIVERSITY PRESS   **ITHACA AND LONDON**

First published 2011 by Cornell University Press
First printing, Cornell Paperbacks, 2015

Printed in the United States of America

Library of Congress Cataloging-in-Publication Data

Mampilly, Zachariah Cherian, 1977–
    Rebel rulers : insurgent governance and civilian life during war / Zachariah Cherian Mampilly.
        p. cm.
    Includes bibliographical references and index.
    ISBN 978-0-8014-4913-0 (cloth : alk. paper)
    ISBN 978-1-5017-0068-2 (pbk. : alk. paper)
  1. Insurgency—Sri Lanka. 2. Insurgency—Sudan. 3. Insurgency—Congo (Democratic Republic) 4. Civilians in war—Sri Lanka. 5. Civilians in war—Sudan. 6. Civilians in war—Congo (Democratic Republic) 7. Sri Lanka—History—Civil War, 1983–2009. 8. Sudan—History—Civil War, 1983–2005. 9. Congo (Democratic Republic)—Politics and government—1997– I. Title.
    DS489.84.M356   2011
    321—dc22   2011005004

Cornell University Press strives to use environmentally responsible suppliers and materials to the fullest extent possible in the publishing of its books. Such materials include vegetable-based, low-VOC inks and acid-free papers that are recycled, totally chlorine-free, or partly composed of nonwood fibers. For further information, visit our website at www.cornellpress.cornell.edu.

Cloth printing   10 9 8 7 6 5 4 3 2 1
Paperback printing   10 9 8 7 6 5 4 3 2 1

For my late father, Cherian, who taught me to be critical, and for my mother, Saroj, who showed me how to be strong

This language of the "leap" is evocative; revolutionary action requires a moment in which one refuses the status quo.... The "clear leap" implies a work of imagination, the ability to believe that a different future might be possible, despite the seeming inevitability of a crushing present. It does not concede the future to the present, but imagines it as something still in the balance, something that can be fought over.

—Grace Kyungwon Hong, "The Future of Our Worlds"

Contents

Illustrations

Preface

During the 1997–98 academic year, I was a visiting student at the University of Dar es Salaam in Tanzania. It was famous for fermenting rebellion from its heyday in the 1970s, when giants such as Walter Rodney strolled the campus preaching the perils of underdevelopment, and perhaps no other university in the world has played as formative a role in shaping the thoughts and actions of such a preponderance of contemporary rebel leaders. A brief roll call of individuals affiliated directly with the campus includes prominent insurgents turned leaders such as Yoweri Museveni, founder of the National Resistance Movement/Army (NRM/A) and now president of Uganda; the late John Garang, founder of the Sudan People's Liberation Movement/Army (SPLM/A) and the former vice president of Sudan; the late Laurent Kabila, leader of multiple Congolese insurgencies from the 1960s to the 1990s and the former president of the Democratic Republic of Congo; and widely known figures such as Ruth First, the South African communist leader.[1]

Despite being at least a generation removed from its pinnacle as the intellectual hotbed for the anticolonial and antiapartheid struggles, Chuo Kikuu cha Dar es Salaam (its widely used Kiswahili moniker) in 1997 was a university again caught within a maelstrom of broader social and political changes affecting the region. Arriving on campus in August of that year, I divided my time between courses, thesis work on the local Asian community, days at the beach, and nights listening to the emerging sounds of East African hip-hop (bongo flava). Although I had little understanding of the complex web of wars taking place in the region, one thing was immediately apparent: both the country and the region were in the midst of a broader transformation that has fundamentally reshaped East and

---

1. Issa Shivji, another prominent intellectual only recently retired from the university (affectionately known as the Hill), documented its history in his memoirs. His ruminations (1996, 32–44) on university life capture both the sense of possibility and the disillusionment felt by those who believed that it could become the center of radical politics in the region. As a member of the University Students African Revolutionary Front (USARF), Shivji recalls visits to campus by seminal political and intellectual figures including Stokely Carmichael, Cheddi Jagan, Gora Ebrahim, C. L. R. James, and A. M. Babu, among others. Composed of students from around eastern and southern Africa, USARF members met weekly and engaged in efforts to support radical groups, including the Frente de Libertação de Moçambique (Liberation Front of Mozambique, FRELIMO) insurgency in neighboring Mozambique. Museveni was a founder and leader of the group, and Garang was a member during his time at the Hill.

Central Africa over the past two decades. Domestically, Tanzania was dealing with a wrenching shift away from the statecentric socialist policies it had pursued during the reign of Julius Nyerere, who had stepped down under pressure in 1993 but continued to exert substantial influence over political debates in the region. Regionally, the end of the Cold War had triggered violent disruptions along Tanzania's western borders, with troubles in Burundi followed by the breakout of the horrendous violence in Rwanda that threatened to pull the entire region into the maelstrom. In 1996, two years after the Rwandan Genocide, this is precisely what happened as Mobutu Sese Seko, abandoned by his Western allies, fled the region under pressure from an invading army led by Congolese exiles, several of whom, like Laurent Kabila, had bided their time in Dar es Salaam under Nyerere's munificent gaze.

While taking a yearlong seminar on Central African history with the exiled Congolese Marxist academic Ernest Wamba dia Wamba, I had only a vague sense that he was about to make a direct contribution to the latest chapter of Congo's tumultuous history. Wamba dia Wamba and Kabila both had close ties to Nyerere. And the Tanzanian president had introduced each man to the rising regional hegemons—Yoweri Museveni and Paul Kagame, the Ugandan and Rwandan presidents, respectively. But though both Congolese leaders moved in similar circles, the distaste that Wamba dia Wamba had for Kabila—whom he regarded as little more than a charlatan—was palpable. Kabila's networking with power brokers in Dar es Salaam paid off handsomely in 1996 when he was plucked from relative obscurity to be the Congolese face of the insurgency that rose to power in Zaire. Wamba dia Wamba, despite active efforts to engage with the now-president Kabila, was consistently rebuffed as the new Congolese administration began to resemble the Mobutu regime it had just replaced. And just two months after I returned to the United States, this thoughtful and soft-spoken academic went on to become the president of a new insurgency that broke out in August of 1998, again with Rwandan and Ugandan support. His professed desire (which I've always perceived as genuine) to bring about a revolution in Congo based on Maoist principles of popular organization was incompatible with the widely held perception of the insurgency he led as a particularly heinous example of African brutality. This contrast led me to the first question that has driven my research ever since: What explains the gap between the intentions of insurgent leaders and their actual behavior on the front lines?

After finishing my undergraduate degree in 1999, I returned to Africa—this time to Nigeria during the transition from military rule—where I went to work for a local human rights organization, the Constitutional Rights Project in Lagos. At the time, Lagos was a city in flux, just barely coming to terms with the ruinous effects of the dictatorial Sani Abacha regime. Abacha, according to the widely accepted sordid—yet darkly humorous—account of what happened, was killed a year before my arrival by a lethal combination of an overdose of Viagra and four Indian prostitutes flown in by private jet for his final dalliance. In office, he had presided over the extended atrophy of the Nigerian state, transforming a once-expansive state bureaucracy into little more than a corrupt appendage of the military. This state of affairs was succinctly captured by the alternate translation of the acronym for the National Electric Power Authority (NEPA), referred to more commonly as Never Expect Power Always.[2] While Afrobeat and Pentecostal sounds blared out of bus windows, I negotiated a streetscape in which block by block, area boys (local gangs) competed with corrupt police to extort a population beaten down by five years of dictatorial rule. Living in a rundown part of Surulere and working in areas that had born the brunt of the breakdown of Nigerian political and social institutions led me to a second question that has occupied my imagination for the past decade: What happens when the state disappears?

It was perhaps inevitable that these two questions would come to shape my research focus, though when I first began this project, I could scarcely have foreseen the scope of the book you have in front of you. But with hindsight, the questions that have nagged me since my earlier days in Tanzania and Nigeria frame much of my analysis below. What I have come to realize and what I hope that I am able to communicate below is the importance of understanding political and social structures in relation to the actual lived experiences of individuals on the ground. For too many of the world's people, formal state institutions are paper entities. Into this void many other forms of authority can and do emerge, shaped by the agency of countless civilians whose stories are too often ignored by academics unable to account for the microlevel processes that commonly determine human experiences in the developing world. As both a political scientist and a scholar concerned with representing those who often cannot speak their own stories, I hope that I have done an accurate job of describing such structures and practices from the top down as well as from the bottom up.

The fact that I visited areas of the map controlled by insurgents often puzzles those interested enough to ask about my research. They are often curious about how I was able to safely visit the areas that I did in the process of researching this book. What I came to discover during my fieldwork is that the true image of any place is revealed only with proximity. From afar what may look like sporadic or random actions and events—and hence off limits to researchers—can evince surprising patterns and sturdiness from a closer vantage point. The key, of

---

2. Rotimi Babatunde, a friend and playwright living in Lagos, explained to me that after NEPA was half privatized and renamed National Electric Power, Public Limited Company (NEP, Plc), the wordplay was adjusted to "Never Expect Power, Please Light Candle."

course, is to have a knowledgeable network on the ground that can help you avoid the pitfalls while pointing you toward what's important. And as always, good luck and an American passport don't hurt.

To the individuals and institutions that have shepherded this project from its inception I am truly grateful. In Uganda, I am indebted to Ham Namakkajjo for giving me a place to crash on my frequent stops in Kampala. Faculty at Makerere University and the Centre for Basic Research, including Joe Oloka-Onyango and Simba Kayunga, helped put me in touch with a wide variety of experts on conflict in the region. The same applies to Zachary Lomo of the Refugee Law Project and Marcel Akpovo and the Amnesty International office in Kampala. Without their regional expertise, I know I would have been lost.

In Sudan, I am grateful to the staff of Jesuit Refugee Services, especially Tracy O'Heir and Aden Raj, who helped me into South Sudan for the first time and provided me with a bed, food, and excellent conversation in Nimule. Geoffrey Mangwe was patient as I plotted my travels. And though I decided not to take his advice to go by motorcycle, he was the first to make visiting Sudan imaginable. In Cairo, Natalie Forcier showed me around neighborhoods filled with young Southern Sudanese, introducing me to the city's vibrant diasporic community. And Bakry Al-Jack patiently answered my questions and shared his own network in South Sudan. In D.R. Congo, I am grateful to Marcos Lorenzana, who gave me a safe place to stay and a stiff drink when soldiers decided to harass me out of my hotel room. And Jason Stearns has been generous with his extraordinary knowledge and networks on the ground. In Sri Lanka, Karunyan Arulanantham, Hari Chandran, and Arjunan Ethirveerasingam helped me with some difficult travels, putting me in touch with all the right people. And faculty members of the Department of Political Science at the University of Colombo were supportive of my research and full of information on the conflict.

Much of the work for this book was done in the Department of Political Science at the University of California, Los Angeles. UCLA is an extraordinary university in a fascinating city, and I am grateful for the time I was able to spend there. I was lucky to have the support of Michael Ross, who gave me insightful feedback on my work at every step of the way. Richard Sklar and Daniel Posner shared their deep knowledge generously. In addition, other colleagues read parts of the manuscript, often challenging me to take the analysis further and in different directions. I am especially thankful to Adrian Felix, Bryan Rhodes, Cesar Zucco, Raquel Zamora, Paul Osher, Fred Lee, Dan Young, Joe Wright, Xin Zhang, Anoop Sarbahi, and Kim Dionne. In addition, the Race and Ethnic Politics (REP) program provided me with a home in the department. I am grateful to Tamura Howard, Lahra Smith, Hector Perla, Murrell Brooks, Dontraneil Clayborne, Natasha Behl, Marie Elena Guadamuz, Laura Rodriguez, Chris Lee, Dena

Montague, Alfonso Gonzales, and all the other members of the REP collective for their intellectual and personal support.

At UCLA I am also indebted to Raymond Rocco for his wisdom and for the best job in the university, working with the freshman summer program for low-income and first-generation college students. Steve Commins provided contacts and access to cutting-edge research in addition to his sage advice. Sondra Hale offered the right encouragement at just the right times. And Mark Sawyer has been a friend and guide into the machinations of academia. I also owe a special thanks to Glenda Jones, the former graduate student adviser.

Edmond Keller and the Globalization Research Center-Africa provided me with key funding at an important juncture in my work. UCLA's International Institute provided financial support through the Alice Belkin Scholarship, and the Institute for Global Conflict and Cooperation provided me with a writing fellowship at a key juncture. The Department of Political Science was generous with financial support and gave me the opportunity to teach my own seminar related to my research, an experience that allowed me to tap the minds of some very bright undergraduate students.

At Vassar I have profited from a highly congenial and supportive work environment with an exceptional group of faculty and thoughtful students. In addition, I am grateful to multiple faculty research funds that allowed me to return to Sudan in the summer of 2008, to D.R. Congo in the summer of 2009, and to Sri Lanka early in 2010. Vassar also provided funds to help with the publication of this book, for which I am truly grateful. I've also benefited from the research assistance of several impressive and promising undergraduate research assistants, including Frances Meyo, Bonnie Velez, Ayse Yildirim, and especially Carola Beeney and Rachel Hui.

I have been privileged to discuss my ideas on the subject of rebel governance in a variety of stimulating environments. The graduate seminar at Nuffield College, Oxford University, invited me to present portions of this project in March of 2007. The Order, Conflict and Violence Program at Yale University welcomed me to do the same in February of 2008. The Program in African Studies at Northwestern University invited me out in February of 2010. And finally, the Hansen Lecture series at San Diego State University gave me one last opportunity to test my ideas for this book in front of an audience in April 2010. I am truly grateful to the organizers of each. I've also presented portions of this book at a variety of other forums, including the Working Group in African Political Economy at UCLA and the Africana Seminar Series at Vassar, as well as panels at the annual meetings of the American Political Science Association, the International Studies Association, the African Studies Association, the Western Political Science Association, and the Sudan Studies Association.

The penultimate draft of this book was prepared during a monthlong residency at the Rockefeller Foundation's Bellagio Center in Italy. I am grateful to Pilar Palacio and the entire staff of the center for making my time productive and enjoyable. I'm also indebted to the diverse group of residents with whom I shared my time for the numerous stimulating conversations about my work and, more important, theirs.

The book has benefited from the guidance of many. First and foremost, my editor, Roger Haydon, and two anonymous reviewers at Cornell University Press pushed me in thoughtful and productive ways. Nelson Kasfir has been a singular influence and advocate for this project. Ana Arjona, Severine Autesserre, and Pierre Englebert were extraordinarily generous with advice on how to improve the book. Rotimi Babatunde, Christine Cheng, Benson Eluma, Susan Fassig, Amir Idris, Arthur Rhodes, Ingrid Samset, Lee Seymour, Tyrone Simpson, Paul Staniland, and Jeevan Thiagarajah read chapters, provided feedback, and shared their own work. Simba Kayunga, Nagalingam Ethirveerasingam, Jeremy Weinstein, Will Reno, Denis Tull, Stathis Kalyvas, Elisabeth Wood, and Carolyn Nordstrom offered their work and advice generously.

I would be remiss if I did not mention the support of my undergrad and M.A. advisers. At Tufts I owe the largest debt to Pearl Robinson and Jeanne Penvenne but also to Sugata Bose, Modhumita Roy, and Sherman Teichman. At the University of Dar es Salaam, Elaine Wamba was generous with her time and compassion. And the late Philippe Wamba I consider an intellectual mentor. At Columbia I thank Andrea Bartoli, Anthony Marx, Al Stepan, and especially, Mahmood Mamdani, who shared his sage advice on this project from its inception. And Sylvia Lane of North Central High School in Indianapolis, I thank you for getting me to college when many others were ready to give up.

My family has been supportive of my work from day one, and I cannot begin to express my deep gratitude for this. My siblings, Shobita and Thomas, and mother, Saroj, have all managed to thrive, despite the loss of our father more than a decade and a half ago. They remain my inspiration. My extended family—Sheila, Sam, Amit, Zachary, and Priya Johnson—have always brought me back from challenging periods with love and laughter. I also owe thanks to my in-laws, Carrie Mampilly, Lori Johnson, Raj and Rani Gowrinathan, Ramanan Gowrinathan, and Shanthi and Swapneel Shah. And to my five nephews—Cherian, Makana, Tadashi, Sohan, and Sathiyan—all born during significant junctures in this project, I look forward to watching you grow up to become confident young men who perhaps one day will read this book.

My friends have been supportive of my work and have helped at every step of the way to make this possible. I owe special thanks to Varun Soni, Nitin Puri, Emery Wright, Chrissy Greer, Jerome Lebleu, Rena Tucker, and Seth Markle, who have kept me humble and laughing throughout. Rishi Manchanda, Biju Matthew, Dileepan Sivapathasundaram, David Baker, and Saba Waheed helped me to remember that academic work has little use if it is not grounded in the concerns of real people. In addition to being a close friend, Dustin Ross came through with the beautiful maps showing the areas of rebel control scattered through the case studies. I owe a debt of gratitude to Adam Branch, who not only accompanied me on my first visits to Congo and Sudan but has always been a friend and influence on my own work.

Finally, to my wife, Nimmi Gowrinathan—at every step you have been my partner. And though our mutual career choices may leave others wondering about our suitability to be parents, I'm honored and thrilled to have brought our son, Cherian "Che" Raja, into this world with you.

Abbreviations

ADP	Alliance Démocratique des Peuple (D.R. Congo)
ANC	African National Congress (South Africa)
AFDL	Alliance des Forces Démocratiques pour la Libération du Congo
CAAP	Conflict-affected areas program (Sri Lanka)
CANS	Civil Authority of the New Sudan
CBO	Community-based organization
CDC	County Development Committee (Sudan)
CJP	Commission Justice et Paix (D.R. Congo)
CNDP	Congrès National pour la Défense du Peuple (D.R. Congo)
CNRD	Conseil National de Résistance pour la Démocratie (D.R. Congo)
CPA	comprehensive peace agreement (Sudan)
CPB	Communist Party of Burma
CPN-M	Communist Party of Nepal-Maoist
CRS	Catholic Relief Services
ELN	Ejército de Liberación Nacional (Colombia)
EPLF	Eritrean People's Liberation Front
FACE	Friends of African Children Educational Foundation (Sudan)
FALINTIL	Forças Armadas da Libertação Nacional de Timor-Leste
FAR	Forces Armées Rwandaises
FARC	Fuerzas Armadas Revolucionarias de Colombia
FLC	Front de Libération du Congo
FLN	Front de Libération Nationale (Algeria)
FMLN	El Frente Farabundo Martí para la Liberación Nacional (El Salvador)
FP	Federal Party (Sri Lanka)
FRELIMO	Frente de Libertação de Moçambique
GAM	Gerakan Aceh Merdeka
GoI	Government of India
GoS	Government of Sudan
GoSL	Government of Sri Lanka
GoSS	Government of South Sudan
HEC	High Executive Council (Sudan)
IAS	International Aid Sweden
ICC	International Criminal Court

ICG	International Crisis Group
IDP	internally displaced person
IHL	International Humanitarian Law
INGO	international nongovernmental organization
IPKF	Indian Peacekeeping Force
JIU	joint integration unit (Sudan)
JRS	Jesuit Refugee Services
JVP	Janatha Vimukthi Peramuna (Sri Lanka)
KDP	Kurdish Democratic Party
LRA	Lord's Resistance Army (Uganda)
LTTE	Liberation Tigers of Tamil Eelam (Sri Lanka)
MAGRIVI	Mutuelle Agricole des Virunga (D.R. Congo)
MLC	Mouvement pour la Libération du Congo
MNC	multinational corporation
MNLF	Moro National Liberation Front (Philippines)
MONUC	Mission de l' Organisation des Nations Unies en République Démocratique du Congo
MoU	memorandum of understanding
MRLZ	Mouvement Révolutionnaire pour la Libération du Zaire
MSF	Médecins Sans Frontiers
NCP	National Congress Party (Sudan)
NDA	National Democratic Alliance (Sudan)
NGO	nongovernmental organization
NRM/A	National Resistance Movement/Army (Uganda)
NPFL	National Patriotic Front of Liberia
OCHA	Office for the Coordination of Humanitarian Affairs
OLS	Operation Lifeline Sudan
PAIGC	Partido Africano da Independência da Guiné e Cabo Verde
PDS	Planning and Development Secretariat (Sri Lanka)
PMHC	Political Military High Command (Sudan)
PRP	Parti de la Révolution Populaire (D.R. Congo)
PUK	Patriotic Union of Kurdistan
RCD	Rassemblement Congolais pour la Démocratie
RENAMO	Resistência Nacional Moçambicana
RPF	Rwandan Patriotic Front
RUF	Revolutionary United Front (Sierra Leone)
SAF	Sudan Alliance Forces
SDAT	SPLM Development Assistance Technical Office
SNM	Somalia National Movement
SSIM	South Sudan Independence Movement

SL	Sendero Luminoso (Peru)
SLFP	Sri Lanka Freedom Party
SPLM/A	Sudan People's Liberation Movement/Army
SRRA	Sudan Relief and Rehabilitation Association
SRRC	Sudan Relief and Rehabilitation Commission
SSIM	South Sudan Independence Movement
SSLM	South Sudan Liberation Movement
TAAP	Tsunami-Affected Areas Program (Sri Lanka)
TEEC	Tamil Eelam Educational Council (Sri Lanka)
TEEDO	Tamil Eelam Economic Development Organization (Sri Lanka)
TPD	Tous pour la Paix et le Développement (D.R. Congo)
TPLF	Tigray People's Liberation Front (Ethiopia)
TRO	Tamils Rehabilitation Organization (Sri Lanka)
TUF	Tamil United Front (Sri Lanka)
TULF	Tamil United Liberation Front (Sri Lanka)
UN	United Nations
UNHCR	United Nations High Commissioner for Refugees
UNITA	União Nacional pela Independência Total de Angola
UNP	United National Party (Sri Lanka)
USAID	United States Agency for International Development
USARF	University Students African Revolutionary Front (Tanzania)
ZANU	Zimbabwe African National Union

REBEL RULERS

INTRODUCTION
Governing Rebels

> **Administration is very difficult, very complicated, especially in war-time. Figuring out how to link administration to political values while you are still in the bush is a very serious matter.**
>
> —Ernest Wamba dia Wamba, Congolese rebel leader

> **It must be considered that there is nothing more difficult to carry out, nor more doubtful of success, nor more dangerous to handle, than to initiate a new order of things.**
>
> —Machiavelli, *The Prince and the Discourses*

On June 30, 1963, Isaya Mukirane, a leader of the Bakonzo people of northwestern Uganda, declared the formation of the Rwenzururu Kingdom after leading a secessionist campaign from the newly independent Ugandan state.[1] Earlier, President Milton Obote had proclaimed a state of emergency over the mountainous region seeking to undermine the kingdom's existence (Rubongoya 1995). But despite the best efforts of the Ugandan government, the rebel monarchs did not buckle. Instead, Rwenzururu leaders, in addition to their military wing, organized a complex governmental bureaucracy composed of eleven ministries headed by a cabinet. They also developed a legislature and a public service commission. By 1966 the Rwenzuru "government" had a salaried staff of over one thousand bureaucrats who collected taxes from residents to fund its activities. Despite never gaining national or international recognition, this administration proved more than capable of meeting the needs of the local civilian population, estimated around one hundred thousand strong, through the provision of basic public goods, including a security force and an education system. In some form, the kingdom was able to operate for the next twenty years, during which it continued to maintain a governmental system of impressive sophistication before finally being reintegrated into the Ugandan state in 1982 (Kasfir 2004).

---

1. Nelson Kasfir (2004) offers the most comprehensive analysis of the Bakonzos' attempt to establish a separate state and its significance.

By the early 1980s a vast territorial enclave in the jungles and plains border-ing the Andes mountains in Colombia's southeast fell under the control of the Fuerzas Armadas Revolucionarias de Colombia (Revolutionary Armed Forces of Colombia, FARC), a long-running Marxist insurgency that set about developing a system to govern civilians living within the area.[2] Accounts of the extent of FARC-held areas estimate that at its peak the organization controlled or influ-enced fully 40 percent of the country's territory (Steinberg 2000, 264). During the high point of rebel rule, the insurgent administration provided substantial ser-vices to the inhabitants of its territory, including health and education systems, a police force to maintain stability, courts to adjudicate civil and criminal disputes, and even loans to farmers and small businessmen. It also engaged in extensive public works projects such as building roads and other infrastructure construc-tion (ibid.; Ortiz 2002, 131; Arjona 2009a, 2009c). The insurgent "government" also achieved considerable international validation during peace negotiations that began in 1998, when President Andrés Pastrana effectively partitioned the country in two, officially sanctioning the rebellion's control of the vast region. Setbacks in the past decade have reduced FARC's territorial holding, but the or-ganization still retains control of large portions of the country, where it continues to govern the daily lives of residents.

The performance of governmental functions by violent nonstate actors from across the ideological spectrum has occurred throughout history and is a far more common occurrence than generally recognized. Indeed, the phenomenon predates the twentieth century. Toussaint L'Ouverture's rebel government dur-ing the Haitian civil war at the turn of the eighteenth century stands as one prominent example. Nor are such governing rebellions limited to countries in the developing world. The title of this book, *Rebel Rulers,"* is drawn from a refer-ence in the *New York Times* (1862) to the leadership of the Confederacy during the American Civil War. Recent and ongoing conflicts in countries as diverse as Angola, Colombia, Indonesia, Israel, Nepal, and Russia have all witnessed the construction of elaborate systems for governing civilians by violent groups. Even when we examine an organization whose members are dismissed as terrorists, such as Hezbollah in south Lebanon, an honest appraisal of its strategy must rec-ognize the importance of service provision in generating popular support among its targeted population. To this end, Hezbollah has constructed an administra-tion that runs schools and hospitals, collects garbage, provides drinking water, and engages in other relief and development activities (Silverstein 2007).

---

2. Ana Arjona's emerging work (2010) on the FARC is the most significant analysis of the orga-nization's governance practices.

This contrasts with the dominant perception of rebel groups,[3] especially those in the developing world, which, since the end of the Cold War, have been caricatured as little more than warlords. Although this term is certainly valid as applied to some violent actors, many other contemporary insurgencies take over large territories for extended periods of time, establishing extensive governmental structures and practices through which they rule the civilian population. Why do some rebel organizations establish sophisticated administrations that provide considerable public goods to civilians under their control, while others do little if anything for their denizens? How do insurgent leaders design the ruling structures and practices they develop to provide governmental functions? Why do civilians embrace some rebel rulers as legitimate governmental authorities while others are rejected, often violently? In this book I seek to explain the variation in the ways insurgents govern civilian populations, which I argue is the product of both the initial preferences of the rebel leadership and their interactions with a wide variety of local and international social and political actors.

At a basic level, governance can be characterized as "decisions issued by one actor that a second is expected to obey" and refers to the control of social interactions by both state and nonstate actors (Kahler and Lake 2004, 409). The term "government" has a more formal meaning, generally referring to a bounded organization that has the authority to make laws and regulations *and* the ability to enforce adherence by exercising control over the means of coercion within a defined territory (Tilly 2003, 9). As Rosenau (1992, 12) notes, "Governance is a more encompassing phenomenon than government." He continues:

> It embraces governmental institutions but it also subsumes informal, non-governmental mechanisms, whereby those persons and organizations within its purview move ahead, satisfy their needs, and fulfill their wants....Governance is thus a system of rule that is as dependent on inter-subjective meanings as on formally sanctioned constitutions and charters....It is possible to conceive of governance without government—regulatory mechanisms in a sphere of activity which function effectively even though they are not endowed with formal authority.

---

3. In this book I use the terms "rebels," "rebel group," "rebel organization," "rebellion," "insurgents," "insurgent group," "insurgent organization," and "insurgency" interchangeably. These are armed factions that use violence to challenge the state. I distinguish these from "militias," a broader term encompassing all armed factions that use violence, including those that work alongside government forces. I also distinguish these from "guerrilla," a term that refers to a type of warfare that rebels frequently engage in but that is not limited to rebel organizations, nor is it the only type of warfare that rebels utilize. I also avoid using politically loaded terms such as "revolutionary," "terrorist," and "freedom fighter." See also Nadarajah and Sriskandarajah (2005) and Bhatia (2005) for a fuller discussion of the taxonomy of violent groups.

Evaluating governance by insurgents requires a normative assessment of the ability of a rebel political authority to regulate life within a defined territory. Thus, a "governance system" refers to not only the structures that provide certain public goods but also the practices of rule insurgents adopt. These can be either ad hoc (informal) or bureaucratic (formal). When the provision of public goods is bureaucratized, we can refer to an insurgent "civil administration"—an apparatus distinct from its military organization (obviously the overlaps between the two are often dense and integral for analysis).

In my application of the term "governance" to rebel-controlled territories, I follow Nelson Kasfir (2002, 4) in referring to "the range of possibilities for organization, authority, and responsiveness created between guerillas and civilians." He rightly points out that rebel governance can demonstrate significant variation ranging from "elaborately patterned relationships" to "the absence of any patterned activity."

Insurgents regularly engage in a variety of governance activities, including—but not limited to—providing security from violence orchestrated by the government, its allies, or rival militias; meeting the education and health needs of the population, including establishing a system of food production and distribution; allocating land and other resources to provide opportunities for civilians to engage in their regular livelihood activities (agriculture, small business, etc.); providing shelter to civilian populations, including those displaced by fighting; regulating market transactions; resolving civil disputes; and addressing other social problems such as theft, drug use, and prostitution that commonly accompany situations of internal war. Insurgents also devote considerable attention to less instrumental assertions of power through symbolic actions that complement other ruling practices and structures.

To be clear, my focus throughout this book is only on those groups that have moved beyond mere looting to actually taking control of a specific territory. As Jeremy Weinstein (2007, 84–85) notes, in order to provide collective goods, insurgent organizations "must be of sufficient size and strength to challenge the government for control of specific territories." This can lead to a situation of contested sovereignty, with both contenders claiming some portion of the population that follows its directives.

Though governance has not generated the same attention from academics as other aspects of rebel behavior, an impressive trove of writing by journalists, aid workers, and movement insiders documenting the organization of specific rebellions has been available for some time. These works provide detailed accounts of the historical trajectory of specific insurgent organizations, frequently discussing relations with civilians, either real or imagined. But the focus on governance tends to be tangential to more pressing concerns. Though important, such accounts do not attempt to provide a theoretical framework for understanding rebel governance as a discrete subject of inquiry. Nor do they provide a real sense of the meaning of these systems for civilians caught within war zones as they go about their daily lives. To fill this gap, I traveled to rebel-controlled areas of the Democratic Republic of Congo, Sri Lanka, and Sudan, visiting multiple sites within each, during two separate trips to each location between January 2004 and July 2005.[4] I also revisited each case between 2008 and 2010, returning often to dramatically different situations on the ground. Combining field research with the available secondary sources, I attempt here to explain the underlying factors that shape the differing ways in which rebel leaders interact with local civilian populations through some sort of governance system. Three central concerns drove the field research process:

1. Under what conditions are rebels likely to take seriously the task of providing governance to civilians?
2. Why do rebels adopt certain ruling practices and how do they design their civilian administrations?
3. How do civilians and other actors perceive and respond to governance efforts by insurgents?

The case studies draw heavily on this field research in rebel-controlled areas and provide detailed analyses of the governance strategies of three different contemporary insurgent organizations: specifically, the Liberation Tigers of Tamil Eelam (LTTE) in Sri Lanka, the Rassemblement Congolais pour la Démocratie (Congolese Rally for Democracy, RCD) in D.R. Congo, and the Sudan People's Liberation Movement/Army (SPLM/A) in Sudan. The cases represent the range of outcomes possible when discussing civilian governance by insurgents—a highly effective system of civilian governance in Sri Lanka, a partially effective system in Sudan, and an ineffective system in D.R. Congo. (How I determine effectiveness is explained in greater detail in a later section of this chapter).

In Sri Lanka, the LTTE was able to develop a comprehensive governance system that met most civilian needs and was largely embraced by the civilian population. The system had a capable police force and a functional and regularized judiciary. And through collaboration with the Sri Lankan state it met the educational and health needs of the Tamil population. The insurgency also devoted substantial resources to crafting a facade of statehood, adopting the symbology of the nation-state with considerable effect. The SPLM/A in Sudan took a more circumscribed

---

4. I also conducted research in the United States and other countries, including Rwanda, Uganda, and Egypt for the African cases and India and Canada for Sri Lanka. Each of these countries either had large diasporic populations or other direct connections to the conflicts under examination.

approach to governance, focusing its resources primarily on developing a security system that could ensure stability while incorporating traditional courts for resolving civilian disputes. Efforts to provide other public goods like education and health were more limited and relied heavily on the involvement of the international community, especially transnational aid organizations that proliferated throughout the area of rebel control. The third group studied, the RCD, failed to maintain security or provide public welfare goods to the civilian population living within its territory in eastern D.R. Congo. It is not true, as often claimed, that the organization cared little about civilian governance; rather, multiple efforts to develop a system of governance consistently came up short, and the organization suffered a deep crisis of legitimacy as a result. Understanding why we see the different outcomes in these cases is a central concern of this book.

Drawing on the case studies, I develop a framework for understanding the question of variation in rebel governance outcomes. Though my key assumption is that insurgencies operate in highly context-specific environments, I also believe that there are common processes and challenges that insurgents face in their construction of a civilian governance system. By bringing into the discussion examples of governance efforts by other rebel groups beyond the three case studies, I attempt to disaggregate the general from the specific, providing a framework for understanding variation beyond the cases under examination.

Although millions of civilians reside in rebel-controlled areas and have intimate exposure to the vagaries of life behind the front lines, there are few discrete studies of insurgent governance systems in either the academic or policy literature and virtually none that take a comparative approach.[5] Too often, especially in more recent analyses of rebel behavior, analysts have instead focused on the more salacious aspects of insurgent interactions with civilians, emphasizing recruitment strategies or the use of violence. This tendency, particularly prominent in the post-Collier literature on civil war, tends to distill the nature of a highly complex political organization into its most gasp-inducing components, lending credence to those who view all nonstate armed groups as analogous to criminal organizations. But recruitment and violence, while undeniably important, do not provide much insight into the broader set of interactions that violent organizations constantly engage in with local communities. As seasoned observers of political violence note, even under conditions of widespread warfare "most

---

5. Weinstein (2007) is an important exception to this, though governance is not the primary focus of his work. In October 2009, I was a co-organizer along with Ana Arjona and Nelson Kasfir of the Conference on Rebel Governance held at Yale University. The conference brought together over twenty experts on various insurgent groups to compare and contrast the different governance strategies of each with the goal of initiating a sustained research program on the subject. In September 2010, a follow-up workshop was held at Dartmouth College. At the time of writing, we are in the process of revising the papers for an edited volume.

people most of the time are interacting in non-violent ways" (Tilly 2003, 12). Indeed, even during an outbreak of mass violence, experts estimate that less than one-third of the population, and often just 5 percent, will actively participate in a violent organization (Wood 2003; Lichbach 1995). In short, attempting to understand civilian experiences during war without a grasp of insurgent governance practices requires a willful ignorance of the majority of interactions that shape life in contemporary zones of conflict.

For the myriad of transnational actors engaging in activities behind rebel lines, whether charitable or commercial, there is a practical need to understand the structures that regulate the daily lives of the populations with whom they seek to interact. And understanding rebel governance is also important for what it tells us about the potential for postconflict peace. As several analysts have argued, structures and practices developed at the local level during a crisis have the potential to be turned to more constructive purposes after the termination of fighting (Manor 2006, 14; de Zeeuw 2008). Indeed, the more we know about the relationship between rebel groups and civilians during a protracted conflict, the better we can understand the potential for a rebellion to transition from a militaristic organization to one concerned more about the relatively prosaic governance issues that many profess to be fighting over in the first place (Wood 2000; Pool 2001).

The Problem

Analysts have gone to extensive lengths to document the nature of the state in the developing world, arguing convincingly that the inability of a government to develop a coercive apparatus or achieve a hegemonic position in society can lead nonstate actors to challenge its sovereignty. Much less attention has been paid to the governance practices of these challengers. This statecentric tendency, especially visible within political science studies of governance, is understandable though problematic, for it implies a basic Hobbesian conjecture—that is, if the state is not capable of exerting control, then chaos must ensue.[6] This assumption, that the absence of a strong state will necessarily be followed by anarchic conditions, has limited our understanding of politics in conflict zones. As a result, scholars thus far have not adequately accounted for the performance of governmental functions by nonstate actors.[7]

---

6. A recent corrective is the volume edited by Jennifer Wood and Benoit Dupont (2006). Anthropologists, of course, have long been more comfortable with exploring the multiplicity of ways that power manifests in contemporary society (Nordstrom 2004).

7. Ken Menkhaus's (2004, 2007) interesting work on Somalia deals with the related subject of political order in the face of state collapse. Though similar dynamics are at work in such cases, insurgents in a civil war with a recognized government face a considerably different political environment—one

Whether labeled bandits, militias, rebels, guerrillas, warlords, insurgents, or even freedom fighters and terrorists, organized groups of men and women who engage in conflict with incumbent state governments face a similar dilemma: Should the organization seek to control territory and the corresponding civilian population in pursuit of its broader strategic agenda? Many rebellions, such as the Lord's Resistance Army (LRA) in Uganda, prefer not to take and hold territory, viewing mobility as an advantage too valuable to sacrifice (Branch 2007). Others that do take territory may choose to expel the civilians in their midst, as the Tutsi-led Rwandan Patriotic Front (RPF) did in its wars against the Hutu government of Rwanda (Mamdani 2001). But many other groups do seek the support of the civilian population in the territories they come to control, establishing governance systems that provide collective goods in exchange for civilian consent to rebel rule. This is a strategic decision. Rebel organizations benefit from the increased security as well as the opportunity to signal their relative strength to the incumbent state. And controlling territory also increases their access to local populations with whom they seek collaboration (Weinstein 2007, 163–97).

In short, I am concerned with the production and use of power by a rebel group and the recognition by insurgent leaders that this cannot come through violence alone.[8] In other words, rebel leaders face a problem comparable to that described by Gramsci in his influential discussion of power and the modern state (Gramsci 1992; Anderson 1976). Although Gramsci's analysis dissects the relationship between the modern state and its constituents, his insights are useful for understanding the behavior of rebel leaders seeking to exert control not only over a specific territory but over its corresponding civilian population as well. Specifically, in order to ensure their viability, insurgent leaders cannot only be concerned with the establishment of a coercive apparatus (domination) but must also gain a degree of consent from the civilian population (hegemony).[9] Indeed, it is only by replicating some of the functions and forms of the nation-state—chiefly in regard to state strategies used to generate civilian compliance—that will allow an insurgent organization to derive support for its political authority and achieve some form of legitimacy.

Theorists have posited that the earliest state structures emerged out of attempts to address this challenge. The most famous treatment of the issue is

---

dominated by the counterinsurgent efforts of the incumbent state. See also Roitman (2001) and Raeymaekers and Vlassenroot (2004).

8. In this, I agree with Hannah Arendt (1970, 41–42), who doubts that violence alone can ever be politically productive. Instead, she argues that power is distinct as it relies on relationships with a larger community, while violence can be utilized unilaterally depending upon the possession by an individual of the appropriate weaponry.

9. For a framing of this issue in regard to colonial rule, see Guha (1997) and Young (1994).

Mancur Olson's introduction of the "stationary bandit" as the progenitor of the modern state lineage (Olson 1993; Mann 1986; Tilly 1990). At the most basic level, to paraphrase Olson, the local population can be viewed in one of two ways: either as the support base and occasional beneficiary of the rebels' actions or as a source to be exploited.[10] Olson's rationalist interpretation argues that groups will prefer to be stationary if they can exercise a monopoly on the use of force within a territory because in the long term the rewards of taxation are potentially greater than the petty thievery of the roving bandit. Though it is true that many contemporary rebel groups are little more than roving bandits, many others develop complex relationships with local populations that go beyond mere extraction, particularly when their agendas include any sort of political component. Like governments of traditional states, rebel leaders must negotiate with civilians in exchange for their loyalty—no easy task as civilian demands frequently involve a variety of different and often competing perspectives. In addition, as global forces intersect and transform even the most local processes, insurgent groups are able to draw resources from and face constraints on their behavior through their interactions with transnational actors and networks.

Despite the intriguing parallels between rebel behavior and influential theories on the origin of the nation-state, I do not subscribe to the view that contemporary internal wars represent an elementary form of state building. Instead, it is important to recognize that certain strategies for generating consent by a political authority are transferable outside the sovereign nation-state framework *without* downplaying the modern state's integral role in cultivating and developing such practices. Thus, rather than assume a teleology toward state formation, I am interested in how structures and practices developed by the modern state can be reconfigured and put to productive purposes by competing nodes of power—in this case, rebel organizations. The complicated relationship between rebel governance and state formation will be addressed in greater detail in the next chapter.

Competing Approaches

So far, scholars have failed to adequately account for the phenomenon of insurgent governance. Much of the literature on why conflicts occur in certain states emphasizes the inability of governments to properly carry out their sovereign duties while paying little attention to the political formations that develop in the

---

10. See also Clapham (1998b).

absence of the state.[11] A corollary of this inattention, common among those who focus their gaze on the workings of the international system, is to ignore the existence of such rebel-governed spaces, referring to them instead as "black spots," "ungoverned territories," or some comparably ominous label.[12] Meanwhile, analyses of the behavior and organization of rebel groups tend to emphasize the conditions that lead to the emergence of war (Berdal and Malone 2000; Ross 2002; Ballentine and Sherman 2003; Collier and Hoeffler 2004). Or they focus on how rebels recruit their followers and organize violence against civilians (Gates 2002; Mkandawire 2002; Wood 2003; Kalyvas 2006; Viterna 2006; Humphries and Weinstein 2006; Weinstein 2007).

Still, not enough is yet known about how rebels *govern* the territory they are able to win away from the incumbent government (Mampilly 2007; Wood 2008, 540; Arjona 2009a). Because insurgents are often able to wrest vast territories and populations away from the state controlling them for extended periods, this is a serious omission. One reason for this inattention is the complexity of the subject itself, implicating as it does the entire set of social, political, and economic relations within a defined territorial space over time. Another is the challenge of conducting research in areas of rebel control. But since governance of civilians is often just as important to the viability of the insurgency as its recruitment strategy or its use of violence, the relative negligence thus far is striking (Wickham-Crowley 1987). Furthermore, a better understanding of rebel governance systems may force us to reassess our understanding of the behavior of violent groups, a point I will address in chapter 8.

Two approaches tend to influence most contemporary analyses of rebel behavior. The first, common in first-person and media accounts of war, draws on the works of seminal theorists of guerrilla warfare and stresses the ideological orientation of the rebel leadership. Modern guerrilla warfare came into prominence during the two world wars that ended the Age of Empire, ripping apart Europe and Asia and in the process rendering the twentieth century the bloodiest in human history. Until World War I, European strategists had paid little attention to irregular war, as conflict was previously considered to be the engagement of two professional armies on a designated field of battle (Nabulsi 2001, 11). During World War II, leaders embraced "total war" in which entire populations were viewed as complicit in battle, spawning new forms of large-scale resistance that fused a civilian population with the broader military goals of a particular

---

11. There is a wide literature that follows this model, including Rotberg (2004), Zartman (1995), and Forrest (1998).

12. For example, on this subject see the forum in *International Studies Review* (Stanislawski 2008) or Rabasa (2007).

nation-state. In the process, the carefully cultivated line between professional armies and civilians was torn down (Lindqvist 2003; Chaliand and Blin 2007: 209).[13] An outcome of this transformation was the need for challengers to state authority to marshal ever-greater resources in order to pose a direct challenge to the recognized sovereign.

Two options quickly came to the fore: (1) to fight a clandestine war in hopes of disrupting the incumbent government enough to trigger a political transformation or (2) by appropriating aspects of state sovereignty, to construct a territorial entity that could challenge the incumbent in a more conventional manner. The former relied on having a small cell of committed activists who could function with or without popular support for their actions—the forerunners of today's urban terrorists (Chaliand and Blin 2007). The latter, it has long been argued, required considerable engagement with the local population and made rebel/civilian relations an important area of concern. When to pursue which approach and how best to do it became a central debate for would-be revolutionaries around the world.

Two historical figures stand above all others in framing the debate on how best to pursue the latter option: Mao Zedong and Ernesto "Che" Guevara.[14] In addition, several other communist theorists influenced by Mao and Guevara but seeking to apply their analyses to specific contexts—Frantz Fanon in Algeria, Ho Chi Minh and Vo Nguyen Giap in Vietnam, Regis Debray in Cuba and Latin America, and Amilcar Cabral in Guinea Bissau—put forth and refined a variety of positions on the ideal relationship between rebel organizations and civilians.[15] The thoughts of these guerrilla theorists are still studied outside the academy and remain influential among organizers of contemporary rebellions, both those who proclaim overtly leftist ideals and those who have little interest in Marxist ideas of social and political organization.[16] For example, on my first visit to Southern

---

13. Obviously the same restrictions against attacking civilians was never applied to European militaries operating in the colonies even prior to World War I, where non-combatants were often purposefully targeted by military actions (Lindqvist 2003).

14. Both Mao and Guevara wrote influential manuals on guerrilla warfare, though their thoughts were also disseminated via a variety of media, including speeches, personal journals, and interviews. See Mao Zedong (1961) and Guevara (1969).

15. For a selection of these writings, see Fanon (1968), Giap (2004), Debray (1980), and Cabral (1966).

16. Contrary to popular perceptions, many contemporary insurgent leaders—including those rightfully acknowledged as among the worst, such as Foday Sankoh and Charles Taylor of the Revolutionary United Front (RUF) of Sierra Leone and the National Patriotic Front of Libera (NPFL), respectively—were conversant in insurgent theory and practice. Both Sankoh and Taylor studied rebel theory in a variety of settings, including study groups of revolutionary students in Sankoh's case and U.S. military training in Taylor's, in addition to the common training both received under the tutelage of the Libyan president, Muammar al-Qaddafi.

Sudan in January of 2004, I walked into a local SPLM administrative office and was surrounded with several handmade posters that listed Mao's "Golden Rules" for rebel behavior, most of which are directly concerned with treatment of the peasantry. And I have debated the practicality of Guevara's theories with LTTE administrators and discussed the relevance of Cabral and Ho Chi Minh for contemporary insurgent organizations with a Congolese rebel leader.

In these writings, the establishment of a system of governance is a recurring concern, though there is considerable debate around what role such systems play in advancing the broader agenda of a violent movement and, equally important, how they should be designed. Mao held that a military establishment must remain subservient to the political leadership. He advocated a shift away from guerrilla fighting strategies to the establishment of a conventional military force that could challenge the state on equal footing, though he acknowledged that this was a contingent strategy based on battlefield imperatives. For Mao, the goal was for the political agenda to trump the military strategy during the insurgency. Extending this framework to the organization's interaction with civilians, he envisioned a minimal role for violence in generating support for the rebellion's political agenda. Instead he emphasized the importance of developing appropriate governing structures accompanied by a prolonged period of political mobilization among the peasantry.[17]

In his major strategic treatise, *Guerrilla Warfare*, Guevara also underlined the importance of demonstrating concern for the social welfare of local residents through the provision of public goods.[18] Like Mao, Guevara was chiefly concerned with how to generate collaboration from the civilian population that would reinforce the rebel unit and supply it with essential items. Thus in his works he paid considerable attention to analyzing relations with civilians. He believed that the productive power of violent action could unleash the revolutionary potential of the peasantry immediately but would leave civilians with little time to acclimate to the transformation of the social and political order to which they had become accustomed (even if they never embraced it). In order to soothe the potentially

---

17. Mao's ideas on rebel organization have proved enduring and were utilized by many rebel groups of diverse political persuasions, including the nationalist Zimbabwe African National Union (ZANU); the right-wing, American-supported União Nacional para a Independência Total de Angola (National Union for the Total Independence of Angola, UNITA); the Sinhalese ethnonationalist Janatha Vimukthi Peramuna (People's Liberation Front, JVP) in Sri Lanka; the Viet Minh in Vietnam; and the Communist Party of Nepal-Maoist (CPN-M), to name just a few.

18. Though not as broadly influential as Mao's ideas, Guevara's "foco" theory of war had its adherents among many Latin American groups, including the Ejército de Liberación Nacional (Army of National Liberation, ELN) and to a lesser degree the FARC in Colombia, as well as even less successful groups in Guatemala, Ecuador, and Peru. Guevara's ideas were particularly influential for Uganda's National Resistance Army (NRA) and among the early LTTE cadres in Sri Lanka (Beckett 2001).

disruptive effects of violence, it was essential to establish "civil organizations" that would administer the liberated zones and win over the population, bringing them over to the rebels' cause:

> In view of the importance of relations with the peasants, it is necessary to create organizations that make regulations for them, organizations that exist not only within the liberated area, but also have connections in the adjacent areas. Precisely through these connections it is possible to penetrate a zone for a future enlargement of the guerrilla front. The peasants will sow the seed with oral and written propaganda, with accounts of life in the other zone, of the laws that have already been issued for the protection of the small peasant, of the spirit of sacrifice of the rebel army; in a word, they are creating the necessary atmosphere for helping the rebel troops. (Guevara 1969, 81)

Both men posited that the provision of public goods could have an ameliorating effect on the insurgency's ingrained need to use violence in pursuit of its political agenda. Thus both stressed the importance of inculcating appreciation for the revolutionary agenda in the civilian population through educational outreach. They saw the development of a civil administration and adoption of other ruling practices as the key to reconciling the tension between domination and hegemony—or put another way, between coercion and consent—that all rebel groups seeking to control territory face. As Eqbal Ahmad (1982, 244), a keen firsthand observer of several key revolutionary figures and movements, has pointed out, such movements sought "not simply to inflict military losses on the enemy but to destroy the legitimacy of its government and to establish a rival regime through the creation of 'parallel hierarchies.'"

Ideological orientation is commonly viewed as signaling insurgent leaders' preferences regarding civilian treatment. Insurgencies that profess revolutionary ideologies, it is surmised, are more likely to take up Mao's call and work to win over civilians by fulfilling their daily needs. However, despite the appeal of a simple ideological explanation, active militants, not to mention academic critics, have consistently questioned whether a professed ideology is a sufficient predictor of rebel behavior. More often than not, the proclaimed values of an insurgent command fail to harmonize with its actual treatment of civilians on the ground.

A powerful response to the failings of the ideological model has been to look within the insurgent organization to the actual financial underpinnings that determine the rebellion's viability. In particular, scholars have sought to emphasize material factors in explaining insurgent/civilian relations, and much recent scholarship on civil wars has focused on the source of funding as the primary determinant of rebel behavior. Scholars like Weinstein (2007), applying insights first popularized by the Oxford economist Paul Collier, have posited a dichotomy between insurgencies that draw on external resources (either natural resources or external state patronage) and those that rely on popular support. In his view, insurgents able to draw on economic endowments will demonstrate far less concern for civilian welfare because they have a readily available financial pipeline that can cover start-up costs and the recurring expense of paying recruits for their participation. Hence they will devote far fewer resources to civilian governance issues. This contrasts with organizations that must rely on social endowments, generally by mobilizing collective identities and interpersonal networks. Such resource-poor rebellions must engage in far more extensive mobilization efforts that seek to convince recruits of the long-term payoffs of collaboration. As a result, they are more likely both to have disciplined organizations and to develop complex governance structures that can woo civilian support.

Though attractive, a purely political economy approach leaves much wanting when it comes to understanding rebel behavior around civilian governance questions. The distinction between "opportunistic" and "activist" rebellions, despite its intuitive appeal, does not hold when one looks closely at the actual evolution of different insurgent organizations' governance systems. Rebellions have a wide variety of viable funding sources and demonstrate considerable dexterity in switching between available options. For example, the three insurgencies I examine here relied upon more than a dozen different sources of funding: internal taxation; voluntary or forced contributions from civilians; racketeering, kidnapping, and/or looting of local businesses and civilians; payoffs from multinational corporations; diversion of humanitarian aid from international agencies and nongovernmental organizations (NGOs); patronage from foreign governments; aid provided by international solidarity organizations; contributions from diasporic communities; the sale of drugs and other illicit goods; systematic mineral expropriation; and revenue from controlling key customs checkpoints. It is perhaps plausible that each source of funding had a distinct effect on governance outcomes. But providing convincing explanations of the impact of each of the above funding sources complicates precisely what advocates of such a political economy approach have long found its most appealing attribute, i.e. the intuitiveness and parsimony of its formulation.

A simplistic binary that posits funding sources as having either a negative or positive impact also cannot account for the variation present within such broad categories. For example, consider the effect of external funders which are largely assumed to have a negative impact on civilian governance. What should we make of contributions by ethnic diasporas or foreign solidarity organizations that do not emerge from within the civilian population but are unlikely to have the same negative effect on the rebel/civilian relationship that other external revenue sources like mineral sales or foreign patronage have? Furthermore, insurgencies often adopt multiple funding strategies simultaneously, switching between sources with relative haste as new opportunities open up or old opportunities shut down as a result of events occurring at either the national or international level. Trying to determine the relative influence of a particular funding source is also challenging because of the difficulty of gathering hard data on the real sources of rebel finance. Recent international efforts to curtail sources of insurgent funding have rendered such activities more clandestine than ever, and even movement insiders disagree on the extent to which their organization is dependent on different financial activities.

Indeed, while they are often posited as competing, both the ideological and the political economy approaches tend to share a number of common traits that hinder their usefulness for explaining rebel behavior around governance questions. First, though parsimony is a worthwhile aspiration in theory making, satisfactory answers to complex and prolonged phenomena often cannot be found by focusing on a single factor. In both models, a desire to reduce variation in governance practices to an individual variable (source of funding, ideological orientation) renders them ineffective in explaining a large number of messy cases that do not fit into neat divisions. Second, both approaches tend to be from the top down, vesting agency solely with the rebel leadership. But governance, by definition, is an interactive process. And an assumption of unconstrained agency of the rebel leadership does not hold in the face of actual evidence on the ground that demonstrates that insurgent leaders are far more restricted in their actions, particularly around governance questions. Third, and perhaps most damningly, both approaches assume that all rebellions begin on a path that they are unlikely or unable to depart from—that they are "path dependent."[19] But though the initial conditions of an insurgency are important, evidence from most cases demonstrates that a rebellion can often transform dramatically over the course of its existence, and not always to the detriment of the civilian population, as the political economy model would have it.

Understanding Insurgent Governance: An Interactive Approach

The argument presented in this book is multifaceted and avoids monocausal deterministic models. Variation in civilian governance provision by insurgents, in my view, emerges from a combination of the initial preferences of rebel leaders

---

19. Weinstein's political economy model allows for insurgencies to degenerate but cannot account for groups that move from having little concern for governance issues to developing elaborate governance systems.

and the interaction of insurgent organizations with a variety of other social and political actors active during the conflict itself. As a result, governance is, by nature, an evolutionary process in which the outcome (more or less effective civilian governance) cannot be predicted by a single variable but must rather take into consideration the varying effects of a variety of concurrent processes on the behavior of the insurgent leaders.

I argue that two conditions present at the onset of fighting—the nature of the preconflict relationship between the state and society and the ethnic composition and ultimate strategic objective of the group—will shape the rebel command's preferences for a civilian governance strategy as well as the initial design of its civil administration. Thus I concur with other approaches that stress the importance of the rebel leadership in shaping civilian governance strategies. However, I depart from top-down, path-dependent models because of a key insight revealed during my field research behind rebel lines—governance structures and practices are constantly transformed over the course of the war by a variety of conflict-produced dynamics endogenous to the fighting. These include organizational issues such as the ability of the insurgent leadership to maintain a unified and disciplined command structure; situational issues related to the actions of the incumbent government, civilian communities, and other social and political actors in rebel-held areas; and transnational issues produced by the interaction of rebel leaders with international actors.

My focus is on the broader political environment that insurgents operate within, emphasizing the various constraints and opportunities produced by the insurgent command's relationship with other political and social actors. The key actors shaping the political environment that insurgents operate within include the civilian inhabitants of the area but also traditional leaders, religious institutions, rival militias, humanitarian agencies, international organizations, neighboring states, and private corporations, each of which is driven by its own distinct logic. Ideally, the command will seek to co-opt such actors into its governance project, but frequently, these actors instead challenge insurgent control through a variety of actions that can influence insurgent behavior in subtle and dramatic ways. Either outcome of these interactions can have important effects on governance performance. Thus a convincing explanation of governance variation must include the transformative impact of these interactions on insurgent governance efforts. Put another way, the agency of rebel leaders is restricted by other actors with whom they are forced into interaction. Variations in governance outcomes result from this series of complex negotiations and do not simply reflect the preferences of the rebel command.

Recognizing this dynamic nature of governance provision, I look beyond the formal structures that comprise an insurgent civil administration to the whole constellation of relationships that shape civilian experiences with governance within a rebel-controlled territory. The goal is to explain the mechanisms by which these interactions impact the behavior of the rebel leadership, producing the variation in civilian governance outcomes that we observe. To comprehend this variation, it is essential to understand not only the formal structures of the insurgent civil administration but also under what conditions an organization's efforts produce a broader system of governance that civilians deem effective by choosing to take advantage of the benefits provided by the insurgency.

"Effective governance" denotes a case in which an insurgent group in control of territory demonstrates the following three capacities. First, it must be able to develop a force capable of policing the population, providing a degree of stability that makes the production of other governance functions possible. Second, the organization should develop a dispute resolution mechanism, either through a formal judicial structure or through an ad hoc system. Civilians must regularly utilize this system to resolve disputes against other civilians as well as those that might arise with the rebel organization itself. Third, the organization should develop a capacity to provide other public goods beyond security. For the purposes of this book, I focus on education and health care, though in certain cases other public goods, such as a system to ensure the production and distribution of food, are equally worthy of attention. Again, in order to distinguish between effective and ineffective governance provision, it is essential to understand to what degree civilians make use of these insurgent-derived systems and how capable they are in meeting civilian needs.

Finally, it is useful to understand whether the organization develops feedback mechanisms to foster civilian participation in governmental issues. Rebel leaders may adopt a variety of approaches in their engagement with civilians, ranging from those that choose to issue directives unilaterally—adopting autocratic practices in their interactions with civilians—to those that seek to provide civilians and other actors an opportunity to participate in the decision-making process. However, I do not consider this an essential aspect of an effective governmental system as there is nothing that prohibits an autocratic political authority from developing an effective capacity to provide public goods.[20]

If a group is able to provide security but not other public goods, I deem it as having "partially effective governance." "Noneffective governance" could result from an insurgent group's deciding not to devote any resources to questions of civilian governance, which would produce a paucity of structures and practices

---

20. In the words of Organski and Kugler (1980, 72), "a highly capable political system need not be free, democratic, stable, orderly, representative, participatory, or endowed with any of the other desiderata alluded to by laymen and experts as bases for evaluating the political life of a nation."

for managing a captive population. More commonly, efforts by the insurgent organization to develop a governance system may be ignored or even rebuffed by civilians and other societal actors, and this can result in a similarly ineffective system.

Data and Methods

To make my arguments about the organization of rebel groups and the concomitant effects on civilian populations, I conducted a comparative analysis of three different contemporary insurgent organizations. My reading of the secondary literature helped me—through a process of induction—to generate a series of original hypotheses on the nature of rebel governance, which I then went into the field to assess. I selected this approach for a variety of reasons, but one more than others. Statistical analyses of large data sets can point to a correlation between an independent and a dependent variable but say little about the links between cause and effect (Ross 2004). Instead, I chose to focus on the microlevel mechanisms and processes that connected specific factors with the actual outcomes I observed in the field.

Generating hypotheses in this manner has both advantages and disadvantages. Since few comparative studies have been undertaken on the subject of rebel governance, there was little in the way of prior theoretical work on variation in rebel governance. My approach was necessary to construct a basic framework for the study and to devise the original hypotheses. Perhaps the most important reason for pursuing microlevel case studies is the ability to witness processes at the most local of levels, an arena often overlooked in macrolevel studies of conflict. Though local political dynamics are more fluid and thus harder to neatly categorize than macrolevel factors, they are also more relevant for understanding the dynamics of contemporary internal warfare (Kalyvas 2003, 480; Autesserre 2008). Hence the bulk of this project focused on providing an analysis of the microfoundations of rebel governance through three separate case studies.

Case studies were useful for illuminating these local dynamics and providing insights into the specific factors that shaped the observed outcomes. Since civilian governance tended to vary temporally within a specific case, a broad historical scope allowed me to consider the evolution of these structures and practices over time, highlighting the key moments in which the development of the civil administration accelerated or stalled. Case studies in general are also useful as they shed light on the intermediate factors that mediate between an independent variable and the dependent variable under study (Gerring 2004). Assuming that each case represents like units, as they do in this study, they can also provide the basis for a comparative analysis.[21]

The cases were selected on the basis of both intellectual and pragmatic concerns. My primary concern was to choose prominent cases that covered the range of outcomes on my dependent variable, those in which insurgent organizations were acknowledged to have created an effective system of civilian governance as well as cases in which the rebellion was thought to have failed in this regard. It was also important to ensure that the cases varied along some commonly discussed dimensions. For example, it was important to cover both secessionist and reformist insurgencies because there is a perception that different mechanisms may be at work in each (Sambanis 2001). I also included some continental variation so as to prevent the possibility that the dynamics I was witnessing were not limited to African wars, for example. Finally, I selected cases before and after the Cold War to ensure that historical and/or geopolitical factors did not bias my results. My ability to safely travel behind rebel lines in the case studies was a primary pragmatic concern. In addition, each of the three cases has a substantial body of primary and secondary literature that I could access to corroborate my own observations. Finally, my own linguistic training and cultural expertise with African and South Asian cases was an important factor.

Preliminary field visits to the location of each of my cases combined with my review of the secondary literature allowed me to develop a framework for assessing the key questions I wanted to address for my study of rebel governance. From this initial phase, I refined a series of propositions on the nature of the relationship between insurgents and civilians, which I then went back into the field to assess. To formulate these assessments of individual insurgencies, I relied on a variety of sources and research in the field to develop a comprehensive analysis of each insurgent group. The research process encompassed at least three distinct approaches: (1) interviews with actors in insurgent-controlled areas, (2) participant observation of life in these areas, and (3) documentary and archival evidence. I interviewed rebel leaders and lower-level cadres, members of the local community, civil society leaders, government officials, international agency workers, and private-sector figures, both local and international. In each of the cases, between forty and fifty subjects were interviewed, with several follow-up discussions during return visits to the field sites. The appendix provides more information on the interview process and a list of those interviewed.

---

21. I focus on rebel groups fighting the government for a period of five years or more that were able to wrest control of a distinct piece of territory from the government or its agents. Once in control of the territory, these organizations attempted to create governmental structures with highly variant outcomes.

Participant observation was both a necessary and a particularly challenging component of my project. It was necessary for a variety of reasons, including establishing the context and identifying individuals for the structured interviews, developing a rapport with the civilian communities, and most important, allowing me to directly observe whether rebel public goods were meaningful for civilian livelihoods. I did this primarily by visiting and observing actual service provision sites such as hospitals, schools, prisons, and courts in insurgent-held territories of the three case study countries. I also sought to cross-reference my field research with substantial documentary and archival literature in addition to the relevant academic works. Since rebel governance tends to vary spatially, to get a more accurate picture of rebel/civilian relations, in each case I examined two areas under rebel control—one where the insurgent organization's rule was supported in some way by local inhabitants and the other in which the rebellion's control of the territory was challenged by the local community. This allowed me to examine the impact of this spatial variation on civilian governance practices.

However, as useful as case studies are, what they do not provide is breadth. With the small sample size and method of selection, the generalizability of my findings to the universe of cases can certainly be challenged (Gerring 2004). To mitigate this shortcoming, I examined a selection of secondary sources regarding the governance strategies of other prominent rebellions. Chapter 7 provides an assessment of my hypotheses drawing on these additional cases, and I will refer to them at other points in the text to assess the relevance of my approach to cases beyond these three.

Layout of the Book

In this chapter I have provided some background on the subject of insurgent governance and put forth the reasons why such a study is warranted, in addition to outlining my approach. Chapter 2 addresses the theoretical concerns implicated in such a study. Specifically, I engage the subject from two distinct angles. First, I address the tendency generally associated with scholars of comparative politics to analogize rebel governance to other forms of political order (or disorder). I argue that rather than equating insurgent governance systems with mere criminality or, more generously, with a form of embryonic state building, as recent analyses have attempted to do, it is better to focus on examining the limits and possibilities of establishing political order outside the control of the state, without any normative or teleological assumptions. I also look at the issue from the perspective of those who theorize about the international system. I argue that the statecentric tendency in international relations scholarship continues to inhibit our grasp of spaces on the map that remain outside the control of a particular state entity.

Chapter 3 explains the framework for understanding variation in governance provision by insurgent organizations. I begin by addressing the general concerns faced by any rebellion seeking to foster a consensual relationship with a defined civilian population. I then lay out specific arguments, situating each within an appropriate theoretical context, including political theory and sociological works on the origin of the state, international relations and anthropological work on interventions into civil conflicts by transnational actors, and comparative politics and economics works on the nature of civil conflict and the organization of rebel groups. The purpose is to provide a transferable framework that can illuminate the precise variables that are relevant for understanding rebel behavior on the question of civilian governance. I also introduce the concept of "counter-state sovereignty" as a more precise description of rebel-governed spaces. Understanding insurgent governance systems as sovereign formations is an essential first step in moving beyond the willful ignorance that has historically characterized the international community's engagement with areas of insurgent control toward a more structured basis for recognition.

The next three chapters rely heavily on the fieldwork I conducted in insurgent-held territories of D.R. Congo, Sri Lanka, and Sudan. As all three conflicts were still active to varying degrees during my visits, a minority of informants requested anonymity to be protected from any retribution for sharing their views. Interviews were generally conducted in English or Swahili (in eastern Congo and Southern Sudan). In Sri Lanka and D.R. Congo, some interviews were carried out in either Tamil or French with the assistance of intermediaries. Since some of my arguments treat international agencies and aid organizations as distinct actors rather than passive observers, during my fieldwork I chose not to align myself with any organization so as not to prejudice my observations. This created its own set of challenges in terms of resources and access, but it remains a decision I am comfortable with. I did occasionally take advantage of rides from NGOs into South Sudan, for example, or with the United Nations Mission in Congo, which once flew me into eastern Congo aboard a helicopter, for which I was very grateful. But generally I traveled into and within these regions aboard local buses or my own arranged transport.

In chapter 4, I turn my attention to the LTTE in Sri Lanka. The rebels fought a twenty-six-year war for a separate Tamil state that ended in mid-2009 with the complete victory of government forces. At its high point, rebel forces controlled one-third of the territory in Sri Lanka, predominantly in the Tamil majority areas of the north and east of the island nation. This chapter is based on fieldwork conducted in Kilinochchi, a town in northern Sri Lanka captured by the group in

1998 that served as the de facto capital of the insurgent region. I visited the area in June of 2004 and again in July of 2005. (I returned to Sri Lanka in January 2010 after the defeat of the LTTE organization.) I also visited Batticaloa, the capital of the former eastern province that the insurgents occupied through much of the 1980s but lost control of in 1991. At the time of my first visit, the rebels were a shadowy presence, controlling much of the surrounding rural areas though not the town itself. When I visited in July of 2005, it was at the center of a conflict between a breakaway faction and the main movement.

I examine the surprising institutional interplay that can emerge between an insurgent organization and the incumbent government, even in situations of prolonged internal war, in order to meet civilian needs. To maintain the welfare of civilians, the LTTE, through a convoluted arrangement with the government of Sri Lanka, designed its civil administration to oversee the government's provision of public goods. The arrangement divided service provision between the two opponents, producing a surprisingly innovative hybrid governance structure that underlines the claim often made by sociologists that warfare can produce tremendous dynamism in political forms (Mann 1986; Centeno 2002). The outcome, largely due to these innovations, was a highly effective and comprehensive governance system that claimed a substantial degree of legitimacy among denizens of LTTE territory.

Chapter 5 is an analysis of the SPLM/A in Southern Sudan. Until the signing of a comprehensive peace agreement (CPA) in 2005, the insurgency had waged a twenty-two-year war against the government, fighting for both regional concerns and national reform. This chapter is based on fieldwork conducted in the vast area controlled by the group along the southern border with Uganda in February 2004 and again in February 2005. I compare Yei, the largest town in western Equatoria, the southernmost province in South Sudan, with Rumbek, the largest town in Rumbek County and also the rebel capital throughout much of the war. Both towns had sizable numbers of internally displaced persons (IDPs). In Yei this population was largely Dinka, a community that is the largest demographic group in Southern Sudan as well as the primary ethnic base of the insurgency. And in Rumbek, a traditionally Dinka area, it was the Nuer, the second-largest population in the South, who migrated into the area after fleeing the fighting in their traditional areas further north. In August 2008 I returned to Sudan to visit Juba, the post CPA capital of the South, and Rumbek.

I examine the ways in which the SPLM/A attempted to incorporate transnational NGOs and international agencies into its governance project. Despite these efforts to develop a comprehensive system of governance, the insurgency was able to develop only a partially effective system that did provide a degree of stability in certain areas of South Sudan but failed to meet other basic needs of the beleaguered civilian population. This does not mean that the SPLM/A civil administration was a failure. Instead, I argue that the insurgency's development of a system of governance was driven by the need to foster greater cohesion within a fractious southern population riven by internal ethnic and regional disputes, a purpose for which it proved particularly effective.

I then turn in chapter 6 to a discussion of the RCD-Goma in the Democratic Republic of Congo. The Rwandan- and Ugandan-backed insurgency sought to capture national power in the country through a rapid advance on Kinshasa, the capital city. After the intervention of other neighboring armies on the government's behalf, the rebellion instead got bogged down fighting for control of a massive territorial enclave until the official negotiated end of the war in 2003, though skirmishes continued even after the signing of the peace agreement. The chapter is based on two trips to D.R. Congo, one in March of 2004 and another in March of 2005, during which I visited several towns across the east and central parts of the country. Most important, I made two trips to Goma, the capital of North Kivu province and the base of the RCD-Goma rebel group. I also visited Bukavu, the capital of South Kivu, a city fiercely contested by the rebels and various other militias. (I returned to the region for a follow-up visit in August 2009.)

This chapter focuses on the inability of rebel leaders to gain legitimacy or transcend the perception that they were little more than Rwandan-sponsored Tutsi lackeys. Despite multiple attempts to develop a functional civil administration during its control of much of eastern D.R. Congo, the RCD-Goma failed to establish even a minimally effective governance system. I argue that the insurgency's leaders failed to understand the complexities involved in navigating the parcellized political order that existed in the region prior to the war, thereby relying excessively on coercion and only intermittently on more consensual strategies—an approach that foreshadowed their failure to generate enthusiasm for the movement. The RCD-Goma case can tell us much about the limitations of governance for gaining popular support and the role of ethnicity in constraining rebel leaders' options. It also provides insights into the impact of external state sponsors on the behavior of an insurgent command.

Chapter 7 revisits the framework from chapter 3, drawing on the case studies to assess its merits and faults. Individual discussions of the specific hypotheses allow me to apply direct empirical evidence from the cases in support or negation of the key arguments. The case studies provide material for real-world assessments of the precise mechanisms that underlie each of the nine hypotheses. I also look at a broader sample of rebel groups, using their individual experiences to compare and contrast with the evidence from the three cases under examination. I find considerable support that the framework is transferable in that it can help explain variation in the effectiveness of the governance systems not only of the three case studies under examination but also of other prominent cases as well. I also address the framework's shortcomings, discussing the different ways that the individual propositions would benefit from future research.

Chapter 8 summarizes the main arguments of the book, situating them within broader debates on insurgent behavior, in particular those concerning rebel recruitment and the use of violence. In addition, it serves three other functions. First, I discuss the treatment of rebel organizations in international law, arguing that taking into consideration insurgent governance practices as a precondition for recognition would be an improvement over the ad hoc and schizophrenic approach that currently typifies the international community's engagement with violent actors. Second, I provide some practical recommendations for both the academic and policy worlds on how a greater engagement with the subject of rebel governance can promote better understanding of violent groups more generally. I conclude with an assessment of the evolution of political violence, focusing on how changes in the geopolitical system since the Cold War have limited the viability of territorial insurgencies. Though my discussion is not meant to be exhaustive, I explore what this transformation means for the study of rebel governance in the future.

2

BANDITS, WARLORDS, EMBRYONIC STATES, BLACK SPOTS, AND UNGOVERNED TERRITORIES

The Unwieldy Taxonomy
of Rebel-Governed Areas

The rebels must build an administrative structure to collect taxes, to provide some education and social welfare, and to maintain a modicum of economic activity. A revolutionary guerrilla movement which does not have these administrative concerns and structures to fulfill its obligations to the populace would degenerate into banditry.

—Eqbal Ahmad, "Revolutionary Warfare and Counterinsurgency"

Ungoverned territories generate all manner of security problems, such as civil conflict and humanitarian crises, arms and drug smuggling, piracy, and refugee flows. They threaten regional stability and security and generate demands on U.S. military resources.

—Angel Rabasa, *Ungoverned Territories: Understanding and Reducing Terrorism Risks*

Consider the following. The areas controlled by Sri Lanka's Liberation Tigers of Tamil Eelam during the past two decades in the north and east of the country were knit together through a politico-judicial architecture that directly mimicked the façade of the Sri Lankan state.[1] As central as the insurgents' military ability to control the territory was the performative aspect of the Tiger state, which included impressive physical edifices as well as elaborate costuming of all personnel, who were organized into sophisticated bureaucratic arrangements across military and civil lines. It was no secret that LTTE leaders sought to replicate the trappings of statehood, and across their territory you could find offices adorned with Tiger insignia that claimed to advance a variety of causes such as education,

---

1. The Sri Lankan government defeated the LTTE insurgency in early 2009, killing its senior military and political personnel.

health, gender, and youth concerns. You would also have found a police force, a legal system, and even an LTTE bank. To the casual observer, it was natural to assume that the insurgency was in the process of constructing an "embryonic state" in the north and east of Sri Lanka.

This book, like others before it, draws parallels between the performance of governmental functions by rebel groups and the genesis of the bureaucratic state, arguably the dominant model for examining insurgent governance (Pegg 1998; Kasfir 2002; Tull 2004; Kingston and Spears 2004). Theoretically this is a seductive and useful initial analogy for our discussion, but scratch the surface and it begins to show its limitations. If we accept the argument that the modern state has its origins in the banditry of a bygone era and that contemporary insurgencies face many of the same incentives today, then it does seem logical to view rebel behavior through the state formation lens. But as I argue in this chapter, such a view has serious shortcomings in providing an analytical framework for understanding the subject of insurgent governance. If we move our focus upward, to the international system, the search for state-ness also precludes an honest assessment of how such rebel-controlled spaces interact and intersect with other actors in the international system.

Take the LTTE again. Despite its successful efforts in carving out a territory from which to project statehood and its attempts to earn credit for many of the public goods provided to denizens of this territory, education and health care throughout the war were provided by the Sri Lankan government. The funds for the public goods the organization did provide were largely derived from donations from members of the war-induced diasporic community, who were often forced to navigate the national restrictions imposed by their adopted homes on sending money to insurgent-controlled areas. Both the collection of funds and the provision of services by the Tigers were determined by the nature of the political actor itself—in this case a nonstate violent group—and only vaguely resembled any approach taken by a recognized state authority.[2] Indeed, the Sri Lankan state, leveraging its privilege as a recognized sovereign entity, was able to exert considerable influence not only over the governing structures and practices the rebellion adopted within its territorial space but also over the organization's efforts to position itself as a coequal in the international community.

This does not mean that there is no value in comparing insurgent governance systems with recognized state governments—for clearly there is, particularly when discussing the overt functions performed by each. After all, the emergence

---

2. I am aware of the role migrant remissions can play in supporting state authorities, but the critique here is focused more on a standard type rather than the ways that some states have found to navigate the vagaries of the international system.

of a political authority, regardless of its genesis or trajectory, relies on a distinct relationship with a subject population. And there is much that insurgents have learned about governing a civilian population by closely examining the behavior of incumbent governments. Instead, I am arguing that a blanket imposition of a preconceived model (state formation) onto a dynamic contemporary process (insurgent governance) can hinder analysis in important ways. I believe it is more useful to examine the limitations of the state formation analogy for understanding insurgent governance systems and to attempt to sketch the boundaries and logic of a political order produced outside—and against—the existing state authority.

While students of rebel behavior productively focus on the internal dynamics of rebel organizations, scholars interested in the international system— concerned as they are with the division of geopolitical space into discrete political entities—tend to obsess over the mere existence of territories outside the control of a state, as the above quote taken from a Rand Corporation study demonstrates (Rabasa 2007; see also Stanislawski 2008). These analyses focus on the negative effects on the international system when nonstate actors challenge what are deemed the prerogatives of nation-states, and they show little concern for the actual political formations that may emerge in the state's absence. Relying on the erroneous assumption that territories outside the control of a state are necessarily anarchic, analysts and policymakers have argued that rebel-held areas pose a unique threat to the global order as spaces in which all sorts of nefarious activities will be conducted, including piracy, drug production, and terrorism (Rabasa 2007; Kilcullen 2009, 10).

In this chapter I consider several of the analogic terminologies used to explain insurgent behavior on issues of governance and authority. I argue that the dominant approaches to understanding rebel behavior have failed to adequately account for the existence of insurgent-governed territories. Nor have they successfully provided a sense of the daily lives of civilians caught within such spaces.

I begin with a brief discussion of the warlord analogy that posits rebel groups as mafia-like actors, concerned solely with maximizing economic profit. I then move on to an assessment of the applicability of the banditry-derived state-formation model for analyses of rebel behavior, which I consider the dominant academic model for explaining governance decisions by insurgents. I argue that though this model is useful for what it can tell us about the relationship between civilians and a political authority, it is unproductive to extend the analogy too far, as it falsely encourages analysts to obsess over teleological outcomes rather than focusing on insurgent governance as a discrete analytical category itself. I then consider the ways in which students of the international system have come to understand governing rebels, primarily by treating them as warlords or other criminal actors. Since the advent of the nation-state, the existence of nonstate power formations that adopt sovereign behaviors has been a recurrent concern. I argue that our failure to understand the internal logic and processes of a rebel-produced political order exaggerates the threat that such territories pose to the global system, undermining the ability of international actors to engage with civilians living within these nonstate political arrangements. Instead, the tendency to refer to such spaces as "black spots" or "ungoverned territories" leads analysts and international actors to assume that no political actor worthy of recognition exists and therefore that violence is the only avenue for engagement.

Economic Incentives, State Formation, and Rebel Behavior

Perhaps the most commonly used appellation for describing violent actors that challenge state power and take control of territory is "warlords," a term that re-entered the popular lexicon after the initiation of conflict by American forces in Afghanistan and Iraq. Generally, warlords are thought of as anomalies within the state-formation process. They are ahistorical, economically minded actors, with no compelling raison d'être for their presence in the Westphalian state system. As I discuss below and as is evident from the brief description of the LTTE above, the warlord category can only minimally account for the emergence of complex authority structures in rebel-controlled territories. A more sophisticated approach is offered by authors who connect the performance of governmental functions by rebel groups to the bandit-derived state-formation model used to explain the genesis of the European state (Pegg 1998; Ottaway 2003; Tull 2004; Kingston and Spears 2004; Stokke 2006). Indeed, there is much that can be gained by working backwards to understand the origins of the modern state system and its relevancy to contemporary conflict processes (Thies and Sobek 2010). However, this approach often encourages analysts to conflate rebel behavior with state formation in a way that inhibits a true appreciation of the distinctive environment that insurgents must navigate in their attempts to construct a system of governance to rule over a population and territory. As I will show below, rather than operating within a Hobbesian state of nature, insurgencies interact with a constellation of national and international actors who rigidly structure the political environment in important ways.

From the extant literature, bandits and warlords tend to share the following four characteristics. First, they are economically self-interested nonstate violent actors. Second, their actions betray short-term horizons in pursuit of primarily economic payoffs. Third, they are politically nonideological. And fourth, they tend to proliferate in weak or collapsed states (Marten 2006–7; Hobsbawm 1990;

Reno 1995; Skaperdas 2002; P. Jackson 2003). A corollary of these propositions is that the provision of any public good—rarely surpassing security—is done solely in pursuit of financial gain. Though they share many important characteristics, the categories of bandits and warlords differ in one important way.[3] Those who view rebel groups as bandits romantically connect them to the lineage of the modern state—an embryonic state—while those who view them as warlords regard them as atavistic throwbacks from an earlier period of state formation—historical anachronisms out of place in the contemporary Westphalian order. But must all bandits become states and are all warlords anomalous? Or does the reliance on such archaic categories to interpret contemporary insurgent behavior reveal a straitjacketing of analysis by powerful norms regarding the post-Westphalian division of global territorial space? Put simply, is it useful to regard organizations like those discussed here and many other recent and contemporary insurgencies as mere warlords or even as bandits? Or is there a need to develop new categories beyond our current conceptual frameworks that are better capable of explaining insurgent control of territory?

Rebel Groups as Warlords

The warlord analogy for rebel behavior is drawn out of three historical periods: Britain during the Dark Ages when the country was divided among several feudal lords (after AD 400), the Barons' War of the thirteenth century that again tore the country apart, and China in the 1920s (P. Jackson 2003). Transposing this political form to explain contemporary insurgent behavior has been popular in academic and media analyses, particularly after the recent turn toward political economy analyses of internal war. In this view, the development of governmental structures by violent actors is driven solely by the needs of a profit-maximizing organization seeking to increase its revenue-generating capacity with little regard for the formal juridical realm of international or domestic law. Public goods are provided only in exchange for specific short-term material gains (Skaperdas 2002). In this sense, rebel governance is little different from protection offered by racketeers in search of profit (Gambetta 1993; Reno 1995; Clapham 1998a; Marten 2006). Some analysts go as far as to refer to the territories controlled by putative warlords as "fiefdoms," betraying their reliance on feudal concepts to describe the behavior of modern actors (Vinci 2006, 6).

---

3. Not every analyst follows this division exactly, but these categories are useful as they represent the dominant approaches for understanding rebel behavior. Robert Jackson (2003, 138), for example, reverses the descriptions of their behavior but maintains the distinct categories of "bandits" and "warlords."

Though the warlord appellation may indeed be useful in describing certain contemporary violent actors who take and hold territory, the term has been applied to an extensive gallery of rogues in recent times, particularly after the end of the Cold War, when many states in the developing world were revealed to be incapable of exerting control over their territory without the support of superpower sponsors (P. Jackson 2003, 134). The warlord label is often applied to almost every variety of nonstate violent actor, including many that have little in common. For example, the most frequently cited examples include controversial individuals like Rashid Dostum, a former pro-Soviet militant in Afghanistan; Shamil Basayev, a militant leader in Chechnya; Somali militia leaders such as Mohammed Aidid and his son Hussein Aidid; Joseph Kony of the LRA in Uganda; Jonas Savimbi of UNITA; Foday Sankoh of the RUF in Sierra Leone; and leaders of multiple groups in D.R. Congo such as Jean Pierre Bemba and, more recently, Laurent Nkunda. The term is often extended even to juridically recognized political leaders such as Mobutu Sese Seko in Zaire, Saddam Hussein in Iraq, and Charles Taylor, the former leader of the NPFL, who was elected to the Liberian presidency in 1997 but never managed to shake the label.

Despite the intuitive appeal of analogizing warlords to rebels, it is problematic for a number of reasons. The prioritization of economic agendas that the warlord category implies reduces the action of complex political actors to little more than the behavior of criminal syndicates, rejecting the possibility that actors who employ violence against the state do so for more than just personal gain (Mkandawire 2002; Carayannis 2003, 234).[4] It may be true that contemporary insurgent organizations are not ideological in the traditional Marxist or anticolonial sense, but the motivations that drive contemporary violent groups can hardly be reduced to purely, or even primarily, economic factors.

Furthermore, even groups like Sierra Leone's RUF and Liberia's NPFL—for many the epitome of the insurgent organization as warlord paradigm—were shaped more by revolutionary political ideologies than is often recognized (Abdullah 1998). During the first half of the Sierra Leonean civil war (1991–95), the RUF devoted attention to carving out a rural base from which to fight a conventional war after having suffered heavy losses following an early attempt to take control of diamond mines in the southeast of the country. It was not until 1997, six years into the conflict, that the rebellion actually began to generate revenue from the international criminal syndicates dealing in diamonds (Abdullah 2006).

---

4. For example, even astute authors writing on the situation in Iraq since 2003 refer to the Sunni and Shiite militias that once divided Baghdad between them as "warlords" (Fearon 2007). However, it is certainly unclear what the economic agendas of each of these militias actually were. Even a casual observer would have to concede that the issues that divide Iraq's religious and ethnic communities are more related to pressing political problems such as institutional power sharing, historical injustice, and the foreign occupation itself than to a dispute over oil revenues.

In fact, according to Bangura (2000), both the NPFL and the RUF attempted to develop a system of governance to regulate social and political life in areas directly under their control, and this resulted in significantly lower levels of violence against inhabitants of these areas (Mkandawire 2002). Thus, although it is an attractive shortcut for explaining rebel behavior, the warlord analogy does not aid our understanding of the behavior of violent groups with multiple political motivations who operate within complicated structural environments replete with countervailing tensions produced by the interaction between local authority structures, transnational actors, and the incumbent state itself. This is especially true where insurgent control of territory is more than a fleeting phenomenon, forcing the group to develop and maintain structures for regulating civilian life.

A more nuanced approach is offered by those who link rebel behavior to the state-formation process initiated by early modern European and Asian bandits. Though not generally recognized in media accounts of armed groups where the warlord paradigm tends to reign supreme, this approach arguably represents the dominant academic trend in analyses of rebel governance.

Rebel Groups as Bandits and Embryonic States

Using a related politico-economic logic but positing it instead as driving a telos in the process of consecration are those that adapt the state-formation models of Charles Tilly (1990) and Mancur Olson (1993) to contemporary violent actors. They argue that service provision by rebels may represent embryonic state building—that is, the banditry model of state formation (Pegg 1998; P. Jackson 2003; Tull 2004; Kingston and Spears 2004; Stokke 2006). This approach shares with the literature on warlords an emphasis on the strategies of material accumulation adopted by violent challengers to the state, but it differs by arguing that contemporary rebel groups driven by economic self-interest may actually be replicating the dynamics that gave rise to the modern nation-state. For example, Denis Tull (2004, 19), writing about a rebel-constructed "parastate," argues that "[w]idespread violence and concomitant institutional decay should therefore be seen as neither pathological nor inevitably terminal events, but as possible stages in the ongoing process of state formation."

There is a widespread consensus that the nation-state remains the basic stabilizing unit of the global system, despite the perception that certain forces have chipped away at its dominance.[5] Indeed, except for the few rare circumstances in which the United Nations, regional associations, or imperially minded states

---

5. Some liberal scholars may emphasize the importance of international institutions. Others have argued that we have entered an era of market-based actors. But very few would go as far as saying that either group is more powerful than nation-states at this moment in history.

usurp sovereignty through trusteeships or forms of colonial occupation, the state is the only polity recognized as legitimate by the contemporary international community, having defeated the many other forms of social and political organization that still populated the globe just one century ago (Spruyt 1994; Krasner 1999). Understandably, commentators have long sought to explain how states became the sole holders of both the legal right (juridical) and physical capacity (empirical) to hold power in the international system. Most trace the consolidation of the state system to the insecurity that characterized Europe during the Thirty Years' War of the seventeenth century, which ripped apart the continent despite the myth of a unified Christian realm (Blaney and Inayatullah 2004). As Daniel Philpott (2002, 71) notes, "The Peace of Westphalia [which ended the war] marked a victory of the sovereign state as a form of political authority."

"Bellicist," or "predatory," theory, as it is sometimes called, focuses on the opportunities that waging war provides for state consolidation (Taylor and Botea 2008; Thies and Sobek 2010). In his influential study on the origin of the modern state (1993), Olson provides an appealingly intuitive version of this theoretical model, contrasting the behavior of the stationary bandit with that of a roving bandit. He moves away from the social contract vision of social order drawn from Western liberalism that emphasizes the consent of the governed to consider the material incentives underlying the power structure. In Olson's conception, a bandit has the choice of taking either a consensual or a coercive approach in his dealings with the civilian population. He argues that bandits who decide to transition from roving to stationary (thereby initiating a process of state formation) are not driven by any moral impulse. Instead, the specter of warfare by other rivals pushes bandits concerned with survival to move toward consensual accumulation strategies because the rewards offered through effective taxation of the population are much greater than the mere looting that the roving bandit previously relied upon to generate revenue.[6]

Tilly (1990) provides empirical support for this approach by examining the formation of states in western Europe. During the seventeenth century, continual conflict between political entities produced an emphasis on the "organization of coercion" within a territory in order to foster more efficient "preparation for war" (14). This hostile environment produced political regimes constantly concerned with readying for war and required the marshaling of vast resources to pay for professional armies. Rulers faced several options for the extraction and

---

6. Olson's argument is particularly interesting when contrasted with much of the literature on conflicts that tends to view contemporary rebel groups as warlords or criminal syndicates. By blurring the line between moral concerns and political outcomes, Olson forces us to reconsider the importance of processes deemed criminal in the genesis of new political formations.

accumulation of capital and came to prefer consensual taxation over more coercive methods, as the latter were more likely to produce resistance and potentially make the tax collector a threat to state power. Consensual taxation offered incentives to both the ruler and the ruled. It allowed leaders to raise extensive resources, plan for the long term, and build a standing army, and taxpayers benefited from the increased stability as well as the ability to voice their concerns to a receptive leadership.

Michael Mann (1986) argues that once a political authority is consolidated, waging war provides a convenient pretext for enlarging the bureaucratic infra-structure by increasing revenue flows to state coffers demanded of the citizenry to finance the war machine. Governmental structures developed during war tend to persist even after the conflict ceases, aggrandizing the state apparatus and deepen-ing its penetration into society. In western Europe taxation and waging war also contributed to the forging of national identities as political entities sought to con-solidate their authority by fomenting identarian ties between the population and the nascent political formations. It was through these various linked processes that nation-states emerged as *sovereign* entities with the capacity to govern a distinct territory with a corresponding population (Tilly 1990; Spruyt 1996). Within this formulation, former bandits turned leaders of what can appropriately be deemed embryonic states had little patience for other violent actors who challenged their power and quickly set about suppressing any internal threats to their authority.

Despite the best efforts of stationary bandits to consolidate authority, a glance at the history of Europe demonstrates that not all of them evolved into states, nor was the ascendant sovereign power capable of eliminating every political and economic challenger within its allocated territorial boundaries (P. Jackson 2003). More relevant to our discussion, once the European system of nation-states was exported to the rest of the world, nonstate actors of various sorts continually contested the emerging state authority's presumed sovereign prerogative to re-tain control over the use of violence within a specific territory. Indeed, nonstate actors operated with a degree of impunity within the reified boundaries that international law sought to ascribe to the dominion of specific sovereign state au-thorities. This was particularly true in much of the postcolonial world, where the state authority's claim to sovereignty remains more a juridical fatwa by the inter-national community than an empirical reality (R. Jackson 1990; Herbst 2000).

During the European period of state formation, bandit-held territories were generally devoid of overt political agendas.[7] What is known about these contes-tants to the incumbent power is that they often posed a direct challenge to state

---

7. Certainly, attempts to romanticize their behavior were made by contemporaneous authors. One need only conjure the romantic vision of a proto-Marxian Robin Hood contesting the authority of immoral political and economic elites.

authority, were able to consolidate their control of (primarily) rural territory, and had complex relationships with local populations as well as transnational actors (Hobsbawm 1990; Desai and Eckstein 1990; P. Jackson 2003)[8]. This type of rural banditry was widely prevalent, particularly at the peripheries of the emergent nation-states' hardening territorial boundaries. And it became especially significant during the period of disruption brought about by the state-formation process throughout Europe. This situation should not sound dissimilar to that in the many parts of the world plagued by civil wars today. Rebel groups frequently claim territory and develop civilian governance structures, directly challenging the sovereign prerogatives of recognized state authorities and demonstrating that the nation-state project is at once still ongoing and far from certain of absolute victory. However, the question remains whether the bandit-derived state formation model really is the most appropriate for understanding the construction of political structures by contemporary rebel groups.

Many scholars have attempted to draw direct comparisons between these processes of state formation and the emergence of rebel governance systems. Indeed, connecting the provision of services by violent nonstate actors to state formation has become quite common.[9] Several go as far as arguing that rebel governance systems are, in fact, embryonic or de facto states (Pegg 1998; Joseph 2002; Ottaway 2003). Generally these analyses argue that except for their lack of juridical recognition by the international community, such entities manifest all the attributes of contemporary states and deserve to be treated, at least conceptually, as such:

> States-within-states have imposed effective control over a territory within a larger state and may have an impressive array of institutional structures that, among other things, allow taxes to be collected, services to be provided, and business with other international actors to be conducted. Yet, they lack the very thing that quasi-states do possess: juridical status (Kingston and Spears 2004, 16).

But as I will discuss, it is impossible to disaggregate juridical sovereignty—and the international recognition it bestows—from the ability of a political actor to develop a system of governance. Recognition provides any political actor access to the international system and has direct implications for its governance efforts.

---

8. As noted earlier (note 3), Jackson actually refers to these actors as warlords, contrasting them against roving bandits.

9. For example, Will Reno (2001, 203) refers to "state-building insurgencies." And Paul Kingston and Ian Spears (2004) titled their edited volume on the subject *States-Within-States*. See also Stokke (2006).

Juridical status is therefore an essential distinction between state and rebel modes of governance.

These authors are not alone in arguing that contemporary rebel behavior is best viewed through the state-formation lens.[10] A few scholars have even advocated that such processes maybe a necessary step to solidify weak political systems around the world. Edward Luttwalk (1999), for example, famously argued that internal conflicts should be allowed to run their course to allow a more realistic political realignment to take place. Proponents of this "fight-it-out" thesis believe that a lack of war-making experience in the postcolonial world produced an unstable equilibrium characterized by weak states incapable of responding to challenges to their sovereignty from internal actors (Thies and Sobek 2010). By allowing civil war combatants to prove their empirical abilities by establishing an effective security apparatus and a system for revenue accumulation within the territories they control, a new social contract could be written that would require legitimate governments to either strengthen their relationships with the population or face challenges from new contenders better able to represent the wishes of the public over which they claim dominion (Herbst 2000; Joseph 2002; Tull 2004).

Thus the dominant trend in analyses of a rebel-produced political and social order has been to analogize it to bandit-derived state formation, producing a teleological trajectory that can only depict such efforts as rebels embarking on the path to statehood—inevitably coming up short. Despite the clear progress away from the simplistic warlord analogy, there are several reasons to be wary of comparing rebel administrations to embryonic states including one major theoretical shortcoming, as well as a variety of other limitations.

Political order has long been tied to the presence of a state, and the absence of the state is thought to be the precursor of chaos. For example, in traditional social contract theory, which underlies much of the theorizing on the appropriate relationship between a government and a political order, states are assumed to represent the structural mechanism through which the collective will of a political community can be expressed (Walzer 2004). In fact, the Hobbesian-derived notion that only a state actor can produce political order is among the most powerful norms within contemporary international relations theory. This statist bias goes a long way in explaining why political analysts have devoted so little time to understanding the provision of political and social order by nonstate violent actors (Mbembe 2000; Nordstrom 2004).

The problem for analyses of rebel governance is that by analogizing the existence of political order outside the state to the process by which states are formed,

---

10. Tilly (1985) pointedly warned against viewing the European experience as replicable.

analysts are often forced to see a state where none exists. As Michael Barnett (2001, 48) perceptively notes, analysts too often bundle "state, authority, and territory," making it "difficult to understand complex global relationships and processes that defy and flirt with the neat boundaries." In the case of insurgency, conflating rebel governance with state order forces analysts to awkwardly transpose the state-formation framework onto an actor that actively resists the state's attempts to project order within its ascribed territory.

A closer look at the emergence of the Westphalian system of sovereign national states can shed light on how the norm of statehood came to be so closely aligned with political order. The Peace of Westphalia of 1648, which preceded Hobbes's *Leviathan* by three years, formally acknowledged as an ongoing political project the division and placement of European territory under the control of discrete and autonomous sovereign states (Shearing 2006, 18–21). Underlying this shift was the normative assumption that states were the best entity for aggregating the will of the people, as the immediately prior era, despite pretensions of unity under a continental Christian banner, had been characterized by the coexistence of multiple actors capable of claiming sovereign functions.

Though this is not commonly understood, Hobbes believed that the state of nature was not just the absence of government but *the state of plural governance,* a situation he considered inherently unstable and in need of transcendence (Hobbes 1997).[11] Thus the notion that only the state is capable of producing political and social order is one that the historical record as well as contemporary examples brings into question. But the emergence of nation-states as the basic unit of the international system was not just the result of a post-Hobbesian normative effort. The state system emerged over several centuries as part of a historical process whereby it consistently outperformed other systems, despite the continued presence of challengers coexisting alongside it (Krasner 1999; Philpott 2002).

It is important to keep in mind that what is really at issue with rebel governance is not state formation but rather the formation of a political order outside and against the state. Both Olson and Tilly situate their discussion in a historical period rather dissimilar to our own globalized era. Olson's roving bandit faced a landscape in which multiple actors competed—with none able to exert complete control over a territory. Faced with the choice of either creating order from nothingness or continuing to exploit the anarchic conditions that existed, the first actor to subdue others to its will would be rewarded with vast material resources.

---

11. Hobbes never argued, as is often claimed, that individuals are prone to commit violence against each other without a higher authority. He recognized the family as the most important stabilizing unit of man's nature but thought that consanguinity was an insufficient principle for aggregating the will of larger populations.

It should be emphasized that both Tilly and Olson are really concerned with the emergence and consolidation of what are, by definition, embryonic states and not with those states' relationship to the current international system.

Today, though many civil wars are initiated far away from the center of power, even the most peripheral conflicts never face an open playing field (Herbst 2000). The state does not disappear but rather remains the premier competitor and threat to any non-state-produced political and social order; thus all rebel groups face a major challenge to their political project from the state authority or its allies.[12] The state—in control of far greater resources than any challenger—can penetrate rebel-controlled territories, disrupting any internal political processes or mechanisms that the organization may have employed. Furthermore, the contemporary global order, based as it is on the primacy of the state system, does not allow for much variation from the dominant paradigm that for every piece of territory, a specific state is deemed sovereign.[13] In the face of this paradigm (Barnett 2001), insurgent organizations that provide governance, despite their recognized ability to manifest aspects of empirical state sovereignty (i.e., control over a territory and a population), have never been able to garner juridical recognition for their existence.[14] Thus rebels must always compete with the state, which has a far greater standing in the international community and retains the right to exercise violence within its ascribed territory without fear of condemnation.

These realities go a long way in explaining why many rebel governments are not on the trajectory of embryonic states. Confronted with the difficulty of legitimating their authority in the face of overwhelming odds, many insurgent organizations prefer to retain their empirical gains without risking everything for a doomed transition to statehood (Mampilly 2009). This is also why analysts of contemporary war tend to misunderstand the stability of such systems, preferring instead to focus on an eventual outcome rather than on the actual structures and norms implemented by rebels in a specific place and time. These systems are certainly not permanent, but neither are they merely transitory. Whether we look at the LTTE in Asia, the SPLM/A in Africa, the FARC in Latin America, or even the Irish Republican Army (IRA) in Europe—all of which existed in some form

---

12. Exceptions would be states that actually collapse fully, like Afghanistan or Somalia. But even here, the groups fighting for control of the country are limited to operating in areas demarcated by the international community as the legitimate boundaries of the state.

13. This is a manifestation of what several analysts refer to as the "territorial trap" of international relations theory, in which sovereignty produces an inside/outside dichotomy that views the international system as anarchical and the state system as hierarchical—that is, states produce order internally but operate within an anarchical system (Agnew 1994; Barnett 2001).

14. One prominent exception was the offer by former Colombian President, Andrés Pastrana, to divide the Colombian territory into separate areas of government and FARC control. This approach was widely criticized and abandoned four years later.

for decades—many of the political structures constructed by rebel organizations may in fact be at least as durable as those established in weak states.

This is not to say that there is no such thing as embryonic states but rather that they exist solely in situations where the incumbent state is no longer able or willing to pose a challenge to the nonstate political authority. This is fundamentally distinct from a political environment in which the state remains a constant presence and threat to the rebel order. Nor is it impossible for a rebel civil administration to evolve into an embryonic state. The most obvious way that this could happen would be if the central state collapsed and no single militant group took control of the remaining state shell.[15] Embryonic states can also emerge as the result of a comprehensive peace agreement that delimits a portion of the territory to an insurgent organization either for a definite period of time or indefinitely.[16] And finally, embryonic states may emerge from the forced fragmentation of the state shell by an external power that ensures the autonomy of the nascent political formation.[17]

Another reason to avoid analogizing rebel governance with state formation has to do with the nature of the contemporary global economic system. Advances in transport and communication technologies alongside the emergence of a transnational market economy have fundamentally altered the landscape within which would-be rebel leaders operate (Friedrichs 2001). For example, Miguel Centeno (2002) effectively argues that similar conditions in nineteenth-century Latin America did not produce the same process of state formation that we saw in Europe in the seventeenth and eighteenth centuries.[18] Instead, the progressive globalization of financial resources diminished the need for state authorities to extract revenue from its citizenry in order to fight, as they had in Europe. Instead, elites interested in making war could rely on funds drawn from the transnational banking sector, which by the nineteenth century was able to efficiently move large amounts of capital across borders and even continents. Centeno further proposes that conflict in Latin America may actually have resulted from the *lack* of the European state-formation dynamic—as the state, unable to exert hegemony over its own territory, was vulnerable to challenges from other actors. Thus it is clear

---

15. This dynamic is in effect in Somaliland in the former Somalia, where the incumbent state has not existed in any meaningful sense since at least 1991 (Menkhaus 2004; Bradbury 2008).

16. The Government of South Sudan (GoSS), which emerged after the signing of a peace agreement between Khartoum and the southern rebels in 2005, is one such example. Its life span as an autonomous entity is limited by the date of a referendum to be held in 2011, which will determine whether it is to become a separate state or dissolved into a unified Sudan.

17. The Kurdish authority in northern Iraq, which has long benefited from American support (even prior to the 2003 invasion), is an obvious example as the foreign army rendered the incumbent state challenge to the incipient political entity insignificant.

18. A similar point is made in regard to African conflicts by Stein Eriksen (2005, 1109).

that the trajectory traversed by would-be political regimes during the period of European state formation has not been replicated by other regions during their own periods of state consolidation. This history raises relevant questions about the applicability of the European model to contemporary processes.

Finally, the fact that rebel governments possess de facto, or empirical, sovereignty—the ability of a political authority to exert direct control over a population and a territory—is considered evidence of their budding statehood (Pegg 1998; Spears 2004). Empirical capabilities were once viewed as the hallmark of sovereignty, which itself was viewed as indivisible (Boone 1998). Since rebel political regimes lack only recognition by the international community (commonly referred to as de jure or juridical sovereignty), scholars argue that they deserve to be considered embryonic states.

But contemporary international norms have delinked the two recognized faces of sovereignty (Krasner 1999). Empirical abilities are no longer a precondition for juridical recognition (R. Jackson 1990; Clapham 1996). States across the developing world fail to provide public goods and are unable to exert military control over their assigned territory; however, this does not inhibit them from enjoying the benefits of being recognized as sovereign by the international community, even if this is more an aspiration than reality (R. Jackson 1990; Reno 2001). Thus the fact that an insurgent government may replicate some of the structures and empirical functions of an idealized sovereign state does not mean that it will reap the benefits of internationally sanctioned de jure sovereignty. Such benefits are not merely symbolic. Recognition, as explained by Stephen Krasner (2001, 20), "guarantees access to international organizations and sometimes to international finance" in addition to offering "status to individual leaders." Equally important, it provides a basic framework for engagement, an opportunity to move beyond the ad hoc toward a more a regularized and structured approach for interaction with other legitimate actors (Philpott 1999, 569).

This is a point many rebel leaders echo themselves, viewing their provision of services as just a stepping-stone to the bigger prize of recognition by the international community—an outcome that few ever achieve (Bob 2006).[19] Still, international recognition of nonstate violent groups thus far has rarely been granted on the basis of the empirical abilities of nonstate violent actors. Far more often recognition is driven by broader geopolitical concerns.

Still, it would be naive to downplay the success of the nation-state as it remains the basic building block of the global system. Instead, it is better to examine the

---

19. This was relayed to me by leaders from both the LTTE and the SPLM/A. Both had a very pragmatic view that recognized their position within broader global discourses that can demonize or valorize rebel groups, and they sought to highlight their governance efforts as a corrective.

nature of the international system and demonstrate how it structures both the adoption of sovereign functions by contemporary nonstate actors and the response by the international community.

Rebel Rulers in the International System

International relations scholars tend to consider insurgent control of territory as an existential threat to the state system. By viewing insurgents solely through the warlord lens, they treat rebel-controlled areas as spaces of anarchy on the map, altogether outside the international system itself. Perceived deviations from the standard model, which posits the nation-state as the sole legitimate holder of territory within the international system, have occasioned much hand-wringing as analysts have developed a lexicon for dealing with territories under the control of violent nonstate actors. In a 2008 forum in the journal *International Studies Review,* for example, contributors deemed such areas of the map as "black spots" (Stanislawski 2008). And an edited volume produced in 2007 by the politically influential Rand Corporation on these areas was entitled *Ungoverned Territories* (Rabasa et al. 2007). In a purely legal sense, the formal rule of law of the state does not extend to areas of rebel control—thus the term "ungoverned" maybe warranted if we accept that only state actors may engage in governance. But this fails the basic legal principle of *ex facto jus oritur,* or that law should arise out of fact, a point I develop further in the chapter 8.

More problematically, those who use such terms rarely do so solely in the context of international law but also consider them as accurate descriptors of the on-the-ground dynamics within non-state controlled spaces. The obvious assumption is that because such territories lack a defined state authority, they have been reduced to anarchy, existing without any internal order. As such, their primary function within the international system is destabilizing; they are spaces from which piracy, terrorism and drug trafficking radiate (Rabasa et al. 2007; Kilcullen 2009).

The problem is that few analysts have tried to bring together works that challenge the assumption that states are the sole providers of order with analyses that demonstrate that a variety of nonstate actors can hold territory and govern populations. Instead, writers who deal with civil wars commonly treat them as bounded phenomena encapsulated within the territory of a single state, thereby failing to see how transnational linkages and interactions shape contemporary internal warfare (Gleditsch 2007). At the same time, those who focus on the international system continue to presume anarchy in those areas of the map outside the control of a defined nation-state (Vinci 2008). A more nuanced approach would combine observations on war's capacity to fragment political authority internally with analyses of how nonstate governing authorities interact with the international system, a task I turn my attention to now.

There are two basic questions: first, whether the international system is composed of a single category of like units (nation-states) or whether these units are sufficiently diverse as to warrant multiple categories, and second, whether the domain of anarchy is domestic or international. Mohammed Ayoob (1998, 37) has pointed out that both neoliberalism and neorealism "accept the assumption about the sameness of state," varying only in regard to their relative power measured along several standard metrics. Historically, however, the states that now constitute the developing world, where most internal wars take place, have never had an equal claim to parity within the international system. Indeed, before the founding of the United Nations (UN), sovereignty was largely considered the preserve of European states, which as a category of privileged actors paid little respect to arguments put forth by non-European leaders.[20] Even after the founding of the UN, violations of the sovereignty of recognized governments were commonplace, both during the Cold War struggles between the United States and the Soviet Union and in later years with military interventions by the United States into Afghanistan, Bosnia, Colombia, Haiti, Iraq, Pakistan, Philippines, Uganda, Somalia, Sudan, Yemen, and Yugoslavia.

Even with international institutions, many in the developing world discern a double standard when it comes to the weaker states in the system. This is most apparent at the UN, where the Security Council continues to be dominated by permanent members. But it also applies to newer institutions such as the International Criminal Court, whose interventions have often been criticized for targeting weaker states on behalf of the more powerful (Branch 2007). Some scholars, such as Barry Buzan (1983), have argued that these realities mean that most states in the developing world may constitute an identifiably different class of states with little connection to our standard perception of what a state actually is or does.

Without a consensus on the institutional and ideological character of the state, it is also difficult to make generalizations about the relationship between a governing regime and the society it controls. For example, contrary to the liberal ideal, regimes that govern states with weak empirical sovereignty often view internal challenges to their control as threats, casting certain segments of the population as opponents rather than beneficiaries of the state's munificence. The population, for its part, rightly comes to view the state as a threat to its security

---

20. For example, Haile Selassie's appeal to the League of Nations after the invasion of Ethiopia by Italian forces in 1935 failed to generate even minimal condemnation of the invasion despite wide praise for the appeal's eloquence and moral content.

(Buzan 1983, 65–69). Acknowledging that states vary along a number of important empirical dimensions and therefore that international society already recognizes multiple categories of political actors is an important starting point for coming to terms with the existence of rebel governments. Furthermore, it is important to understand that these challengers to state sovereignty are an integral aspect of the power dynamic within certain state shells, requiring a movement away from the obsession over state weakness towards an appreciation of the need to understand alternate political formations that may emerge. We must also reconsider the standard dichotomy implicit in many international relations analyses regarding the nature and location of anarchy.

A common assumption is that the international system is anarchic whereas the domestic realm is hierarchically organized under the control of a distinct sovereign power (i.e., the state) (Neumann 1998b). Indeed, a stable international system is often assumed to be predicated on well-ordered states under the control of powerful and legitimate sovereigns, as "this prevents the exportation of domestic anarchy to interstate relations" (Ayoob 1998, 40). More critical analyses of the international system question this premise, arguing that for much of the developing world, global politics appears far from anarchic but is instead highly organized, with the great powers structuring the system in hierarchically ordered ways (Escude 1998). These scholars have also questioned the assumption that the domestic realm is hierarchical, pointing to the fact that many Third World states consider the real domain of anarchy to be domestic territorial spaces that remain out of their reach and under the control of nonstate violent actors. For states affected by violent challenges to their sovereignty, the standard formulation that views the international system as anarchic in contrast to a hierarchically ordered domestic political scene with the state at the apex is inverted. Instead of domestic order and international disorder, many developing countries struggle to impose a degree of control over their territory while, at the same time, receiving permanent recognition of their legitimacy from a highly ordered international system (Ayoob 1998; Neumann 1998b).

Part of this confusion is produced by a basic disagreement on what criteria are necessary to designate a political entity as a state within international law. The Montevideo Convention of 1933 that has since become the basis of customary international law specifies four attributes of statehood: (1) permanent population, (2) defined territory, (3) a government, and (4) the capacity to enter into relations with the other states (Stanislawski 2008). This approach presumes a degree of contiguity between the four criteria, or in other words, that there is a relationship between the empirical and juridical dimensions of sovereignty. In the previous section, I questioned the wisdom of bundling together the first three criteria, which are related to the empirical ability of a political entity to project power. Analysts who draw their notions of statehood from these criteria tend to focus on the state's role as the recognized governing authority over a defined, and territorially bounded, human community.

But this approach disregards a fundamental reality that underlines the establishment of the contemporary international system. As Philip Bobbit (2008, 453) notes, "[T]he U.N. Charter was structured by the legal concepts of nation states with *opaque* sovereignty [emphasis in original]"—thereby disregarding the internal politics of a state in determining its membership in international society. This is true even where a regime has clearly committed transgressions beyond the boundaries of international law, up to and including orchestrating genocide against a portion of its population. Formal recognition of statehood, as a result, emphasizes only the fourth criterion of the Montevideo Convention. In this view, the state may serve as the political authority over a defined community, but its existence is not defined by its ability to serve this function; thus the presumed contiguity between the concepts of statehood and authority is uncertain. More important is the recognition of the claim to statehood by the international community, highlighting both the autonomy of the state from the domestic political community and its sustaining entanglements with like units within international society (Asad 2008).[21] This tendency helps explain why even in cases where the recognized authority is a "quasi-state" (R. Jackson 1990)—one with little or no capacity to govern the territory adjudicated to its control—it can remain a viable entity within international law while other actors such as insurgent organizations that may actually demonstrate the capacity to govern a segment of the territory and population fail to garner any recognition at all.

It is tempting to suggest that rebel groups that engage in governance are essentially the inverse of a quasi-state, i.e., a political entity with empirical abilities if not juridical sovereignty. However, such a formulation ignores the often complex relationship between juridical and empirical forms of sovereignty and the ways in which rebel leaders try to navigate between the two. An insurgent organization is not concerned solely with gaining empirical control but also with using its governance of a population and territory to make a claim for greater juridical recognition, which in turn can enhance its governmental abilities. What I propose instead is that nonstate groups in control of territory need to be treated as a distinct category of sovereign actor, more akin to other nonstate

---

21. This is the only way to make sense of the term "government-in-exile," a term that was employed widely during World War II to describe those governments that had fled their territorial base to take up residence elsewhere. A recent example is Somalia (2004–5), where the government resided in exile in neighboring Ethiopia.

systems that have always coexisted and competed with the nation-state.[22] In
effect, what I am suggesting is that the international community reconnect juridical recognition with empirical abilities, at least in the context of evaluating
the behavior of nonstate actors. I will discuss this approach in greater detail in
chapters 3 and 8.

In the real world, such an approach, despite its analytical advantages, is often
rejected on the basis of political rather than intellectual objections. The notion
that authority need not be unitary within a single territory but in fact, can be
both multiple and overlapping[23] continues to generate resistance from state governments inclined to preserve their privilege to exercise dominion over a people
and territory. State authorities in particular have multiple reasons for viewing
insurgent organizations as mere warlordism and hence denying them access to
even elemental juridical recognition within the international system. As Adam
Branch (2007, 183) notes, "[I]nternational criminalization is an excellent strategy for states wishing to rally foreign forces to their side and to delegitimate
political or military opposition."[24]

Resistance can also emerge externally, from an international society predicated on the notion of discrete state authorities mutually respecting and en-
forcing each other's sovereign claims. As Blaney and Inayatullah (2004, 188–89)
note, juridical sovereignty is produced by a "reciprocal recognition" between
state entities, which makes the creation of international society "an inherently
social process." Analysts have pointed out that despite the origins of many Third
World political systems and boundaries as the arbitrary byproducts of colonial
era imperatives, current international norms continue to evidence a strong resistance to legitimizing challenges to a recognized sovereign, for fear of eviscerating state legitimacy more generally (Herbst 2000; Nadarajah and Srikandarajah
2005). It is in this way that the rebel governments most clearly depart from the
state paradigm as recognition of their presence would pose a direct challenge
to an international system that restricts full membership solely to the singular
category of the nation-state. In essence, recognizing a nonstate actor's claim to

---

22. For example, the "shadow networks" described by Carolyn Nordstrom (2004).

23. This resonates with Hedley Bull's (1977, 254) alternate formulation of contemporary global
political order as neomedievalism, "a system of overlapping authority and multiple loyalty." In this
perspective, political authorities share sovereignty over a territory with multiple actors, competing
for supremacy both horizontally with their peers and vertically with vassals.

24. For example, the U.S. government, under pressure from the Sri Lankan government, listed the
Tamils Rehabilitation Organization (TRO), a prominent diasporic humanitarian NGO operating in
LTTE-controlled areas, as a terrorist group, thereby restricting the ability of its international partners
to work in the north and east of the country (see Treasury Department 2007). This was done despite
concern from Human Rights Watch and others about the violent actions orchestrated against the
Tamil population by the Sri Lankan state.

territory would undermine the very opacity of sovereignty that is the corner-stone of the contemporary international system, despite continuing challenges to this principle by well-meaning, if ineffective, human rights activists and international courts.

Although certain groups—such as Forças Armadas da Libertação Nacional de Timor-Leste (Armed Forces for the National Liberation of East Timor, FALINTIL) in East Timor, the Palestine Liberation Organization (PLO) in Israel, and the Irish Republican Army (IRA) in the United Kingdom—have been able to transcend this bias for limited periods, achieving a degree of formal international recognition on an ad hoc basis, these cases remain the exception. Moreover, since the type of recognition they are grudgingly granted is functionally dissimilar to that offered to even the weakest states, making comparisons between the two is an awkward exercise. Instead, as I discuss in greater detail in the next chapter, it is essential to acknowledge that despite the existence of politically ordered territories outside the control of specific governments, the nation-state remains the premier actor within any given geopolitical space. As such it retains the ability to mitigate the adoption of sovereign functions by contemporary armed groups as well the international community's response to these nascent political formations.

This is not to imply that there are no similarities between how states and nonstate actors engage with the international system. As even casual observers of contemporary conflicts understand, a wide variety of transnational actors play an important role in almost all contemporary war zones. Analysts have recognized that the relationship between the state and transnational actors is a key component of how many contemporary regimes, empirically incapable of exerting control, are able to survive (Bayart 1993). Similarly, it is widely recognized that other states, international agencies, NGOs, and multinational corporations (MNCs) work with insurgent structures to reach populations and territories under rebel control. Scholars such as Carolyn Nordstrom (2004) have shown how transnational shadow networks are able to move goods and services in and out of insurgent-controlled territories with surprising regularity, providing basic resources to those living within, including the rebels themselves. However, the nature of these interventions differs widely between state authorities and rebel civil administrations.

For insurgent organizations, the lack of juridical recognition renders any interaction with transnational actors skirting the line between licit and illicit in the eyes of the international community. As such, these interactions are functionally dissimilar to those between recognized state authorities and the same set of transnational actors (R. Jackson 2003; Reno 2001). Still, such resources play an important role in the development and functioning of rebel governance efforts, though they remain ensconced furtively in the shadows, despite their scale and significance.

In this chapter, I have argued that viewing rebel groups as replicating the trajectory of the modern state is limited in important ways. It is more useful to think about insurgent governance systems as an example of both the potential and the limitations of a political and social order produced by nonstate or counterstate actors.

What is the importance of understanding these spaces? Many states across the globe are characterized by fragmented control over their assigned territory and civilian populations. A realistic appraisal of the primary organs of the international system, limited as they are to the voluntary membership of recognized nation-states, needs to begin by accepting that they do not encompass, let alone represent, all the world's territory and population, despite their claims to universality. A variety of nonstate actors, including insurgent organizations, can and do control the fate of civilian communities for substantial periods. Thus, international society must find ways to comprehend such territories or risk abandoning them to those who do not respect basic norms governing transnational engagements. Though warlords concerned solely with wealth maximization offer few opportunities for inclusion, rebel governance systems are a categorically different phenomenon with a varied set of motivations and behaviors and should be understood as such.

The above discussion demonstrates that, generally speaking, the only opportunity for validation of a rebel government lies in making the transition to effective statehood, a transition few are likely to achieve. Thus insurgent organizations that govern territories and population effectively lie in a state of limbo in which they can achieve legitimacy only by becoming a state, but they face tremendous challenges, both normative and structural, to their capacity to do so. Rather than regard them as embryonic, which implies a trajectory toward consummation, it is more productive to reject facile comparisons to preexisting analytical categories and recognize the fundamental challenges rebel governments face in legitimizing their existence.

Treating these actors as worthy of their own analytical category can help analysts understand their internal mechanisms and processes as well as their position within the international system. In the next chapter I introduce the concept of "counterstate sovereignty" as a legal category for nonstate violent groups that develop effective governance systems. By offering insurgent organizations a standardized route to international recognition based on an objective assessment of their governance systems, we can move away from the ad hoc process of recognition toward an approach that focuses on civilian welfare, a discussion I return to in chapter 8.

The stakes of this debate are more than academic. On one hand, recent trends have come to view any nonstate actor involved with violence as illegitimate at best or irrational at worst. On the other hand, some view insurgents as drivers of the state-formation process. Those who conflate insurgency with terrorism reject the possibility that any violent organization can express legitimate dissent against oppressive states. More problematically, they willfully ignore the ability of insurgent organizations to establish order and ensure the welfare of civilians within conflict zones. Those with a more positive take tend to downplay insurgent violence, preferring instead to celebrate an insurgency's transformative potential. In both cases, the effect is to allow purely political considerations to determine international recognition or sanction of any particular rebellion, often to the detriment of civilians caught within. By removing the normative blinders and instead assessing these organizations by their ability to address civilian welfare, we can prioritize human needs in our understanding and treatment of violent groups. The rest of this book is dedicated to removing the cloak of darkness that shrouds rebel-controlled territories through a specific focus on how these sites are organized to address civilian livelihoods. Through a better understanding of variation in insurgent governance, we can move away from demonizing or glorifying such groups to a more clear-eyed view.

3

UNDERSTANDING VARIATION IN INSURGENT GOVERNANCE SYSTEMS

In the shadows of war and politics there came to be surreal turns of cause and effect.

—Michael Ondaatje, *Anil's Ghost*

In revolutions, as well as counterrevolutions and civil wars, there comes a crucial point when people suddenly realize that they have irrevocably broken with the world they have known and accepted all their lives. For different classes and individuals this momentary flash of a new and frightening truth will come at successive points in the collapse of the prevailing system. There are also unique moments and decisions—the storming of a palace, the beheading of a king, and in reverse the overthrow of a revolutionary dictator—after which there is no return. Through these acts a new crime becomes the basis of a new legality. Huge sections of the population become part of a new social order.

—Barrington Moore, *Social Origins of Dictatorship and Democracy*

On a visit to the lakeside city of Goma in eastern D.R. Congo in 2004, I rode through a rotary in the center of town then under the control of the RCD-Goma rebel organization. Workers wearing ragged uniforms displaying the insignia of a defunct municipality were busy tending to a freshly planted garden of flowering shrubs. Struck by the incongruity of attending to the cosmetic appearance of a rotary when surrounded by the combined destruction from years of war and a debilitating volcanic eruption, I asked my *boda-boda* (motorcycle taxi) driver whether these types of superfluous public works projects were common during the war. He simply replied, "Wote wanapenda maua" ("Everyone loves flowers").

It can be difficult to understand the logic that shapes rebel behavior around governance issues. Unlike other discrete aspects of insurgent behavior that analysts have sought to explain, such as the use of violence or recruitment strategies, governance encompasses a much broader set of societal interactions; thus a search for a single, master variable is inevitably quixotic. Understanding rebel

governance entails an appreciation of the complex interactive relationships between a variety of state, nonstate, and transnational actors that in combination
shape the experience of civilians during war. Often, as with the establishment of
a legal system, the logic of rebel behavior is straightforward. And other times, as
with the beautification project in Goma, it is decidedly not.

In this chapter, I provide a framework for understanding rebel behavior on
questions of governance. My approach is to move from the general challenges
facing nonstate actors seeking to construct a political order in a situation of war
to the more specific challenges that emerge from rival actors and locations. Understanding the broader environment that affects all rebel groups seeking to develop governing systems is an essential first step, and so I start here. In particular,
I examine the two central relationships—one with the incumbent state and one
with the inhabitants of the territory they seek to control—that will determine the
nature of the political arena insurgents enter. But equally important is to identify
the distinctive factors that emerge from precise locations affecting the behavior
of insurgents around questions of civilian treatment. Therefore, I move on to a
detailed discussion of hypotheses derived from specific challenges that face nonstate violent actors seeking to govern civilian populations.

Though it is clear that the construction of governance systems by rebels draws
directly from the model of the nation-state, it is imperative to avoid allowing the
parallels between the two to shape our perceptions of the former (Asad 2008,
184). In the previous chapter, I discussed why current analyses that view rebel
governance as being analogous to either state formation or warlordism are incapable of explaining the phenomenon adequately. I argued that instead of approaching the study of rebel governance as merely a threat to legitimate states
(warlordism) or along a presumed trajectory within the state-formation process
(embryonic states), we should assess the subject on its own merits, for its actual
forms and functions during a conflict. Thus it is perhaps more useful to think
about insurgent groups constructing governance structures as an opportunity to
examine the potential and the limitations of a political and social order produced
by a *nonstate* or, more accurately, by a *counterstate*.[1] Rather than analogizing
rebel behavior to preexisting discrete historical categories such as bandits or
warlords, I present the idea of insurgent organizations that develop governance

---

1. "Counterstate" is an underused term for an old category of violent actors that have always existed alongside and against the nation-state. The earliest reference to a counterstate is in Luis Mercier
Vega's 1969 work, *Guerrillas in Latin America: The Technique of the Counter-State*. In his seminal work
on rebel governance Timothy Wickham-Crowley (1987, 478) spoke of a counterstate that "establishes
itself through exchange, in effect establishing a new 'social contract.'" See also Radu (1990) and Castells, Yazawa, and Kiselyova (1996).

structures as "counterstate sovereigns," operating in an interactive fashion with the incumbent state and other nonstate actors, both local and transnational.

Insurgent Governments as Sovereign Formations

As many authors have pointed out, internal warfare fragments political authority (Kalyvas 2006; Fearon 2007). But fragmenting political authority is quite distinct from eradicating it altogether, and in the absence of a centralized, empirical *and* juridical sovereign formation, new configurations of political order are likely to emerge, constructed in some cases by the state or its allies,[2] but also by challengers to it. Like warlordism, control of civilian populations by rebels is an alternate form of nonstate political authority that prioritizes security and emerges where the state is no longer able to exert control. And like embryonic statehood, rebel governance requires a complicated relationship with a defined civilian population that implicates bigger questions about the nature of authority, legitimacy, power, and sovereignty itself. However, it is my contention that rebels governing territory represent neither warlordism nor banditry-derived state formation. How, then, can we best understand this phenomenon? A more useful way of assessing the similarities and differences between the governance systems of insurgents and formally recognized state authorities is to directly compare the parameters of state sovereignty with the political and social order constructed by insurgencies.

There are three issues related to the question of sovereignty: first, the relationship between the political authority and the population; second, the relationship between the political authority and the international system; and third, the actual form and manner of the political authority itself. Analysts have generally recognized two faces of sovereignty (R. Jackson 1990; Krasner 1999).[3] One is an external, socially constructed dimension (discussed in detail in the previous chapter), which, because of the prejudice of an international system predicated on a division of territorial space into nation-states, rebels are incapable

---

2. For example, paramilitaries aligned with the Colombian government have established alternate political orders in areas under their control. See Gutiérrez Sanín and Barón (2005) for an interesting discussion.

3. The classic view of sovereignty is that it is an indivisible characteristic of states. But work over the past two decades has challenged this assumption, arguing instead for a view of sovereignty that treats it as a multifaceted set of characteristics, each of which is worthy of analysis. See Lake (2008) for a discussion of this point.

of appropriating.[4] The other is an internal dimension, which posits a particular relationship between a political authority, a target population, and the territory upon which it resides. Thinking of sovereignty as composed of both a juridical and an empirical dimension (as they are commonly referred to) is useful for understanding the construction of a rebel political authority. Having discussed juridical sovereignty in the previous chapter, in this chapter I focus instead on the question of empirical sovereignty.

William Munro (1996, 116) offers a useful summary of the accepted view on the empirical dimension of state sovereignty:

> In modern social formations the state is the principal institutional locus of political power. The state is seen as the legitimate provider of specified political goods, over which it has sole and universal jurisdiction on the basis of a national collectivity and for which it seeks revenue on that basis.

Compare this with one definition of a rebel government, which can be viewed as the series of institutions established by an insurgent organization to manage relations with civilians living in the territory under its control that set in place a system of taxation and a series of rules (formal or informal) for governing civilian life (Weinstein 2007, 164). The similarity between the two definitions is unsurprising. But Munro (1996, 122) takes his analysis of state power further.

> State power rests, then, not only in coercive capacity or in the influence of dominant social groups but also in political and ideological traditions of control and consent that are not socially fixed.... Consequently the links between the state and society are multivalent and complex, running not only through the regime and the economy but also through the institutions and discourses of the public sphere. In this light, the core problem of governance and state authority is how to incorporate people into a polity and economy in such a way that they accept the particular forms of political and legal authority that are centered on the state and, most broadly, the different ways that various realms of civil society are made subject to the ultimate jurisdiction of the state through its various legal and administrative institutions.

Thus the construction of sovereignty is more than an instrumental process of incentives offered by a political authority and a response from a target population, as it is sometimes framed.

---

4. As I discuss later, however, they do have distinct relationships with actors in the international system (Englebert 2009).

Indeed, sovereignty's internal face implicates power, authority, and legitimacy—three highly contentious terms—in the relationship between a civilian population and a political regime. Removing the teleological assumptions about state formation that bedevil much of the analysis on rebel governance, we can instead recognize empirical sovereignty as a particular type of authority relationship. Unlike control, which is a function of brute force, authority implies a mutual relationship between two actors in which the subordinate actor willingly *consents* to a command by the dominant actor (Lake 2008). Violence can be an important driver of an authority relationship, but a purely coercive relationship between a political regime and a subject population is not one that would be considered authoritative. Authority requires a degree of consent even if this is partially derived from the coercive capacity of the political regime. Power then rests not only with the ability of a political actor to use violence but also with its ability to generate consent. As Hannah Arendt (1970, 41–42) notes, "Indeed one of the most obvious distinctions between power and violence is that power always stands in need of numbers, whereas violence up to a point can manage without them because it relies on implements." In social contract theory, legitimacy refers to an authority relationship that achieves the appropriate combination of coercion and consent between the political regime and the subject population.

Understanding how power, authority, and legitimacy intersect on the question of governance by rebel groups is an essential task when discussing rebel/civilian relations. In their engagement with the incumbent state, insurgents have a variety of options for dealing with civilian populations that they come into contact with. Many groups have little interest in holding territory, choosing to engage with local communities primarily through violence. But insurgents that rely on terror alone must be satisfied with operating as roving bandits, as the LRA has done over the past two decades in Central Africa. Terror can stifle opposition but cannot engender loyalty and support from the civilian population. Indeed, until the post–September 11 expansion of the "terrorist" designation to any nonstate group that uses violence, this was a common criterion that analysts used to distinguish between an insurgency and a terrorist group (Ahmad 1982).

Other rebellions choose to liberate territory but have no intention of engaging the accompanying population. In order to do this it is necessary to depopulate the territory of local communities, often using violence or the threat of violence to motivate civilians to flee. For example, the RPF adopted this approach in northern Rwanda because it distrusted the surrounding Hutu communities in the areas under its control (Mamdani 2001, 186–89). Though both of these approaches to dealing with civilians have been adopted by contemporary insurgent groups, viewing them as representative ignores the tremendous diversity of strategies that rebels can avail in managing civilian populations. It also tends to overestimate the efficacy of coercive tools for consummating the insurgent agenda, as violence alone is often an insufficient basis for mounting an effective challenge to state power over time.

Many other insurgent groups view civilian collaboration as an elemental component of their political strategy. Coercion is an essential tool for insurgent leaders as they vie to take control of a territory away from the incumbent state in line with their strategic objectives. But once an insurgency gains control, an overreliance on coercive means will limit its ability to generate popular support for its agenda, an important factor that can determine its capacity to retain its military position (Ahmad 1982, 249; Kasfir 2004). As Stathis Kalyvas (2006, 114) explains, "[F]ear alone does not suffice to sustain rule in the long term; however, it operates as a first-order condition that makes the production of loyalty possible." Indeed, many insurgencies find civilian support to be an essential concern in pursuit of their organizational ambitions.

The idea that insurgents frequently develop consensual relationships with civilian populations is not debated, but can these governance systems ever gain legitimacy? Theoretically, this is certainly a possibility. Theorists have shown how the legitimacy of state authorities, rather than being static, is deeply contingent on the behavior of the political regime and hence can always be contested by alternate political entities (Tilly 1990; Wickham-Crowley 1987). During an internal war, civilian support is rarely determined at the onset of fighting but rather is malleable, contingent on the behavior of the belligerents over the course of the conflict (Kalyvas 2006, 101–3). In addition, scholars have shown how authority relationships are not limited to formal governments but can also exist in the kinds of informal relationships that humans commonly develop (Roitman 2001, 2005; Wickham-Crowley 1987). These realities can lead to a contest between the state and its competitors over which is the legitimate authority. As with the state, an "asymmetrical exchange relationship" may develop between a nonstate political regime and the population it seeks to govern (Wickham-Crowley 1987, 475). This relationship, based on mutual and unequal exchange, relies on a combination of coercion and consent that over time can produce an informal social contract that can render an insurgent government a legitimate authority, thereby bolstering its position in its competition with the incumbent state.

Challengers to a recognized political authority begin with their weapons aimed at the old order but diverge on the question of how to prevent those same weapons from turning on the population they purport to be fighting for.[5] Indeed, one of the biggest challenges for leaders of an insurgency is how to resist

---

5. I thank Raquel Zamora for helping clarify this for me.

the brutal efficiency of coercive tools if they hope to mobilize civilians behind their cause (Ahmad 1970). The fact that ignoring the importance of generating civilian support through other political means beyond violence can have serious costs is an important motivating impulse for contemporary rebel leaders. Discontented civilians living in rebel territory can pose a number of challenges to a command. These can be expressed nonviolently through noncompliance with insurgent directives or, rarely, by autonomous civil society organizations that are able to express discontent openly. Or more threateningly, civilians may choose to collaborate with the state, providing crucial information and engaging in actions of sabotage against insurgent rule. They may even form militias (with or without state support) that violently challenge the insurgency's control of territory.

Once in control of territory, rebel leaders choose between relying on violence to quell internal discontent and finding alternative means of winning civilian support. At a basic level, controlling territory allows insurgents to offer utilitarian benefits to civilians in ways that groups without territory could never do (Kriger 1992, 169). Rebel organizations that choose to pursue nonviolent options have several potential strategies for inducing civilian collaboration and limiting challenges to their rule. Kalyvas (2006, 124) identifies six mechanisms that allow a rebel organization in control of territory to push the civilian inhabitants toward the insurgent agenda, including two integral components of governance: "shielding" and "provision of benefits." Shielding refers to protection from threats of violence by a rival violent actor. In conditions of overt warfare, the ability to provide a modicum of stability can be a powerful lure to civilians seeking refuge. And the provision of other benefits, including but not limited to the establishment of schools and hospitals, can provide a powerful incentive for civilians to support insurgent rule, even if only passively.

From the perspective of the insurgent organization, reaching out to the larger noncombatant population makes tactical sense. Even in situations of mass mobilization, only a tiny sliver of the population is likely to participate actively. Mark Lichbach (1995, 18), for example, estimates that only about 5 percent of any population is made up of active and militant participants; others have put the upper limit of civilian participation at well below a third of the total population (Wood 2003). The key for rebel leaders is to ensure that this passive majority does not turn on the insurgency as a result of the organizations' negative behavior or more attractive conditions offered by rival actors. As a collective good rather than a selective benefit, civilian governance by guerrillas can extend beyond simply generating individual participation (13). Since civilians in rebel-controlled areas can and do enjoy these goods without directly participating in the insurgency, the provision of public goods can be viewed as part of a broader program to generate legitimacy and support for the rebel regime.

In short, though a reliance on force alone may be an essential precondition for rebels to gain control over a territory and population, it is not a sustainable strategy over the life of the conflict, as civilian commitment to the insurgent cause remains susceptible to overtures from other political actors. For states dealing with internal insurgencies, this principle has long been recognized and serves as the basis for counterinsurgent strategies, which commonly focus on severing the ties between an insurgent organization and its civilian support base. The basic strategy of all governments fighting insurgencies has been to use a mix of sticks and carrots to wean the population away from supporting the rebel group without engaging in activities that push them into the rebel camp (Rich and Stubbs 1997; Kilcullen 2009). Rebel governance efforts cannot be merely rhetorical but must either produce public goods that surpass those on offer from competitors or face the possibility of civilian defection and other overt or covert resistance to rebel rule. As Wickham-Crowley (1987, 493) found in his study of guerrilla governments in Latin America, an organization that is unsuccessful in developing effective governance functions must rely to a greater extent on terror to ensure civilian compliance, often with detrimental effects on the insurgency's likelihood of achieving its objectives.

It is in this competition for civilian loyalty that rebel governments most closely draw inspiration from the nation-state; that is, in order to gain legitimacy for their political authority, rebels do not rely on force alone but also engage in activities that generate a degree of consent from the population. For the rebel command, the challenge is to balance its use of violence in dealing with civilians with its need for civilian support—the Gramscian balance between domination and hegemony (Gramsci 1992; P. Anderson 1976).[6] Extrapolating from the above, it is the provision of governance and the establishment of an informal social contract that will determine whether a group will be able to derive support for its political authority and achieve some form of legitimacy, a key factor in shaping the nature and scope of its challenge to state power (Ahmad 1982).

The Gramscian formulation of state power is also useful because it recognizes the decentralized nature of power within society, emphasizing the need for the political authority to manufacture consent through nonmaterial means. When I apply the term "governance" to rebel behavior, I have in mind the process by which rebel leaders develop both the structures necessary to provide goods *and* the practices that enforce their legitimacy (Wood and Dupont 2006, 2). This broader approach to understanding governance has its origin in the observation that at its most basic, a system of governance entails not just formal institutions but all the

---

6. For a framing of this issue in regard to colonial rule, see Guha (1997) and Young (1994).

practices and norms that regulate the daily life of civilians as well. The advantage of understanding governance broadly as the ability "to structure the possible field of action of others" (Foucault 1982, 220; Rosenau and Czempiel 1992) is that it allows us to look beyond the formal structures of the political authority to interrogate the discourses and other normative behaviors that shape civilian life.

This formulation encompasses legitimation strategies that incorporate the production of political power through methods other than the provision of goods, including, commonly, the adoption of cultural symbols. While the contemporary state is imbued with legitimacy through its presumed contiguity with a cultural nation based on which it claims the right to rule, a rebel government, even one representing a nationalist claim, cannot take for granted its affiliation with a specific population, since a civil war by definition renders that claim permanently a field of contestation. Thus rebels often seek to legitimate their authority through replicating the forms of the nation-state itself, a fact that forces us to consider how sovereignty is constructed symbolically and how this applies to rebel behavior. Put another way, I am concerned with not just the structures of the civil administration but also the political culture of an insurgency and its role in legitimizing the authority of a particular organization. The notion of insurgent political culture encompasses "the values, norms, practices, beliefs, and collective identity of insurgents." As Wood argues (2003, 19), rather than remain a static enterprise, political culture tends to evolve in tandem with "the experiences of the conflict itself, namely, previous rebellious actions, repression, and the ongoing interpretation of events by the participants themselves."

Such symbolic behaviors are the bridge between the external and internal faces of sovereignty, encompassing the performative elements that signify a sovereign entity to other nation-states, as well as being a strategy for a political regime to demonstrate the legitimacy of its rule to a subject population (Weber 1998). In addition to developing a civil administrative structure to woo civilian support then, rebel groups also rely on symbolic actions as a cost-efficient way for the political authority to generate compliance by reproducing the symbols of the sovereign nation-state. Since a rebel political regime does not possess legitimacy in the same manner as a juridically sanctioned government, it attempts instead to burnish the legitimacy of its governance system by mimicking the symbolic behavior of the nation-state.

Indeed, one of the more striking aspects of insurgent behavior is the length that some rebels go to project their power symbolically, often with little obvious instrumental value to their actual military goals. These practices, which they often adopt with gusto, may include such idiosyncratic practices as the costuming of personnel according to distinctive military arrangements, the adoption of official flags and mottoes, the burial of the dead in extravagant cemeteries (the LTTE in

Figure 3.1. An LTTE cemetery in the northern province of Sri Lanka, May 2004. Courtesy Ananthan Sinnadurai.

Sri Lanka), the printing of a "national" currency with no local value (attempted by the SPLM/A's Bank of New Sudan), and the composition of national anthems for unborn nations, as was the case during the struggle in D.R. Congo waged by Laurent Nkunda's Congrès National pour la Défense du Peuple.

Performative elements are designed by rebel leaders to promote a degree of consent among the governed and are hence an important element of rebel governance systems. They are part of the broader Gramscian program of building consent through the provision of specific public goods as well as the deployment of discursive practices and symbolic actions drawn from the insurgent political culture. Thus, while many rebel leaders may act in ways that betray their own rhetorical constructions of their cause, this criticism does not render their actions and comments meaningless. Instead, it is important to recognize that the intended audience for these actions may not be the international or even national community but rather a clearly defined subject population and perhaps the affiliated diasporic community, who are better primed to comprehend the meaning of the rebel command's symbolic maneuvering.

In short, symbolic and empirical aspects of sovereignty are mutually reinforcing, and rebels address both with the goal of legitimating their political authority.
The hope is that through consistent efforts to normalize the social and political
order by developing a comprehensive system of governance, rebel leaders can,
over time, legitimize the insurgent political authority in the eyes of civilians:
"Therefore, as the guerrilla government grows and strengthens itself, we can observe the shifting of the exchange equation toward a reciprocal set of obligations,
and the emergence of a more clearly defined set of interlocking rights and duties for both governors and governed" (Wickham-Crowley 1987, 483). But since
authority is deeply contingent on the behavior of the political regime, insurgent
governments that fail to maintain their end of the social contract can just as easily
lose popular support; thus the development and maintenance of a governance
system are continuing concerns (492). Though rebels may never fully appropriate the sovereign realm of nation-states, it is clear that sovereign behaviors, in
both the empirical and symbolic sense, influence and even drive rebel behavior
on the question of civilian governance. But without the juridical sanction offered by the international community, insurgent claims to sovereign status are
perpetually incomplete, as the incumbent state power, by virtue of its juridical
status, retains considerable scope for affecting rebel civilian governance efforts
(Englebert 2009).

Insurgent Governance and the State

**With regard to the enemy, we should never underestimate them.
If we do, we will inevitably meet with failure.**

—Ho Chi Minh, quoted in Vo Nguyen Giap, *Fighting under Siege*

Conflict between an incumbent government and a violent armed group in control of territory requires us to distinguish the "state," the entity granted juridical
sovereignty, from the "state shell," the territorial area delimited as a discrete unit
in the international system (Vinci 2008, 303). The fragmenting of sovereignty
induced by a civil war does not cause the state to disappear; rather, its ability to
exert its complete sovereign prerogatives is reduced to only a portion of the state
shell.[7] It may be tempting to theorize that the rump state is no more powerful

---

7. Even in states with seemingly comprehensive empirical control, territories often remain outside the direct grasp of the state's legal apparatus. For example, urban slums controlled by criminal
gangs often operate outside the direct control of the state authority. Consider the favelas of Brazil for
one prominent case.

than the new political entities that emerge within the state shell—that the fragmenting of sovereignty renders the state shell a space of anarchy with no single actor capable of exerting control. However, this ignores the significant advantage that the state is accorded as a result of its juridical recognition, even in a situation of fragmented control (Englebert 2009). Despite its diminished capacity, the incumbent government retains the ability to affect political life throughout the entire state shell. Thus there is a relationship between empirical and juridical sovereignty that cannot and should not be ignored by incumbents, particularly in their dealings with nonstate actors in internal wars, where this effect is particularly evident.

The complicated relationship between rebel governance efforts and the incumbent state is predicated on the struggle for territorial control, as the shifting nature of the battlefield requires insurgents to develop governance systems that evolve in response to various state challenges to their position. Control refers to the ability of a rebel group to exert its power over a defined territorial space and to induce collaboration from the civilian population living within this area. It is generally a product of the military abilities of the insurgent group and is defined by the rebellion's capacity to defend the population from external threats. When speaking of a rebel-controlled territory, it is important to recognize that territorial control can vary widely within a defined area. Control is never a fixed attribute but evolves as the rebel military organization generates victories or suffers setbacks on the battlefield. Indeed, rebel control tends to swing dramatically both spatially within the area of operation and temporally in response to the ebb and flow in the rhythm of the conflict itself. Generally, three zones of control can be identified: (1) areas under the control of the insurgent group, (2) areas of divided or contested control, and (3) areas under the control of the incumbent state (Kalvyas 2006).

This forces us to consider how territorial control influences the governance project of any particular insurgent group. In the competition for power between a state and an insurgency, the question of control often emerges as determinative because the effectiveness of the political authority can vary widely by the degree of control a particular insurgent group is able to exert over a given territory at a specific time. The rebel command will decide to engage different areas with varying levels of commitment, choosing to devote greater resources to strategically important towns or villages than to others less central to the conflict dynamics. Rebel leaders must navigate between their desire to foster more permanent governance structures that demonstrate their actual control of a territory and population and the realities of a violent engagement where the ability to expediently abandon a position in the face of strategic shifts is essential to the survival of the group itself. It is not unusual for a rebellion to develop a pockmarked map of towns and villages under its control, leaving adjacent population centers to the control of the state authority.

In a situation of contested control, the state may choose to use "hearts and minds" strategies, common to most counterinsurgent campaigns, to woo the population away from the rebel authority. However, in areas under insurgent control, states tend to engage with the civilian population mostly through violence (Wood 2003, 121; Weinstein 2007, 27). In these areas, the incumbent state has a variety of tools that can disrupt efforts by the rebel organization to develop governmental functions. These can be direct, through military means, whether combat with rebel forces or the use of indiscriminate bombing. States also frequently deploy militias by funding, supplying, and directing their efforts against rebel targets, with considerable effectiveness (Gutiérrez Sanín 2004). State efforts can also be indirect, through restrictions on essential supplies or other controls on people and goods that undermine the ability of any emergent rebel-derived political order to survive. States may even attempt forced population movements that can deny insurgents their popular base of support, though this strategy is contingent on first taking control of territory away from the rebellion.

The fact that rebels copy the forms and structures of the nation-state is often a strategic necessity to deal with the counterinsurgent strategies of the incumbent state. As Mao (1961) made clear, marshaling a political force capable of challenging the incumbent government is often the only option for any violent actor hoping to challenge the overwhelming advantages that nation-states continue to hold over their challengers. These advantages emerge internally within a specific territory, where nation-states can rely on their supposed filial relationship with a national population. And internationally, nation-states benefit in two ways from the recognition of their monopoly on violence: militarily, it allows them to access the latest weaponry—the production and distribution of which generally continues to be regulated by other states—as well as politically, where nation-states generally remain capable of using violence with minimal prohibition from the international community.

Thus it is essential to recognize that rebel governments are engaged in a convoluted and interactive relationship with the state—not only in its actual physical manifestation as the focus of its violent actions but also as an idea, both internally as the predominant form of political community, and externally as the unit upon which the international system is based. This reality has a direct impact on the governance strategies of insurgent leaders as they seek to respond to strategic shifts in the conflict dynamics produced by the behavior of the state incumbent. As Wood (2003, 28) succinctly notes in the case of El Salvador, "The change in government strategy led to a change in insurgent strategy as well." As the international system transforms from one built on the nation-state as the basic political unit to one in which the nation-state is no longer the sole or even dominant form of political authority, its centrality in shaping the behavior of violent groups is likely to change as well (Tambiah 1996, 11). But for now, and the foreseeable future, the nation-state will remain the basic building block of the international system, despite the prognostications of several prominent and thoughtful observers.[8]

In brief, I define rebel governance systems as possessing counterstate sovereignty for the following reasons. They are counterstate actors in that their competitive relationship with the state is the premier impulse that motivates every aspect of their civilian governance project. They are sovereign in that they not only adopt many of the empirical functions of the state but also seek to gain a degree of legitimacy by mimicking the trappings of the nation-state itself. It is through these empirical and symbolic behaviors that they make a claim for juridical recognition within international society, a discussion I will return to in the chapter 8.

On the Behavior of Counterstate Sovereigns

An insurgent organization is a collection of men and women joining together at great risk to pursue a common agenda with little chance of success. Despite occasional proclamations to the contrary, these organizations tend to be top-down entities, with tremendous power invested in the leadership. Throughout the following discussion, the rebel leadership is treated as the primary agent shaping the organization's governance efforts, though a central assumption I make is that an insurgent command operates in a highly constrained environment. Different rebel commands respond to similar pressures from various actors that dictate the effectiveness of the governance system they develop. My intention is not to proclaim any laws of rebel behavior but rather to explore this political environment that insurgent leaders navigate while also highlighting its exceedingly dynamic nature.

As Kasfir (2005) demonstrates in his discussion of the National Resistance Army in Uganda, leaders of the insurgency struggled to find the appropriate balance between their desire to construct governance structures and the realities of the battlefield. Though they generally prioritized the military struggle over civilian governance, this was not an automatic outcome and required a careful calculation of the costs and benefits of their eventual decisions. In a similar fashion, all rebel leaders must decide when and how to divert resources away from the

---

8. Philip Bobbit's (2003, 2008) discussion of the market state, which calls for an international system that recognizes it as the basis for international regimes, is one of the more thoughtful examples.

military battle with the incumbent and redirect them toward civilian governance. These resources are not purely financial but also include the insurgent personnel that would have to leave the battlefield to oversee the civil administration. My focus, then, is on comparing the distinct strategies pursued by rebel leaders to establish structures and practices by which to govern a civilian population.

As discussed in greater detail in chapter 1, my approach diverges from foundational analyses by rebel theorists that assume the unconstrained agency of rebel leaders on questions of governance (Mao 1961; Guevara 1969). In this view, rebel leaders develop governance systems in line with their ideological beliefs, i.e., from the top down. Though leaders may exert considerable influence in the initial phases of the war in regard to recruitment strategies, as well as during the latter phases of the war in regard to peace negotiations, their agency during the fighting is highly constrained by the behavior of other actors. For this reason, I also diverge from the political economy perspective that has dominated the study of rebel groups in political science and economics.[9] Since natural resource endowments often remain static—or at least do not fluctuate wildly—they do not hold the key for understanding processes that exhibit considerable variation both temporally during different phases of the fighting and spatially according to the degree of territorial control by the state or the rebel group.

My concern in the case studies that follow this chapter is with the effectiveness of rebel governance efforts, which I assess by examining several sectors that illustrate the ability of various organizations to govern a civilian population: first, strategic services, including a police force and judicial mechanism; second, technical services such as the provision of health and education; and third, the development of legislative bodies or other feedback mechanisms that seek to represent the population on the ground (Wickham-Crowley 1987). These sectors correspond with what are generally agreed upon as the three core functions of modern government, namely, security, welfare, and representation. State theorists view these three functions as being interconnected. In this view, "security constitutes a precondition for welfare and political participation, while welfare reduces conflicts and political representation allows for non-violent resolution of conflicts. Likewise, welfare increases the capacity and propensity for political participation, while representation promotes economic development and social justice" (Stokke 2006, 5).

Despite a desire to demonstrate long-term horizons in the construction of civil administrative structures, rebel leaders seek solutions that evince an instrumental understanding of the shifting terrain of the battlefield—and they adopt

---

9. For examples see Weinstein (2007) and Collier and Hoeffler (2004). Relevant critiques have been leveled by Gutiérrez Sanín (2008).

governance strategies accordingly. In my own field research, I learned that the provision of services by insurgent organizations is rarely a concern at the outset of fighting, as groups do not come into control of territory until some time after the initial phases of the war. For the first few weeks and even months after fighting breaks out, military engagements tend to paralyze civilian social and economic life dramatically, reducing interactions to the most local of levels. Thus, generally speaking, a sufficient period of territorial control is a precondition for the attempt by any insurgent group to construct a civilian governance apparatus.[10] As a consequence, public welfare provision beyond defending the population is rarely an immediate imperative for a rebel command that seeks to rule over civilian subjects (Wickham-Crowley 1987, 486).

Indeed, when rebels come into control of a distinct territory and population, I found that the establishment of a force capable of policing the population, followed by a broader judicial mechanism to regulate disputes, was often the first step taken by any rebel group and easily the most important. This follows from the discussion of control and the importance of regulating the means of violence, an essential precondition for the development of a comprehensive system of governance. The establishment of security structures allows an insurgency to demonstrate its relative power to civilians, in addition to laying claim to a key component of Weberian sovereignty, that is, the monopoly over the use of violence within a specific territory. As a famous rebel theorist noted, a system of law provides a degree of stability to a rebel-controlled territory allowing civilians to "normalize" their life under rebel rule (Guevara 1969, 83).

Without a functioning security system, it is difficult for rebels to gain the credibility they would otherwise have as the dominant force in control of a specific territory. It enables them to initiate a process of providing additional collective goods (Weinstein 2007, 26–27) by allowing interaction with transnational actors, many of whom understandably choose to stay away during intense periods of fighting. Furthermore, since the rebel army already possesses effective instruments of coercion, a police force is not nearly as cumbersome to establish as other public goods like social welfare programs or legislative bodies. Unsurprisingly then, the establishment of a police force followed by the development of a broader legal mechanism, either informal or formal, is the highest priority for any leadership and is often the key determinant as to whether the rebel group is able to make the transition from a roving insurgency to a stationary one (Wickham-Crowley 1987, 482–83).

---

10. This explains why the cases of rebel governance comprise only a fraction of the total number of insurgent organizations, as many violent groups either fail to take and hold territory for a sufficient period of time to build a robust administration or simply choose to operate in a roving fashion.

The provision of other public welfare items such as health and education is often viewed as a secondary concern, though occasionally rebels may attempt to provide these services even before they build an effective security system. As with security, the delivery of services can also be ad hoc (informal) or bureaucratic (formal), with the establishment of specific structures within the civil administration explicitly to provide public goods. Legislative bodies or some other mechanism to foster civilian participation in administrative decision making ranks last with rebel leaders, again unsurprisingly, as most tend to have an autocratic predisposition in their ideas for what is best for their subjects.

As discussed in chapter 1, in the assessments of specific insurgencies, I consider insurgent governance efforts effective when the following conditions are met. First, a force capable of policing the local population must be developed. Second, a broader dispute resolution mechanism should be put in place. Third, additional public welfare goods should be provided. For the purposes of this book, I focus on the development of educational and health systems. And finally, the civilian population must regularly and willingly avail itself of the structures—both formal and informal—that make up the governance system. Notice that I do not consider representation a necessary condition of effective insurgent governance. An insurgent organization that is able to develop only effective policing and judicial practices is considered to have partially effective governance, and obviously, an insurgency unable to meet any of the above conditions would be considered to have non-effective governance.

Governance entails more than just the actual structures that comprise the rebel civil administration. Since rebels often interact with, or attempt to co-opt into their governance project, other nonstate actors engaged in service provision, it is essential to look beyond the formal structures to the whole set of relationships that shape the provision of public goods within a rebel-controlled territory. Thus, beyond the effectiveness of insurgent structures for distributing public goods, I am also concerned with the role of other political actors and their intersection with insurgent governance systems. Since these relationships may not always be formalized, it is necessary to understand the complex practices of rules that create the bargaining context between insurgents, other political actors operating in conflict zones, and civilians (Kahler and Lake 2004, 412). Indeed, as the case studies make clear, understanding the complex web of interactions between insurgent organizations, the incumbent state, the civilian population, civil society actors, and transnational actors is essential for understanding the capacity of different rebel governance systems.

Thus the construction of a rebel governance system is an iterative process whereby the adoption of specific practices and structures is responsive to the behavior of a number of diverse political actors, each operating within a specific local and international context. For example, actions occurring at the most local of levels may push rebel leaders to adjust their governance system to dissipate the threat posed to the organization's strategic objectives (Kalyvas 2003, 487). Indeed, insurgent governance systems constantly evolve as a result of demands articulated from multiple locations. From the bottom up, civilian demands or situations created by the local population can alter rebel behavior. And from above, the imbrication of global forces on the conduct of an internal war can affect rebel behavior, as transnational actors insert themselves into local political, economic, and social processes in ways that rebels must take into consideration (Branch and Mampilly 2005; Gleditsch 2007; Mampilly 2009). At each step of the conflict, insurgent leaders refine their governance strategy in response to these dynamics, adopting or rejecting approaches in an evolutionary fashion. Because rebel governing systems lack the seeming permanence of their state counterparts, they are more able to transform dramatically over time, though as I argue below, they are constrained by the historical context and political environment in which they operate.

Factors in the Development of Civilian Governance

Civil wars are complex and ambiguous phenomena that resist efforts to be categorized along a single dimension. Instead, the shifting nature of the battlefield muddles our understanding of even the most seemingly straightforward conflict. As a result, the question of rebel behavior does not lend itself to monocausal explanations or simplistic binary formulations. Rather than focusing on a single preexisting condition, it is better to think about contemporary rebel leaders as engaging in a series of interactive relationships with a variety of political and economic actors. In a messy world where global forces shape local conflicts that are likely to have their own transnational impacts, this should not be surprising. A single master variable is thus impossible to identify, though it is possible, as I assert below, to identify several key challenges that affect the development of civilian governance by insurgent leaders. As explained above, some factors are present at the onset of fighting, while others surface as a result of fluctuations on the battlefield.

These factors emerge from three separate levels that the insurgent command must constantly engage—from below, from within, and from above the organization. From below, rebel groups face pressure from the denizens of the areas under their control. The civilian population is as important for its own actions and beliefs as it is for its general composition on racial, ethnic, religious, and ideological grounds. From within, rebel groups must take into consideration individuals or factions representing oppositional perspectives, whether based on cultural or ideological differences or even just greed. From above, rebel groups interact with transnational actors, including international agencies like the United Nations and World Bank, MNCs, NGOs, churches and other religious organizations, diasporas, and states.[11] However, I do not mean to imply that these categories are exclusive; rather, it is the interactive relationship between the three levels that is central to my analysis, as I discuss in greater detail in the case studies that follow this chapter.

From Below: Civilian Demands Affecting Insurgent Governance

> **With regard to the people, if the army can win their affection, confidence, and admiration, it will surely win victory.**
>
> —Ho Chi Minh, quoted in Vo Nguyen Giap, *Fighting under Siege*

Recent comparative analyses of rebel behavior have tended to treat populations as static—responsive solely to the behavior of the insurgent organization or to other actors—rather than constituting an active agent capable of influencing events. Thus, scholars of insurgent/civilian relations have emphasized such factors as the resource environment the rebel group operates within (Weinstein 2007), the organizational capacity of the leadership (Kasfir 2005), the geographic surroundings of the rebellion (Herbst 2000), and whether the group operates in rural or urban areas (Mkandawire 2002). Each of these approaches tends to view the population as generic, malleable by external forces, and incapable of shaping the behavior of the rebel command. However, as Kalyvas (2003, 481) notes, "The locus of agency is as likely to be at the bottom as the top, so civilians cannot be treated as passive, manipulated, or invisible actors; indeed they often manipulate central actors to settle their own conflicts."

The tendency to elide the role of civilians at the local level was not always the norm. Earlier analysts of insurgent behavior often focused on the relationship between the rebel command and local communities, arguing that insurgents must generate collaboration from the population for a variety of instrumental concerns. Consider one analysis of rebel behavior from 1970:

> The guerrilla concern with mass support is understandable even on purely military grounds. Mobility, for example, depends on the

---

11. To some degree, diasporas operate at all three levels, though I categorize them as operating from above.

availability of food, shelter, road gangs, labor for laying mines and booby traps, messengers and stretcher-bearers—services which require active and clandestine civilian cooperation right under the enemy's nose.... Intelligence depends on intimate contacts with the population to the extent that it develops into a widely based rebel infrastructure which includes women, old men and children.... Lastly, popular support is essential because the disparity of military strength rules out a clear-cut victory by the insurgents, and the struggle tends to be a war of attrition in which the guerrillas' morale is their trump card; morale cannot be sustained in isolation from one's people. (Ahmad 1982, 246)

Thus the removal of civilian agency from studies of rebel behavior is a problematic and unwarranted omission.

Indeed, the impact of conflict on local populations is the main concern of this book, and it is imperative to recognize that civilians are rarely only victims in war zones (Lubkemann 2008). Civilians are never passive or invisible actors and can manipulate the tenor of rebel governance efforts through the explicit demands they make on an insurgent command, usually in line with their own local preferences. They have a variety of ways of responding to rebel control, including wholesale support, limited or coerced participation, public and private protest, disengagement (by fleeing the rebel territory), covert and overt collaboration with the incumbent state, and even violent rejection through the formation of local militias. An insurgent organization's most immediate tool for ensuring compliance is always its ability to deploy coercive tactics, often with stunning brutality, upon civilians under its control. Still, civilians do not lack agency in their interactions with rebel groups and generally have strong preferences that remain even after they come under the control of a rebel organization (Kriger 1992). The essential dynamic to recognize is that the decision by a population to either embrace or reject a specific rebel organization is a strategic one. And the ways it goes about doing this can affect the behavior of insurgent leaders, who must partially structure their governance systems to respond to civilian demands.

Another common tendency of comparative analyses of rebel organizations is to separate the behavior of the group from the social and historical conditions that precede the conflict. Rebel groups are often treated as ahistorical phenomena emerging whole from raw materials more accessible to statistical analyses such as geographic location, population dispersion, economic inequality, and access to natural resources. Though the predilection for statistical solutions is understandable, it is clear that in this case, analysts ignore historical factors with great risk, for there is evidence that the complex preconflict relationship between the people and the state affects the structure and behavior of rebel groups, particularly as it

pertains to questions of governance. Thus it is dangerous to treat civilian populations as little more than cattle, responding herdlike to generic stimuli. Instead,
it must be recognized that preconflict preferences can have an important effect
on civilian acceptance of various insurgent organizations. For example, during
the civil war in Zimbabwe, Norma Kriger (1992, 147) documents how the war
deprived peasants of a number of government services that they had become accustomed to, including "public transport, marketing, cattle dipping, clinics, and
schooling for their children." This had important consequences for the guerrillas
of the Zimbabwe African National Union (ZANU) as they sought to rally popular support behind their liberation struggle.

Variations in civilian preferences can be produced by several historical factors.
These would include whether the preconflict society was habituated to paying
taxes, whether it had a say in politics, whether it was a multicultural society, and
how the state's bureaucratic structures reflected such differences. I argue that the
preconflict relationship between the state government and the civilian population has a determinative impact on the effectiveness of rebel governance systems
as insurgent leaders respond to demands made by civilians conditioned by their
relationship to the preconflict political authority. The task is to determine a way
to distinguish between those populations likely to make claims upon the political authority and the types of claims they are likely to make, which I turn
to now.

STATE PENETRATION: HABITUATION

The state-society paradigm that forms a significant strand in the comparative
politics literature of the past two decades has done much to demonstrate how
the past lingers in reconfigurations of political order, especially in the postcolony
(Migdal 1988). A good summation of this perspective is provided by Atul Kohli
(2002, 90):

> Taking history seriously suggests instead a shared belief that the past in-
> fluences the present and, as a result, that satisfactory causal explanations
> must have a strong over-time component. This analytical standpoint
> follows in part from taking institutions seriously. As patterned beliefs
> and practices, institutions take time to root. Once rooted, institutions
> mold behavior. Political outcomes are thus partially path-dependent,
> influenced by institutions of an earlier origin, forcing state-society
> scholars to be sensitive to the impact of the past on the present.

If we are to heed these insights, then we must account for the influence that the
prior relationship between state and society—particularly the social dynamics

produced by this relationship—has on the development of new structures and practices of rule triggered by the outbreak of violence (North 1990; Mkandawire 2002). It is my contention that only through an understanding of the preconflict state-society relationship can we grasp the modalities that produce diverse insurgent governance efforts across cases, as various civilian populations, politically habituated in differing ways, make distinct demands upon the rebel political authority.

Understanding the fiscal relationship between state and society is one way of distinguishing the idiosyncrasies of certain populations that insurgents come into contact with in their operations. As Joseph Schumpeter noted, "The spirit of a people, its cultural level, its social structure, the deeds its policy may prepare—all this and more is written in its fiscal history" (cited in M. Moore 2004, 298). Historically, most non-Western political regimes began with international recognition of their juridical sovereignty over the boundaries left behind by the colonial powers, despite their physical incapacity to enforce them (R. Jackson 1990). Over time, international norms have protected even the empirically weakest states, often when they could not protect themselves (Herbst 2000, 106). While some non-Western states, such as India, have developed, in true Tillyan fashion, a governmental structure based on the progressive expansion of the taxation apparatus across the population, many others have followed a divergent fiscal path based on a much narrower capital accumulation model, namely, rents.

In Europe the progressive expansion of state power was tempered by the development of an active and vibrant civil society. Thus, as the bureaucratic apparatus penetrated deeper into society, citizens developed an active response to state power through the institutions of civil society (Young 1994; Migdal 2004). In much of the developing world, however, civil society was stillborn. Colonial rulers were little concerned with the development of a viable state project and were hostile to empowering societal actors to respond to the encroaching state apparatus. Rather, profit drove the state-formation process, with coercion serving as the basis for extraction. Hence the state apparatus that developed in much of the colonial world was primarily concerned with institutionalizing the "machinery of permanent domination" in order to maximize the accumulation imperative (Young 1994, 95). Crawford Young (1994) argues that the colonial state's emphasis on profit required it to develop a strategy of accumulation predicated on the manipulation of traditional elites rather than a broader integration of the civilian population into the institutions of the state. This strategy facilitated the extraction of natural resources once potential oppositional figures had been co-opted or coerced into compliance.

Faced with a dwindling to nonexistent tax base, many independence leaders across Africa and Asia could not emulate the revenue-accumulation model based on the taxation of the citizenry (hereafter referred to as "merchant states") adopted by their former colonial masters in their home countries. Instead, they turned to the quick financial rewards offered through the collection of rents from foreign investments in natural resources and from lucrative strategic political alliances, both of which were plentiful during the heyday of the Cold War. The rentier state emerged in response to a globalized world order that rewarded local political elites with large economic surpluses based on their control of native resources and their mutually profitable relationship with agents in more developed countries (Mkandawire 2002; Moore 2004). These financial resources accrued to political elites recognized as the legitimate sovereign, even if this recognition was more an international fatwa than an empirical reality (R. Jackson 1990; Herbst 2000; Reno 2001; Moore 2004). Scholars have convincingly argued that state authorities that rely on rents possess greater autonomy from the will of the general public because the government has little need to develop a broad tax base, preferring instead to either buy off noncooperative citizens or build a coercive apparatus capable of keeping the population in line (Mkandawire 2002; Moore 2004).

As I have argued thus far, the variation evident in rebel governance systems is a function of the different pressures on the insurgent command; primary among these are demands articulated by the civilian population under insurgent control. Thus examining the history of the penetration of the state into society is one method for distinguishing between the types of demands likely to be made by different populations that insurgencies come into contact with. This is in keeping with an observation made by Mahmood Mamdani (2001, 22):

> Political identities exist in their own right. They are a direct consequence of the history of state formation, and not of market or culture formation. If economic identities are a consequence of the history of development of markets, and cultural identities of the development of communities that share a common language and meaning, political identities need to be understood as a specific consequence of the history of state formation.

Mamdani's contention that "[e]very state form generates specific political identities" (23) is useful for grasping the postcolonial differences between states that rely on the citizenry for fiscal support (merchant) and those that rely on other sources of funding (rentier) and the varying political arrangements that come into being as a result of the development and penetration of the state administration. Specifically, what I am arguing is that in order to understand the type of relationship a local community is likely to have with a rebel government, it is important to understand how and to what degree that community was integrated politically into the preconflict state through the expansion of the government bureaucracy.[12]

Two distinct visions of the civilian population related to the penetration of the state apparatus into society emerge from the preceding discussion. As a material form of power, taxation can serve as a useful proxy for understanding the relationship between a political regime and its subjects (Bates and Dau 1985; Roitman 2005). In the rentier state, populations have no sense of ownership over political decision making since they are not required to fund the state through taxation (M. Moore 2004).[13] Therefore, a disengaged government produces an apolitical population, disconnected from the local machinations of the presumably ineffective public bureaucracy. In contrast, in the merchant state, an active population is heavily invested in political decision making through its direct financial contributions. Citizens in these states aggressively seek to limit the behavior of the state authority in a way that is beneficial for the overall well-being of the polity.

To summarize, theorists have shown how the nature of the state is determined by its fiscal prerogatives. A corollary of this argument is that two types of civilian populations will emerge in response to the fiscal strategy adopted by a specific state. My argument is that the different types of populations produced by the above state forms affect rebel governance in determinative ways. Thus, civilians politically habituated by rentier state fiscal policies are unaware of their ability to influence the political authority, a condition that carries over to political formations that develop in the face of a conflict-produced state withdrawal. In merchant states, where the bureaucratic structures penetrate deeply into the public psyche and are capable of both collecting taxes and providing significant amounts of public goods, civilians are habituated to having a say in political affairs. They understand that welfare provision is reciprocal in nature, often in proportion to their support for the established political authority (Timmons 2006). In both cases, it is up to the rebel command to determine how to deal with the civilian population, and its ability to establish political structures that respond to the demands articulated by the local community will determine the success

---

12. I use "penetration" to mean more than just the idea of "governmental capacity" discussed by other authors and used to compare the relative capacity of governments in different states. Governmental capacity refers to the "extent to which governmental agents control resources, activities, and populations within the government's territory" but does not take into consideration the territorial variation in capacity common to most contemporary rentier states (Tilly 2003, 41).

13. This is not to imply that no community within the state has dense relations with the state authority. Some communities are the favored recipients of state largesse and enjoy considerable benefits from this relationship. However, without an underlying mechanism driving the state/society relationship, there is considerable variation between communities within these states, each of which may have distinct relationships with the central government.

or failure of the organization's governance project. Failure to do so may open the group to internal challenges, both political and militant, from the civilian population. The above discussion provides us with the basis for hypothesis 1a.

> **H1a: If an insurgency emerges in a state with minimal penetration into society, it is less likely to develop an effective governance system than one that emerges in a state that penetrated deeply into society.**

STATE PENETRATION: COOPTATION

State penetration also produces a secondary effect that shapes rebel governance beyond civilian demands. To mitigate civilian challenges, rebel leaders must often tap into and even co-opt preexisting institutions and networks of power, which are themselves the direct product of the preconflict relationship between the incumbent state and political actors (Migdal 2004). Merchant states are characterized by more effective social control resulting from the denser interactions between the state and significant social groups that allow citizens to be more demanding in their interactions with the political authority. However, in the rentier state, the lack of a functional state bureaucracy opens up the path to alternate forms of governance by nonstate actors. In the preconflict period, political and social order is likely to be provided by an ad hoc array of political actors, including religious institutions, charitable organizations, private corporations, trade networks, and traditional authorities (Bierschenk and De Sardan 1997). Such a divided authority structure can create significant obstacles for rebel leaders as they seek to develop their own structures and practices of governance, forcing them to negotiate with a multiplicity of different actors in their efforts to build a governing system (Raeymaekers, Menkhaus, and Vlassenroot 2008). This compares with the legacy of a highly penetrated state, a situation in which rebels confront cohesive institutions and networks of power. This provides us with hypothesis 1b.

> **H1b: If an insurgency emerges in a state with high penetration into society, it is more likely to be able to co-opt preexisting institutions and networks into its civil administration, thereby improving governance provision.**

I also argue that the preconflict degree of interaction between the state and civilians will influence the scope for institutional innovation by an insurgent organization, again as a result of the legacy of state penetration into a territory before the outbreak of a conflict. The design of rebel governance systems is the least likely to depart from preexisting patterns and institutions when the preconflict society is characterized by a high degree of state penetration. In this case, the group will likely incorporate, fully or in part, the governmental structures and practices established in the preconflict period. This is done primarily through the replacement of government bureaucrats with personnel selected by the insurgency. Much of the bureaucratic framework will remain the same, with only specific changes made to accommodate the needs and desires of the new rulers.[14]

In certain cases, rebel groups may be forced to share the administration of their territory with the incumbent government they are fighting, assuming they are unable to devote the material resources necessary to keep the bureaucracy functional and a suitable joint mechanism can be designed. This approach may entail the division of service provision into various sectors, alternately allocated to either the state authority or the insurgent civil administration—for example, health and education may be left to the government while the legal system is reconstituted by the rebels. In chapter 4 I provide a fuller discussion of this dynamic, looking at the case of the LTTE in Sri Lanka.

On the other hand, insurgents that take over areas where the preconflict political regime has failed to penetrate into society are likely to develop more innovative, yet less effective, structures and practices to govern the civilian population. In this case, rebel leaders may have to start from scratch, establishing a completely new governance strategy for each of the sectors based on their own prerogatives. Alternatively, they may be able to negotiate with the nonstate actors that assumed the role of providing order in areas where the state does not exist. Either way, this approach requires massive efforts by the organization to develop and staff new structures or to engage in complex negotiations with nonstate actors like aid organizations, religious institutions, and traditional authorities that continue to provide civilian services even after the rebels take control.

From Within: Internal Dynamics Affecting Insurgent Governance

With regard to discipline, an order from above must be obeyed by every combatant; a report to the upper ranks must be honest, timely, realistic....Rewards and punishment must be just and clearsighted....With regard to the troops, a commander must understand their speech and behavior, their joys and sorrows, their food and clothing; he must take utmost care of these things.

—Ho Chi Minh, quoted in Vo Nguyen Giap, *Fighting under Siege*

---

14. This was the approach adopted by the Eritrean People's Liberation Front in Ethiopia, for example (Pool 2001).

Frantz Fanon, the Martinican consigliere to Algeria's Front de Libération Na-
tionale (FLN), sagely warned insurgent leaders to be conscientious about the
two struggles all revolutionary groups must face: against the enemy and against
internal tensions within the movement (1968). Rebel leaders must address both
of these imperatives when developing their organizational strategy.[15] Fanon's
admonishments are useful for understanding how would-be insurgent leaders
define their struggle, both to the population from which they elicit support and
to actors outside the movement. First, leaders must decide whether their objective is the overthrow of a central government or the secession of a specific
territory. This is generally determined by the behavior of the government and
the ability of rebel leaders to convince members of the target population of the
appropriate type of violent response varying forms of state oppression warrant.
For example, political and economic marginalization of a particular ethnic community would naturally entail a different response to state power from political
entrepreneurs than an insurgency that seeks to rectify perceived corruption by a
national political elite.

Though focusing on the misbehavior of the government may be sufficient
in garnering support for a particular grievance, the rebel command must also
develop a message directed internally that can rally the target population behind
its distinct strategy of resistance against the preexisting order. This is essential for
an organization to garner the support necessary to represent the struggle among
competing internal alternatives that may chip away at the movement's cohesive-
ness from within. For example, the Eritrean People's Liberation Front (EPLF) in
Ethiopia competed against other rebel factions for primacy. A coterie of leaders
agreed that a violent struggle for Eritrean autonomy was warranted but differed,
often fiercely, on how best to achieve it.[16] Whether embracing Maoist principles or
relying on Koranic injunctions, the appropriate internal organizational strategy
can help mitigate potentially disruptive cleavages. Both the internal and external
messages adopted by the command affect the development of a rebel governance
system and deserve closer attention. I will discuss the external dimension first.

The message articulated externally by insurgent leaders comprises both strategic and ideological components. Strategically, there are two basic objectives
that a rebel organization can espouse: overthrowing the central government or
carving out a discrete territory from the state shell that corresponds with the

---

15. See, for example, the Proclamation of the Algerian National Front issued in November
1954, which clearly identifies both internal and external objectives for the group. http://historicaltex
tarchive.com/sections.php?op=viewarticle&artid=10.

16. The same struggle between groups to represent the broader movement occurred in each of
my case studies.

aspirations of the target population.[17] As tactical actors, leaders will frame their struggle in either national or regional terms on the basis of their calculation of which approach provides the greatest stimulus to their military objective. By and large, rebel leaders will share the same objective of their struggle with both their internal and external audience; that is, a group that claims to its target population that it has secessionist ambitions will proclaim those same ambitions to external actors. This is not always the case, however. In some cases, insurgent leaders may decide that it is to their strategic advantage to remain ambiguous, delivering a secessionist message to their internal audience while advocating a more nationalist position to the external audience. This was the case with the SPLM/A in Sudan, and scholars continue to argue over whether it deserves to be classified as a secessionist or nationalist movement (Johnson 2009).[18] The decision on how to frame the strategic objective of the struggle triggers certain consequences for civilian governance that warrant attention here. I will return to the question of ideology in the next section.

SECESSIONISM AND ETHNONATIONALISM

Commentators have pointed out the relative advantages for elites seeking to mobilize the population by adopting ethnic claims rather than relying on other societal cleavages such as class or gender (B. Anderson 1983; Horowitz 1985; Tambiah 1996; Wimmer 1997). Inherent in this argument is the notion that ethnic or nationalist appeals are perceived as more salient than other types of claims and hence more useful as the basis for garnering support for any collective enterprise. Historical factors have caused ethnic claims to take on even greater salience in the developing world. As colonial authorities openly manipulated ethnic identity as a tool of political control, the postcolonial state bureaucracies of many countries remained ethnicized despite the efforts of some nationalist leaders to foster a new, unitary national identity (Mamdani 1996). The forcible imposition of the nation-state framework upon disparate collections of ethnic communities that often had only limited interaction prior to the arrival of the European powers resulted in counterclaims to state power emanating primarily from ethnonationalist subgroups (Tambiah 1996; Wimmer 1997). Elite political entrepreneurs sought to capture state power by manipulating ethnicity to their

---

17. In his influential typology, Christopher Clapham (1998b) refers to such insurgencies as either reformist (center-seeking) or separatist (secessionist).

18. From my experiences, I characterize the SPLM/A as a secessionist movement, though the ambiguity on this question was central to the strategy of the rebel leadership. As one Southern Sudanese scholar explained to me, "Garang may have proclaimed his nationalist intentions to the international community, but in the south, we knew the truth" (interview with Jok).

own ends, generally by showering rewards upon the ethnic communities that supported their rule while marginalizing those that did not.

Through this process, ethnicity has come to take on highly instrumental overtones directly affecting the livelihood of citizens in most postcolonial societies. In much of the world, access to political and civil rights, in addition to material benefits, continues to be determined by membership in the "right" ethnic community. Since exclusion from political and economic opportunities is often ethnicized, it is unsurprising that appeals to ethnic solidarity often serve as the basis for insurgent collective action. But claims that rely on distinguishing a segment of the population from the rest of the society also generate their own expectations within the ethnic community. Unlike groups that seek power at the national level, ethnonationalist groups have a greater immediate need to prove their ability to improve the material welfare of their target populations. As Stanley Tambiah (1996, 17) reminds us, ethnonationalism is more than just a reaction to an oppressive or irrelevant state; it is also the articulation of a desire by communities "to achieve their own regional and local sociopolitical formations."

Insurgent organizations must frequently choose between various strategies in deciding how to interact with the different communities inhabiting their areas of control. It is not uncommon for a rebel group to use horrific and seemingly random violence in one village while behaving with significant restraint when engaging with civilians in a neighboring village. Though no less abhorrent than the behavior of an organization that treats all civilians with hostility, this variation in civilian treatment by a single organization is telling. All insurgencies that seek popular support treat some communities as potential collaborators requiring restraint and certain positive inducements, while at the same time, for a variety of reasons, they treat other communities only with violence. However, rebellions that seek power at the center have greater leeway because the intended audience for their actions includes potentially the entire population.

This contrasts with secessionist groups, which define the target audiences for their various actions (both violent and nonviolent) more narrowly. As a result, secessionist leaders face a higher barrier as they draw from a more limited constituency for support. Because they must convince their ethnic kin of the potential payoffs likely to accrue in the short term if they support the rebellion, they are more susceptible to criticisms and demands from within. In addition, the ethnic population targeted for mobilization is likely to face harassment on the basis of its collective ascriptive identity—rather than individual political allegiances— thereby further raising the costs to the community if the insurgency is unable to provide a degree of stability. Thus I argue that insurgent organizations with a secessionist or ethnonationalist agenda have a vested interest in proving their ability to serve as de facto governments in areas they come to control as their

Table 3.1 Effectiveness of insurgent governance systems

	LOW STATE PENETRATION	HIGH STATE PENETRATION
Center-seeking	low	partial
Secessionist	partial	high

ability to garner support from a specific population will be directly shaped by their governance performance. The relationship is addressed by hypothesis 2.

> **H2: If the insurgency is secessionist or ethnonationalist, it is more likely to develop an effective system of governance than groups that seek to capture power at the center.**

Secessionist leaders may also be positively influenced by the international community's clear preference for nation-state-like actors. International humanitarian law, for example, has long privileged struggles for "national liberation" over other types of violent movements (Sassoli 2006). This bias is echoed in the clear preference of transnational activist networks to throw their weight behind movements of cultural preservation that seek a degree of political autonomy (Bob 2006), over the more messy "reformist" insurgencies that seek to capture power at the center.

Both hypotheses 1 and 2 are generally evident at the onset of fighting; table 3.1 summarizes the expected outcomes. Combined, they provide us with a reasonable starting point for assessing the initial governmental preferences of various insurgent commands. However, as discussed earlier, many other factors that affect rebel behavior around governance questions are endogenously driven by the conflict dynamics, emerging from a variety of locations only after the initiation of fighting. I turn to these now.

IDEOLOGY

The other component of an organization's external message has to do with how rebel leaders publicly position themselves ideologically. The relationship of ideology to governance provision has a commonly hypothesized positive correlation—groups that openly embrace a left-leaning agenda are more likely to evince concern for the well-being of the civilian population.[19] However, publicly professing a leftist orientation does not require a rebel command to follow the

---

19. This is also true for secessionist movements that frame their struggle as part of a broader ideologically driven attempt to reform the nation itself. This dynamic was evident in such overtly ethnic conflicts as those in Eritrea, Rwanda, Sri Lanka, and Sudan.

organizational strategies of prominent revolutionary thinkers. For example, how should we categorize a rebellion that adopts the moniker Communist or Maoist in its name but does not follow Maoist principles when it comes to civilian mobilization? In general, the ideological agenda professed by an insurgency to an external audience is primarily rhetorical and has little direct influence on the behavior of insurgents in their relations with civilian populations.

This does not render ideology irrelevant when it comes to civilian governance systems. A more nuanced take on the question recognizes that ideological influences do not find expression solely in outward articulations but can also be reflected in the internal organizational strategy that the leadership adopts. This internal influence of ideology may be hard to discern during the initial phases of a conflict, but it can and does become salient when organizations decide how to develop their civilian governance capabilities. Any organization, including those run by violent actors, will deploy the relevant knowledge that can help create rules that best contribute to achieving a particular goal (Barnett and Finnemore 1999, 707), generally unencumbered by the external allegiances the organization may profess.

For example, a secessionist insurgency may choose to implement a Maoist strategy for organizing its political authority (as with the National Socialist Council of Nagaland in India), while a rebellion seeking to take power nationally may adopt an internal organizational strategy based on religious principles (as with the Union of Islamic Courts in Somalia). The paradigmatic example of a gap between the internal influence of ideology and the external message a group expounds is surely that of União Nacional para a Independência Total de Angola, a right-wing group supported by the United States during the Cold War, which adopted an organizational strategy derived directly from Maoist precepts.

Indeed, regardless of how they frame their external message, rebel leaders are not bound to any particular organizational strategy and can and do switch over time on the basis of strategic considerations. Thus I argue that ideology is salient for an insurgency only when it shapes the internal organizational strategy adopted by the leadership. In particular, leaders who take seriously Maoist ideas—specifically, Mao's emphasis on conventional warfare, disciplined cadre, a prolonged period of political mobilization, and the development of broad-based civil administrative structures that function to incorporate the peasantry into the insurgent organization—must devote considerable resources to their governance efforts. This provides the basis for hypothesis 3.

H3: If an insurgency chooses to implement a Maoist organizational structure, it is more likely to develop an effective governance system.

INTERNAL CLEAVAGES

Another internal organizational factor that can affect the design of rebel civil administrations is related to the composition of the local community and the cleavages that exist prior to the outbreak of conflict. Fanon's second admonition on the dangers of intragroup tension is relevant here. Though desirable, full hierarchical control within any organization is never possible; some degree of tensions between internal factions is inevitable (Barnett and Finnemore 1999, 724). Factions may compete as a result of differences over how to allocate material resources, the political agenda for the group, the real or imagined cultural or ethnic orientation of the organization, or some combination of all three. Such internal divisions can lead each faction to perceive the organization's overall mission in fundamentally different ways, with significant effects on rebel governance efforts. For example, Wood (2006), in her study of sexual violence, has shown how the command and control structure of a rebel group can have a determinative impact on its relations with civilians. In worst-case scenarios, these divisions may even lead to the fracturing of the broader movement and the emergence of multiple militant rivals to the original organization. Understanding the sources of factionalization and how they contribute to the different organizational structures of various insurgencies is therefore an important task.

There are two questions to address in regard to the above. First, how and why are some insurgent organizations able to suppress internal cleavages and forge a unified command while others get ripped apart by similar tensions? Internal dynamics often reflect relationships between local communities and the insurgent leadership in constitutive ways. And the ability of rebel leaders to incorporate representatives from constituent factions within their organization is a key determinant of the type of command—either unified or divided—a group will have.

Preconflict cleavages at the local level tend to persist and affect rebel behavior once fighting begins, regardless of the stated cause of the war (Kalyvas 2003, 478–80). If the movement is multiethnic, multireligious, or multiregional, tensions between component factions due to perceived dominance or mistreatment on either side can bubble to the surface (Jok and Hutchinson 1999). Such local-level economic, racial, ethnic, religious, and regional differences all impact the behavior of rebel leaders as they attempt to cajole or coerce a less-than-complacent population into accepting their governance system. Any attempts at consolidating their rule will require rebel leaders to carefully assess the nature of the population they seek to control, paying particular attention to mitigating potential cleavages that could emerge. Indeed, preexisting internal cleavages can have a wide variety of consequences for insurgent organizations. And the leaders must devote considerable attention and resources to ensuring that they do not undermine the ability of the organization to pursue its goals effectively.

Second, it is critical to understand how a divided or unified command affects the internal organization of a rebel group and its ability to develop a system of civilian governance. More dramatically, if the command actually splits into multiple rival factions, how does contested territorial control shape insurgent governance efforts? Rebel leaders able to establish a unified command that exerts its control throughout the entire organization and corresponding territory—despite internal competition—are more capable of implementing a cohesive system of governance than an organization divided into competing factions. This resonates with Guevara's (1999, 79) observation on the perils of a contentious command: "I stressed the need for a single command at the front; the dispersion of independent forces was unacceptable, especially when one saw the tendency to anarchy and rivalry that led to extremes of violence among one or another of the groups." If the leadership can establish an undisputed political authority over its territory, it strengthens its ability to offer protection to its chief supporters, extract more resources, and wage war (Tilly 1990, 181). This provides us with hypothesis 4a.

> **H4a: If an insurgency is able to form a unified political command either through subjugating competing factions or through incorporating them into a single command, it is more likely to develop an effective system of governance than an organization riven by multiple and competing poles of power.**

The elimination of internal rivals as a precondition for the forceful implementation of a new political and social order is not a new lesson but one acknowledged as early as the Russian Revolution. Vladimir Lenin, the leader of the Bolsheviks and a keen student of the French revolutionary period, understood that the fall of Maximilien Robespierre had much to do with his failure to wipe out internal competitors to the new order the revolutionaries were in the process of establishing. To avoid a similar fate, the Bolsheviks, upon achieving their own victory in Russia, assiduously went about wiping out other aspirants to power (Chaliand and Blin 2007, 203).

In the contemporary period, during most of the violent conflict in Sri Lanka, the LTTE was the unquestioned representative of the broader Tamil movement, a position achieved through the systematic destruction or the forced incorporation of competing factions. This contrasts with groups such as the Moro National Liberation Front (MNLF) in the Philippines and El Frente Farabundo Martí para la Liberación Nacional (FMLN) in El Salvador, both of which were coalitions of preexisting factions that never coagulated into a unified command. Other groups like the SPLM/A and the RCD began as unified entities but failed to prevent internal challenges from ripping apart the leadership into multiple competing factions. Such divisions are frequently accompanied by brutal internecine warfare with devastating costs borne by the civilian population.

If the local community an insurgency seeks to mobilize is divided into diverse political constituencies, leaders must constantly adjust their behavior and establish mechanisms to prevent these societal schisms from partitioning the rebel organization itself. Thus rebels also have a need to take into account population composition when developing their governance systems, as hypothesis 4b argues.

> **H4b: If an insurgency fails to compensate minority factions through the design of the civil administration, a rupture is probable.**

Notice that this hypothesis does not claim to directly explain the effectiveness of the rebel government. Rather, it helps explain the role of the civil administration in mitigating cleavages between members of the target population. Insurgent groups often bring together factions with assorted origins and differing agendas—despite outward claims of unity. Managing these differences and satisfying the demands of component factions is a vital imperative for all rebel commands. In certain cases, the need to incorporate diverse factions into the broader cause may even trigger forms of "distributive politics," in which leaders from the dominant faction overcompensate subordinate factions by designing governance systems that are especially responsive to the needs of a minority in order to win support. Still, perceived mistreatment of a specific group can be cause for a split within the rebel organization itself as opportunistic leaders rally minority sentiments against the established leadership. Such a split occurred in all three of my case studies, and as I show there, these crises often force insurgencies to take more seriously the task of bolstering their civilian governance efforts.

CONFLICT INTENSITY

The construction of an insurgent system of governance is an evolutionary process, with the development of structures and practices responding directly to shifts in the conflict. Such temporal variation in the degree of conflict is a persistent feature of all civil wars as insurgents and incumbents suffer setbacks or achieve gains for any number of reasons. Just as they will focus on developing civilian governance when faced with a potential internal crisis, insurgents also tend to focus on civilian needs according to the degree of active conflict with the incumbent state. This leads us to hypothesis 5.

> **H5: If a civil war exhibits periods of relative peace—through either a stalemate or a ceasefire—the insurgents are more likely to devote resources to the civil administration, and this results in a more effective governance system over time.**

During periods of active warfare, rebel leaders naturally prioritize military needs over civilian administration. Conversely, governance efforts are likely to become more sustained during times when military conflict is diminished. Furthermore, the signing of a ceasefire or just a lull in fighting can trigger a jockeying for spoils among the organization's constituent factions that may have lain dormant during more active fighting, forcing the rebel leadership to respond. Such periods may witness a "ratcheting up" effect in the quality of civilian governance as structures developed during these periods tend to persist even after fighting resumes, thus aggrandizing the governance system over time. Here also civilian agency can play a role as the population becomes accustomed to a greater degree of service provision and will actively seek to ensure the continuing enlargement of the civil administration. However, this effect presumes that rebel territorial control will remain stable during shifts in the conflict dynamics, an assumption that may not hold after the breakdown of a ceasefire or an increase in battlefield hostilities that result in the loss of territory by the insurgency.

When fighting rages, security concerns also make it far more difficult for transnational actors to access rebel-held territory. In addition, both the state and rebel authority are likely to place restrictions on movement during such periods out of fear of being infiltrated by enemy interlopers. This contrasts with periods of relative calm when transnational actors tend to engage more directly with rebel political structures. Such actors rush in to rebel zones of control in the immediate aftermath of a ceasefire or other extended period of stability, sharply increasing the interaction of global forces with dynamics on the ground, the effects of which I investigate in the next section.

From Above: Transnational Actors Affecting Insurgent Governance

It is a truism worth repeating that internal wars can rarely be contained within the territorial boundaries of a single state. Both international relations and area studies theorists have discussed the increased impacts of transnational actors on civil war dynamics (Stein and Lobell 1997; Callaghy, Kassimir, and Latham 2001; Gleditsch 2007). Internal wars rely on arms flows and military support from across borders and can produce massive population dislocations that initiate further interventions by state actors on both sides of ostensibly domestic disputes (Keller 1997). Furthermore, nonstate actors such as aid organizations, international agencies, diasporas, religious institutions, and corporations all intervene in war zones while pursuing their own diverse agendas.

Scholars have discussed at length how transnational actors interact with local authority structures within conflict zones. Analysts have highlighted the importance of "transboundary formations" that "link global, regional, national, and local forces through structures, networks, and discourses that have wide-ranging impact, both benign and malign." These global interactions "play a major role in creating, transforming, and destroying forms of order and authority" (Callaghy, Kassimir, and Latham 2001, 5). Anthropological discourses have highlighted how such transboundary formations can sustain societal actors, including violent groups, outside the purview of the state (Guyer 1994; Callaghy 2001; Ferguson and Gupta 2002). Others have discussed the emergence of localized political orders produced by humanitarian actors—termed "mobile sovereignty"—characterized by the ceding of empirical sovereignty to a "transnational mobile apparatus" that moves from crisis to crisis (Pandolfi 2003). Ronald Kassimir (2001, 109) points out that these actors not only play a role in the provision of services usually deemed the responsibility of the state but may also claim the right to represent an affected population.[20]

The ability of transnational nonstate actors to impact and even replace governmental institutions in both government and insurgent-controlled territories has clearly been well established (Callaghy, Kassimir, and Latham 2001; Nordstrom 2004). These processes linking rebel groups to broader global forces that play determinative roles in fostering or destroying local order are functionally similar to those encapsulated in the concept of "extraversion," in which state elites are able to consolidate power through their interactions with the international community (Bayart 1993). Despite the reluctance of the official organs of the international community to legitimate counterstate sovereigns, the overwhelming presence of different transnational actors within the territories controlled by rebel organizations directly serves to link such spaces to the formal world system. Thus it is important to consider the impact of transnational actors on rebel behavior as it pertains to civilian governance.

Rebel leaders remain acutely aware of the potential benefits (and risks) of hitching a ride on the transnational gravy train and will often seek to incorporate their relationships with such actors into their political project (Bob 2006). As Marie-Joelle Zahar (2001, 60) argues, since insurgencies "see themselves as either governments-in-waiting or as independent political entities," they seek legitimacy by interacting with transnational actors, providing the "international community with an opportunity to engage such groups on issues of treatment of

---

20. This applies to both state and nonstate actors. For example, international agencies such as the United Nations High Commissioner for Refugees (UNHCR) and NGOs such as the Red Cross may claim responsibility over entire refugee or IDP populations. Similarly, states may make irredentist claims, as witnessed, for example, by the government of Rwanda's repeated attempts to influence the Rwandophone population of eastern Congo.

civilians." In short, transnational actors perform an array of essential functions in contemporary conflict zones, and rebel leaders will often work to find the correct balance in their interactions with these important groups. As a result, different categories of transnational actors produce distinctive effects on insurgent behavior regarding civilian governance.

However, despite recognizing the integral role that the international community plays in fomenting and fostering contemporary violent conflicts, attention has generally focused on the economic agendas driving international actors to intervene in rebel-controlled territories and the resulting configurations of power that result (Chingono 1996; Reno 1998, 2001; Nordstrom 2001, 2004). Carolyn Nordstrom (2004), for example, describes the complex networks of formal and nonformal actors that funnel material goods across state borders and into rebel-controlled territories. Less attention has been devoted to the political interventions required on the ground to make such transactions possible. For rebels, providing a modicum of political order on the ground both results from their interactions with transnational actors and is an effort undertaken to woo such actors to their territory in the first place.

Of all such actors frequently present within rebel-controlled territories, nongovernmental organizations, both national and international (INGO), have received perhaps the most attention. The NGO category includes organizations with considerable diversity of structure and function. Generally, I am referring to any nonstate organization serving a noncommercial function, including those established by professional charitable organizations such as the Red Cross, religious institutions such as Catholic Relief Services, and organizations established by ethnic diasporas.

Important critical assessments of the political and social problems that result when such organizations have an unmediated relationship with local populations have been made for some time now. Most start with the basic observation that NGOs must distribute aid according to their own institutional imperatives. As a result, even in nonconflict periods, local civil or political institutions have little or no control over the distribution of these transnational resources (DeMars 1994). The risk is that populations may become habituated to making appeals for assistance to unaccountable international bodies instead of holding existing political entities accountable and that this may lead to the evisceration of both the legitimacy and the capacity of local political authorities (Mamdani 1993; Tvedt 1994; African Rights 1995). In insurgent-controlled territories, this competitive dynamic can to lead to tensions between the rebel leadership and the NGO, leaving the latter vulnerable to violent reproach by the insurgents. Such threats can cause NGOs to unexpectedly pull out, revealing the shallow roots these organizations have within war-torn societies and wreaking havoc on any societal formations that may have congealed in their presence.

Also of concern are situations where armed groups position themselves between an aid organization and the local population—and mediate the relationship to their own advantage (Keen 1994; de Waal 1997a; African Rights 1997). There are several ways that insurgents have done this. For example, an insurgency may be able to insert its own "linkage personnel" into the NGO to monitor and influence the actions of aid organizations. More problematically, rebel armies have circumvented aid through force. Either way, aid intended for noncombatant populations may instead be used to provide sustenance to rebel troops (Lischer 2003). Aid may also contribute to a politics of patronage by allowing the insurgency to funnel resources to its collaborators while withholding aid from those not as enthusiastic in their support. The presence of aid organizations can also preclude the need for an insurgency to build an inclusive democratic constituency as NGOs rush in to claim responsibility for the provision of specific public goods, allowing rebels to define their dominion solely in military terms (M. Anderson 1999). On a more positive note, the participation of NGOs in transnational activist networks may pressure insurgents to temper their use of violence and improve their treatment of civilians in exchange for the legitimacy granted them through their association with these representatives of the international community (Bob 2006).

This last function is especially apparent when discussing organizations associated with religious institutions, which are a subset of the broader NGO category—though distinct in important ways. While most aid organizations rely on their own material endowments to build constituencies, communities facing violent conflicts commonly turn to churches and other religious institutions for assistance, both material and spiritual (Nolan-Haley 2002). In many societies, religious leaders serve as countervailing authority figures to the political class, a dynamic even more evident during times when the political leadership is in question. Tapped into transnational activist networks but intimately local in their structure and operations, religious institutions are often the only functional welfare providers in the initial phases of a conflict. Even after a rebel organization takes over a territory, churches and mosques often remain a key support for beleaguered communities providing services and sanctuary, at least to their own constituents, and often to other needy individuals as well.

Though religious leaders can be co-opted into either progovernment or prorebel positions, they commonly strive to remain autonomous from the political regime in power (interviews with Pasinya, D.R. Congo, and Okello, Sudan). Indeed, religious leaders commonly challenge rebel organizations, openly criticizing insurgents with a relative degree of impunity (interview with Miller,

Sri Lanka). In ways that few other societal actors can, religious leaders are able to articulate political positions that can undermine support for the rebellion among the local civilian population as well as in the international arena. The transnational networks that tie all but the most parochial churches or mosques into hierarchies located outside the country can be immediately mobilized to bear witness and place pressure on rebel groups that abuse religious sensibilities. And like other charitable organizations, religious groups funnel substantial financial resources through their own humanitarian organizations into rebel territories, building and staffing schools, hospitals, and other public goods required by needy civilians.

Members of ethnic diasporas also engage with insurgent organizations, providing financial and political support to insurgent leaders and sustenance to their conflict-affected kin (Byman 2001).[21] Analysts have rightly focused on diasporas' significant financial contributions to rebel groups, providing cash for battlefield expenses and other resources and expertise that can support a budding insurgency (Fearon and Laitin 2003; Collier and Hoeffler 2004). But these analyses mostly focus on diaspora support for the insurgent army, ignoring the fact that members are often more involved in humanitarian issues. Diaspora members have an existential bond with the conflict, including material, emotional, and familial ties to the land and people left behind. Individual members operate within humanitarian NGOs, international agencies, foreign governments, and private corporations directing attention and material support to their chosen cause. Diaspora members also operate in concert with insurgent organizations, providing direct support to, and pressure upon, rebel leaders through their own humanitarian efforts. This is not to say that all or even most diasporic activities necessarily reflect the will of the inhabitants of insurgent territories. Diaspora members possess their own perception of the broader conflict situation and its toll on civilians. Through their link to a rebel command, they may push for their preferred vision of what level of suffering is acceptable (Shain and Barth 2003), even if these preferences are painful for the communities left behind.

Rebel leaders often rely on diaspora members to perform a number of roles within the organization, including serving as ambassadors and lobbyists in their adopted countries and as hosts for delegations looking for material support abroad. In this way, diasporic organizations can function as the equivalent of foreign missions (interviews with Tamil diaspora members; Shain and Barth

---

21. Though it may appear that diasporas are of concern only for secessionist movements based on ethnic or religious interests, I share the constructivist view that identities are fluid. Thus conflicts that may not be identified by a particular ethnic or religious grievance may come to imbue ethnic valences through the efforts of enterprising leaders. For example, the SPLM/A succeeded in uniting ethnic groups that had had significant historical and contemporary conflicts, such as the Dinka and Nuer, behind a unified Southern Sudanese identity.

2003). This trust is not misplaced. Members of the diaspora are often more quali-fied to understand the importance of human rights and other discourses on the global perception of an insurgency and are thus better able to shape the image of the organization outside the home country. And support from diaspora mem-bers can go beyond their considerable activities in their adopted countries (Shain 1989). Members of the diaspora frequently serve in important political positions within rebel groups. Expertise and connections gained in their adopted homes make them particularly adept at performing nonmilitary functions within an insurgent political wing. Humanitarian organizations, staffed by members of the diaspora and funded through donations raised among community members abroad, can operate in close conjunction with a rebel command while carefully avoiding any direct legal connections to it, thereby avoiding the legal prohibitions often attached to violent groups operating abroad. In fact, in several cases, the humanitarian organizations established by diasporas may even take over the pro-vision of services like health and education entirely, in addition to engaging in a wide range of other developmental activities including building shelters, digging wells, and ensuring food security (see chapters 4 and 5 for two examples).

Though similar to NGOs in certain ways, international agencies like the World Bank and the United Nations shape relations between insurgents and local com-munities in their own distinct fashion (Barnett 2001). Mandated to provide hu-manitarian aid, such agencies willingly work with rebel authorities to ensure the passage of aid convoys and distribution of humanitarian resources. Such recog-nition from international agencies can legitimize insurgent claims to represent a specific population, opening opportunities for the co-optation of the agency's activities in a manner similar to insurgents' intervention with NGOs (Mampilly 2009). The presence of international organizations in a rebel-controlled terri-tory is also a powerful signal to other transnational actors such as corporations and aid organizations that they may enter areas they previously shied away from. International agencies are also an important source of funds for the relief and development efforts of aid organizations in conflict zones.

But this is not the extent of the relationship. Military personnel deployed through the auspices of international peacekeeping missions can impact the re-lationship between insurgent groups and local communities. Current UN think-ing, based on lessons learned from the difficult Security Council-authorized American intervention in Somalia, attempts to design interventions to take into account the on-the-ground power dynamics, underscoring the need to forge al-liances with the recognized power brokers (Mortimer 1998). Rebel organizations deemed worthy of partnering with international agencies can access substantial material resources and even military support from peacekeepers, providing a tre-mendous incentive to insurgent leaders to reconcile their own agenda with the needs of the international agency.

The final category of transnational actors that commonly operate within contemporary conflict zones, and perhaps the most controversial, are multinational corporations. While both NGOs and international agencies profess to work in the interests of the civilian population on the ground, foreign corporations are explicit about their focus on profit, an attitude that inevitably affects the livelihoods of local communities (Reno 1998). Illegal logging, mining, and other industries that rely on resource extraction all require rebel organizations to privilege the needs of the multinational corporations over the inhabitants of surrounding area. To this end, foreign corporations strike deals directly with rebel leaders that can prove highly lucrative, and since rebel organizations are often willing to go to great extremes to collude with potential corporate partners, there is less need for insurgent leaders to generate support internally (Reno 2001; Ross 2002). Natural resources are rarely evenly spread geographically but rather exist in highly desirable resource enclaves—thus rebel control of these territories is prone to constant competition from a variety of actors, most prominently the state itself (Leonard and Strauss 2003). Just as they provide support to insurgent armies, corporations can provide government forces with the resources necessary to subvert rebel control of these enclaves (Obi 2001). Rebel leaders who defy commercial demands may also face direct challenges to their control over territory from private security firms hired by foreign corporations to protect their interests.

As the above discussion shows, rebel leaders react to resources and constraints produced by an increasingly transnational world, going as far as "marketing" their rebellion to actors in the international community (Bob 2006). However, analyses of rebel organizations' relationships with transnational actors fail to delineate the precise effects of such interactions on the primary insurgent interface with the civilian population, the rebel civil administration. As a result, they tend to assume only a negative impact on civilian governance, an assumption that ignores the nuances of such complicated interactions. Not every transnational interaction will have the same effect on rebel governance efforts. Indeed, different categories of transnational actors have their own views regarding civilian treatment formed prior to their engagement with various militant groups. These preferences can include deep concern, passive lack of interest, or outright hostility toward local residents. As a result, they will determine if and how transnational actors engage with a particular rebel organization and the concomitant effects of the intervention on civilian governance. The question is, when do such transnational relationships negatively affect insurgent civilian governance efforts? And when are they likely to have a more positive impact? The various categories of transnational actors play two important roles—as supporters or competitors—that can affect the behavior of rebel leaders.

SUPPORTERS

First, transnational actors function as *supporters* of rebel organizations by providing resources that impact their ability and desire to grapple with civilian governance concerns. Insurgencies with a limited resource base have a strong incentive to develop relations with transnational actors in order to generate financial resources and to take advantage of the credibility provided by such associations (Zahar 2001). Insurgencies are commonly assumed to draw such support from two types of transnational actors: private corporations and other states. Both are explicit about their self-interested engagement with rebel groups, offering leaders direct financial payments and other material support in exchange for assistance in pursuit of specific material or strategic gains (Ross 2002). In the early phases of a rebellion, when such resources are likely to be essential, the effect is often to undermine civilian agency on questions of governance by reducing the need for the rebel organization to mobilize popular support (Weinstein 2007).

It is reasonable to assume that support drawn from foreign corporations and other states will have a detrimental effect on civilian governance efforts. However, funding sources are not the sole determinant of rebel governance outcomes. Variation in rebel financing strategies over time is an important constraint on the impact of economic factors. Variation may be caused by a shift in political alliances between states or the collapse of a commodities market, and many insurgencies, particularly those with life spans measured in years rather than months, must be able to constantly adjust their fiscal strategies to adapt to changing conditions or risk collapse. When faced with a dramatic shift in their funding source, many groups do succumb, of course. But many others prove more durable, constantly shifting between available funding strategies, which may include patronage from an external state, the sale of natural resources or more illicit goods, or the extortion, smuggling, and taxation of civilians and commercial or charitable organizations.

More important, state and private organizations are not the only transnational actors that provide support to rebel organizations. Many others engage in conflict zones for ostensibly humanitarian purposes. The manner in which rebels can benefit from these relationships has been discussed, most prominently in the notion of a "substitution effect" that allows insurgent leaders to neglect civilian welfare in favor of more military concerns (De Mars 1994; de Waal 1997a; M. Anderson 1999, 2001). However, organizations concerned with civilian welfare issues, including foreign NGOs, international agencies, diasporic organizations, and religious institutions, may also have a positive impact on rebel behavior if an effective coordinating mechanism can be established. Incorporating such actors into an insurgency's governance system can stimulate the development of the civil administration by providing resources, services, and expertise that can supplement the organization's own capacity to meet civilian needs. For rebels, such collaborations provide an effective way to address civilian welfare without actually diverting limited financial resources or personnel. For humanitarian organizations, working with insurgents can ease access to populations affected by the fighting. Rebels may also provide security for development and relief projects and may even offer their own local expertise to supplement these efforts.

For example, rebel organizations have successfully incorporated INGOs into their governance project. By forcing aid groups to work within a contractual framework that delineates the specific activities they will be allowed to engage in, the areas in which they can operate, and any other requirements regarding the hiring of personnel or the payment of duty to the political authority, many insurgent organizations have successfully inserted themselves between the aid organization and the population they seek to serve (DeMars 1994; de Waal 1997a; Branch and Mampilly 2005). This brings us to hypothesis 6.

> **H6: If an insurgency is able to co-opt humanitarian organizations into its governance project, then it is more likely to develop an effective system of governance.**

COMPETITORS

If the rebellion fails to co-opt transnational actors into its governance system, however, it may come to view transnational organizations and networks as *competitors* in the battle for the hearts and minds of civilians. This can occur in one of three ways. First, insurgent civilian governance can be negatively affected in situations in which insurgents fail to take into account the needs of local trading networks and foreign corporations with commercial interests in rebel-controlled territory. Whether through the hiring of private security firms or shoring up government military forces, private actors have repeatedly shown their willingness to challenge the insurgency's control over territory, generally to the detriment of the civilian population caught within.

Second, by providing basic services to a receptive population, aid organizations that refuse to fall in line with the insurgent program can undercut the revolutionary promises made by rebel leaders, offering immediate rewards instead of weak promises for a better future. In India, for example, Naxalite insurgents expelled all charitable organizations operating in territories under their control out of fear that the NGOs were improving peasant welfare and hence reducing the salience of their violent appeals.[22]

---

22. I thank Biju Mathew for his insights on the behavior of the Naxalites.

Third, human rights activists and journalists, both local and international, are tapped into transnational activist networks that can mobilize international public opinion against insurgencies that exploit civilians or that rely on excessive coercion to ensure civilian compliance. Similarly, religious institutions, with their transnational networks of believers, have proved particularly effective in mobilizing international public opinion against the behavior of undisciplined violent groups. For example, the Community of St. Egidio, a Catholic lay organization credited with negotiating an end to the Mozambican civil war, operates in seventy countries and has fifty thousand members. When a conflict erupts in one location, local members immediately share their experiences with the community abroad. Members of St. Egidio include faculty of top Western universities, government officials, UN workers, and many others who have proved able and willing to intervene in conflicts in substantive ways.

Though private competitors generally have a harmful impact on insurgent civilian governance efforts, the effect of noncommercial competitors is decidedly more mixed. In many cases, the activities of recalcitrant NGOs or critical human rights activists are likely to push the insurgent command to become defensive about its treatment of civilians. This can lead rebel organizations to work to hide their abuses from the international community to the detriment of affected communities. However, in certain cases, such pressure may push the insurgent command to take more seriously the task of addressing civilian needs, particularly if it perceives that such a change in behavior will produce more positive coverage for the rebellion in national and international circles.

H7: If an insurgent leadership faces challenges to its rule from local and transnational civil society actors, then it may develop a more effective system of governance under certain conditions.

The wording of this hypothesis is purposefully conditional as it relies on idiosyncratic factors that may push the organization to take more seriously the task of civilian governance. For example, the presence of a rival organization competing for the loyalties of transnational actors may pressure insurgents to devote more attention to civilian needs. In situations where insurgent control is complete, however, the same pressure from transnational actors may simply push the organization to expel or imprison any or all competitors.

The above discussion provides a framework for understanding the complex dynamics that affect the behavior of rebel leaders in regard to the provision of civilian governance. The purpose of this chapter has been to situate each of the nine hypotheses within the appropriate theoretical literature and to detail the mechanisms and processes that link cause with effect. In the rest of the book we will examine how well these hypotheses explain variation in the provision of public goods by insurgent organizations. I proceed in the following two ways. First, three detailed case studies of contemporary rebel groups (chapters 4–6) based on repeat visits to rebel-controlled areas provide an opportunity to examine the framework's strengths and limitations for explaining the varied outcomes that occurred during recent struggles in Sri Lanka, Sudan, and the D. R. Congo. Chapter 7 then seeks to evaluate the framework systematically through a comparative analysis of different insurgencies, drawing on the case studies as well as examples culled from other recent conflicts. I find considerable support for most of the framework, though the effects of several of the individual propositions are not fully borne out.

4

THE TWO FACES OF THE TIGER
Sri Lanka's Liberation Tigers of Tamil Eelam

Oh Tamil! You are like a pouncing Tiger, Enter the battle front with a smile.

—Kasi Ananthan

During the war in Sri Lanka, crossing into insurgent territory from land controlled by the incumbent government felt no different than crossing the militarized border between India and Pakistan.[1] A mile of no-man's-land walled off with razor wire separated the Government of Sri Lanka's (GoSL's) immigration post from its LTTE facsimile. On both sides of the partition, uniformed young men and women dutifully asked similar questions in different idioms—Tamil and Sinhala. Baggage was slowly unpacked and repacked haphazardly. And though the atmosphere was tense, both sides exhibited an eerie calm in their interactions with outsiders. A foreign visitor was treated no more vigilantly than he would have been checking-in at LAX. Lurking beneath the surface, however, was a wariness reserved for those members of the rival ethnic community who tried to cross between the two sides of the divided country, a fury reserved for one's own reflection.

---

1. The epigraph to this chapter was written by the Sri Lankan Tamil nationalist poet Kasi Ananthan in the 1960s prior to the founding of the LTTE. The poem references the Chola Kingdom, which ruled parts of southern India and Sri Lanka from the ninth to the thirteenth centuries. The kingdom's emblem depicted a tiger, from which the LTTE eventually drew its inspiration. Research for this chapter was conducted during two separate visits to LTTE-controlled areas between early 2004 and mid-2005, with a follow-up visit to Colombo in early 2010. In 2004 and 2010 I was traveling with Nimmi Gowrinathan, with whom several of these interviews were conducted. The chapter focuses on the prolonged period of LTTE control of much of the north and east of the country and does not address LTTE governance practices during the final phase of the war, which began with renewed fighting between government and rebel forces in mid-2007.

As with the conflict in Sri Lanka, the nature of the LTTE system of governance resulted from the negatively symbiotic relationship between the Sinhalese and Tamils who share the island nation. A hybrid administrative system that mixed both government and insurgent civil and political institutions controlled the lives of the inhabitants of the Tamil-dominated areas of the combined north and east provinces. In line with my arguments about secessionist groups operating in areas with historically dense interactions between state and society, life in Tiger territory was impressively stable, with a clear political authority responsible for providing extensive public goods. In this chapter I focus on the organization of the LTTE, the once-dominant rebel organization operating on the island. With a troop strength estimated at twenty thousand, the Tamil insurgency was arguably one of the best organized nonstate military forces ever assembled, with the capacity to fight on land, at sea, and in the air.

The rebels controlled vast parts of the north and east of Sri Lanka for extended periods throughout the duration of the conflict from 1983 to early 2009. Despite the open warfare between the two sides, the Sri Lankan government had a strong incentive to keep a connection to the population living within LTTE-held territory and continued to provide public goods to rebel-controlled areas throughout the war. I show how the insurgents and the government came to accept this convoluted power-sharing arrangement. I argue that the rebel command, faced with the legacy of strong state institutions that had penetrated deep into the Tamil areas and psyche, had little choice but to work with the government to establish a joint mechanism to ensure a continuity of services for a population long accustomed to receiving a substantial amount of public goods from the state. On the government side, retaining a link to the Tamil population living in LTTE-controlled territory was crucial to limiting the insurgency's claim to sovereign status. The resulting agreement ensured that that those living within rebel territory were able to receive a steady provision of public services through the cooperation of the rebellion's civil administration with the state bureaucracy.

Sri Lanka is a country of approximately twenty million people sharing an island of roughly sixty-five thousand square kilometers, slightly smaller than Ireland, off the southeastern corner of India (see figure 4.1). From its earliest postcolonial incarnation, Sri Lanka's government has long been a formal democracy with a vigorous emphasis on redistributing resources across the citizenry (Snodgrass 1999). At the time of its independence in 1948, the British viewed Ceylon, as the country was known then, as the most promising of the empire's extensive holdings in Asia. Even without the benefit of any particularly lucrative natural resource, in 1960 Sri Lanka had a per capita income comparable to that of South Korea and significantly higher than that of either Indonesia or Thailand.

Compared with other former colonies, Sri Lanka also benefited from extensive colonial infrastructure and an effective and efficient bureaucratic apparatus

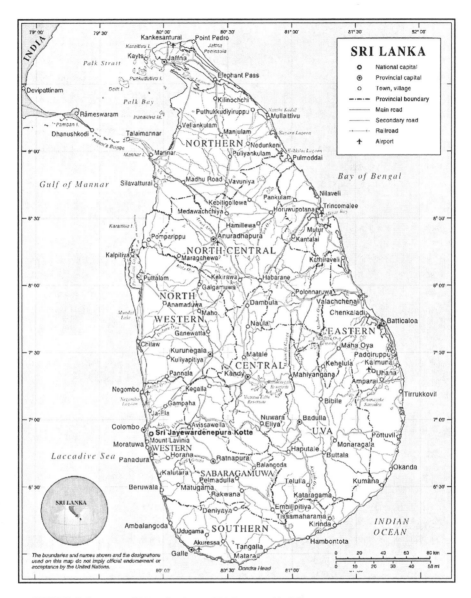

FIGURE 4.1. Map of Sri Lanka. *Source*: UN Cartographic Office.

that penetrated deeply into every corner of the island nation (Kelegama 1999). As a result, in the postindependence period, the country managed a respectable economic growth rate of just below 5 percent (Sanderatne 2000, 29). For much of this time, the government provided substantial welfare benefits to its population, including food subsidies, health care, education, and subsidized transportation

(Jenne 2003). At the same time, for close to three decades, the country was divided by a brutal ethnic conflict between the Tamil and Sinhalese communities that left approximately one hundred thousand dead and over a million displaced. In the next section I provide a history of the conflict. I show how colonial rule incorporated the Tamil minority into a unitary state structure while at the same time radically upsetting the demographic balance between the two ethnic communities that share the island nation. This troubled history of incorporation into the state eventually came to determine the nature and scope of the LTTE governance project.

Background of the Conflict

Split between a majority Sinhalese community accounting for approximately 74 percent of the population and a minority Tamil community of slightly less than 18 percent, Sri Lanka's ethnic mélange is somewhat similar to the ethnic makeup of Rwanda or Burundi. These similarities to the Central African cases persist when considering that at independence in 1948, Ceylon's minority Tamil population boasted higher education and income rates than the Sinhalese population, as did the minority Tutsis in Rwanda and Burundi. And though Tamils make up a majority of the population in the north and east of the country, almost half of the Tamil population has long lived in all corners of the island, with an especially significant community in the capital, Colombo.[2] However, unlike those in Rwanda and Burundi, where the two communities have fought in cyclical bouts of spectacular violence, Sri Lanka's ethnic tensions simmered on low for the first three decades after independence. After the outbreak of war in 1983, the country witnessed a considerable amount of death and destruction, only occasionally garnering the kind of attention given to similar ethnic conflagrations in Bosnia, Rwanda, and Darfur.

The Tamil community is divided between an autochthonous population constituting about two-thirds of the total and Indian or Estate Tamils,[3] who constitute the remaining third and are concentrated in the rural highlands located in the Sinhala-dominated central part of the country (Samaranayake 2002; Sivathamby 2005). A regional difference also exists between Sri Lankan Tamils who live in the north and those who live in the east, with the former taking pride in

---

2. More precisely, Tambiah (1986) estimates that fully 47 percent of the Tamil population lived outside the N&E Province. Conflict-related demographic shifts make accurate calculations difficult for the contemporary period.

3. As I discuss below, this community is composed of the remnants of the indentured servant population brought by the British to Sri Lanka from India to work in the colonial plantation economy prior to independence.

historically having had greater autonomy than the latter. Tamils in the east were more incorporated into the Sinhala kingdom before the arrival of the Portuguese (Sivathamby 2005), and even today the province has a more diverse demographic mix than the north. The great majority of Tamils profess Hinduism (Saivite) and speak the Dravidian Tamil language, while the bulk of Sinhalese practice Theravada Buddhism and speak Sinhala, a language that is Sanskritic in origin. Both groups also have sizable Christian (encompassing Catholic and other Christian dominations) populations, the legacy of Portuguese, Dutch, and British missionaries. The remaining population of the country consists of a sizable population of Muslims (7%), who are recognized as constituting a separate ethnic community despite their racial and linguistic connection to the Tamils,[4] and a small community of Eurasians (<1%), commonly referred to as Burghers, which formed through intermixing of the indigenous population with Europeans.

As it did in other parts of the colonized world, European rule in South Asia forced diverse communities with limited prior interaction into contact in often uneasy arrangements. This was true with the Tamil minority concentrated in the north and east of Sri Lanka, whose relationship to the central Ceylonese authority before the arrival of the Portuguese rotated between extended periods of incorporation and disengagement (Tambiah 1986). When the European powers first arrived in 1517, the Sinhala and Tamil populations lived in semiautonomous kingdoms under the nominal suzerainty of Sinhala kings, who controlled the entire island through a Buddhist-Sinhala administrative bureaucracy. Tamils may have occupied a lesser position in society, but local and regional sociopolitical arrangements were far more important than any islandwide political or ethnic hierarchy (Seneviratna 2001). Though people were certainly aware of the ethnic divide, it never emerged in a violent manner.[5]

Colonialism weakened the country's Buddhist Sinhala institutions. The Portuguese, who sought to use the island as a trading point, attacked the Buddhist political hierarchy, turning land over to the control of Roman Catholic orders. The Dutch followed briefly before being replaced in 1796 by the burgeoning British Empire, which had taken great interest in expanding its consolidation of the South Asian region. The British, like the Portuguese and Dutch before them,

---

4. The Muslim community was caught between the two sides in the conflict. Muslims were targeted by the LTTE for not supporting the Tamil cause sufficiently despite their common linguistic heritage. They were also not granted status as an autonomous community and were excluded from negotiations between the GoSL and LTTE. At the same time, they did benefit from the ability to move between the two communities and owned many of the transport and trading companies operating in the country. There was thus a high degree of economic interdependence between the Tamil and Muslim communities (Goodhand and Lewer 1999).

5. Contemporary Sinhalese nationalists often point to this period as proof that a federal solution is unnecessary and that both communities can live—and have lived—under a benign, unitary Sinhalese government.

continued to usurp local political authorities, replacing indigenous chieftaincies with their own provincial administration. British administrators further undermined the special position that the Buddhist clergy held within the Sinhalese state, reducing it to no greater a position than that of other religions on the island. At the same time, the British built roads across the island and generally contributed to infrastructural development across the colony, often with better success than they had had in the Indian behemoth to the north, largely because of Ceylon's relatively small size. They also developed a strong educational system that utilized both Sinhala and Tamil at the primary level, bringing both communities together in an English medium setting at the secondary level (De Silva 1999). Though these institutions were spread throughout Ceylon, the colonial power favored the Tamil population because it believed that community was better suited to serve in the civil service.[6] Thus, through colonial policies that favored the minority population, the Tamil community was asymmetrically incorporated into the bureaucratic framework of the colonial Ceylonese state. For example, at independence, Tamils made up 30 percent of the civil service and fully 40 percent of the armed forces (Rotberg 1999).

The British also established a system of plantations for the cultivation of commercial crops, mainly rubber and tea. It was the construction of this plantation economy that was to irrevocably change Ceylon's ethnic balance for the worse. Needing a workforce to staff the booming plantation economy, in 1825 the British began importing Tamils from the much larger community in south India, operating on the naive assumption that a similar culture and geographic terrain would provide for an easy assimilation into Ceylonese life.[7] This labor transfer served to alter the population balance between the Sinhalese and Tamils of Ceylon in a way that exacerbated preexisting fears among the majority that it was likely to be overrun by an influx of Tamils from India (Seneviratna 2001, 13). This fear of India remains potent even today, and politicians and intellectuals frequently tap into fears of Tamil mass migration to justify exclusionary policies. As the colonial period came to a close, changes in the demographic balance between the two communities, combined with the elevated position of native Tamils—who were overrepresented within the colonial civil service, army, and educational institutions—contributed to feelings of insecurity on the part of the Sinhalese majority in regard to its own position in Ceylonese society.

---

6. Tambiah (1986) explains this perception as resulting not from an innate capacity of Tamils for serving in the bureaucracy but from the lack of other economic opportunities in the north of the country, which pushed the Tamil population to disproportionately take advantage of the newly opened missionary schools in the region.

7. Although this migration has not warranted the same attention as the transportation of Indians to Africa and the Caribbean after the abolition of African slavery, it is part of the same trend and actually predates these more distant migrations.

At independence in 1948, Ceylon boasted an educated workforce with a high literacy rate but also a divided electorate in which the minority Tamil community occupied a higher social and economic position than the majority community. Sri Lanka adopted a Westminster parliamentary system based on a one-person-one-vote formula that naturally favored the Sinhalese while offering little in the way of protection for the minority communities—a surprising omission considering the extensive protections offered minorities in the Indian constitution that came into existence around the same time. The departing British had initially wanted more protections in the constitution in response to demands from the Tamil leadership and sought to placate these demands by forcing the adoption of section 29 of what became known as the Soulbury Constitution. Section 29 made it illegal to make any law discriminatory to, in favor of, or adverse to any one community that was not equally applicable to the other communities.[8] Concurrently, Tamil political leaders led a failed effort to unite all of Sri Lanka's minorities in a demand for a power-sharing arrangement that would have given this minority coalition a fifty-fifty power split (Jeyaraj 2001). Thus at independence section 29 was the only constitutional provision offering any protection to Ceylon's various minority communities.

Tensions between the two communities emerged almost immediately in the postindependence era as nationalistic Sinhalese politicians sought to make an issue of the migrant Tamil population brought from India as labor in the colonial economy. These migrants were denied membership in the new nation as the Sinhalese-controlled parliament adopted the nativist option, passing a series of laws including the Ceylon Citizenship Act (1948), the India-Pakistan Residents Act (1949), and the Ceylon Parliamentary Elections Act (1949) that effectively rendered the Indian Tamils stateless and denied them even meager political rights. As a result of these and other exclusionary policies, 50 percent of the Indian Tamils were repatriated to India by the 1970s (Jenne 2003). The exclusion of the Indian Tamils was attributable to Sinhalese fears of a bloc Tamil vote that would give the minority community too much power in the new parliament. An unintended consequence of this policy was to reify the idea of a unified Tamil community as indigenous Tamil politicians began to embrace their transported Indian ethnic kin. Although Ceylon Tamils had always identified with the Indian Tamils on a linguistic level, the communities were separated geographically in

---

8. The relevant parts of section 29 of the constitution reads as follows: "(1) Subject to the provisions of this Order, Parliament shall have power to make laws for the peace, order and good government of the Island. (2) No such law shall—(a) prohibit or restrict the free exercise of any religion; or (b) make persons of any community or religion liable to disabilities or restrictions to which persons of other communities or religions are not made liable; or (c) confer on persons of any community or religion any privilege or advantage which is not conferred on persons of other communities or religions."

terms of both their origins and where they lived on the island. Ceylon Tamils also tended to look down upon the working-class Indian Tamils as they were primarily drawn from lower-caste and lower-class communities in India (Sivathamby 2005). The unified Tamil leadership eventually grasped the significance of the state's repatriation efforts and began an organized effort to challenge these policies within the new parliament, though with little success (interview with N. Ethirveerasingam).

At the dawn of independence Sri Lanka had a competitive economy that exported tea, rubber, coconuts, and other commercial crops. Under the populist rule of the Sinhala-dominated United National Party (UNP), the government committed itself to provide a wide range of public goods to the population, including subsidized food, education, medical care, and transportation (Snodgrass 1999). The appeals to ethnic consciousness by the Sri Lankan government were built upon this economic populism, which both major Sinhalese parties, the UNP and the Sri Lanka Freedom Party (SLFP), used to woo support among the majority population. However, as early as the 1950s, economic spending could not keep up with the significant welfare benefits offered to the population. In response, politicians from both the UNP and the SLFP shifted strategies by escalating their ethnic rhetoric to garner support.

In 1956 the SLFP came to power under the leadership of the new prime minister, Solomon Bandaranaike, who rode a wave of Buddhist nationalism fomented by his party to shift attention away from the declining economy. At first, he sought to position Sri Lanka as nonaligned in the emerging Cold War global order, and he openly embraced socialist welfare policies and significant state intervention in the economy. Bandaranaike also initially recognized the perils of an unadulterated Sinhala chauvinism, and in 1958 he did attempt to give the Tamils a degree of autonomy in the north and east provinces by devolving fiscal and political matters to the provincial level. He also attempted to recognize Tamil as an official language. However, once unleashed, Sinhalese nationalism could not be contained, and Bandaranaike soon found himself portrayed as disloyal by even more extremist elements who had taken control of the UNP. Forced to pull back on commitments made to Tamils and facing increased pressure from Sinhalese rivals, Bandaranaike decreed Sinhala the national language. He also set into place policies that discriminated against Tamils in the armed forces, civil service, and university admissions. Tamils had made up 60 percent of the professionals employed by the state at independence, but this number fell to under 10 percent by 1970. In the administrative service, the drop was from 30 percent to less than 5 percent during the same period. And most dramatically, in the armed services, the percentage of Tamils went from 40 to less than 1 (Rotberg 1999). In higher education these exclusionary policies culminated in 1972 with the placement of strict quotas on the number of Tamils allowed entry into universities. Faced with a stagnating economy and contentious intra-Sinhala political disputes, Sinhalese politicians were more than comfortable in using patronage to ensure voter loyalty, a method that culminated in the almost total exclusion of the Tamil community from the military, civil service, and academic sectors by the early 1970s.

The Emergence of a Tamil Movement

The history of the Tamil movement in Ceylon reveals a clear slide away from a policy of responsive cooperation led by an integrationist political party to territorially defined autonomy demands and finally to an all-out secessionist war led by a violent insurgent group. At independence the majority of the Tamil people believed their future lay with the nascent Ceylonese nation. Throughout the island, there was a general recognition by the Tamil community that the government was a generous one that, despite its other faults, did not discriminate when doling out the considerable benefits offered to all citizens (interview with N. Ethirveerasingam). The prevailing sentiment within the community was that secessionism and even federalism held little appeal and that the Tamils' continued prosperity required active participation in Ceylon's economic and political life. So entrenched was this belief that discussions of federalism, let alone secessionism, were largely absent from the political discourse of this period, with a few marginal exceptions. This position was reflected in the leadership of the Tamil community under G. G. Ponnambalam, who led the All Ceylon Tamil Congress into a cooperative alliance with the ruling UNP government. It was not until a breakaway faction led by S. J. V. Chelvanayagam formed the Federal Party (FP) that the community began to perceive itself as a territorially defined minority population deserving of greater autonomy within a federal Sri Lanka. When the Sinhalese nationalist SLFP came to power in 1956, the FP, which up to that point had had little electoral success, swept the polls in the two Tamil majority provinces, reflecting the deepening ethnic polarization of the country (Jeyaraj 2001).

The FP's rise was a response to the 1956 decision to make Sinhala the official language of the island. A legal challenge was initiated that charged the new linguistic policy with violating section 29 of the constitution. After Tamil leaders succeeded in a lower court in declaring the law a constitutional violation because of its clear anti-Tamil bias, the Sri Lankan government appealed the case all the way to the supreme court, which refused to rule on the issue. In the Ceylonese judicial system at the time, a privy council sat as the highest constitutional order, empowered to make decisions on the constitutionality of the cases that came before it. The privy council found that the Tamil legal challenge had merit and sent the case back to the supreme court for a decision. But the government, under Sirimavo Bandaranaike—who had come to power in 1960 after the assassination of her husband by a nationalist Buddhist monk—decided instead to simply circumvent the constitution. She did this by forming a presidential constitutional commission to write a new constitution, despite technically lacking the power to alter the old one, which had been vested with the parliament instead. Bandaranaike's gamble paid off, and in 1972 a new constitution was ratified that enshrined Sinhala as the official language and rendered the previous challenge to the linguistic policy null and void. Referring to this incident as the tipping point at which the community shifted from viewing the conflict as one to be waged nonviolently to considering a more militant option, a longtime activist within the Tamil movement told me, "Tamils had no choice but to take up arms because it was the government who rebelled against us [by changing the constitution]" (interview with N. Ethirveerasingam). It was also at this point that Ceylon dropped its name, adopting the ancient Sanskritic appellation Sri Lanka, or "resplendent land" in English.

By 1972 the Tamil community faced a progressive marginalization of its social position through three decades of unconstrained Sinhala nationalism. Though initially divided by descent, religion, and caste, the community had come together and unified its various political parties under the Tamil Unified Front (TUF). The emergence of TUF represented the coalescing of an elite Tamil response to the consistent transformation of a multiracial albeit unitary Sri Lankan state into an overtly Sinhalese-Buddhist one. Initially engaged in constitutional and peaceful political protest against this discrimination, the community took a more strident turn in 1976 with the Vadukkodai Resolution, which called for a separate Tamil homeland. To reflect this new position, it renamed its coalition the Tamil United Liberation Front (TULF). The hardening of the Tamil position reflected a similar stance within the Sinhala community, which in 1977 brought to power the nationalist government of Junius Jayawardene at the head of a rejuvenated UNP.[9]

Having never resolved the persistent economic crisis, Jayawardene approached the Western powers for aid by adopting promarket economic reforms and in the process turning his back on the Non-Aligned Movement (NAM) and the socialist policies of his predecessors (Tambiah 1986, 30–31; Sanderatne 2000). Scholars

---

9. Indian Tamils actually supported the UNP in great numbers as Jayawardene brought the Ceylon Workers' Congress, a trade union that most Indian Tamils supported, into the government. Exploiting such preexisting cleavages within the Tamil community has been a common and effective strategy used by different Sri Lankan leaders.

have argued that as the first country in South Asia to liberalize its economy, Sri Lanka was a preferred destination for the largesse of international financial institutions such as the World Bank, the International Monetary Fund, and the Asian Development Bank, as well as donor nations such as Japan (Richardson 2004; Bastian 2006, 2007). The shift to international financing exacerbated ethnic tensions, and Jayawardene's term in office was characterized by an intensification of the conflict (Gunasinghe 2004; Richardson 2004). But reliance on the Western powers also constrained the government's behavior during the war in important ways, a point I discuss in greater detail later on.

Unable to win any political concessions from the government, a younger generation of Tamils from less economically prosperous backgrounds and hailing from outside the urbanized Tamil elite began articulating a more aggressive nationalism and calling for a violent response to perceived Sinhala oppression. This generation came of age never having experienced the multiethnic coexistence that had characterized the childhoods of the older generation of Tamil politicians, whom they viewed as being disconnected from the concerns of the Tamil masses (interview with Ponnambalam). Under the leadership of Vellupillai Prabhakharan, a charismatic eighteen-year-old from a rural Tamil family in the north, the LTTE emerged as one of several militant insurgent groups (Jeyaraj 1985; Swamy 2002; Roberts 2009). By this point, both populations had concretized their positions in keeping with the supposed distinctiveness of their respective ethnic histories. And the conflict had taken a violent turn that few could have predicted would be as bloody as it turned out to be.

Origins of the Liberation Tigers of Tamil Eelam

> **We wish to state clearly and emphatically that we are not a group of amateur armed adventurists roaming in the jungles with romantic illusions, nor are we a band of terrorists or vandals who kill and destroy at random for anarchic reasons....We are not in any way isolated and alienated from the popular masses, but immersed in and integrated with the popular will, the collective soul of our nation.**
>
> —Open letter from Prabhakharan to Ranasinghe Premadasa, prime minister of Sri Lanka, in 1979

Support for the LTTE increased dramatically after the killing of thirteen government soldiers in 1983. This incident provoked widespread anti-Tamil riots throughout Sinhala-majority areas on the island, including in the capital city, Colombo. Estimates for the number of Tamils killed by Sinhala mobs range from

350 to 2,000 depending on the source. Though accounts of the riots remain contentious, there is general agreement that the government turned a blind eye to the destruction. Many argue that the violence was orchestrated with the collusion of the UNP government, as evidenced by the use of voter rolls to target Tamil homes and businesses and the lack of response once the violence began (Tambiah 1986). The killing of the soldiers triggered the outbreak of Eelam War I,[10] which began with government forces engaging in heavy fighting with the LTTE in the north of the country. In the south, where large numbers of Tamils had lived alongside the majority Sinhala community for generations, the riots led to a massive emigration of Tamils out of Sri Lanka to the West. Estimates put the size of the Sri Lankan Tamil diaspora at over seven hundred thousand scattered in close-knit communities in North America, Europe, and Australia (Daniels 1997).

As with many war-induced refugee flows, many of those who left Sri Lanka at the first signs of the conflict were professionals who had the resources to flee the country. Members of this community have been financially successful in their adopted countries and have continued to harbor deep-seated resentment at the suffering they faced in their home country (Daniels 1997). This anger motivated the wealthy and not-so-wealthy within the diaspora to contribute substantial resources for the LTTE's efforts, estimated at up to $2 million a month at its peak (Subramaniam 2000). Throughout the life of the insurgency, it received considerable financial and other support from the Tamil diaspora through both voluntary and involuntary contributions, which, according to one report, contributed as much as 80 percent of the group's revenues at different points. This was collected through taxes on diaspora members in the United Kingdom, Canada, Australia, and to a lesser degree, the United States (Chalk 2000; Human Rights Watch 2006). Members donated proceeds—often under pressure from Tamil activists—from gas stations, restaurants, and other businesses they ran in their adopted countries (interviews with Tamil diaspora members). Despite this significant financial role for the diaspora, most knowledgeable observers agree that community members abroad had little influence on the military decision making by the top LTTE brass, though as I discuss below, they did play a significant role in supporting the organization's governance efforts (interview with Sivaram).

In its earliest incarnation, the organization received significant financial and material support from the government of India (GoI) and the state government of Tamil Nadu in India's south, including military training in India and shipments of small arms such as grenades, mortars, land mines, and other conventional weapons. New Delhi viewed the LTTE as a potential tool in its pursuit

---

10. Eelam is the name given to the longed-for Tamil homeland in the north and the east of Sri Lanka.

of hegemony in the South Asian region and used the insurgency to punish the GoSL for turning away from the Non-Aligned Movement that India continued to spearhead until the end of the Cold War. Meanwhile, the Tamil Nadu government provided considerable resources to the insurgents in response to populist mobilization in the state calling for protection of ethnic Tamil kin living across the Palk Strait in Sri Lanka. The support from the Tamil Nadu government was extensive and included the establishment of camps for the training of rebel cadres, with the GoI providing both the armaments and the expertise to use them.

Indian support for the Tigers came to an end in 1987 after the ascension to the office of prime minister by Rajiv Gandhi, the reluctant scion of India's Nehru dynasty. Soon after taking power, Gandhi signed the Indo–Sri Lanka accords, which brought an end to the immediate fighting and established the Indian Peacekeeping Force (IPKF) in Sri Lanka to disarm the LTTE. However, the peacekeepers soon generated resentment, both from the rebels for their heavy-handed tactics in Tamil areas and from the Sinhalese public out of fear of an invasion of the entire island by India (Rotberg 1999).[11] The fear of Indian imperialism led directly to a violent uprising among nationalist Sinhalese elements known as the Janatha Vimukthi Peramuna (People's Liberation Front, JVP). Faced with an internal popular insurrection, the administration secretly formed an unlikely alliance with the rebel army, providing the Tamil insurgents with weapons to help them push the IPKF out of the country. In 1990 after sustaining and inflicting great losses, they succeeded (Bose 1994). Prabhakharan's resentment for the Indian incursion was great, and he satisfied his desire for revenge in 1991 at a rally near Madras, the capital of Tamil Nadu, by ordering the assassination of Rajiv Gandhi, who had ordered troops in to Sri Lanka in the first place. In response, the Indian and Tamil Nadu governments turned on the insurgents, cutting off all official support and actively cracking down on any remaining Tamil militants operating in India, though the organization did eventually win back a degree of popular support in Tamil Nadu (C. Smith 1999).

Sri Lanka is divided into nine provinces and twenty-five districts. In 1987, after the arrival of the Indian peacekeepers, the historically Tamil-dominated (73% of the total inhabitants) north and east provinces were unified into a single unit and placed under emergency control by Colombo.[12] By placing the northeast under Colombo's control, the GoSL was able to dissolve the elected provincial

---

11. Despite the IPKF's presence in Sri Lanka, Indian sympathy for the Tamil cause did not end, even within the Indian armed forces. According to Major General Arjun Ray, who served with the IPKF in Sri Lanka, many within the force had great sympathies for the LTTE cadres, who were admired for their fighting acumen (interview with Ray).

12. Since the unification of the northern and eastern provinces, people refer to the combined region as the northeast. In this book I use "N&E Province," "northeast," and "northeastern"

assembly, a standard feature of the other seven provinces. In these provinces, funds from the central government were allocated to the provincial assembly, which made decisions regarding funding for education and health matters, for example. In the combined N&E Province, this power was transferred to the governor, a position appointed by Colombo. The northeast did have a nonelected provincial council composed of members selected by the governor, but neither the government nor especially the insurgents took the council very seriously. It is generally agreed that the combined province received less than its due from the finance commission, which was supposed to determine fiscal allocations to the provinces under a standardized though complex revenue-sharing formula (interview with Lankanesan).

After the withdrawal of the IPKF, rebel leaders were forced to organize their group to deal with three separate challenges. First, the organization was suddenly left in control of much of the north of the country that had been occupied by the peacekeeping force from 1987 to 1990, including the Jaffna Peninsula. Second, the group was forced to reorganize its internal operations without the patronage of the external state sponsor that had guided the insurgency from its origins. And third, the LTTE had to deal with a renewed outbreak of fighting, known as Eelam War II, with the invigorated government forces, who had honed their counterinsurgent skills by brutally suppressing for a second time the violent revolt of the JVP that broke out in the south of the country during the IPKF occupation of the north.[13] As I discuss in the next section, these internal crises forced the LTTE to restructure and empower its political wing in order to compensate for the loss of support from India. They also required the insurgents to develop a broader-based movement that could handle the rejuvenated government forces.

In 1994, running on a peace platform at the head of a left-leaning coalition known as the People's Alliance, Chandrika Kumaratunga (the daughter of the Bandaranaikes) won the presidential election by promising to cut a deal with the Tamil insurgents. The emergence of Kumaratunga brought to an end seventeen years of unbroken UNP rule during which the country's long-standing ethnic dispute had turned shockingly violent. Despite an initial pause in the fighting that followed a unilateral ceasefire announced by the government, the LTTE grew wary of Kumaratunga's overtures, and fighting recommenced, initiating Eelam War III. In 1998, after making some significant gains in territory, the rebel command surprised the Sri Lankan political leadership by calling for talks and

---

interchangeably to refer to the province. In January 2007, the province was again separated into its two constituent parts.

13. The first JVP rebellion occurred in 1971 and was initially more a Marxist-oriented struggle than the revolt of ethnic chauvinists it became.

offering a unilateral ceasefire (Rotberg 1999). Although the war continued for three more years, the secret talks that had been initiated in 1998 culminated in the signing of a ceasefire agreement between rebel leaders and the government in 2002.

At the time of the ceasefire, the country was divided between "clear" areas directly under the control of the GoSL and "unclear areas" under the control of the rebels. However, as I discuss below, the situation was more fluid, with the LTTE retaining the ability to influence events in clear areas throughout the northeast despite having suffered setbacks, particularly around Batticaloa in the east (interview with Lankanesan) (see figure 4.2).[14] Civilians I spoke with in the region agreed that living in a clear area provided greater access to government services, whereas unclear areas were thought to be more safe (interviews with anonymous civilians; interview with Jeyanesan).

Prime Minister Ranil Wickremasinghe of the UNP signed the ceasefire. He had come to power through parliamentary elections in 2001 and shared that power in an uneasy cohabitation arrangement with Kumaratunga, who continued as president. The terms of the ceasefire agreement called for a federal solution to the crisis in Sri Lanka with the creation of a semiautonomous province under the control of the Tamil leadership. However, many Sinhala nationalists viewed the agreement as too conciliatory and overly generous to the LTTE, and negotiations toward a final settlement stalled. In 2004, Kumaratunga dissolved parliament, and Wickremasinghe prepared to contest the presidential elections of 2005, hoping to gain a mandate for a final negotiated settlement with the insurgents.[15] However, dissatisfied with the tenor of the peace negotiations, the rebels called an election boycott in Tamil areas, effectively denying the presidency to the UNP and clearing the way for the SLFP candidate, Mahinda Rajapaksa, to come to power at the head of a Sinhalese nationalist coalition that promised to revisit the terms of the agreement between the government and the Tigers. Rakapaksa's election led to a dramatic escalation of the government's military offensive, which succeeded in wiping out the LTTE and killing its top leaders in early 2009 following a two-year siege of rebel-controlled territories that destroyed much of the two provinces.

---

14. According to Goodhand and Lewer (1999, 74), writing before the ceasefire, "A cleared area is assumed to be one that is under the control of the Sri Lankan Armed Forces, where there is no 'terrorist' presence, there is a level of protection and stability and the population is receiving the same public entitlements as elsewhere in the country. 'Uncleared' areas are those which remain under the military control of the LTTE."

15. Interestingly, LTTE leaders had studied aspects of the Machakos Protocol, which ended the war in South Sudan, and had hoped to reach a deal comparable to the one the SPLM/A achieved (interview with Sivaram). See also Wijemanne (2002).

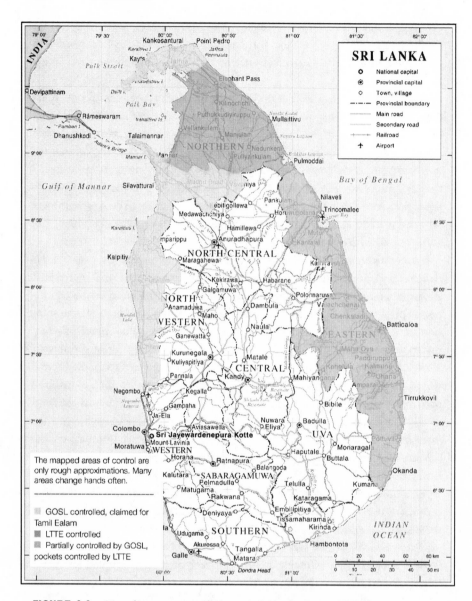

FIGURE 4.2. Map of insurgent-controlled areas in Sri Lanka. *Source*: Dustin Ross.

Establishment of the LTTE Civil Administration

Although the LTTE soon became the preeminent insurgent group representing the Tamil movement, from the beginning it faced serious challenges to its leadership by other paramilitary groups such as the People's Liberation Organization of

Tamil Eelam, Tamil Eelam Liberation Organization, Eelam People's Revolutionary Liberation Front, Eelam Revolutionary Organisation, Eelam People's Democratic Party, the Rafik Group, and a faction led by Colonel Karuna, the former
LTTE number two (Jeyaraj 1985). The Sri Lankan government often provided
both overt and covert support for these other Tamil factions, and the struggles
between them and the LTTE proved to be particularly gruesome on all sides, with
abductions and torture of each other's cadres common—so much so that several
commentators have labeled the war in Sri Lanka a "dirty war" (Nordstrom 1992;
Rajasingham-Senanayake 1999).

As a result, when it came to the establishment of a governmental authority, the
rebel leadership was consistently preoccupied with maintaining a brutal coercive
apparatus over its charges above all else. Faced with competition from other factions, the LTTE sought to establish its dominion by repeatedly punishing those
perceived to be sympathetic to these factions. This was especially true during
the first four years of the war (1983–87), when the group controlled little territory, instead operating alongside existing government institutions and focusing
mainly on wiping out its competitors. Even at this early stage, the LTTE stood out
among its competitors for its ability to organize itself under a unified command
structure with top-down control over the entire organization and for its instrumental use of violence in clearing the political space of the northeast (interview
with Sivaram; Swamy 2002). As a result, though the command was technically
divided between a military office (M.O.) and a political office (P.O.), in practice
political personnel were generally drawn from the military wing; only rarely were
civilians incorporated who had not first proved their loyalty to the organization
on the battlefield (Bose 1994, 125). The consistent failure of the organization to
separate the P.O. from the M.O. undermined the autonomy of the political wing
from the inception of the rebellion.

From 1983 to 1987, in areas the rebels controlled, the administration of justice and the police force remained in the hands of the incumbent government
(interview with N. Ethirveerasingam). The LTTE first established a civilian administration during tripartite peace negotiations between the group and the Sri
Lankan and Indian governments in 1987. Prior to this a planning commission
did exist within the P.O., but it did little. Civilian governance efforts accelerated
dramatically after the withdrawal of the Indian peacekeepers in 1990 as insurgent
leaders sought to build structures to fill the political vacuum opened by the Indians' departure. Claiming the role of the protector of the Tamil people, the LTTE
established a Tamil Eelam secretariat to replace the P.O. and to serve as the official political wing. The secretariat gave the insurgent organization control over
"hotels, transport, education, local bodies, cultural activities, media, and food
distribution" (Swamy 2002, 213) while also providing a new source of revenue to
offset the loss of Indian support.

The first nonsecurity component of the nascent civil administration was a broad development structure named the Tamil Eelam Economic Development Organization (TEEDO). Its initial purpose was to assess damage done to rebel territory during the war and coordinate efforts for developing these areas. In 1994 several commissions were established by TEEDO that included government civil servants, university personnel, and civil society actors who provided assessments of the basic costs and needs of reconstruction for each sector. Town-hall meetings were held to provide local Tamil residents and civil society actors the opportunity to give feedback on the plans for reconstruction and development. Through this process, the LTTE published a series of reports that detailed the needs of the N&E Province and provided a blueprint for moving forward. These reports were released alongside the Sri Lankan government's own assessments of the province's needs.

Over time, these TEEDO-appointed commissions began to specialize in specific sectors and were spun off into their own agencies within the civil administration. As discussed in the next section, the administration grew to include education and health ministries, a legal system comprising both a police force and a judiciary based on the LTTE's own legal code, a comprehensive tax authority, and even a Bank of Tamileelam, which had six branches at its peak (DeClercq 2004). The construction of the civil administration was designed to demonstrate the capacity of the rebel organization not only to the local inhabitants but also to three separate external audiences: the government, the international community, and the Tamil diaspora (which had long provided direct financial support and professional expertise for the organization's nonsecurity governance work) (interviews with Maran and Puleedevan; Chalk 2000).

After the withdrawal of the IPKF and the resumption of fighting between the government and the insurgents in 1990, the N&E Province was subjected to an economic embargo encompassing over sixty items, including basic consumer, medicinal, and other daily goods such as fertilizer (Sarvananthan 2005). It continued until the ceasefire in 2002 and was reinitiated after fighting recommenced in 2006. The embargo had a profound impact on life in rebel-controlled territory, particularly in the provision of health care, which required many of the goods prohibited by the government for having military and civilian usages. With the advent of Norwegian-led peace talks in February 2002, the LTTE began a concerted effort to separate the military wing from the civil apparatus even further (Mampilly 2009). Though the N&E Province under rebel rule suffered considerable decline in several key indicators, including health, education, and infrastructure, the overall status of these indicators was low only in relation to their values in the rest of the country. For example, in 2001, while 17 percent of children were born underweight across Sri Lanka, the average in the N&E

Province was 26 percent (Sarvananthan 2005, 27). Although this was a significant difference, considering that the LTTE had long controlled the majority of the territory in this province, what is surprising is how close the two numbers actually were. A closer look at the organizational structure of the civil administration can shed some light on how the insurgency was able to achieve these impressive results.

The Structure of the Civil Administration

At the top of the organizational structure of the LTTE was the supreme leader, the late Prabhakharan, who fostered a personality cult around his distinctive mix of Tamil nationalism and socialist rhetoric (De Mel 2007). Prabhakharan gained fame among the Tamil population for his bravery in battle against the incumbent state and his ruthlessness in dealing with dissidents within the Tamil movement. He sat at the head of the Central Governing Committee, which united all aspects of the organization, both military and political, under a single command. Within this structure existed the political secretariat, which encompassed the civil administration (*Atasialthurai* in Tamil) and was headed by the *porupalar* (in Tamil, or person responsible in English) (interview with N. Ethirveerasingam). This position was long held by Thamilchelvam, the most prominent LTTE political administrator, until his death in 2006. The bureaucracy was divided into several ministries, including those for finance, justice, protection (police), economic development, health, and education, each headed by a secretary (also referred to as porupalar) (Neeran 1996). It was a top-down structure with specialized sectors serving to implement decisions made by the insurgent leadership (interview with Sivaram).

As mentioned above, during the war Sri Lanka was divided into eight provinces after the unification of the N&E Province, large parts of which had been controlled by the insurgents since 1990. Each province was further subdivided into approximately three or four districts. In the rebel-controlled province, each district was assigned a district-level porupalar who served to ensure that sectoral directives issued by the head porupalar were implemented at the district level. As I discuss in the next section, in Tiger territory, the government continued to provide education and health throughout the war. It was the role of the district porupalar to ensure that the GoSL administrators followed LTTE policy in the provision of these public goods. Even in the clear areas of the province that supposedly remained under government control, the LTTE appointed a porupalar to monitor government administrators, though with less direct effect on civilian governance (interview with N. Ethirveerasingam).

Service Provision: The Civil Administration and the Government

During its reign over the northeast, the LTTE developed numerous governmental structures and embraced ruling practices that vigorously asserted its dominion throughout the territory under its control. Underneath Tiger flags fluttering in the wind, civilians passed through a landscape replete with symbolic expressions of nationhood—uniformed traffic police, elaborate war memorials, posters commemorating the fallen, and pamphlets and newsletters advertising public campaigns on social issues—all accompanied by insurgent radio and TV broadcasts that penetrated the airwaves, consistently reminding them of the regime in power.[16]

The actual provision of services within LTTE-controlled territory, despite the overwhelming proliferation of symbolic claims to sovereignty, is a challenge to understand because of the complex interface between state and rebel governmental efforts. The real purpose of several ministries within the insurgent civil administration was to regulate and supplement the services provided by the Sri Lankan government. Other ministries, particularly in the security sector (including the police and the judiciary) remained completely under the control of the insurgents. But when it came to health, education, and several other sectors, the rebels worked alongside government institutions to meet the needs of the civilian population. Faced with a population accustomed since independence to the continuous provision of public services, the rebellion had little choice but to work with preexisting institutions to ensure civilian welfare.

In a practice left over from colonial rule, every district in Sri Lanka is assigned a government agent (GA) (known as the district secretary since 1997) who is responsible for implementing directives promulgated by the central government. Sri Lanka's unitary structure gave these administrators considerable influence in ensuring that policies mandated by the center were implemented throughout the country. This remained true even in rebel areas, where the government assigned GAs to each district in the N&E Province. Although officially a government choice, the individual selected was generally someone acceptable to the rebel civil administration, often a Tamil member of the GoSL civil service.

If the assignment of district-level supervisors by the government in the persona of the GA seems reminiscent of the LTTE district porupalar, this was clearly no inadvertent decision. In 1990 after the withdrawal of the IPKF and the establishment of the rebel civil administration, insurgent leaders approached

---

16. For a more extensive discussion of the LTTE's use of symbols, see Roberts (2009).

their government counterparts, asking them to resume service provision in the northeast (interview with Puleedevan). The insurgency modeled its own civil administration on the government's bureaucratic framework with the intention of designing a structure that could both control and fill in the gaps of the government's agencies. Thus the district porupalar position intentionally mirrored the GA position and was designed to regulate it. This approach guided the design of several relevant rebel ministries, though not of the security system, which the LTTE maintained as its own preserve.

In the country's other provinces, democratically elected provincial assemblies served as a countervailing force to the power of the GAs, providing a necessary degree of local control over Sri Lanka's centripetal tendencies. In the N&E Province during the war, the governor-appointed, nonelected provincial council was created to substitute for the lack of a provincial assembly. However, the LTTE prevented it from gaining much legitimacy, fearing that an effective and representative council could undermine its claim that no institutional solution to the woes of the province was possible (interview with Lankanesan). This left the area bereft of an officially sanctioned oppositional structure, a void the insurgent organization attempted to fill with its own civil administration. Thus the provincial council, through which flowed 80 percent of the funds allocated to reconstruction by the government, determined where and how to allocate these funds unconstrained by any officially recognized democratic feedback mechanism (interview with Sivananthan). Instead, in the conflict zone, the LTTE's civil administration was the only structure capable of determining the direction of these allocations. In effect, the government knowingly ceded control over state fiscal expropriations to the insurgents.

Why the Government Compromised on Governance

There are two obvious questions that come to mind. First, why did the government continue providing services to a segment of the population that had violently challenged its sovereignty? And second, why did it allow the insurgents any say in this process? One reason for the GoSL's approach was Sri Lanka's dependence on the generosity of the donor community, which increased dramatically after the liberalization of the economy in 1977. Donors, weary of the brutality that accompanied the crushing of the JVP, did not want to be seen as bankrolling a regime that allowed any further embarrassing humanitarian disasters. As long as the Sri Lankan government ensured that the conflict did not affect the performance of the economy while continuing to implement economic liberalization, Western donors were content to focus on economic performance (Bastian 2006, 2007). The fact that the economic base of the country had long been centered in the western province around Colombo made this a surprisingly viable strategy. Thus, under the watchful gaze of the international community, which communicated its fear of any negative publicity directly to the receptive Sri Lankan leadership, the government had a strong incentive (through conditions on aid tied to human rights) to manage the conflict with the LTTE without allowing any great humanitarian catastrophes (Uyangoda 2008). The best way to do this was to ensure the material welfare of the civilian population in the northeast, even while engaging in brutal combat with the Tamil rebels.

A second answer, according to several interviews I conducted with government officials, was that service provision provided the government with an essential—if tenuous—link to the Tamil population. The prevailing assumption was that if the government abdicated responsibility to provide services to the Tamil community, nothing would connect the people of the N&E Province with the government that still claimed dominion over them.[17] Therefore, the official government strategy across multiple administrations was to wean the population away from the insurgents by providing public goods. The Sinhalese political elite did not uniformly embrace this approach. A division existed between Kumaratunga and other factions within her government that pushed for the cutting off of financial support to LTTE territories. Though these opposition forces did not have the political clout to force her hand, they were able to undermine Kumaratunga's efforts, rendering service provision in the northeast less substantial than in the other provinces (interview with N. Ethirveerasingam).

Finally, the decision to give the group a say in governance questions reflected the recognition by the government that cutting off public goods to the northeast would force the LTTE to develop more extensive civil administrative structures, further burnishing the group's image as a Tamil government-in-waiting (interview with Lankanesan). The government preferred to negotiate directly with the rebel leaders about service provision because they feared that the insurgents might set up a comprehensive parallel administration as a testament to their secessionist credentials. Partly as a result of this dependency on the Sri Lankan state, the organization did much to promote the idea that it was an autonomous government, devoting considerable attention to symbolic projections of power within its territory. I was able to visit a massive LTTE graveyard—one of many in the region—where, in a dramatic gesture, the organization had elaborately

---

17. This was probably a wise decision, to judge from a comparable international situation. After the first Gulf War, Saddam Hussein hoped to punish the northern Kurdish population by cutting off the region from supply lines in the south of the country. Instead of devastating the population as he hoped, it triggered the development of an autonomous Kurdish government in the north that only solidified Kurdish secessionist claims.

buried its dead to demonstrate the sacrifices of its cadres to the civilian population.[18] This was despite the fact that most of the dead were Hindus and generally should have been cremated in line with the traditions of the faith. Thus, despite the distaste both sides had for the arrangement, a compromise system that would allow preexisting institutions to remain while granting the rebels a say in the nature of service provision was the only viable option.

As a result, throughout the N&E Province in areas of rebel control, there was a bifurcated political command with a dual authority structure composed of representatives from both the government and the insurgent civil administration. In practice this meant that the GA operating in any district under LTTE influence walked a very fine line between ensuring that government mandates were carried out uniformly in all districts and respecting the wishes of the insurgent administrators, as relayed to him by the district porupalar. Considering the fraught nature of their position, civil servants appointed by the government to work in rebel territory had a remarkably congenial relationship with their LTTE counterparts. This is attributable to the government's appointment of ethnic Tamils to work in the northeast who, as a group, were generally sympathetic to the needs of the civilian population, even if individuals did not support the LTTE in particular (interview with Lankanesan).[19]

The insurgency benefited more from this arrangement, as it was able to keep the residents of Eelam satisfied without having to direct its limited resources to providing services to civilians. In addition, the organization was known to forcibly impose taxes on the population within its territory, up to 12 percent for those working in government professions (Human Rights Watch 2006). Because the government paid the salaries of teachers, doctors, nurses, and other professionals in the health and education sectors (Mukarji 2000, 48), the rebel tax authority knew that these employees had the money available to pay taxes.[20] In effect, it was able to skim funds for its operations from government disbursements used to pay civil servants.[21]

---

18. The majority of these graveyards have now been destroyed by the government seeking to prevent any lingering memories of the LTTE's presence.

19. LTTE leaders told me that they directly selected the personnel to work within government agencies and that these people were then incorporated by the GoSL, but I never received confirmation (or denial) of this from government employees.

20. Having diverse sources of funding provided the organization with greater stability if any one source was cut off, as it had experienced several times earlier in its history. Besides receiving support from internal sources such as taxes and running its own businesses and external sources such as the diaspora and the Indian government (until 1987), the LTTE was also accused of raising funds through criminal enterprises such as international drug and weapons trafficking and extortion and racketeering within its territory (Jenne 2003; Chalk 2000).

21. This does not mean that the GoSL was blind to this strategy but rather that it accepted it as a necessary cost of keeping a connection to the people in insurgent territory. Indeed, the insurgency

The Provision of Services in North and East Sri Lanka

The Security System

When the LTTE first came into control of territory in the mid-1980s, its first priority was to establish an ad hoc force capable of policing the population (Sambandan 2003). Like other rebel groups, the organization sought to develop a formal security system primarily to ensure compliance with its rule and normalize civilian life under rebel control. To this end a police force with stations scattered across rebel territory came into being in 1990. As Anton Balasingham, the LTTE's chief political adviser, explained in 2002, "There are huge populations here and we have to administer them for the purpose of maintaining...social order and cohesion; we need to have certain institutions.... Police stations are necessary instruments to maintain law and order because we cannot allow anarchy and social disorder in areas controlled by us" (TamilNet 2002b). A Tamil former constable of the Sri Lankan police established a police academy with the capacity to train three hundred cadets a year. At its peak, the force eventually grew to approximately three thousand officers deployed across rebel-held areas (Bulathsinghala 2003a, 2003b). Over time, the police force came to be a legitimate and respected local institution. Civilian informants confirmed that the rebel police had a high degree of legitimacy and viewed the force as an uncorrupt and important stabilizing factor in the region.

The LTTE adopted a more expansive approach in regard to the judiciary. Instead of viewing the judicial system solely as a source of stability, the insurgents initially hoped to use it to generate revenue from the population. By establishing a system of land courts, the organization was able to establish an agreed-upon value for private property through a joint consultation with the property holder. This allowed the civil administration to establish an annual tax on all properties, providing it with an immediate and steady source of income, particularly from relatively wealthy members of the diaspora concerned about their property holdings back home. At the same time, it put control over a key resource, land, squarely within the jurisdiction of the rebel's embryonic civil administration (interview with N. Ethirveerasingam).

While establishing the land courts, the fledgling insurgent organization continued to use the government's legal codes and structures to administer justice.

---

was forced to rely on such strategies to compensate for the total lack of foreign investments in this part of the country. This deficiency resulted from an active policy by the government to prevent investment in LTTE-controlled areas, which would provide the group with the ability to strike lucrative financial arrangements with foreign investors. This did change briefly after the signing of the ceasefire, when many diaspora members were allowed to initiate projects in the northeast.

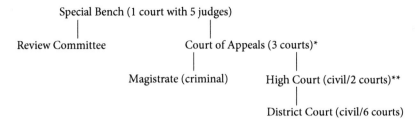

Special Bench (1 court with 5 judges)

Review Committee   Court of Appeals (3 courts)*

Magistrate (criminal)   High Court (civil/2 courts)**

District Court (civil/6 courts)

*Only the Kilinochchi Court of Appeals functioned during the war
**These were located in Kilinochchi and Mullativu

FIGURE 4.3.   Structure of the LTTE legal system.

Informal mediation boards referred to as *inakka saphai* in Tamil were set up at the village level, but they did little.[22] It was only after the withdrawal of the IPKF that the rebels tried to establish a formal judicial system composed of committees of respectable persons, including retired civil servants and teachers. But its disorganized approach to administering justice led to widespread complaints (TamilNet 1997). Recognizing that the prosecution of crimes and the resolution of civil disputes were important points of contact with the civilian population it sought to control, the command turned its attention to establishing a comprehensive legal system that would fit its agenda more closely. To this end, a law college with the capacity to train three hundred lawyers a year was set up, and by 1992 a system of courts was put into place across rebel territory (Kamalendran 2004). Enacted in 1994, the Tamil Eelam Penal Code set out the maximum and minimum sentencing requirements, mandating the death penalty for a variety of offenses, including murder, rape, and treachery (treason) as it was explained to me by an LTTE magistrate (interview with Anpu).

The legal system adapted elements of the British-influenced Sri Lankan Penal Code, combining them with customary practices based on the LTTE interpretation of the Tamil cultural norms known as *thesavalamai* that regulate inheritance, marriage, and other civil practices (interview with Puleedevan; TamilNet 2003). The Thesavalamai Code was actually laid out by a Dutch legal scholar in 1707 and based on his interpretation of the customs of Tamils in ancient India and Sri Lanka. It was used as the framework for regulating civil issues in the Tamil areas throughout the colonial period. Even in contemporary Sri Lanka, marriage and inheritance laws for Sri Lankan Tamils are influenced by the code (Muttettuwegama 2001). The insurgency modified and further expanded the code while

22. See the interview with the LTTE judicial chief, Joseph Pararajasingham (TamilNet 2003).

integrating it into its own legal system, excluding those cultural norms that did not fit in with its social agenda. For example, while the colonial interpretation of the code provided extensive regulations regarding such unpleasant subjects as caste and dowry, they were excised from the LTTE version.

Perhaps the area where the code fit most closely with the rebel agenda was with control of land transfers. According to the LTTE's reading of the code, land transfers could be made only to relatives or local community members (interview with N. Ethirveerasingam). The main purpose of this strategy was to prevent Sinhalese and other outsiders (Muslims and nonloyal Tamils) from buying land in traditionally Tamil areas, a sensitive subject considering the government's consistent use of population transfers to the northeast to change the demographic balance in the region. By incorporating Tamil cultural norms into their legal regulations on property transfers, the rebellion was able to gain legitimacy for its judicial approach while also keeping close control over this very contentious and lucrative (through taxes on property) issue.

There was a single legal system for both civilians and the rebel cadres in Eelam, run by lawyers and judges trained in the law college, almost all of whom had experience in the military ranks (interviews with Lankanesan and Anpu). A small number of lawyers were even sent by the rebels to India and Australia to receive advanced legal training, while others were trained by Tamil lawyers with experience in both the government and insurgent legal systems (Kamalendran 2004). The LTTE used public meetings and local media such as cheaply published pamphlets to spread awareness about the legal system. According to civilian informants, justice was administered very quickly, usually in two or three days for most civil disputes. Furthermore, there was a perception that most judgments were favorable to poorer sectors of the community. The insurgent organization went to great pains to demonstrate the incorruptibility of the legal system in rebel areas, and there was a general perception that crime was a greater concern in the government-controlled areas or areas of divided control in the northeast. The rebels also ensured that legal services were accessible to all, charging most a flat fee of less than $20—which covered the cost of the court-appointed lawyer—while also providing free legal advice for the poor. Thus, in areas directly under the control of the Tigers, the system proved to be effective and well received by the population. According to the LTTE, by 2002, over 23,000 cases had been tried in the rebel court system, with fewer than 5 percent of decisions being appealed by disputants (TamilNet 2002a).[23]

As discussed earlier, the rebels controlled not the entire N&E Province but rather a patchwork of territories, tending to cede control to government forces

---

23. Though I never received an independent confirmation of these numbers, I did see considerable evidence of detailed record keeping during a visit to an LTTE court in Kilinochchi in 2005.

in many urban areas, including important towns such as Jaffna, Trincomalee, and Batticaloa. Although these clear areas were technically under the control of government forces, the Tigers had an impressive ability to influence daily life even in towns outside their nominal control. Tamils in government-controlled areas of the northeast would frequently cross into rebel territory to file complaints in the insurgent judicial system. The rebels would then issue a summons to the defendants requesting their presence in an LTTE court (interview with Jeyanesan; TamilNet 1997). As a result, civilians in areas of divided control essentially had two legal systems to choose from and generally decided according to their own perceptions of the relative benefits of each. The impact on the insurgency was mixed. In the north, where the distinction between government control and rebel control was easier to discern and was more stable, the insurgent legal system was quite popular and regularly utilized by civilians. However, in the east, where control tended to shift erratically, this was an especially despised facet of the system. Civilian informants complained that competing legal systems interfered with their daily life because supporters of the rebellion would often use LTTE courts to overrule judgments made by the official Sri Lankan legal system.

The Health System

Undoubtedly the health infrastructure in the northeast was undermined by the war-induced embargo on goods to a much greater degree than were other sectors that were not as reliant on highly skilled personnel or the timely provision of a diverse array of supplies such as education. In the east there were no government hospitals operating in rebel-held areas. This was a result of the fact that the insurgency controlled only rural parts of the region and no major population centers. However, aid organizations such as Médecins Sans Frontières, the International Committee of the Red Cross, and the diasporic Tamils Rehabilitation Organization (TRO) provided a limited number of mobile health centers within rebel territory, though physicians did not generally staff these. Civilians with more serious medical conditions were forced to travel to government-controlled towns for treatment (interview with Sivam). This was a normal difficulty of life during the war for civilians who had to cross the border between the two zones of control before it was closed every evening at six, if it was opened at all on that day.

In the north, Kilinochchi, the largest town under rebel control, had a large government-run hospital staffed by a crew of doctors and nurses paid for through government allocations. However, the entire health service sector suffered from chronic shortages of supplies due to the embargo. When the conflict was active, most medicines were categorized as restricted, and no new health facilities were constructed because of a ban on the transportation of cement to rebel areas (interview with Damian). But the ban was generally relaxed or even lifted during ceasefires and other lulls in fighting, and this led to improved capacity. Throughout the war there was a chronic shortage of personnel due to a general hesitation by qualified Tamils to work in rebel areas. Although all medical personnel received salaries from the government, individuals had to self-select to work in the northeast, a commitment many were understandably afraid to make. As a result, with a population of approximately 150,000 people, Kilinochchi only had fifteen doctors and seven assistant doctors working in 2005. This is compared with a countrywide average of approximately fifty doctors per 100,000 people, more than three times as many as in rebel-held areas. According to a local doctor I spoke with on a visit to the Kilinochchi hospital in 2005, about twenty nurses served this population, around a sixth of the actual number necessary for adequate health care provision (interview with Sathyamourthy).

The organization played little more than an advisory role when it came to the provision of health; this contrasts with its involvement in the education sector (discussed below), where the rebellion had a proactive community-based effort to control the quality of education within its territory. Instead, the health sector looked to international agencies such as UNICEF to make up for its shortcomings, though as I discuss below, it was not until the ceasefire of 2002 that NGOs and international agencies began entering the region in significant numbers.

The Education System

During an internal war, daily life is regularly disrupted by the rhythm of the fighting, which can quickly vacillate between periods of extended calm and brutal confrontations. It was no different during the war in Sri Lanka. However, despite the frequent shifts in battle and the regular border closures and embargoes on goods that resulted, the education system in LTTE areas was remarkable for its ability to provide a degree of continuity despite these interruptions. To understand the importance of education in the northeast, it is essential to recognize the historical educational opportunities that had long prevailed in the Tamil regions of the country. As discussed earlier, the British established an extensive system of missionary schools within the northeast, hoping to incorporate the Tamil community into the colonial bureaucracy. The unofficial first city of the Sri Lankan Tamils, Jaffna, was favored by the British, and during the colonial era had a larger number of schools than anywhere else outside the Colombo/Kandy area.[24]

---

24. Jaffna has always been revered as the cultural and intellectual sanctuary for the Tamils and has produced many of the most important leaders of the Tamil movement (interview with Sivaram; Roberts 2009).

After independence, the populist policies of the new Ceylon government covered educational expenses for all citizens. In the northeast this included the payment of fees for students attending missionary schools and salaries for the teachers. This financial support continued till 1960, when Bandaranaike nationalized schools, taking power away from the missionaries who had run the educational infrastructure in the region from colonial times. Though nationalization was disruptive, the European missionaries who had set up the schools ceded power to native Tamil converts, who continued to maintain the high educational standards already in place. As a result, before the war Tamils in the N&E Province had the highest educational levels on the island. The Sri Lankan education system empowered the provincial governments to make decisions regarding the curriculum, hiring of teachers, location and construction of schools, and other issues affecting education in the provinces (interview with Lankanesan). Provincial education offices were given a degree of flexibility in these matters, though they were also expected to implement mandates issued by the Ministry of Education in Colombo. Such a decentralized structure was necessary given the linguistic differences between provinces, especially in the northeast, which required a Tamil curriculum.

During the war the LTTE established the Tamil Eelam Education Council (TEEC) to coordinate the provision of education with the provincial representatives. The council functioned as the Ministry of Education within the rebel civil administration under the leadership of a secretary of education. Its purpose was to encourage the establishment of civil society–based advisory committees in every district that would be composed of parents and educators to regulate and supplement the provision of education (Ethirveerasingam 1999). The ability to send their children to school was a frequent concern in my interviews with civilians living inside rebel territory, and it reinforced the common perception that Sri Lankan Tamils place a superlative emphasis on education as a means for social uplift. This parental concern for their children's education also provided the insurgency with a proactive community that the advisory committees could tap into. During the war, when the school system was interrupted by the lack of either teachers or materials, members of the council could pitch in and supplement the government education system (interview with N. Ethirveerasingam). This provided schools with a degree of continuity necessary to compensate for the frequent breaks in education provision due to the war.

Even during the difficult days of the embargo, students in the northeast had impressively high pass rates. For example, in 2002, prior to the ceasefire, a total of 1,994 primary and secondary schools operated throughout the province with a total enrollment of 648,000, according to government figures (Ministry of Education 2002, cited in United Nations 2003). The UN estimated that about

FIGURE 4.4. Children attend school in an LTTE-controlled village, 2005. *Source*: Author's collection.

50,000 children were out of school during Tiger rule in the northeast, and it put the student dropout rate at 15 percent, almost four times the national average (United Nations 2003). Though this was relatively high compared with national performance benchmarks, it is worth pointing out that a 15 percent dropout rate is remarkably low for an area affected by more than two decades of almost continuous conflict. Though no figures exist that specifically separate the number of schools in rebel areas from the number in areas controlled by the government in the N&E Province, it is reasonable to assume that the actual number of dropouts was higher in Tiger territory than in government-controlled territories. However, considering the extent of insurgent control over the population in the province, a substantially higher dropout rate would clearly have been reflected in the provincewide number, which it is not.

In the east, teachers preferred to live in the government-controlled capital, Batticaloa, traveling into rebel territory daily. Since this entailed passing through a series of checkpoints and traversing some very difficult terrain, teachers often missed class altogether (interviews with Jeyanesan and local teachers). In the north, where rebel territorial control was more uniform, schools could draw teachers from within rebel territory and hence provide a more consistent educational experience to the student population. Accounts by civilian informants and my own personal observations indicate that during the war a functioning education system up to the upper secondary level existed throughout the N&E Province, although students were required to travel to schools located in towns controlled by the government if they wanted to continue beyond this point (interview with Sivam).

The Impact of the Ceasefire and the Role of NGOs

The 2002 ceasefire initiated the continued evolution of the Atasialthurai into an even more complex structure as the political leadership sought to adjust the governance system in response to the rapid changes affecting the northeast.[25] The civil administration was transformed in two different ways. First, in response to the easing of travel restrictions between the two former provinces, the rebel leadership sought to centralize the administration by transferring powers once given to the eastern commanders back to the north. And second, it was forced

---

25. For a comprehensive assessment of the 2002 ceasefire, see the contributions to the edited volume by Keethaponcalan and Jayawardana (2009).

to deal with the influx of postconflict aid brought by international agencies and INGOs to the region.

Despite the unification of the northern and eastern provinces, the distance between the two and the difficulty of traveling from one through government territory to reach the other meant that prior to the ceasefire, the insurgency's second in command, Colonel Karuna Amman (nom de guerre of Vinayagamoorthy Muralitharan), exercised considerable autonomy over the eastern province. During the war the insurgent administration functioned in a quasi-federal manner with substantial powers allocated to the regional command, especially in regard to civilian governance concerns, though Karuna was expected to defer to Prabhakharan on most military issues. The ceasefire altered this dynamic, and for the first time members of the LTTE could travel relatively freely between the two regions.

The central command used this opportunity to claim greater power for the civil administration away from the eastern commanders. The judiciary, the police force, and the income tax offices were all made to report to the center and not to the regional command, a measure that directly undermined Karuna's authority in his home region. Karuna's split from the main faction in 2004 was directly related to the increasing centralization of governance brought about in the context of the ceasefire. He was able to appeal to latent dissatisfaction due to the perceived discrimination against the eastern Tamils by the northern Tamil population.[26] As evidence of this discrimination, he cited numbers demonstrating the underrepresentation of eastern Tamils in leadership positions and their overrepresentation in casualty figures (Jeyaraj 2004). His split, however, left the LTTE with no internal opposition, allowing Prabhakharan to continue the process of centralizing authority under his direct command.

In its earlier manifestations, a secretariat for NGOs existed within the political secretariat to coordinate humanitarian efforts, but it had a limited scope that reflected the relative paucity of international aid organizations in wartime Sri Lanka. During the war several types of relief organizations did operate throughout the northeast, but as a category, they did not have the same influence as they do in other contemporary war zones. This is largely attributable to the relatively solid service provision that characterized life in the province before and during the conflict and the LTTE's suspicion of and general aversion to foreign organizations operating within its territory. Thus, prior to the early 1990s—when the fall

---

26. There is insufficient space here to recount the history of relations between the northern and eastern Tamil communities. Generally it is fair to say that the eastern Tamils did support the LTTE but were wary of its unwillingness to give the east greater say in the organization of the movement. Many in the east perceived this as a preference for the interests of the north (interview with Miller).

of the Soviet Union brought about an influx of Western money geared directly toward the promotion of so-called civil society initiatives—there were few NGOs except those that came out of the churches or other big charitable organizations (Goodhand and Lewer 1999).[27]

The exception to this was the TRO, established by Tamil refugees and members of the diaspora in 1985 to provide support for reconstruction efforts in rebel areas as well as relief for the growing refugee population in India. It is difficult to pinpoint the exact relationship between the LTTE and TRO. As an NGO, TRO operated in fifteen countries, including Sri Lanka, and it went out of its way to prove its autonomy from the rebel organization (Tamils Rehabilitation Organization 2004). Although TRO's claim to autonomy was partially true, according to one community leader who remained in the Kilinochchi area throughout the conflict, insurgent leaders wanted a Tamil organization that could handle developmental affairs, so they backed TRO soon after it commenced operations in the region (interview with Nagendran). It is probably best to think of TRO as something between a quasi-rebel structure and an independent aid group as the vast majority of its activities did not directly involve the insurgent organization, though it is also true that it would never have had the type of reach it did without its close ties to the LTTE. Approximately 50 percent of TRO's volunteers were foreigners, predominantly Australians, and many were not members of the Tamil diaspora. Rather, non-Tamil foreigners were motivated to work with the organization through exposure to publicity exercises, mostly informal, organized by members of the Tamil diaspora in Australia, Canada, the United Kingdom, and the United States.

Even when INGOs first began trickling into the region in the early 1990s, the vast majority of service provision remained under the shared control of the rebels and the government. The ceasefire, at least in its first and second years, led to hopes by many within the international community that Sri Lanka had turned a corner and was deserving of large aid projects to encourage the nascent peace process. This produced a flood of developmental INGOs, flush with money from international agencies such as the World Bank and the Asian Development Bank into LTTE-controlled areas of the northeast. This influx spurred the development of new structures within the rebel civil administration that sought to keep control over the development process (interview with Mathy).[28] The organization

---

27. Estimates I heard in the region put the number of INGOs operating in LTTE areas at around five or six, including the Red Cross, Oxfam, and CARE (interview with Nagendran).

28. Mathy was one of the organization's many female cadres, though somewhat unique in her position of prominence within the civil administration. During our conversation, she laughed at my question about the presence of female fighters in the LTTE, joking that every academic or journalist

was determined to be perceived as a reliable partner, creating the Planning and Development Secretariat (PDS) in January of 2004 to coordinate NGO activity within insurgent territory. According to one rebel leader, the pace by which other sectors within the secretariat were spun off into their own agencies increased as well. The PDS required that NGOs be registered, submit their plans for approval, and find a local partner organization, which the command hoped would promote capacity building within their Tamil constituency (interview with Puleedevan). The goal was for community-based organizations (CBOs) to take control of international aid projects fostering local ownership over the development process.

In a gleaming new office building in the official rebel capital during the war, Kilinochchi, I spoke with the managing director of the PDS in July 2004. A twenty-something former fighter, Maran spoke impeccable English and had a tremendous grasp of issues affecting development and reconstruction throughout Eelam. According to him, the role of the PDS was to formulate a general development agenda for the province, set standards for any work done, and guide actors on where and how to set up projects. The secretariat's role increased significantly after the tsunami of December 2004 when the region witnessed an almost unimaginable influx of foreign aid organizations into the region. When the tsunami hit, PDS had only one office in Kilinochchi. However, the disaster triggered an expansion of the PDS, and district offices were opened across rebel territory to handle the newly arrived aid agencies (interview with Mathy). The stated goal of the rebellion following the tsunami was to ensure that donors viewed the PDS as the speediest means for implementing recovery programs, though it also recognized the legal constraints that donors faced in their home countries, where the LTTE was labeled a terrorist organization, especially in the aftermath of September 11, 2001.[29] According to one knowledgeable observer, the rebels hoped to change this perception and "wanted to use the opportunity [the tsunami] to gain legitimacy" (interview with Lankanesan).

Not surprisingly, considering their history of cooperation, distribution of tsunami aid brought the newly created insurgent aid distribution mechanisms together with their government counterparts. During the war, the Conflict-Affected Areas Program (CAAP) was funded primarily by government allocations, and international organizations had little role. However, the Tsunami-Affected Areas Program (TAAP) was supported primarily through external funds and caused

---

she met wanted to know about this issue. She insisted it was of no particular relevance for her personally.

29. International agencies were not as affected by these national restrictions, and the World Bank held several meetings with the LTTE leadership in order to determine ways of providing funds directly to the group, though it was generally recognized that only a comprehensive peace agreement would allow funds to flow unconstrained. See Mampilly (2009) for a full discussion.

both sides (GoSL and LTTE) to recognize the importance of working together to maintain control over the process of aid distribution (interview with Sivananthan). A joint mechanism was established between the belligerents to distribute the substantial financial resources flowing into the country. A consortium was established comprising representatives from the government, the rebels, and the INGOs that was designed to give all three a voice in regulating the behavior of aid organizations involved in tsunami reconstruction efforts (interview with Puleedevan). All sides viewed it as an opportunity to bring the LTTE into the mainstream, and the rebellion initially earned plaudits for its effective reconstruction programs (interview with Sivananthan). In many ways, this brief posttsunami period represented the pinnacle of the LTTE governance system.

However, the goodwill created through this deepening relationship between both sides was short-lived, as tensions arose about other issues, including the perceived dithering of government negotiators over a final settlement and the LTTE's general unwillingness to accept anything short of an independent state. These factors eventually unraveled the peace process in 2007, leading to the complete victory of government forces over the insurgency in early 2009.[30] During this final phase of the war, civilian governance in rebel-held territory went through a rapid process of decline, as the organization devoted its resources to its military wing in an ultimately unsuccessful effort to preserve its shrinking territorial base.

The Sri Lankan case demonstrates the lengths to which a secessionist organization was willing to go in order to generate support from the civilian population in a protracted civil war. Faced with the entrenched preferences of the Tamil population, which, since independence, had been able to access extensive public goods from the government, the insurgency would have risked alienating its support base if it had tinkered unsuccessfully with the provision of education or other public goods. At the same time, the incumbent government was wary of losing its tangible connection to the areas of the country that remained outside its control during the war. In recognition of these competing imperatives, the two enemies were forced to accept a joint system and work together to maintain service provision to civilians living in rebel areas. Underlying both rebel and government behavior was a subtle but persistent struggle, as the insurgent group attempted to present itself as the natural representative of the Tamil people while the government sought to limit this perception among both the residents of Tiger territory and the international community.

---

30. For a more detailed discussion of the posttsunami transformation of the conflict in Sri Lanka see Uyangoda (2005, 2008).

Though the government was successful in getting the LTTE labeled an international pariah, the fact that the rebel leadership had only one domestic actor to negotiate with—albeit the incumbent state—in order to meet civilian needs meant that international condemnation had a relatively minor impact on the insurgency's governance capacity. As a result, efforts by the state to demonize the organization among its civilian base of support fell flat, largely as a result of its own sustained contributions to LTTE governance efforts. This state of affairs persisted until the tsunami encouraged insurgent leaders to attempt a failed break from their financial dependency on the Sri Lankan state, an effort that contributed to the broader unraveling that eventually led to the organization's demise (Mampilly 2009).

The logic underlying the organization's choice of governance strategy is fairly straightforward and easily comprehensible, if not necessarily available to every insurgent group, as the next two case studies demonstrate. Because the state bureaucracy was highly effective in distributing public goods, the insurgent organization was able to position itself as a replacement to the Sri Lankan government by appropriating the machinery of the state itself. Combined with the substantial efforts the organization took to promulgate an effective symbolic display of its hegemony in the areas under its control, the LTTE case drew most directly from the model of the nation-state to successfully entrench its rule among its civilian subjects. The end result was to render the organization's efforts among the most substantial examples ever seen of civilian governance provision by an insurgent group. The LTTE was able to develop a comprehensive governmental apparatus that achieved deep legitimacy within the society under its control. Indeed, in rebel-held areas, most civilians came to view the LTTE political regime as the sovereign authority itself, despite its continued reliance on the incumbent for support.

5

BUILDING A NEW SUDAN

The Sudan People's Liberation Movement/Army

**Bear in mind that Nationalism is the mother of widows.
Sovereignty is the grandmother of orphans.**

—David Aoloch Bion, "The Infidels"

Before my first visit to New Sudan, I wandered around Kampala, Uganda, in search of a "visa" from the SPLM/A's representative in the city. I was told to find the offices of an aid organization run by Sudanese exiles with close ties to the rebel group. But after presenting our request to the director in front of a room filled with Southern Sudanese, we were met with blank stares and abject silence.[1] Dismayed but not defeated, we managed to arrange a meeting with an SPLA commander at a popular Kampala café frequented by Sudanese exiles. Over milky tea, Commander Riak Jeroboam, the insurgency's representative in Uganda, made a few phone calls on his cell phone. A personalized letter of introduction soon materialized. A return visit to the director, whose demeanor had instantly changed from hostile to enthusiastic once he had the letter, led to our securing an impressively professional light blue cardboard travel certificate—after we parted with two passport-size photos and $35. After traveling overland through northern Uganda to the insurgent-controlled town Nimule along the southern Sudanese border, I was struck by the sense of normalcy we encountered. Two years of calm following a ceasefire had allowed the rebels to expand their governance capacity, and they now proudly presided over an effective security system

---

1. On my first visit to Sudan in 2004 I traveled to Yei and Nimule with Adam Branch, an assistant professor of political science at San Diego State University. I returned to South Sudan by myself in 2005. In 2008 I traveled to Juba and Rumbek with Arthur Rhodes. Several of the interviews cited in this chapter were conducted jointly with them.

and, in conjunction with foreign aid groups who had flocked to the region, a rudimentary health and education system as well. However, though the civil administration was impressive in scope, conversations with civilians, aid workers, rebel soldiers, and bureaucrats revealed that it was still a work in progress rather than a comprehensive system of civilian governance.

Until the signing of the ceasefire agreement in 2002, the war in South Sudan had been one of the world's longest and most destructive conflicts, spanning more than two decades directly and indirectly causing the deaths of at least two million people. During the twenty years of its existence, the SPLM/A morphed from its origins as a conglomeration of various discontented southern militias into one of the most structured and fearsome rebel armies in contemporary Africa. The signing of a comprehensive peace agreement (CPA) in early 2005 brought the organization into the government and transformed the former guerrilla army into a political party, albeit one with the ability to go back to war if it ever believed that the conditions of the peace agreement were being broached.[2]

I examine the development of the insurgent civil administration, tracing its origins to internal tensions between the insurgent army's constituent factions. In line with my arguments about a secessionist group operating in a territory with minimal preconflict state penetration, the SPLM/A did attempt to develop civilian governance capacities early on in its control of vast portions of Southern Sudan. However, the process of constructing a civil administration really took off only in response to internal challenges to the leadership's rule, triggered partially by accusations of civilian mistreatment. These challenges forced the command to acknowledge the importance of developing a governing system to improve relations between the insurgency and the local communities living under rebel control. Eventually, insurgent leaders embraced the development of a civilian administration, hoping it would help the rebellion become the fulcrum around which a Southern Sudanese resistance could cohere.

Faced with a political landscape with little to no penetration by state institutions, the SPLM/A deserves credit for its innovative efforts to turn transnational

---

2. The agreement provided for a federal solution to Sudan's long-standing tensions between its northern and southern regions, including a fifty-fifty split of the all-important oil revenues. Under the agreement the longtime leader of the SPLM/A, John Garang, was made vice president, though a helicopter crash ended his life in July of 2005. The agreement stipulated that in six years time southerners would be allowed to vote on whether or not they want independence. In January 2011, they will likely vote for secession, though it is yet to be seen whether the ongoing crises in the south, as well as those in Darfur and Khordofan, may undermine the independence process. During the transition period, the SPLA is allowed to remain an autonomous army, though the agreement requires the organization to contribute troops to joint integration units (JIUs) that will become the basis of a new integrated national army if the referendum holds the country together. Meanwhile, the SPLM has been transformed into an autonomous political party in control of the new, semiautonomous Government of South Sudan (GoSS). It lost out to the National Congress Party (NCP) in the national elections scheduled for 2010, but did win a significant number of elected positions at a variety of levels.

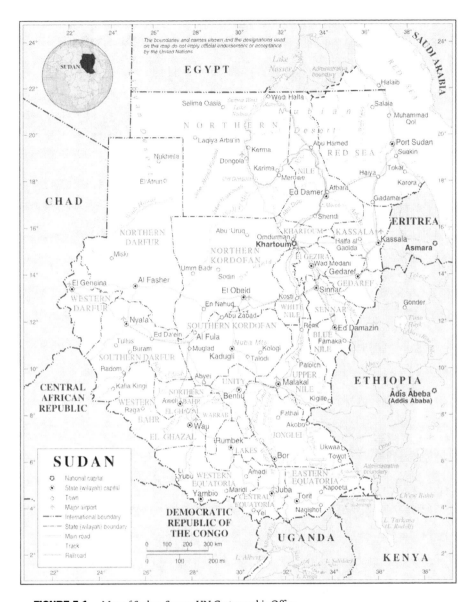

FIGURE 5.1. Map of Sudan. *Source*: UN Cartographic Office.

NGOs into supporters of its governance project. This approach allowed it to begin the process of providing to South Sudan what it always lacked—a meaningful administrative capacity. However, as I show in this chapter, actual service provision varied widely across the territory of New Sudan. In addition, insurgent leaders' reliance on international agencies and NGOs made the Southern

Sudanese landscape particularly susceptible to the opinions and actions of transnational actors, with mixed impacts for its governance capacity.

My analysis is based on an examination of two separate towns that remained under rebel rule for much of the latter part of the conflict, a fact that allowed me to explore some of the internal variation typical of most insurgent governance efforts. Rumbek and Yei were chosen to reflect the Dinka/ non-Dinka split within SPLM/A-controlled territory. During the war, both towns had similarly sized populations but varied dramatically in terms of their ethnic makeup and proximity to the fighting. Rumbek's majority Dinka population and frontline location contrasted starkly with Yei's Equatorian majority and relative stability along the border with Uganda, with distinct implications for SPLM/A governance efforts.

Though some observers have been unimpressed by the SPLM/A's governance project, I argue that the establishment of administrative structures and governing practices served other functions for the organization that warrant serious consideration. Premier among these was the success of the rebel command in integrating previously antagonistic elements into its broader agenda by developing a civil administrative structure that privileged local autonomy over central control. I connect the organization's approach to civilian governance to the history of neglect that characterized the south's relationship with the Khartoum government. With little preexisting infrastructure, the leadership's only option for developing a civilian governance system without diverting its limited resources was to co-opt the plethora of transnational actors engaging in developmental activities in the south. I argue that by limiting the civil administration's role to managing service provision by other nonstate actors operating within New Sudan, the rebel leadership was able to exert a degree of control over the developmental and humanitarian activities in its territory. At the same time, this low-cost approach allowed the rebel rulers to empower local level administrators, fostering greater cohesion within the southern population generally.

Background to the Conflict

The conflict in Southern Sudan is often perceived as one between an Arab and Muslim north, which has controlled the central government in the independence period, and the African and Christian south, which has been subject to varying degrees of economic and social marginalization and political and religious repression. Although it is true that the Khartoum-based government has consistently exploited the south while brutally suppressing opposition to its rule, closer examination reveals that the north-south divide is only one of many political divisions in contemporary Sudan. Sudan, Africa's largest country, is home to dozens of ethnic groups speaking hundreds of languages. There are a significant number of "Africans"—Christians, Muslims, and those adhering to traditional beliefs—in the north and a significant number of Muslims in the south. Thus, though religion has been a language in which politics and violence have been expressed, it cannot be seen as the cause of the conflict nor as its main reason for continuing.

Likewise, although race is often portrayed as the cause of the conflict, there are Arabs within the SPLM/A, just as there are Africans who support the regime.[3] The conflict being fought in Darfur against the Government of Sudan (GoS) by those identified as both Muslim and African demonstrates the difficulty of defining clear cleavages in a country as expansive and diverse as Sudan. Many analysts of, and participants in, the struggle have made clear that the conflict in Sudan, rather than being caused by racial or religious differences, is anchored in unequal development and political exclusion that has taken place in the context of easily politicized racial and religious identities (Abdel Salam and De Waal 2001).

The historical neglect of the south by the north has antecedents that predate colonial rule and are often traced to the rule of the Mahdi regime in the nineteenth century and even earlier (Idris 2001).[4] Indeed, at no point in the relationship between the two was the south ever treated as an equal partner in the construction of the Sudanese nation. In fact, the south has long been "stateless" and has actively resisted attempts to incorporate it into any of the major states of the region (Johnson 1998). Many commentators point to this precolonial relationship between the north and south as a cause of the current conflict. "Today's lurid crop of massive insecurity, enslavement, repression, and genocide was first sown generations ago" (Daly 1993, 1). This history of marginalization is central to the development of the insurgent government, as I will argue in this chapter.

North and south really came into administrative contact with the advent of the Anglo-Egyptian Condominium period (1899–1955), during which England ruled the Sudan through its Egyptian pawn. The two regions were ruled separately, with the financial profitability of the north serving as a convenient pretext for an unequal development policy that fostered further racial separation (Idris 2001). The north received a far greater percentage of the developmental disbursements for health and education from the colonial government. In

---

3. Johnson (2003) identifies multiple conflicts in the north and other parts of Sudan, including the Nuba Mountains and Darfur.

4. Before the Mahdiyya, Sudan was a part of the dying Ottoman Empire. The Ottomans viewed Sudan as little more than a site for levying tributes and stripping assets, including slaves. It never attempted to develop the region, and no functional bureaucracy was ever established.

addition, business opportunities created through British economic interests were concentrated in the north fostering the development of a northern economic elite with easy access to the newly minted colonial political institutions (Daly 1993). The south, meanwhile, was of interest only strategically, as a result of the long-standing British desire to control the Nile River, which wound through it (Yongo-Bure 1993). In the south, the British adopted a policy of separation that claimed to be a way to keep the region free from Arab/Muslim influence, allowing it to develop in its own "natural" way. However, scholars have argued that the British chose not to develop an educated and skilled native elite to provide administration in the region out of fear that this could lead to the emergence of a discontented nationalist southern intelligentsia (Tvedt 1994).[5]

This logic was taken to its natural extreme with the adoption of the southern policy in 1930, when development of the region was essentially abandoned. Administration was limited to a few Egyptian and Sudanese clerks and education left to Christian missionaries of various denominations. By 1949, when the south finally opened its first secondary school, the few remaining colonial institutions were in demise and the region had become a political and economic backwater. British policy had left South Sudan among the least developed regions in all of Africa (Idris 2005).

In 1956, Sudan gained independence under the unionist government of Ismail al-Azhari. In its hurry to abandon Sudan, the British colonial government passed control of the country to a tiny Arab elite who had comprised the exclusively Arab "nationalist" movement. Sudan's new nationalist leadership viewed the remaining 70 percent of the country as superfluous to its conception of the new nation. As a result, the south was further marginalized from any meaningful political and economic development. At best it was viewed as a poor relative worthy of little more than contempt or, more commonly, outright hostility. In practical terms, this meant that little attention was devoted to the development of the region while at the same time much was done to ensure that the region's resources could be funneled to benefit Khartoum and the surrounding environs (a process that accelerated after the discovery of oil in Bentiu in 1978). Since the people of the south were often viewed as expendable by northern leaders, the bureaucratic presence of the government remained scant (Prunier and Gisselquist 2003). The government eschewed seeking a balance between consent and coercion in favor of a rather harsh and uncontested force meant to keep the population compliant.

---

5. Experiences elsewhere in the colonial world had taught the British that promoting liberal values among a colonized elite could backfire, with this elite serving as the fulcrum around which nationalist struggles could emerge. Thus in Sudan, as in many parts of Africa, indirect-rule systems were put in place that relied on co-opting traditional authority systems in the place of a Westernized local political elite. See Mamdani (1996).

As a result, even at this early point, the country began convulsing under the strain of southern disaffection, witnessing a series of riots that left more than three hundred dead (Daly 1993). During the next decade, conditions in the south deteriorated, reaching their nadir in 1964 when war broke out between the two regions.

The First Anya Nya War

Of the forty million people in Sudan, only around one-quarter live in the south. The region is characterized by tremendous diversity and is home to 50 percent of the languages spoken in the country (Johnson 1998). It is a politically contested space with no historically unified Southern Sudanese identity. What common identity does exist seems to be based primarily on common repression by, and resistance to, the Khartoum regime.[6] But equally prominent are the divisions between the many ethnic groups in the south. The first Anya Nya war, as it came to be known, was fought by a collection of small southern militias, many with roots in the province of Equatoria along the northern Uganda border. Initially, the various guerrilla bands operated autonomously along ethnic lines, even going as far as to proclaim the establishment of their own republics, such as the Sue River Republic of Samuel Abujohn and the Anyidi Republic of Akuot Atem.

Six years later, in 1970, Joseph Lagu—an Equatorian leader who received support from Israel through the brokerage of Idi Amin—consolidated these groups into a single force that came to be known as the Southern Sudan Liberation Movement (SSLM) (Johnson and Prunier 1993). The war wreaked further havoc on the southern landscape, which was already seriously underdeveloped, as the government targeted infrastructure including roads, bridges, agricultural fields, and even schools for destruction (Yongo-Bure 1993). In 1969 an army coup with Colonel Jafar Muhammad Nimeiri at its head overthrew the government in the north. Initially promising a new vision for Sudan, the coup leaders formed a ten-man revolutionary command council that soon fell victim to infighting. This prompted a second coup attempt that threatened Nimeiri's hold on power but failed to overthrow him—instead triggering a purge of the council's progressive elements. This infighting helped Nimeiri recognize the importance of ending the southern war if he was to going to consolidate his control of the government. In March of 1972, under the auspices of the All-African Council of Churches, the

---

6. SPLM/A leaders and many academic authors imply that this identity forged through conflict is sufficiently coherent to prevent schisms in the postconflict era. See Abdel Salam and de Waal (2001, 220). For the SPLM/A view, see Wondu (2002).

Addis Ababa Agreement formally ended the conflict between the Government of Sudan and the SSLM.

The Regional Self-Government Act for the Southern Provinces emerged out of this accord and was willingly accepted by the former rebel leaders. The act created a single region out of the south, one with its own governing body made up of a regional assembly and a High Executive Council (HEC). The southern government had a significant degree of autonomy, though the act stopped short of embracing a truly federal arrangement for the country (Alier 1990, 89–99; Lesch 1998, 46–47). However, this arrangement was quickly undermined by the machinations of both Nimeiri and the southern leadership (Malok 2009). Although the agreement called for the development of the political and administrative institutions that the south had always lacked, only a small portion of the budget was actually allocated by the central government. With limited financial resources, there was little southern leaders could do because the region was completely bereft of the skilled manpower necessary to staff its newly empowered institutions. According to one account, the administrative and professional personnel in the south during the interwar period were among the smallest and least educated in the world (Tvedt 1994, 73). To fill this administrative void, foreign aid organizations began entering the region, particularly Equatoria, the southernmost province, where NGOs went as far as taking control of several public sectors (Rolandsen 2005).[7] Still, the two regions persisted in an uneasy peace, at least until the construction of the Jonglei Canal in 1977 reignited tensions between the two halves of the country. The canal ran through the Upper Nile province, displacing southern communities and denying them access to dry-season grazing land for their cattle (Prunier and Gisselquist 2003).

In the north, Nimeiri was beset with a challenge from Islamists to whom he found himself increasingly beholden.[8] The reforms that he proposed to bring the Sudanese constitution in line with Islamic law only further exacerbated the growing tensions between the regions. On the economic front, the years 1978 to 1982 witnessed a progressive deepening of Sudan's external debt, which had risen

---

7. According to Tvedt (1994, 91), from the mid-1970s to the mid-1980s it was the very efficiency of NGOs operating in the region that led them to undermine state authority. "I will argue that, in Southern Sudan, the NGOs contributed unintentionally to the erosion of the authority of a very weak state.... The NGOs put up their own administration and authority systems thereby undermining the state institutions without establishing viable alternative structures."

8. After Nimeiri had abandoned his supporters in the Communist Party in 1971, he was forced to rely on the Islamists in order to survive, famously embracing them in a public display in 1977. For their part, under the leadership of Hassan al-Turabi, the impressively professional and credentialed social base of the Islamist movement recognized the strategic value of entering the civil service and economy in vast numbers, greatly exaggerating their power relative to their actual base of support in the country (Prunier and Gisselquist 2003).

to over $5 billion dollars. The discovery of significant oil deposits near Bentiu led Nimeiri to believe that the regime's salvation lay with the untapped black gold, causing him to calculate—wrongly as it turns out—that the Addis Ababa Agreement was no longer essential to his survival (Johnson 1998, 46). Since Bentiu lay within territory demarcated as part of the south, Nimeiri forcibly adjusted the country's administrative boundaries to remove the oil fields from the jurisdiction of the southern regional government, much to the chagrin of the area's leaders. Feeling pressure on both the economic and political fronts, Nimeiri pandered to his major supporters, the Islamists, by increasing his Islamization policies, even going as far as declaring sharia (Islamic law). Southern leaders resented this move, viewing it as a deliberate attempt to undermine the autonomy of the southern region (Arou and Yongo-Bure 1988).

At the same time, schisms began to reappear in the south, and non-Dinka politicians promoted a "redivision" of the region into its three constituent parts (Equatoria, Bahr el Ghazal, and Upper Nile) by mobilizing popular fear among non-Dinka of Dinka domination of the unified southern administration—a movement commonly known by the Bari word *Kokora* (Dak 1988, 191–93).[9] Initially, non-Dinka occupied many of the positions in the southern government, but throughout the 1970s they began to assert their demographic strength and were able to quickly increase their numbers in the leadership. This culminated in the replacement of the Equatorian former SSLM leader (and prominent Kokora supporter) Joseph Lagu at the top of the regional government by Abel Alier, a Dinka nationalist. Alier promptly filled half the ministerial posts in the HEC with Dinka supporters, spreading insecurity among non-Dinka groups that rendered the entire southern government vulnerable (Johnson 1998, 53). This played into Khartoum's agenda to foster factionalism in the region and manipulate southern political institutions (Malok 2009, 93). When the HEC consistently refused to redivide the south, Nimeiri did it himself by decree in June 1983, assigning to the three newly reformulated provinces a greatly reduced degree of autonomy (Lesch 1998, 51).

This redivision was one of the triggers for the second southern rebellion, as it resulted in replacement of the federal structure by one entailing increased central control from Khartoum (Malok 2009).[10] Thus the new insurgency was fighting in

---

9. For an account of the divisions that plagued southern politics leading up to the SPLM/A rebellion, see Badal (1994). Badal relates the history of the resentment of Dinka hegemony within the south; he quotes Lieutenant General Lagu, the Madi leader of Anya Nya, as stating, "It is time we cut the Dinka down to their original size. They must go home, they have nothing to do in Equatoria" (120). See also Lagu (1980). For a more recent account, see Johnson (1998).

10. John Garang, the founder and leader of the SPLA, did not agree with the importance of the Kokora as a trigger for the war, pointing out that the rebel army had gone into the bush before

part to preserve a status quo ante that many Southern Sudanese did not want. To be clear, some in the south, particularly in Equatoria, did want a redivision of the region in order to be free from what they perceived as Dinka hegemony, but even these proponents were not satisfied by the more centralized structure imposed on them by Khartoum (Johnson 2003).

Origins of the Sudan People's Liberation Movement/Army

On top of his progressive weakening of the southern government and his attempts to reorganize the country's boundaries in order to control the oil resources, it was Nimeiri's movement toward Sudan's Islamists that set into motion events that birthed the new southern rebellion. Nimeri had long walked a balancing line between his desire to keep Sudan united and the pressure from Islamist parties that wanted to declare the country an Islamic state. His embrace of Islamism culminated with his proclamation of sharia, which proved to be the proverbial straw that broke the camel's back.

Unlike other cases wherein a small group of dedicated activists rally public support around a budding insurgent cause, the SPLA's military capacity was present at birth. The war began with a series of defections by southern fighters in the national army, including many who had fought in the first Anya Nya war. The effect of this was that the organization had little need to devote resources toward generating popular support in its initial phases, and as a result it paid little attention to civilian relations.

In July 1983, the Marxist government of Mengistu Haile Mariam (commonly referred to as the Derg or Dergue) in neighboring Ethiopia brought the disparate southern militant groups together. Mengistu had long harbored resentment against the Sudanese military for its support of the Eritrean secessionists, and in revenge he cultivated leftist insurgencies in the south (Johnson and Prunier 1993; Malok 2009, 156). At the Ethiopians' insistence, the newly founded insurgent organization decided against a separate military and political wing, instead combining the two under the leadership of John Garang, Mengistu's choice for leader of the fledgling rebel army. Too young to have played a significant role in the first southern rebellion, Garang had been encouraged by Anya Nya leaders to join

---

the redivision. Still, he did admit that it was an important factor. See his interview in the Sudanese newspaper the *Heritage* (1987: 4).

the National Army and continue his education.[11] Eventually he rose to the position of colonel after receiving military training at Fort Benning in Georgia. The selection of Garang, a Dinka, over former non-Dinka Anya Nya fighters who held senior positions in the first war contributed from the outset to tensions between the rebel army's constituent ethnic groups. Openly recognizing the risk of being perceived as a Dinka ethnonationalist movement since its inception, the organization tried to transcend the problems of polarized racial, religious, and ethnic identities by calling for a "New Sudan" based on national unity and equal development (Lesch 1998, 88–92).[12]

The dominance of the Dinka within the insurgent organization was not surprising considering the demographic strength of the community in the region. Approximately a third of the southern population is Dinka, far exceeding the next-largest community, the Nuer. Dinka have long lived and clashed with the Arab-ized[13] ethnic groups that occupy lands close to their traditional holdings. Their demographic strength notwithstanding, it is also important to recognize the historical position of the Dinka within Sudanese society. More a conglomeration of distinct subgroups than an organized ethnopolitical identity, the Dinka were passed over for positions in the colonial government in favor of communities viewed as better able to handle the demands of bureaucratic life. According to Johnson (1998, 50), "the majority of clerks, police and soldiers in the South were drawn from Equatoria and western Bahr al-Ghazal." This educational advantage explains why it was from among the Equatorian population, and not the Dinka, that the first Anya Nya received its leadership.

Despite Garang's attempts to frame the SPLM/A's struggle in an inclusive manner, tensions between the various ethnic groups in the south plagued the rebellion from the start. As one longtime observer and participant in the struggle simply put it, "In South Sudan, ethnicity affects everything" (interview with Aljack). Indeed, tensions between southern ethnic groups have broken into all-out conflict several times since independence. The Sudanese government has long found it expedient and cost-effective to promote schisms within the southern opposition. Though it would be an exaggeration to lay blame solely on the government for

---

11. Despite his formal training in the Sudanese military prior to founding the SPLA, Garang was not unfamiliar with revolutionary activity and insurgent theory. At the University of Dar es Salaam, where he studied in the late 1960s, Garang became a member of the university's radical student association, USARF, an organization that once claimed Yoweri Museveni as its president.

12. In its founding manifesto, the SPLM/A went so far as to state "that the principal objective of the SPLM/A is not separation from the South." Cited in Atem (1999).

13. "Arabized" is a contentious (though more precise term than "Arab") used to refer to groups that have adopted elements of Arab culture, primarily the Arabic language and the Islamic faith. In this context, it is primarily used to refer to groups like the Messeriya who are historically nomadic groups that live in the border areas between north and south Sudan.

these tensions, it has been Machiavellian in its attempts to fragment the southern resistance. Despite their professed socialist bearings, insurgent leaders initially did little to build support with the non-Dinka population. Even at the earliest phases of the rebellion's history, non-Dinka lacked a prominent role within the leadership, especially when considering their predominance in the first rebellion. Worse, non-Dinka were frequently subjected to atrocities at the hands of the rebels (Human Rights Watch 1994; Sudan Human Rights Association 2003), and many viewed the group as a vehicle of Dinka domination not dissimilar to the Khartoum government.

The SPLM/A treated Equatoria in particular as occupied territory,[14] moving large numbers of Dinka into the province, where they would have better access to relief aid and avoid the worse fighting further north.[15] This massive, violent demographic shift meant that during the war, in parts of Equatoria, internally displaced Dinka outnumbered remaining non-Dinka by three to one. Those who remained found themselves subject to political and economic marginalization in their own homes. In response, several small ethnic militias emerged throughout Equatoria to challenge the authority of the SPLM/A, though none posed a real challenge to its military might.

By 1989 the group had merged with several other factions, achieving impressive military victories over GoS forces and gaining control over two-thirds of the south, including several large towns (Prunier and Gisselquist 2003). Political power rested with the Political Military High Command (PMHC), which exercised absolute control over all civil and military affairs (Akol 2009; Malok 2009). In 1991 the SPLM/A lost its key supporter when Mengistu's regime collapsed. Ethiopia had long provided both funds and logistical support to the insurgent organization, and throughout its brief history, the rebels had maintained rear bases in the country. These bases were utilized for a variety of purposes, including serving as a critical refuge for the rebellion away from Khartoum's advances and an important source of nonmilitary and military goods. The organization's effective radio broadcast, which served to educate the southern population about the insurgency's agenda, also originated in the Ethiopian bases and was shut down after the collapse of Mengistu.

The new Ethiopian regime, led by the former rebels of the Tigray People's Liberation Front (TPLF), had little patience for the Sudanese rebels—tarnished as they were by their affiliation with Mengistu—and quickly expelled them from Ethiopian

---

14. As Johnson (1998, 70) writes, the inhabitants of Yei saw the SPLM/A as an "army of occupation."

15. A 1994 USAID estimate put the number of IDPs in SPLM/A-held territory at around 1.5 million during the war; in Equatoria the number was probably several hundred thousand, although in interviews we were confidently told by (mostly Equatorian) informants that the actual number was in the millions.

territory. The collapse of the friendly regime next door also triggered a massive influx of hundreds of thousands of refugees back into the south from refugee camps in Ethiopia (Johnson 2003, 88). The insurgent organization was ill prepared to deal with this population, having long pursued a strategy of funneling civilians across the border to sanctuaries in Ethiopia in order to avoid devoting resources to structures capable of providing basic services to the conflict-affected population.[16]

At this inopportune moment, the Nuer, who make up the second-largest segment of the southern population after the Dinka, began making both violent and nonviolent demands for greater representation within the rebel leadership, further adding to the organization's woes (Scroggins 2004; Jok and Hutchinson 1999).[17] In August 1991, several Nuer commanders led by Dr. Riek Machar,[18] a member of the PMHC, attempted a coup to replace Garang. Along with Dr. Lam Akol,[19] the Nuer leaders claimed that under Garang's leadership, the rebel army had consistently abused the human rights of civilians within its territory. More relevant to our discussion, the coup leaders accused the PMHC of failing to establish an effective and democratic civilian governance system for rebel-held territories (interview with Gumbiri; Atem 1999; Akol 2009). The Nuer faction was initially known as the SPLM/A-Nasir, named for the town in Upper Nile where Machar was commander. Eventually, he rejected Garang's vision of a united New Sudan, instead adopting the overtly secessionist appellation the Southern Sudan Independence Movement (SSIM) (interview with Aljack). Whether Machar actually cared about governance or was merely opportunistically exploiting a legitimate concern articulated by the civilian population, the split he orchestrated demonstrates the consequences of the insurgent command's failure to address demands for services and representation from the civilian population, particularly when these deficiencies could be ethnicized by opportunistic factional leaders.

The war between the two factions was extraordinarily bloody, and both sides commonly targeted civilians. Open conflict lasted from 1991 to 1999 and produced many more civilian deaths than did the battle against the Khartoum government. Although the Nasir faction, which framed itself as the champion of the

---

16. Pushing civilians across the border to a friendly neighboring country is one possible mechanism by which neighboring state support might undermine insurgent governance performance.

17. Many observers viewed Mengistu as the real reason for Dinka/Nuer solidarity, and they trace the split between the communities directly to his demise (interview with Butler).

18. Machar gained a degree of notoriety after he married Emma McCune, a British aid worker who worked with Street Kids International, an aid group that sought to build schools in South Sudan. Even after their marriage she continued to work with the agency. McCune served as Machar's greatest supporter, using her connections to the international community to promote a kinder, gentler version of the commander that many thought duplicitous in view of his actual behavior. See Scroggins (2004).

19. Lam Akol, another member of the high command, presents his version of events and in particular his critique of Garang's leadership in Akol (2009).

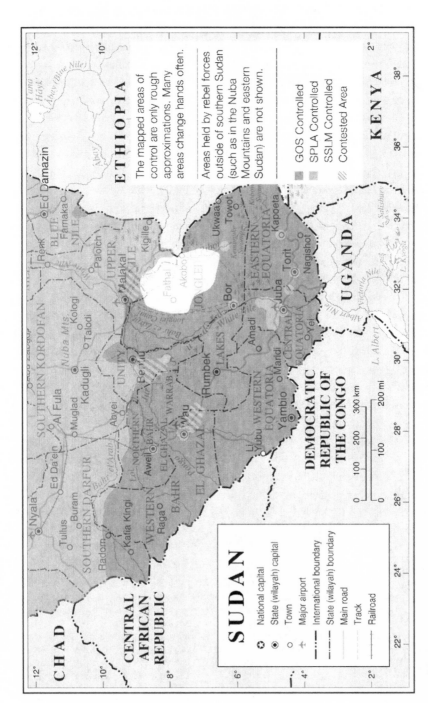

FIGURE 5.2. Map of insurgent-controlled areas in Sudan. *Source:* Dustin Ross.

Nuer, did tap into deep-seated political grievances, it undermined its own potential to replace the SPLM/A as the dominant rebel organization in Southern Sudan by accepting extensive support from Khartoum (Jok and Hutchinson 1999). Like Garang before him,[20] Machar was known to be skillful at garnering support from transnational actors, and it is doubtful whether his faction would have been able to survive if personnel from international aid agencies had not been so willing to throw their support behind him early on, directing aid to the areas under SSIM control (Scroggins 2004, 299). Personnel from these INGOs eventually cooled on the splinter group when a recording made of an attack on a Dinka town in 1991 was circulated among the expatriate community. The video dashed any perceptions that Machar represented a new, liberal path away from the autocratic tendencies of Garang, arguably preventing a wholesale shift in transnational support away from the SPLM/A to Machar's faction (ibid; Rolandsen 2005). The SSIM's reliance on and comeuppance from transnational actors is a good example of the crucial role that such actors can play in contemporary conflict zones, both building up and tearing down would-be insurgent leaders.

The intrasouth conflict was not resolved until 1999, when Machar agreed to rejoin the SPLM/A after a peace initiative brought about by churches and other local leaders.[21] The split had a substantial impact on the insurgent organization. The rebellion lost most of its territory as government forces took advantage of the split, launching a series of effective military offensives. In addition, the rebel army lost a large number of troops to the SSIM, and its civilian base was significantly reduced as well (Rolandsen 2005). The split also pushed the organization away from its national focus toward a more secessionist position in response to Machar's use of independence rhetoric (Jok and Hutchinson 1999). The leadership had initially refrained from using secessionist language out of deference to its Ethiopian patron—which was engaged in its own bloody struggle against Eritrean secessionists in the 1980s. After the loss of Ethiopian support, both the SPLM/A and the SSIM sought to draw popular support by offering their followers total independence from the Sudanese state. Eritrea's gaining of independence in 1993, long a taboo within both Africa and the international community, had created a secessionist precedent that the leadership quickly embraced. However, in propaganda materials, the insurgency stressed its nationally focused agenda while sending signals to its internal constituency that secession was certainly on the table (interview with Jok).

---

20. Garang often sent off missives to the media to correct what he perceived as misperceptions about the SPLM/A. See his letters and essays in Garang (1992).

21. Not all those who supported the breakaway faction rejoined the SPLA. Some, like the South Sudan Liberation Movement, remained loyal to Khartoum and even held on to large pieces of territory during the war. See figure 5.2.

Forced to recognize the explosive resentment of the insurgency by a segment of the population they claimed to be fighting for, Garang and other leaders made attempts to alleviate the tensions between Dinka and non-Dinka. Militarily, they were able to gain some support from southern populations as a result of Khartoum's indiscriminate retaliation on areas suspected of supporting the rebels (Johnson and Prunier 1993). Politically, the group initiated a south-south dialogue that sought to clarify the responsibilities of the political wing, which had long languished under the dominance of the military wing.

Concomitant with these demands for genuine local self-government and ethnic inclusion from below, the National Democratic Alliance (NDA) put pressure on the rebel leadership to respect demands for local autonomy. The NDA was an umbrella organization that came together after the bloodless coup that brought a military junta led by Colonel Omar Al-Bashir to power in 1989. Prior to the coup, the SPLM/A had worked together with many of the organizations that formed the NDA, which included the major northern opposition political parties and several armed groups and trade unions (Akol 2009, 220). In keeping with the 1995 Asmara Declaration put forth by the NDA, participating in the coalition compelled the southern rebels to embrace democratic values by acknowledging, "the fact that unity of the Sudan cannot be durably based on force or coercion but on justice and the free-consent of all the various groups in the Sudan" (cited in Abdel Salam and de Waal 2001, 203).

Establishment of the SPLM/A Civil Administration

Service provision in the region had first been formalized in 1989 by the Sudan Relief and Rehabilitation Association (SRRA), a diasporic NGO created to provide basic services to populations living under rebel control. Although the SRRA had actually commenced operations in 1986 in scattered parts of Ethiopia, it was not until a widespread famine in 1988 killed an estimated 250,000 people that the organization moved into Sudan. The famine triggered a massive reentry of foreign NGOs under the auspices of Operation Lifeline Sudan (OLS), a consortium of UN agencies and prominent relief NGOs set up to oversee the distribution of aid in the region.[22] The SRRA's influence grew in response to this increased transnational intervention into insurgent territory as the high command recognized the importance of having an institutional body capable of representing the

---

22. Tvedt (1994, 89) writes that "in Southern Sudan the NGOs came to play a very important role already in the 1970s," calling Southern Sudan "an early and natural place for NGO involvement."

organization within the aid distribution process (Akol 2009, 129–38). The goal for the restructured SRRA was to have both a presence on the ground within Sudan and representation for the SPLM/A abroad through the SRRA office located in Nairobi. By 1990 the SRRA had begun operating in many areas of the south, serving as both a coordinator of relief operations and often the de facto political authority and civil administration for the southern rebellion (interview with Gumbiri).

The insurgent organization had begun to establish a civil authority structure (independent of the SRRA) in the early 1990s in response to the overmilitarization of life in the region after the successful capture of large territories in 1989. The main task of the nascent civil administration was to mobilize human and material resources for the organization (Atem 1999). Quotas related to the provision of new recruits and other material resources were imposed on traditional leaders. Unmet demands could lead to chiefs' being fined or removed from power. The civilian population also provided the rebels with the majority of their food needs, as well as labor power and beasts of burden. Although the situation was not anarchical because NGOs and religious institutions labored to provide a modicum of social and political order, the administrative capacity of the organization at the time was minimal, reflecting the whims and initiative of local political leaders (interviews with Sowinska and Gideon).

The conflicts between southern ethnic groups led the insurgent command to recognize that decentralizing the political apparatus was essential if they were to retain and regain support from non-Dinka ethnic groups and be able to win national and international legitimacy (interviews with Arop and Gumbiri).[23] These internal tensions combined with pressure from aid organizations, churches, and international agencies and provoked the insurgent command into beginning a process of governance reform (Rolandsen 2005). In September 1991, the PMHC, the highest executive and legislative body of the SPLM/A, initiated a transformation of the civil administration (Johnson 2003). The meeting that produced what came to be known as the Torit Resolutions took place shortly after Machar's break from the organization, though the subject of civilian governance reform had been discussed prior to the attempted coup.[24] This led to a series of smaller conferences of the high command, where it was decided to hold a convention to restructure the organization's governmental structures and practices. Between March and April of 1994, a national convention of SPLM/A members met to

---

23. In Equatoria, a regional conference in 2001 and a convention in 2002 led to a call by political and civil society leaders for the decentralization of government in the south and constitutional and legal reforms that would guarantee the self-rule of Equatoria free from Dinka dominance.

24. For an insider's account of the internal deliberations, see Malok (2009).

discuss the establishment of a civil administration. This meeting led to, in 1995, the Conference on Civil Society and the Organization of Civil Authority in Himman-New Cush, at which the Civil Authority of the New Sudan (CANS) was initiated to rectify a situation characterized by one rebel administrator as "jungle law" (interview with Wani).[25]

From its humble origins in 1994, CANS quickly became more formalized, with a clearly defined governmental ethos that sought to establish autonomous political structures distinct from the military command. It was to be run by civilians or former fighters, and the insurgency's emphasis—at least in its rhetoric—on democratic, representative local government increased. As the rebel political wing wrote in its "Peace through Development: Perspectives and Prospects in the Sudan," published in February 2000,

> From the perspective of the SPLM, a peaceful resolution of the conflict in the Sudan will be achieved through a comprehensive development strategy that depends on a sustainable system of participatory democracy and good governance. On the other hand, participatory democracy and good governance rely on the establishment of a broadbased civil authority, such as CANS. (Sudan People's Liberation Movement 2000, 10)

CANS encompassed a civil administration formally independent of the military command, with its own civilian police force, judicial system, and even a Department of Wildlife. In theory, the civil authority was to be institutionally distinct from the military command structure, and during the war, CANS and SPLM/A officials often attested to the autonomy of the civilian governance structures. However, confidential discussions with aid workers, church officials, and regular civilians who regularly dealt with the civil administration made clear that they saw the local government's autonomy from the rebel army as a project to be realized rather than a reality.[26] These informants perceived that the SPLM/A high command continued to make politically sensitive decisions nominally under the control of the civil authority. Moreover, all CANS officials were ex-rebels, a fact that led to an intermeshing of civilian and military culture through personal ties and influence (Johnson 1998, 67). A military ethos inevitably permeated the

---

25. The conference and its aftermath are detailed in Rolandsen (2005). See also the description of this process in Sudan People's Liberation Movement (2000). A third conference was held in 1997 examining the tense relationship between the SPLM/A and Christian religious leaders. It resulted in an agreement between both sides to support each other's agendas by cooperating on a variety of issues. In March of 2008, a second national convention was held in Juba.

26. These interviews were conducted in early 2004, before the comprehensive peace agreement was signed.

civil administration as a result. In short, and despite claims to the contrary, the military wing continually held exclusive power throughout the war. There was a "fusion" of powers in the rebel organization, as one human rights lawyer claimed (interview with Lomo), or as one analyst wrote at the time, "the administrative structure is not democratically based, but rather reflects a militaristic top-down approach" (Riehl 2001, 11).

Still, when I visited in 2004, my informants credited insurgent leaders for making a genuine effort to demilitarize the local government, and they had seen substantive changes in this direction immediately after the signing of the ceasefire in 2002. The goal was for the autonomy of CANS regarding reconstruction and development activities to proceed in step with the devolution of genuine political authority to the civil administration from the rebel military structure. Thus, CANS was intended to represent not only an evolution of local government but an evolution of the entire structure of the rebel leadership as the political wing began to realize a degree of autonomy away from the military command.

In the context of political and economic marginalization, the insurgent leadership intended for a decentralized and autonomous civil administration to address the ethnicized grievances of the southern population. The question of political equality was intermingled with the question of economic and social equality from the beginning of the conflict. As the passage from "Peace through Development" cited above makes clear, decentralization of local government was intended as much to promote inclusive economic development—by devolving service provision and development activities to local levels—as to promote political inclusion. Thus the SPLA command intended for CANS to address local grievances, ameliorating concerns about its autocratic behavior and ideally engendering loyalty to the rebel government from the disparate ethnic communities of the south. In practice, the weakness of the higher levels of CANS meant there was wide variation in its effectiveness in different areas. On the ground, the political composition of the local area played a key role in the way CANS was enacted across New Sudan. But rather than discredit the insurgency's efforts, this variation actually allowed the command to claim to have empowered local authorities on civilian governance issues without actually delegating military power away from the central command.

From 1994 on, the SRRA (renamed the Sudan Relief and Rehabilitation Commission, SRRC) underwent significant restructuring in response to the reforms proposed to CANS. The SRRC handed off some of the many responsibilities it had accrued throughout the 1990s—education, health, agriculture, communications, economic development—to the civil administration and refocused its efforts on humanitarian relief (interview with Arop). During a visit to the region shortly before the signing of a comprehensive peace agreement that ended the war and formally brought the rebels into government in early 2005, it was clear to me that like most institutions in Southern Sudan, the relationship between the two service provision bodies remained overlapping, as many of the activities that were nominally under the auspices of CANS were still in the hands of the SRRC.[27]

The Structure of the Civil Administration

The task of decentralization was made slightly easier by the high command's early decision to divide rebel-held territory into nonethnic specific zones of command. Many other multiethnic insurgencies take the path of least resistance, dividing their territory into ethnic-specific zones. The danger with this approach is that it tends to reify ethnic identity as the basis for political participation, fostering tensions between the organization's constituent communities. By contrast, the SPLM/A divided its territory on the basis of the preconflict multiethnic provinces and subprovinces (Johnson 1998). This was an attempt to prevent competition for political influence among different ethnic groups at the regional level, though the split between the Dinka and Nuer factions of the organization exposed the limits of this strategy.

As discussed, the basic objective of the 1994 reforms was to devolve power to a hierarchy of local authorities, delegating the provision of services away from the central command. This bottom-up approach began at the village, or *boma,* level. Resurrecting the colonial strategy of co-opting traditional authorities, the boma was given a bifurcated political authority, split between an ethnically determined chief and a boma administrator. The traditional chief was generally selected by the local village community, advised by a council of elders, and primarily served to resolve disputes between community members. The boma administrator, meanwhile, was appointed by the insurgency to serve as the organization's liaison to the village.

Above this level, a *payam* was composed of four to six bomas. The administrative structure of the payam was more elaborate. A payam administrator was the highest authority figure and liaison to the rebels, overseeing legislative, executive, and judicial bodies. Each payam had a legislature composed mostly of elected members and some appointed members. Payam legislatures did meet, generally in an unstructured manner, but the precise purpose of this body was never fully articulated, and so its impact was less than substantial. Instead, the executive branch was the local authority of primary relevance for the civilian population.

---

27. In areas outside the control of the SPLM/A, the ruling National Congress Party set up the rival Coordinating Council of South Sudan as its official southern branch. Observers claimed that its primary purpose seemed to be to undermine the efficacy of CANS.

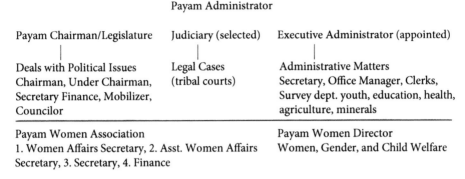

FIGURE 5.3. Structure of the *payam* administration.

Led by an executive administrator, who was appointed by the rebels with an eye toward selecting someone acceptable to the local population, often an indigene, this branch was responsible for the daily administration of the payam.

The county level sat above the payam. Counties covered large areas, often encompassing regions that were disconnected from each other—especially given the condition of Southern Sudanese roads during the war. A county commissioner appointed from among personnel within insurgent ranks led each county. The county administration was responsible for setting and collecting taxes, including a general poll tax taken from all able-bodied adults and market fees—though the commissioner of Yei County related in an interview that taxation was primarily a token action (interview with Lokule). It is hard to discern the actual amount of tax taken by the SPLM/A, but considering the general poverty levels that prevailed, it is doubtful that much could have been extracted from the population. However, the local authority did manage to siphon off significant aid from locals through a personal tax taken from whatever relief supplies civilians were able to solicit from foreign aid organizations (interviews with foreign aid workers).

At the county level, several agencies were mandated to provide services to local communities. One of these was the County Development Committee (CDC), whose purpose was to plan, coordinate, and evaluate development programs in the county. It served as the mechanism through which the development activities of the SRRC were to be transferred to the civil administration (interview with Khamis). The CDC came into existence in 1999 and was meant to serve as a liaison between INGOs and the population. The staff worked closely with the SPLM Development Assistance Technical Office (SDAT), an insurgent body based in Nairobi that received substantial funding from the United States Agency for International Development (USAID) to develop a model for promoting development within insurgent-held territory. Despite the rebellion's desire to promulgate a standardized development agenda at the county level, most agencies at this level never developed the capacity to implement these programs across such a vast territory during the war.

Above the county level, a zonal/regional commander appointed by the high command served as the highest military and civilian authority. Regional commanders controlled vast areas such as Equatoria, Bahr-el-Ghazal, and Upper Nile, each of which was partitioned according to the old multiethnic provincial boundaries. These zones, while important as military commands, had little to do with civil administration, which really became a concern at the county level and below.

At the national, zonal/regional, county, and payam levels, legislative councils were created and designed to allow a degree of democratic feedback into the governance system. At the payam level, the congress consisted of 600 members, and subsets of this level were to comprise the 1,800 delegates of the county congress. Subsets from each of the county legislatures would comprise the regional congress of 2,400 members, and subsets from the regional level would comprise the national congress of 3,000 members (Stiansen 2002). However, it became clear in interviews with SPLM/A personnel that despite the sophisticated design of the legislative system (or perhaps because of it), these were little more than paper institutions, especially at the higher levels. While many individual county and payam congresses met frequently, the regional and national congresses met rarely, if at all. Furthermore, meetings tended to be ad hoc and unfocused. Even in cases where elections were held for legislators, executive approval from SPLM/A commanders was required before they were allowed to occupy their seats in the various congresses.[28] On paper, the structure was genuinely impressive and made many provisions to ensure representation from all groups—seats were reserved for women at each level, for example. However, the command was ultimately more concerned with constructing the facade of democratic institutions to impress international donors than with actually gathering feedback on the provision of services to local communities; and these legislative bodies, at all levels, had scant influence on civilian governance practices in New Sudan.

Service Provision: The Civil Administration and NGOs

The majority of the health, educational, infrastructural, and, in places, nutritional needs of the Southern Sudanese during the war were fulfilled by foreign aid

---

28. See also Metelits (2004).

organizations. The presence of NGOs after the 1988 famine was so overwhelming that one researcher asked, "Is New Sudan actually the first NGO-istan?" (Riehl 2001, 4). A robust critical literature on aid operations in Southern Sudan developed in response to the establishment of Operation Lifeline Sudan, providing an important starting point for the consideration of the relationship between aid organizations and the insurgency in the provision of services to the population.

As recounted above, immediately before the initiation of conflict in 1983, international aid organizations had come to play a significant role in the provision of services to the south. The outbreak of conflict led to a rapid exodus of these organizations out of the war zone, and it was not until the famine of 1988 that NGOs decided to reenter in significant numbers under the auspices of OLS (Minear 1991). Initially the pace of reentry was slow as many thought that war would soon be ending; thus OLS retained an informal nature, mainly a series of agreements that allowed foreign aid organizations to operate in the south under the protection of the United Nations (Rolandsen 2005). As there was no military force offering protection, OLS instead relied on agreements with the various combatants to ensure safe passage for all international personnel (Akol 2009, 133). Different factions of the southern resistance competed for aid by offering safer environs than others. The inability of one faction to provide a stable environment could lead aid organizations to move their operations from one faction's territory to another that could provide better security (Rolandsen 2005).

In order to regularize the international intervention, "ground rules" specifying the precise roles and duties of OLS and the SRRA, as well as the security arrangements expected of all violent factions operating in the region, were drafted in 1995 (Malok 2009, 181). OLS also pushed both to develop the capacity of indigenous community organizations and to foster the growth of the rebel civil administration because the ad hoc nature of transnational aid interventions into the region required local partners in order to be effective (Riehl 2001). By this point, annual expenditures for OLS were put at over $100 million (Riehl 2001), and more than fifty international and national agencies and NGOs operated throughout the region thanks to its efforts (Crossley 2004).

As discussed in detail in chapter 3, there are many useful critiques of the impacts of foreign-funded, NGO-implemented relief and humanitarian aid on war zones. In relation to Sudan, commentators have long questioned the impact of transnational actors on rebel behavior, highlighting the various strategies insurgent leaders use to take advantage of their presence. International humanitarian organizations follow their own institutional imperatives in determining aid allocations, often creating a culture of dependency among local communities and undermining indigenous forms of political and social order. Worse, insurgents are often able to siphon material and financial resources that enrich rebel coffers by inserting themselves between international aid efforts and the civilian populations they claim to serve.

In South Sudan, humanitarian organizations came to accept that a certain portion of any aid given was taken by the insurgency or competing violent militias, either as part of an agreement or through other means. Indeed, this was formalized in the ground rules, which allowed the SPLM/A to tax personnel working with foreign agencies, including Sudanese working for the UN (Crossley 2004). Thievery of aid supplies was also a daily reality in the south. Rebel officials would commandeer vehicles, radios, and other technology, putting them to use for personal or military purposes. But more commonly the SRRA would insist on controlling the aid distribution process. This allowed the rebels to skim off a portion of each shipment while also directing aid to reward supporters or segments of the population they hoped to win over (interview with Gumbiri).[29]

As long as humanitarian organizations were willing to provide the rebellion with the ability to enrich itself and direct where a portion of the aid went, they were left alone to control the nature and content of the programs they administered in rebel territory. Insurgent leaders initially viewed such organizations as little more than a lucrative resource. But this golden goose vision of NGOs was eventually replaced by increased resentment toward the entire aid distribution framework set in place by OLS, particularly as it developed into an autonomous political and economic behemoth that was perceived as threatening to the rebel claim of authority in South Sudan (Riehl 2001). The challenge for the command was how to subordinate INGOs to local political institutions through the strategic intervention of the civil administration in the process of aid distribution (Branch and Mampilly 2005). To a large extent, this was the underlying principle driving the design of the civil administration, prior to which the organization lacked a structural mechanism for intervening between aid organizations and the civilian population they worked with (DeMars 1994; Human Rights Watch 1994, 174–89; Karim et al. 1996).

The insurgency attempted to gain a degree of control over NGOs and the distribution of foreign funds through a number of strategies, including expelling aid groups unwilling to obey SPLM/A dictates or respond to concerns about infiltration by Khartoum. For example, using a provision of the ground rules that stipulated that foreign organizations must not endanger the security of the area, the rebellion expelled the French aid organization Action Contre le Faim for a

---

29. The SRRA could also rely on its close relationship with USAID, the source of much aid into the region. Under the leadership of Gordon Wagner, a known SPLA partisan, USAID made it clear to NGOs that sought its support that they would have to go through SRRA structures (interview with Butler). See also O'Toole Salinas and D'Silva (1999).

perceived security breach in 1997 (Kuol 1999, 16). In 2000 a formal instrument of control was introduced through the use of a memorandum of understanding (MoU) as a mechanism to control NGOs.[30] Every aid group was required to sign an MoU with the rebel organization and abide by these terms at risk of expulsion. As the executive director of the town of Yei put it, "NGOs have to fit into our own program" (interview with Mukhtar). Through the use of the MoU the rebel government sought to avoid the random patchwork of neglect and overprovision of services commonly seen in areas of dense NGO activity.[31]

SPLM/A efforts to control the behavior of aid organizations operating within its territory naturally generated considerable resistance from international personnel who doubted the organization's capacity to play a productive role in relief and development efforts. In the words of Adele Sowinska, who worked for Catholic Relief Services (CRS) in the region for over a decade, "Many NGOs wanted to run the country themselves." Over time, the congruity between insurgent aspirations and the desires of foreign aid organizations forced most to fall in line with the insurgent program. As Sowinska explained to me, "I never saw us as part of the SPLA, but we did respond to the same priorities that they saw."

Among officials with the civil administration, there was a broad awareness of the pitfalls of dependence upon foreign aid. Administrators frequently related their reluctance to accept foreign aid, seeing themselves as trying to navigate a course between two contradictory imperatives. On one hand it was openly acknowledged that a degree of foreign aid was necessary if the local administration was not to lose support because of popular dissatisfaction with continued poverty and lack of services. On the other hand, there was an understanding that long-term dependence upon foreign aid could undermine the social and political coherence of the south, putting the insurgent political project at the mercy of donor governments and foreign philanthropists (interview with Mukhtar).[32] Controlling the aid distribution process, it was thought, would allow the organization to

---

30. Riehl (2001, 9) claims that the MoU effected no fundamental change: "A fully implemented and carried out MOU would in fact have been a serious coup d'etat attempt in NGO-istan but it failed due to the underdeveloped administrative capacity of the SRRA to oversee, coordinate, re-direct, and sanction project implementations of INGOs....In the case of South Sudan the political directive and development coordination remained widely in the hands of INGOs and their networks." A critical perception of the SPLM/A's civil administration is echoed in earlier studies by African Rights (1995, 1997). Rolandsen (2005, 64–71) summarizes both perspectives in his work.

31. The MoU also served a more strategic purpose for the insurgency. Faced with Khartoum's strategy of placing informants within foreign aid organizations (generally non-Dinka government sympathizers), the SPLM used the MoU as a useful mechanism for monitoring personnel working within such groups (interviews with Gideon and Gumbiri; Kuol 1999, 16).

32. Riehl (1994, 13–15) points out the SPLM/A's increased awareness of the threat posed by international aid but argues that nevertheless INGOs held "political domination... in nearly all fields except for military defence."

build the capacity of its civil administration through foreign funding, without succumbing to the imperatives of the transnational mobile aid apparatus.

In order to navigate this course, CANS leaders sought to authorize aid programs that could be transferred to the civil administration over time. They also ensured that the distribution of foreign funds, resources, and services went through their own structures so that the population looked to the rebel government for resources instead of going directly to foreign aid groups and bypassing the rebel civil administration. Having earlier decentralized decision making concerning the distribution of development funds meant that increasingly it was the most local of authorities—the county, payam, and boma levels—that were empowered to decide who would receive resources for reconstruction and development and who was excluded. This allowed insurgent leaders to distribute foreign aid in a way that was perceived as ethnically fair, though it also led to tensions at the local level as administrators funneled resources to ethnic kin at the expense of other displaced communities. By devolving the aid distribution process to the local level, the insurgent command was able to eradicate what many saw as Dinka dominance within the civil administration's political structures and to consolidate its political project in South Sudan.

With the termination of open fighting in the south in 2002, the civil administration became regularized, the administrative capacity of CANS increased, and the insurgency's control over foreign aid organizations improved to the point where it was able to begin mediating between these organizations and the civilian population. In the next section, I will look at specific sectors and analyze the impact of the civil administration's attempt to provide services to the civilian population.

The Provision of Services in South Sudan

My assessment of the rebel governance system is based on a comparison of two towns of similar size and importance that were under SPLM/A control for large stretches of the war. Since governance often varies widely within specific rebel territories, such a comparison provides a more balanced assessment of the group's behavior, particularly since the two chosen towns reflect the Dinka/non-Dinka split among the insurgency's ethnic constituencies. Rumbek, captured by the rebels in 1997, is the largest town in Rumbek County, an area with a total population of close to 370,000 people. More than 90 percent of the population is of Dinka origin, though the community is split among different subgroups. It is also home to a sizable population of displaced Nuer (UNORHCS 2004a). Rumbek served as the base of the insurgency during the war and was home to many key offices of the rebel government.[33]

Yei is the largest town in western Equatoria, the southernmost province in Southern Sudan, located just across the border from Uganda. It is the seat of Yei County, which has a population estimated at 320,000 people with close to 80,000 in the town itself (UNORHCS 2004b). The area is traditionally populated by Pajulu, Makaraka, Kakwa, Lugbara, and Kelico, collectively referred to as Equatorians. Yei County is known to be among the most fertile in Sudan with sufficient rainfall to produce agricultural surpluses. When fighting spread to Equatoria in the 1990s, many Equatorians fled to Uganda, Zaire, and Kenya, where their ethnic kin across the different borders reluctantly accepted them.[34] After the SPLM/A captured Yei in 1997, it became home to large numbers of Dinka from the north who fled southward to the relative peace the town offered.[35] Many of these internally displaced people settled into agricultural lifestyles around Yei, and their presence was a point of tension for the local Equatorian population that remained.

The Security System

As with most insurgencies, the first priority addressed by the nascent rebel civil administration was the establishment of a semblance of law and order within its territory. In general, observers and participants agree that the SPLM/A's concern at the time was with ensuring military discipline and suppressing internal dissent rather than responding to civilian needs (Akol 2009), although as early as 1985 the insurgency was able to establish a rudimentary system to control rampant cattle raiding—an omnipresent problem in much of Dinka territory, where cattle is the primary source of wealth (Johnson 2003). In July of 1984, the insurgents promulgated the Penal and Disciplinary Laws of the SPLM, combining customary practices with formal military law into a complex multilayered system. Three tiers of military courts were established to maintain discipline among the rebel cadres with punishments such as the death penalty for rape and looting (Johnson 1998, 68; Kuol 1999). The harshness of the penal code caused some resentment among members of the SPLM/A rank and file, including many who eventually

33. After the signing of the CPA, Rumbek was replaced as the capital of the south by Juba, which had remained under the control of the Government of Sudan through much of the conflict.

34. Estimates of the refugee population put the number at around five hundred thousand (McLaughlin 2004).

35. The town continued to be attacked by GoS forces, but these were limited to intermittent air raids and ended in 2002.

broke away from the organization (Akol 2009, 271). However, the system is also credited with having reduced abuses against civilians by undisciplined cadres (interview with Sebit).

At the same time, the organization sought to co-opt traditional authorities and customary legal mechanisms into a more comprehensive judicial system capable of responding to disputes between civilians, not just to complaints of misbehavior against rebel soldiers. Like many parts of the formerly colonized world, South Sudan at independence had absorbed certain legal practices from the colonizing power, including those aspects of colonial legal theory that drew a line between civil and customary law. These systems distinguished between modern and foreign and traditional and indigenous legal practices, circumscribing narrow jurisdictions for each and in the process reifying both categories (Mamdani 1996). In such bifurcated systems, customary law was drawn from various conceptions of "tribal traditions," which were generally thought to be more deliberative and interpretive than punitive. The insurgent command sought to utilize these traditional courts to resolve disputes within any particular ethnic community. This was a community defined as a tribal unit, in which decisions as to the most important resources, including land and cattle, were made exclusively by those seen as embodying that tribal custom—chiefs and elders.

Initially chiefs had been viewed as relics, as the insurgency imbibed the Marxist disdain for traditional authorities from its Ethiopian patron. But after the collapse of the Derg regime, the SPLM sought to foster better relations with the chiefs, a challenge made more difficult because Khartoum had spent considerable efforts and resources in wooing traditional authorities to the government side. After the Addis Ababa agreement of 1972, traditional chiefs were elected to their positions by their ethnic constituencies. But viewing this process as democratic would be a grand overstatement. In the idealized version, it was meant to ensure that the provision of justice was legitimized by the presumed kinship connection between a tribal community and its traditional chief. And if the selection of chiefs had been left to members of the community, then this might have been the case. But Khartoum frequently intervened in the succession disputes, a practice the insurgency embraced with gusto once it was in control, even influencing which chiefs were selected in the first place (Johnson 1998, 106). As a result, the legitimacy and relevance of traditional courts for civilians varied widely across rebel territory despite the insurgency's desire to incorporate chiefs into their judicial system.

Early on, the insurgent organization failed to clearly define the precise responsibilities of the traditional courts and their relationship to the SPLM/A military organization. As a result, civilians commonly preferred to approach military commanders to resolve contentious disputes because the traditional courts were seen as ineffective (Kuol 1999). After the first SPLM/A national convention in

1994, the 1984 act was partially repealed (though certain provisions remained in force till after the ceasefire in 2002). The broader reform process initiated at the national convention pushed the organization to formalize customary law to handle civilian grievances. A hierarchy of traditional courts from the boma to the county level was recognized, with chiefs empowered to make judgments based on a mixture of customary law, sharia (where applicable), and guidelines handed down by the SPLM (Johnson 1998, 69; interview with Leonardi).

Despite misgivings, the insurgent command was unable to avoid the legacy of ethnically defined traditional authorities in the legal realm. Southerners were highly aware of the issues surrounding ethnic-based political divisions, and the topic had been the subject of intense debate for decades among intellectuals and political leaders in the region (Badal 1994). The fear was that an ethnic-based judicial system would set the stage for the management of the population through the manipulation of politicized ethnicities, in a fashion reminiscent of the approach employed by the colonial authorities. However, in order to rectify perceptions of Dinka ethnic dominance, judicial power was allocated along ethnic lines. For the rebel judiciary, people were defined first as members of tribes, and the accountability and representativeness of the tribal judiciary were seen as being ensured by the correspondence assumed between members of the tribe and the chief.

As a result, prior to the ceasefire in 2002, the local judiciary was composed of a series of tribal courts headed by a hierarchy of chiefs (Sundnes 2004). To mitigate against the overethnicization of life in the south, SPLM/A commanders did travel through rebel territory, allowing civilians to appeal judgments issued by traditional authorities. But more commonly, appeals went to a body of traditional elders, whose autonomy was growing, at least within particular ethnic communities. The insurgent leadership also resurrected the colonial-era policy of placing land tenure under customary law, giving exclusive power of interpretation to a tribally defined chief and further enriching the power of the traditional chiefs (Kuol 1997; Johnson 1998, 65–70). Appeals on land issues also went to a body of elders (Sudan People's Liberation Movement 2000, 16–20).[36] By most accounts, this system was widely viewed as legitimate by the civilian population, at least for resolving intraethnic conflicts (Sundnes 2004). Anecdotally, it does seem that the system had greater legitimacy around Rumbek, where many of the chiefs were Dinka and often ardent supporters of the rebels, versus their counterparts in Yei and Equatoria, where support was not as strong (Leonardi 2007).

Since the traditional legal system was by definition ethnicized, the military justice system of the rebellion served to allot justice interethnically where

---

36. Donald Wani, an assistant payam administrator, confirmed this in an interview.

necessary. Comparable to the system of military police used by governments else-where in the world, the SPLM/A's Code of Rules regulated the behavior of cadres and served to prevent civilian abuse by irresponsible soldiers.[37] The system was known to be particularly harsh, with execution often serving as the punishment for a variety of crimes, including rape, robbery, and insubordination (interviews with White and Sowinska). Civilians had a choice as to where to take their dis-putes and usually approached the military courts only for dealings outside their kin group. Since the insurgent army was such an omnipresent force, integrating most able-bodied men and many women into its ranks, the military justice sys-tem served as the de facto judiciary for governing relations between members of different southern ethnic communities. This was made possible because the percentage of the population involved with the insurgency in some capacity gave the military justice system a very broad jurisdiction.

The decision to bifurcate the legal system proved to be effective for dealing with civilian disputes within New Sudan. By formalizing customary law and co-opting traditional courts for intraethnic disputes, the insurgents successfully drew on preexisting legal practices that had been entrenched for generations within the southern population (Johnson 1998). And where this approach failed to solve law-and-order issues, the insurgency built its own system for dealing with interethnic conflicts by constructing an alternate military-based justice mechanism that took advantage of the rebel army's multiethnic membership. As with most systems in South Sudan during the war, it is hard to gauge how consistently punishments were meted out for transgressions. But informants in the region testified that both the traditional courts and the SPLM/A legal system were more than trivial, serv-ing to regulate daily life for both rebel cadres and the civilian population.[38]

The Education System

Whereas preconflict judicial traditions offered some materials upon which the insurgent organization could construct its own system, health and educational

---

37. Soldiers were ordered by their commanders to stay five kilometers away from civilian sites, but the ability to enforce this directive varied by the commander in charge. Soldiers I spoke with recounted tales of witnessing harsh punishments meted out to cadres for looting civilians (interview with Sebit).

38. Human Rights Watch (1994, 239) disagreed with the effectiveness and adherence to the rule of law of this legal system, though its assessment was made prior to the reform initiated by CANS: "Despite an eleven-year history of controlling a large population and territory, the SPLM/A has not developed anything approaching a system of justice and due process." As they pointed out at the time, "customary Southern Sudanese law continues to be applied in SPLM/A areas" (241). Understanding the convoluted relationship between the insurgency and customary authorities was not the purpose of the report, and hence it largely misses this important dimension.

needs in the south had long been ignored by the Khartoum government. The SPLM/A had two choices in response: either the organization could devote substantial human and material resources toward building effective educational and health services from scratch, or it had to find an innovative way of dealing with these two issues without devoting large amounts of resources. The organization chose the latter, adopting an approach that sought to appropriate the mobile transnational aid apparatus into their provision of such public welfare items, with decidedly mixed results.

In 1981, barely two years before the war broke out, the three provinces of Southern Sudan—Bahr al-Ghazal, Upper Nile, and Equatoria—had just under 600 primary schools,[39] fewer than 100 intermediate schools, and only 14 secondary schools.[40] In the capital city of Khartoum, by contrast, there were 541 elementary schools, 234 intermediate schools, and 55 secondary schools. In the central region there were an astonishing 1,796 primary schools, 547 intermediate schools, and 60 secondary schools, a fact that clearly reflected the priorities of the Khartoum regime. As a further indication of the south's marginalization, even sparsely populated Darfur had 675 primary schools, 108 intermediate schools, and 11 secondary schools. Surprising as it may seem, these numbers actually represented progress from the date of independence, when Southern Sudan had had only two secondary schools (Scroggins 2004, 175).

Notwithstanding the region's deep educational crisis, the political leadership in South Sudan has often come from the most educated segment of society. During the first war, when the leadership of the Anya Nya forces was drawn primarily from Equatoria, the government purposefully targeted the educated as troublemakers and traitors of Islam. This trend continued with the second war, and many of the leaders of the insurgency were among the most educated in the region; these included Garang himself, who had gone so far as to earn his Ph.D. in agricultural economics from the University of Iowa. Other SPLA leaders also received Ph.D.s, including the eventual SSIM leaders Riek Machar and Lam Akol, a fact that led civilians to apply the mordant nickname "the doctors' war" to the fratricidal intraregional struggle.

Despite the educational background of many commanders, during the early phases of the war the insurgency gained a reputation as being antieducation. Indeed, the SPLA was initially hostile to aid organizations that sought to meet

---

39. Equatoria did have an additional 176 private primary schools, while Bahr el Ghazal had 36 and Upper Nile had 1. However, at the intermediate and secondary levels, only three private schools existed throughout the south.

40. Statistics on schools are drawn from a 1983 report produced by the Sudan Department of Statistics (cited in Yongo-Bure 1988, 348–50).

the educational needs of children in areas under its control (Scroggins 2004). According to several outside observers, the rebellion's reliance on child soldiers, like that of many insurgencies, put it in conflict with broader international norms regarding children's right to education (interview with White). In the early days of the war the leadership took a hands-off approach to the education projects promoted by the UN through various NGOs, preferring to run a parallel education system set up by the insurgent controlled Friends of African Children Educational (FACE) foundation. The FACE system was designed to serve both educational and more instrumental purposes for the insurgency with children contributing to industrial and agricultural endeavors as part of their school day. In addition, FACE schools became fertile recruiting ground for the rebel army. Sebit, a former child soldier recruited by the SPLA, recounted to me that he had initially joined the insurgency ostensibly to attend school along the Ugandan border. Though he did receive some education, he always understood that when the time came, he would be expected to play his part on the front lines, as he was eventually called to do. Faced with criticism from the international community that FACE schools were more labor and military training camps than they were educational sites, Garang eventually shut them down (Scroggins 2004).

Over time, pressure from international agencies combined with demands from civilians, forcing the command to reevaluate its apathy toward education provision. By the late 1990s, after the reforms in various sectors of the civil administration discussed above, CANS, with funding from Care International, established an education secretariat to begin the process of addressing the dire educational needs of the region. Of particular importance were the churches, many of which provided the only educational facilities for students throughout the conflict, generally with minimal support from the insurgent civil administration. As one Catholic priest who lived through the war explained to me, church officials eventually acquiesced to the insurgency's overtures, despite continuing mistrust, largely out of a desire to see improvements in the dismal educational conditions for civilians (interview with Okello). With the approval of the churches and working closely with both religious and secular aid organizations, including Jesuit Refugee Services (JRS), International Aid Sweden (IAS), Across, and UNICEF, the secretariat began the difficult process of developing an education system in rebel territory.

In one example, JRS, which entered South Sudan in 1997, was actually contacted by the education secretariat through the SRRC and asked to run educational programs in Nimule and Kajo Keji (interview with Raj). By 2004 the program had close to forty thousand students in both primary and secondary education across New Sudan. As with all foreign aid organizations operating in the region, JRS was required to sign an MoU with the civil administration forcing it to hire local staff from among former rebel cadres to serve as liaisons between the organization and the SRRC. In some cases these individuals remained relatively aloof from the educational programs, giving the appearance that the stipulation to hire local personnel was designed more as an employment program for former soldiers than as a genuine method for overseeing the behavior of the aid organization. In Nimule, the liaison officer, an elderly Equatorian gentleman, provided a library of historical information but seemed to know little about JRS programs on the ground. However, in other areas, such "linkage personnel" clearly wore multiple hats and were very influential within the aid program, the civil administration, and the local community as well. For example, in 2005, shortly before the signing of the CPA, I spoke with the education officer with IAS in Yei. He was a local former fighter who also served as the county education coordinator, a volunteer position that was the highest administrator in the county's education bureaucracy. Based out of the IAS office, he was involved both in the development of educational strategies through his position in the civil administration as well as with their implementation through his work with the aid organization (interview with Luther).[41]

The insurgency devised ground rules for education and was able to maintain them through both the MoU and the use of such linkage personnel. Every boma had a representative to the education secretariat known as the school supervisor, who was selected from the local community to coordinate educational activities. Education projects were funded primarily by contributions from aid organizations but also from funds raised through parent-teacher associations established by the secretariat. The community decided on the location of the schools and even appointed the teachers, who also served on a volunteer basis (Stiansen 2002). The curriculum varied across regions and was often determined by whether students had the opportunity to continue their education in neighboring countries. Thus both Ugandan and Kenyan curriculums were used (interview with Raj). Although schools were used to foster a national identity—youngsters were taught in class to think of Garang as president, the SPLM/A as the government, and its policies as national programs (Crossley 2004)—the secretariat was never able to develop an indigenous Sudanese curriculum during the war, primarily because students who hoped to continue their education generally left the country to seek opportunities in neighboring countries.

In line with other reforms proposed by the national convention, the civil administration allowed local initiative to be the central driver of educational capacity in South Sudan. The education secretariat sought to empower the most local

---

41. He also presumably received a salary for his work with the group, though I chose not to ask.

FIGURE 5.4.   Malnourished children in an SPLA-controlled town in Equatoria, South Sudan, 2004. *Source*: Author's collection.

of levels to manage their educational needs, including the right to determine who was eligible to attend primary school. As a result, though in theory every boma was meant to have a primary school, significant variation between regions prevailed. In Rumbek County, where Dinka predominated, only around 12 percent of the children attended primary school in 2004 (UNORHCS 2004a, 11). However, in Yei County, the enrollment rate was significantly higher at 43 percent (UNORHCS 2004b, 11). Part of the discrepancy between the two is related to the ethnic composition of each area. In Yei, cultural attitudes toward education tended to be more positive, especially in regard to educating girls (38% of pupils in Yei were girls versus only 8% in Rumbek) (UNORHCS 2004a, 2004b).[42]

In 2002, at the time of the ceasefire, of the 1.4 million school-age children in Southern Sudan, slightly over 300,000 were enrolled in schools; this figure represented only about one in five students, or 22 percent of the total school-age population. These students were being taught by 8,655 teachers, for a student/teacher ratio of approximately 1:35. Put more starkly, at the time of the ceasefire, the

---

42. I was told by several informants that the Dinka tend to view educating girls as spoiling them. See also Sundnes (2004).

region had one teacher for every 162 school-age children. Only 27 percent of the student body was female, and fully 94 percent of the teachers were men according to a 2003 UNICEF report (cited in UNORHCS 2004b, 11). These numbers clearly show the depth of the education crisis in the region, which continued even after the signing of the CPA in 2005, and beyond.

Despite its failures, the SPLM/A deserves recognition for two innovations. First, the organization managed to co-opt many of the international aid organizations operating in the region into its educational system, an approach mirrored in its efforts to provide health services, as I discuss below. And second, governance of educational issues was successfully devolved to the local level, helping the organization address ethnic tensions that had long threatened to tear it apart.

The Health System

As with education, the Khartoum government has long allowed and even promoted vast regional disparities in the provision of health care. In 1980 the three provinces of the south were serviced by only 31 hospitals, a measly 5 health centers, and 108 dispensaries. Meanwhile, Khartoum alone had 22 hospitals, 35 health centers, and 57 dispensaries. And Central province accounted for 42 hospitals, 74 health centers, and 259 dispensaries (Yongo-Bure 1988). During the initial stages of the conflict, when Mengistu directed financial and other resources to the organization, the insurgent leadership encouraged civilians to move into Ethiopia to take advantage of refugee camps where food and medical supplies were available (Johnson 2003). With the loss of Ethiopian support and the corresponding restructuring of the civil administration, the rebels looked to international aid organizations to take the lead in the development of a local health system.

By the latter part of the war, a three-tiered health system largely funded by foreign aid organizations but amply staffed with SPLM/A personnel was operating in New Sudan. The first tier, the primary health care units (PHCUs) were run by community health workers who received a basic nine-month training course and were mostly drawn from the local community. According to one health worker, PHCUs were designed to provide health education and basic health care for malaria, diarrhea, and other common ailments (interview with Deng). At this level, workers did not receive salaries for their services (Stiansen 2002). Above the PHCUs, the primary health care centers (PHCC) were capable of providing a much wider array of medicines for treating diseases that commonly plagued the southern population, such as tuberculosis, kala-azar, sleeping sickness, and leprosy. These centers had beds for patients and laboratories capable of running basic medical tests. By the time of the ceasefire in 2002, South Sudan also had seventeen general hospitals operating above the PHCCs that could provide all of the above services, with several even offering basic surgical procedures (UNORHCS 2004b, 12).

Both the PHCCs and the general hospitals were largely run by foreign aid organizations, which paid salaries for all workers, while the PHCUs were designed to be staffed solely by SPLM personnel (interview with Deng). The entire system was managed by the county health department, which was run through a collaboration of international aid workers with rebel administrative personnel. As with education, the actual provision of health care during the war varied widely according to local conditions. However, local initiative was rarely enough to develop and run a complex health care system. Obtaining the resources required in terms of both medical personnel and supplies to staff and run hospitals in areas with active fighting often proved insurmountably difficult. The insurgency did try to gain control of the process by fusing its own personnel with the resources of INGOs through the use of the MoU and linkage personnel. But unlike the teachers and administrators in the education system, many of whom openly supported the insurgency's goals, health workers, regardless of national origin, took a more agnostic approach to the politics of the region, focusing instead on the onerous task of providing basic health care to civilians in South Sudan. Thus the availability of health services in the region was determined primarily by the willingness and ability of aid organizations to provide resources and had little to do with insurgent initiatives.

International efforts were generally concentrated in areas where the insurgents could provide a degree of stability. The government's penchant for attacking health facilities, despite OLS prohibitions, meant that in practice, large areas remained out of reach of even basic health operations throughout the war.[43] In comparison, Yei County, one of the most stable within all of New Sudan, had sixty-two health facilities, including three hospitals, six PHCCs, and fifty-three PHCUs, while Rumbek County, located closer to the war's front line, had forty facilities, including three hospitals, ten PHCCs, and twenty-seven PHCUs (UNORHCS 2004a, 2004b).

In early 2005, during a visit to the impressive general hospital in Yei County, which had five wards with a total of 150 beds, I spoke with local Sudanese hired as staff. The hospital provided secondary health care to those civilians who could make the often arduous trip. Since 1997, shortly after the SPLA came into control of the town, it had been funded and operated by the openly partisan relief organization Norwegian People's Aid (NPA). NPA played a central role in shoring

---

43. According to the U.S. Committee on Refugees, in 2000 alone there were 113 bombings by GoS forces against civilian and humanitarian sites (cited in Prunier and Gisselquist 2003).

up the insurgency's governance capacity across a variety of sectors. At this hospital the organization paid for medical supplies and the salaries of local staff and also provided international medical volunteers, though the facility had a chronic shortage of qualified personnel (interview with Sworo). As the matron of the hospital, a nurse from Equatoria who had been in her position for two years, explained to me, the SPLM/A's primary contribution to health services in the region was to keep out of the way of the day-to-day operations in the hospitals and PHCCs. But by directing health resources to Equatoria, an area known for challenging the insurgency's pro-Dinka bias, the insurgent command again demonstrated its savvy manipulation of civilian governance by prioritizing the needs of factions representing oppositional perspectives.

Although many have pointed to the weaknesses in the SPLM/A's governance system, it is important to remember that governmental capacity in the region was never substantial either during the colonial era or for the brief periods in which the south was directly governed by Khartoum. Even after the first Anya Nya war, when a semiautonomous southern government ruled the region, the lack of functioning institutions and qualified personnel meant that the leadership was never able to administer the region effectively (Johnson 2003, 105). As for the insurgency itself, the question remains whether it was able to meet the basic needs of the civilian population. The answer would be mixed. Though the security system established by the rebel organization was effective and came to be viewed as legitimate, the provision of health and education varied widely, reflecting local conditions and initiatives. The historical lack of educational and health infrastructure in the south hampered the ability of the group to provide these basic services. When these handicaps were combined with the twin problems of ethnic factionalism and corruption, both resulting from the weakness of the command to impose order throughout the bureaucratic infrastructure, it is doubtful that the insurgency could ever have developed effective health and education systems.

The organization does deserve credit, however, for having adapted the civil administration to respond to demands from its diverse constituent communities for greater autonomy over local affairs. Under Garang, the leadership responded to pressure from below by constructing a civil administrative structure that was flexible enough to incorporate non-SPLM/A organizations while remaining responsive to local initiatives. By appropriating the efforts of aid organizations to provide services, funds, and skills to the population, the rebels were able to share credit for welfare provision in New Sudan without diverting resources from their military effort. They were also able to tap into skills present within the civilian population, encouraging inhabitants of New Sudan to take control of their daily existence while also endearing them to the broader agenda of the insurgency. This was particularly important in non-Dinka areas, where, according to one longtime observer, the "devolution of administration...began to give people the feeling that the Movement was their movement, and the struggle was their struggle" (Johnson 2003, 108).

6

RESURRECTING BULA MATARI

The Rassemblement Congolais pour la
Démocratie-Goma

This is hell's system. The fire is raging but we don't get burned.

—Koffi Olomide

In 1964 Pierre Mulele, a deputy of Patrice Lumumba—the deposed prime minister and former independence leader—began a rebellion in the western Congolese
province of Kwilu. He soon came to control an area the size of Belgium, where
he ruled his followers with a mix of socialist rhetoric and assurances of magical
protection. Despite limited resources, Mulele attempted to organize an ambitious
governmental structure within his territory, distinguishing between the military
and political commands, with departments focused on medical welfare, social
affairs, and popular support (Welch 1975). Soon after, in the eastern part of the
country (contemporary South Kivu), Laurent Kabila, a former government bu-
reaucrat, came into control of a vast area under the auspices of his "Afro-Marxist"
militant organization, the Parti de la Révolution Populaire (Party of the Popular
Revolution, PRP) (Kayunga 2000). Kabila's enclave engaged in collective agriculture and mineral smuggling, often conniving with Mobutu's own military commanders (Dunn 2002, 54–55). The history of Congo is littered with examples
of such nonstate violent groups taking territory and constructing governance
systems.[1] However, none of the Congolese rebel governments—including those
that emerged out of more recent wars—have achieved the level of sophistication

---

1. Under Mobutu, Congo was renamed Zaire in 1971. It retained this appellation until 1997,
when the country's name was returned to a variation of its pre-Mobutu form. I use the historically
appropriate form in this chapter and thus refer alternately to either Congo, Zaire, or the Democratic
Republic of Congo (D.R. Congo) depending on the time period.

found in many other parts of the world, including neighboring Uganda, where the impressive Rwenzururu Kingdom came into existence around the same time as these early Congolese groups.

The back-to-back wars that racked the Democratic Republic of Congo through the latter part of the 1990s brought the country screaming into the twenty-first century in worse condition than at almost any other period in its short and often tumultuous postcolonial existence. At points during the conflict, civilians in the eastern areas of the country experienced a dystopia frequently compared to the anarchical visions of Thomas Hobbes. Unsurprisingly, this conflagration, which drew in countless fighters from neighboring countries, became viewed as intractable, and the country itself came to epitomize the worst of the post–Cold War African battle grounds. But even amid the seeming chaos, a reconfiguration of political and social order was occurring in ways dissimilar to that described in the previous two chapters. Whereas the Sri Lankan and Sudanese rebels built governmental structures and practices to enforce order within the territories they came to control, the Rassemblement Congolais pour la Démocratie (RCD), a product of foreign machinations from its inception, often appeared either uninterested or incapable of establishing order within its territory, abandoning the task to other nonstate actors.[2]

Most commentators tend to view the leaders of the RCD and its offshoots (most prominently the RCD-Goma, referred to as RCD-G below) harshly for their oppressive and frequent use of force against civilians under their control. But to characterize the behavior of the rebels as driven solely by the engine of violence ignores their sustained attempts to address the extraordinarily complex political situation within the vast territory they controlled. Focused on the capital, Kinshasa, but forced to confront a tangled political environment in the eastern provinces, the RCD-G made discernible efforts to forge a political hierarchy using a variety of strategies. These attempts may all be judged failures—as one resident of RCD territory during the war succinctly put it, under rebel rule "people did not live with a hope of life" (interview with Patrick). But in their failure they shed light on the strategies available to reformist insurgencies operating in conditions where the political authority is unclear, the population is nonsupportive and even hostile, infrastructure is minimal, interethnic tensions are high, and involvement from the international community is either malicious, illicit, or inconsequential.

---

2. As I discuss below, soon after the conflict broke out, the RCD split into several factions, including the RCD-Goma. Since the RCD-Goma was the dominant faction, I focus mostly on its behavior. I refer to the RCD-Goma when discussing the group after the split and to the RCD when discussing the undivided organization.

In this chapter I chart the trajectory of the RCD's civilian governance project, situating it within a broader narrative of neglect that characterized relations between the center and the periphery in Zaire during the rule of Mobutu Sese Seko. Under Mobutu, the state withdrew from vast portions of the country's territory, leaving behind a minimalist bureaucratic apparatus that interacted with local actors in complex and unique political arrangements. As the state withered away, Zaireans were forced to turn toward civil society and other nonstate actors such as aid organizations, traditional authorities, business associations, and religious institutions, all of which negotiated with the remnants of the Mobutuist state to provide a semblance of social order to their highly localized constituencies. With the advent of the first war in 1996, state retraction accelerated, leaving behind a multiplicity of diverse institutional arrangements that the invaders from the east were forced to interact with—either by coercing these actors into submission or finding other ways to co-opt them into the agenda of the new political authority.

The failure of the rebellion's governance project primarily resulted from the rebel command's inability to negotiate with this alternate political and economic configuration that had emerged in the east prior to the outbreak of conflict. The insurgent organization too often resorted to coercion to subdue challengers to its rule. I argue that three factors help explain this failure. First, the rebel leadership did not address concerns about the ethnic and national affiliation of the rebellion. Second, the command was unable to resolve internal tensions between different factions that undermined its ability to implement a coherent political agenda. And finally, focused on the political kingdom in Kinshasa and reliant on foreign markets and governments for revenue, the leaders struggled to develop the local expertise required to achieve hegemony over territory far from the capital. This led the leaders to neglect the internal forces that were pushing them to take seriously the concerns of civil society and other nonstate actors that had emerged as the primary providers of political order in the region.

Research for this chapter was conducted largely in the RCD-G base areas in the easternmost provinces of the D.R. Congo, which I visited in early 2004 and again in early 2005.[3] North and South Kivu are the most densely populated provinces in Congo. Inhabitants of these provinces have long been oriented more toward the East African countries with which they share borders than with the capital,

---

3. During my research visits I traveled to eastern Congo from the Ugandan capital, Kampala, via the Rwandan capital, Kigali—once on board a United Nations helicopter and once along the Kigali/Goma road aboard a local bus. In addition to Bukavu and Goma, I also visited Kisangani in the center of the country and Bunia in the troubled Ituri region. I returned to eastern Congo for a final round of interviews in August of 2009, traveling with Jason Stearns, with whom I conducted several interviews jointly.

Kinshasa.[4] Rebel control of the two Kivus was primarily an urban phenomenon, with control of the rural areas often shifting among an assortment of militarized actors (interview with Kahorha). This insecurity limited my ability to visit rural locations; thus most of my research was conducted in the Kivu's two largest cities. Bukavu, the capital of South Kivu, is a once-major industrial city on the southern banks of Lake Kivu with a population of close to half a million people. During the war, RCD control of the city was intermittent as the insurgents faced sustained challenges to their rule from a variety of local and national actors. Goma, the capital of North Kivu, is located on the northern edge of Lake Kivu, and has a population of close to four hundred thousand, with another hundred thousand in the surrounding areas. It served as the base for the RCD during the war and was the city most directly under the control of the insurgency.

Background to the Conflict

Ernesto "Che" Guevara arrived in East Africa in April of 1965 with aspirations of spreading his doctrine of insurgency and Marxist revolution across the continent. Barely a year after the doomed rebellion of Pierre Mulele had broken out, Guevara crossed into Congo from neighboring Tanzania shortly after his arrival in Africa. In total, he spent close to two years in the country working with the rebel forces of Laurent Kabila's PRP. Despite his experiences in multiple Latin American war zones, Guevara was overwhelmed by the complex dynamics of the Congolese situation. He quickly came to realize that the insurgency was riven by multiple factions and infiltrated by a seemingly countless number of foreign interlopers, including those from his own adopted home of Cuba. After a prolonged attempt to organize the Congolese rebels, Guevara departed the region in disgust. Soon after, in 1968, Mulele followed Lumumba to an early grave, ending the most serious challenges to the young regime of Joseph Mobutu. Having orchestrated the assassinations of his two greatest rivals—Lumumba and Mulele—as well as co-opting or defeating countless other challengers such as Kabila, Mobutu quickly set out to consolidate his control over the country he immediately christened Zaire.

Guevara's account of the war is revealing in that many of the conditions that he faced on the ground were replicated during later fighting between the Kinshasa government and another insurgent force that had come to power in the Kivus, the

---

4. Tull (2004, 57) points out that the Kivus are closer (as the crow flies) to five other national capitals than they are to Kinshasa.

RCD.[5] In his reflections on his time in Congo, Guevara (1999) stressed the need for a rebel group to structure political and social life in the areas under its control, something he accused the Congolese rebels of failing to do. Consistent with his earlier advocacy for following violent actions with civilian-friendly policies,[6] Guevara urged the Congolese rebels to take advantage of the "liberated zone" opened up by Kabila, administering it effectively so that it could become a productive contributor to the war efforts by serving as a shining example of rebel competence. He discussed at length his frustrations with the PRP's failure to address civilian needs by providing basic services such as education and health that, he believed, could have fostered loyalty among the inhabitants of the region. Guevara had initially hoped to develop Kabila's enclave for use as a training ground for both Congolese and other African rebel groups, but frustrated by the behavior of the PRP cadres, he soon gave up in favor of a doomed return to Latin America.

Guevara was also cognizant of other factors that continue to shape the politics of insurgency in eastern Congo today, including the significance of ethnic membership, which he decried but failed to comprehend. The power of cultural issues to adversely affect political outcomes was something that his Marxist politics—with its emphasis on material attachments—could not quite synthesize. His analysis of the emerging transnationalism of civil wars, which he highlighted in a discussion of the role that international aid organizations like the Red Cross were beginning to play in rebel-controlled territories, was far more prescient.

State and Society in Zaire

The failure of the Mulele and Kabila insurgencies and numerous others to mount a serious challenge to the Congolese state allowed the renamed Mobutu Sese Seko Kuku Ngbendu Wa Za Banga to mold Zaire according to his own prerogatives.[7] Commentators have examined at length the "deflation" of the state under Mobutu's regime from 1965 to 1997, stressing the ways in which the state progressively retracted from vast areas under its de jure control (Young and Turner 1985; Nzongola-Ntalaja 2002). Although Zaire was the epitome of a rentier state, characterized by a limited degree of state penetration in the bulk of the country, Mobutu

---

5. According to Severine Autesserre, who spent considerable time in the region during the war, RCD rebels often referenced Guevara's presence in the region and attempted to appropriate his legacy. Personal communication, 2007.

6. Guevara's theory is briefly discussed in chapter 1. See Guevara (1969) for a full discussion.

7. The former Joseph Mobutu took this name in 1972. It roughly translates as "the all-powerful warrior who, because of his endurance and inflexible will to win, will go from conquest to conquest, leaving fire in his wake."

nimbly deployed a cultural nationalist offensive to generate loyalty and ensure subservience to his regime. By adopting a doctrine of "Zairois" to reinforce the idea and territoriality of the Zairean nation, he was able to imbue the citizenry with a strong sense of nationality without offering any meaningful interactions with the actual institutions of the state. A glance at the history of state formation in Zaire offers some clues as to how nationalist loyalties penetrated so deeply into the Congolese psyche despite the government's eventually being revealed as little more than smoke and mirrors.

In many ways, Mobutu's governance of the Congo should be viewed not as exceptional but rather as the continuation of colonial practices that often retrofitted precolonial forms of authority to serve the new political regime (Young and Turner 1985; Tull 2004). Upon first assuming power, Mobutu faced a political and economic landscape molded by the colonial imperative of resource extraction. Infrastructure across the country was erratic and designed primarily to generate revenue for state coffers through the sale of copper, diamonds, timber, and other natural resources. Under Mobutu, state power continued to rest on the extraction of a single resource, copper, which also served as the principal source of fiscal revenue during the colonial period. Indeed, from 1920 to 1990, copper consistently provided the bulk of government revenue and foreign exchange (Nest, Grignon, and Kisangani 2006, 18). After deposing Lumumba and claiming the presidency for himself, Mobutu wasted little time before nationalizing the mining and other industries. Between 1960 and 1975, Gecamines, the name given to the nationalized copper mining company, continued to provide between 50 and 80 percent of state revenue.

Initially Mobutu used the economic resources offered by the copper wealth to build an impressive physical and bureaucratic infrastructure directly under the control of the central state:

> At first the Mobutu regime seemed successful, building on the autocratic heritage of the colonial state to create a remarkably unified and centralized polity—with exorbitant pretensions. At its zenith in the mid-1970s, Mobutu had built a command state with himself at its helm, erecting an extravagant personality cult around his role as president and enforcing his rule through a single national party. (C. Young 2006, 302)

But reliance on the copper market rendered Mobutu's state construction agenda precarious, and the collapse of the market in 1975 exposed the weak underpinnings of a single commodity-driven economy. This fiscal collapse forced Mobutu to shift his populist developmental agenda to a nationalist approach heavy on cultural symbolism but sparse on material improvements. Though copper exploitation had allowed Mobutu to build infrastructure as a tool of political patronage, the loss of financial revenues led him to hitch Zaire's political fortunes to Cold War politics in order to maintain a steady source of revenue. By the late 1970s, Mobutu had abandoned most state development projects and presided over an extended period of atrophy during which ambitious infrastructural projects initiated across the expansive country were left to rot (Callaghy 1984; Young and Turner 1985). At this point the Mobutuist state, having failed to establish empirical control over its territory, shifted to political repression and cultural nationalism to establish a highly personalized hegemony over the population (Schatzberg 1988).

By the 1980s, growing corruption claimed an ever-greater portion of public finances and led to a steady decline in the state's ability to perform key functions. The loss of state capacity encompassed two elements (Young and Turner 1985). First, the state was unable to provide even basic services despite continued attempts at revenue collection as government ministries were hollowed out into ineffective shells of their former selves. Second, the Zairean public lost faith in the state's ability to govern, instead turning to other institutions to assume the responsibilities that the state no longer performed. This is not to say that the state disappeared. Starved of even the most basic resources, including salaries, local government officials were left to fend for themselves. In fact, they were empowered to do so by the central government, which turned a blind eye to the many compensatory mechanisms established by officials to make up for fiscal shortfalls (Tull 2004, 65). Bureaucrats quickly reverted to extracting revenue directly from civilians or from private capital, maintaining a facade of state control despite the many deficiencies in basic service provision.

Mobutu's gamble for Cold War relevancy allowed the regime to soldier on (McCalpin 2002). Controlling Congo, which was a lucrative prize for both the NATO Alliance and the Soviet Union, became an important goal for the Western trio of Belgium, France, and the United States, each with its own motivation and distinct history with the country. The "troika" willingly provided financial sustenance to prop up the Mobutu regime—while ignoring its obvious failures—in order to prevent the Soviets from stepping into the fray. Lacking an internal revenue base, Mobutu cut funding for public services including health, education, and basic infrastructure, dramatically reducing the size of the state bureaucracy. Between the revenue from the copper industry and foreign aid, throughout his three decades in office, Mobutu never looked to the Zairean population to generate fiscal resources.

However, as the Cold War came to an end in the late 1980s, Zaire's importance to the new world order declined, and the United States lost interest in bankrolling an aging kleptocrat. By the early 1990s, production of copper had declined by over 90 percent from its heyday, and hyperinflation set in (C. Young 2006, 304). Per capita national revenue decreased from $377 in 1958 to $117 in 1993.[8] In a

---

8. Van Acker and Vlassenroot (2000, par. 13), cited in Autesserre (2006).

country the size of Western Europe, Mobutu's regime eventually withdrew into itself, spurring the development of novel political formations to compensate for the absence of state power (Romkema and Vlassenroot 2002; International Crisis Group 2003a). Civilians under Mobutu had few meaningful interactions with the state, coming to view it as an unwelcome burden and relying instead on local political and social institutions to fill the void. Tribal or traditional authorities, religious institutions, private businesses, and aid organizations stepped into the void, dividing up sovereign functions to provide a modicum of social order.

Eastern Congo before the Outbreak of War

Congo today has a population of close to sixty million people. Road density is the lowest on the African continent, and the bulk of the population lives in densely populated border areas, with the expansive forested interior largely unpopulated. North and South Kivu, located along the eastern border with Rwanda and Burundi, are among the most densely populated provinces in the country, with a combined population estimated at close to five million. The population concentration, especially in North Kivu, combined with the diversity of ethnic groups sharing the provinces, has long led to disputes over land between the different communities (Vlassenroot and Huggins 2004).

Laurent Kabila was not the only insurgent leader to notice that Congo's eastern provinces were an ideal place from which to launch a rebellion (Prunier 2001; C. Young 2002). The area is cut off from the capital by the vast Congo Basin and other impenetrable geographical features. In addition, the linguistic prominence of Swahili, a language spoken only in the east and parts of the south, added to the region's isolation. Furthermore, the area is surrounded by the Great Lakes and has long borders with Tanzania, Uganda, Rwanda, Burundi, and Sudan, providing easy escape routes and a steady revenue stream through control over customs checkpoints for budding insurgent organizations (interview with Tegera). Even during the copper boom, the Mobutuist state had difficulty establishing its control over the eastern provinces, especially North and South Kivu and Katanga, where powerful chieftaincies resisted attempts at direct control. To compensate, it reverted to strategies of intermediary rule by co-opting or replacing dissenting chiefs. In addition, Mobutu sought to exert control over the local economy by extending patronage to select economic partners (Tull 2004, 55). Thus few infrastructural and development projects were undertaken in the region, a situation that led to a contentious relationship between the central government and the eastern provinces throughout the postindependence history of the country.

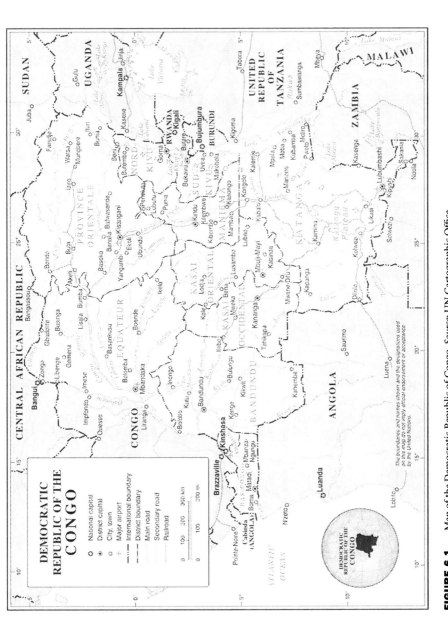

FIGURE 6.1. Map of the Democratic Republic of Congo. *Source:* UN Cartographic Office.

The diminution of the state following the copper bust in 1975 did not signal the end of the state's presence but rather, further entrenched Mobutu's policy of patronizing local agents to minimize challenges to his power. Agents of the state continued to operate throughout the country, working with the new political actors that emerged in the wake of state withdrawal. This was especially true in the Kivus, which in the 1980s and 1990s had begun looking across the eastern border toward Uganda and Rwanda, with which they shared linguistic, histori-cal, ethnic, and cultural connections, instead of west toward the distant Zairean capital of Kinshasa (Englebert 2003). Unlike Southern Sudan, where the state never penetrated deeply, eastern Zaire was characterized by a complex arrange-ment that established political order through interactions between active agents of a distant state and multiple categories of nonstate political and economic actors. Central and regional offices of the government continued to be staffed by personnel who generated income through fees and other kickbacks charged to civilians. Working hand in hand with private companies and regional trading networks, state agents ensured a steady extraction of the region's extensive re-sources with few benefits for the surrounding communities. They provided little to residents in the way of meaningful public services, whether health, educa-tion, infrastructure, or even a consistent legal system. Instead, aid organizations and religious institutions, in conjunction with local chiefs, stepped in to pro-vide some public goods and construct other developmental projects (C. Young 2006, 316).

Traditional chiefs, known as *bami* (the plural of *mwami*), have long had a substantive influence on the politics of the Kivus. Indeed, throughout modern Congolese history, membership in a specific ethnic community has determined one's access to land and other aspects of economic and social power (Nzongola-Ntalaja 2002). Prior to the colonial period, ethnic membership was a product of a patron/client relationship, whereby a local mwami granted clients rights to land usage in exchange for their loyalty and tribute. Although altered slightly by the political regimes that followed, the basic framework that restricted land access to the discretion of the local traditional authority reinforced the instrumental value of ethnic membership for successive generations of Congolese citizens.

After independence, two types of citizenship coexisted alongside each other. National citizenship gave all individuals political and civil rights, while ethnic citizenship provided those with membership in an officially sanctioned native authority access to economic and social rights, including access to land. This par-titioning of rights further strengthened traditional authorities, who now had the ability to allocate land, as well as issue identity cards, run local markets, and ad-minister customary justice (Mamdani 2001, 238). Thus competition for power, whether economic, social, or political, came to take on ethnic valences, with ethnicity at the center of disputes over land, political positions, and economic markets. This was especially true at the local level, but even at the national level, access to the political sphere came to be determined by one's ethnic identity.

In the eastern provinces of the country, which border the densely populated corners of Rwanda, Burundi, and Uganda—areas from which ethnic communities have migrated freely across borders since precolonial times—ethnic disputes also came to encompass questions over who was indigenous and what indigenousness itself entailed (S. Jackson 2006). At the center of these debates in the Kivus was the Congolese Rwandophone community (both Hutu and Tutsi), which had long been viewed with suspicion by other eastern Congolese ethnicities. Close to 50 percent of the inhabitants of the Kivus are members of the Rwandaphone community, a category that refers to several subgroups that share the Kinyarwanda language.[9] Congolese Rwandophones share linguistic and cultural connections with people in Rwanda and Burundi, and their presence in other nations of Central and East Africa has often been contentious because of the enduring perception that they are foreign to any area outside the two tiny countries. The bulk of this population was brought to Congo from Burundi and Rwanda to serve as labor during the colonial regime, though a significant portion of the community predated this labor migration (Mamdani 2001).

At times incorporated and favored by the Mobutu regime and at other times disenfranchised by the state, both Tutsi and Hutu vacillated between brief periods of recognition by the state and periods of increased nativism, during which their very presence in Zaire came into question by the government and other ethnic communities. At independence in 1960, the "fundamental law" granted most of the Rwandophone community partial citizenship but failed to recognize them as indigenous. For members of the community to gain access to land, they had to pay tribute to the local customary authority, under whose jurisdiction they remained (Mamdani 2001).

The community's fortunes improved in 1966 when policies favoring the Banyarwanda elite were put into place as a result of the efforts of Barthelemy Bisengimana, a Tutsi from North Kivu, who served as chief of staff of the presidential

---

9. The Rwandophone community is not a unified entity, though it is often perceived as such by non-Kinyarwanda speakers. There are divisions between the Hutu and Tutsi communities and even within each of these two categories. I will use "Rwandophone" to refer to the entire population of Kinyarwanda speakers in the region. "Banyarwanda" is generally used to refer to the Congolese Tutsis community of North Kivu, which constitutes the majority of the Tutsi population. The term "Banyamulenge" refers to a subgroup of the Tutsi community that is concentrated in the high plateaus of South Kivu. However, during my interviews, people often used this term to refer to any member of the Congolese Tutsi community. This created some confusion about which portion of the community they were actually referring to and reflected the false perception held by many that this internally fractious community is actually a threatening monolithic ethnic identity.

office, a high-ranking position in Mobutu's regime (Prunier 2001, 148). The Nationality Legislation of 1972 granted members of the Rwandophone community who had been resident in Congolese territory before 1950 equal citizenship within the Zairean nation. But this relatively prosperous period for the community came to an end in 1981 with the passing of a law that severely restricted the ability of members of the community to claim citizenship, pushing some elements to begin contemplating what avenues were available for reclaiming their right to remain in the country (ibid.; Mamdani 2001).

The exclusion of the Rwandophone community paralleled the demise of Mobutu's economic and political project through the 1970s. An economic downturn so severe might have brought down many other political leaders, but Mobutu survived by further ethnicizing Zairean politics. In the Kivus he ethnicized the distribution of land in areas already experiencing high rates of population growth (Tull 2004, 82). Key to this strategy was identifying certain ethnic communities as fully a part of the Zairean nation and entitled to the complete benefits of citizenship, including their own native authority for controlling the distribution of land. This move allowed Mobutu to reinforce the idea of who qualified as Zairean by clearly demarcating who was not. To its detriment, the Rwandophone community was identified as alien and denied its own native authority. The competition for recognition this produced in the Kivus naturally escalated the value of ethnic membership and strengthened cleavages between ethnic communities, allowing Mobutu to reinforce his position as the premier source of patronage in the country. In tandem, he also implemented a hypernationalist political-cultural agenda to reinforce in the cultural sphere his own idiosyncratic ideas about what constituted a Congolese/Zairean person. By instilling in the population a strong sense of national identity through these Zairois, or *authenticité*, policies, Mobutu sought to unify the Zairean population, presenting himself as the symbolic father of the nation (Prunier 2001).

There were two legacies of this strategy in the Kivus. First, the presence of those considered nonindigenous in the region became a continually contested issue—sometimes violently—by those interested in defending the benefits of indigenousness. If not for the overbearing presence of Mobutu's coercive apparatus, large-scale ethnic violence in the Congo might have emerged by the end of the 1980s (Autesserre 2006, 54). Second, in the words of one Congolese activist, "99 percent of Congolese want to remain one country" (interview with Akpovo). Mobutu's nationalist offensive limited the viability of secessionist appeals, as most Congolese citizens, even today, commonly express their opinion that the country should remain indivisible (Weiss and Carayannis 2005). Consequently, all the insurgencies that emerged in the 1990s framed their struggles as national in focus (interview with Elaine Wamba; Englebert 2003).

These tendencies came to a head in 1990, triggered by the war between the Front Patriotique du Rwanda (Rwandan Patriotic Front, RPF) and the government of Juvenal Habyarimana in neighboring Rwanda (Prunier 1997). During the war, the RPF, a force that originated among the vast Tutsi diaspora in Uganda, made use of diasporic networks in North Kivu, where it established a rear base. Mobutu, fearing the emergence of an antagonistic military power to his east, threw his weight behind Rwanda's Hutu president while fostering divisions between Hutu and Tutsi within the Zairean Rwandophone community. Although distinct, the two communities in Zaire had never been characterized by the same degree of antagonism as their neighbors in Rwanda and Burundi, where they engaged in cycles of extreme violence (Newbury 1993). Sensing an opportunity to improve their situation by tying their fortunes to the RPF, many Tutsi in eastern Congo supported the rebels, often enlisting in the Rwandan forces (Longman 2002)—a decision many in the community would come to regret. Some of their Hutu counterparts also joined the RPF, but most used the opportunity to differentiate themselves from their Rwandophone Tutsi brethren by claiming they were indigenous, a position grudgingly accepted by many local traditional authorities. As tensions rose, violent conflict broke out in 1993 between the Congolese Rwandophone community and the so-called autochthonous groups in the region,[10] claiming fourteen thousand lives and displacing more than two hundred thousand (Tull 2004, 104).

After the genocide and subsequent victory of the RPF in 1994, over one million (mainly Hutu) Rwandan refugees arrived in eastern Zaire, fleeing retribution by the new Tutsi government. Among this refugee population were a significant number of fighters from the former government forces, the Forces Armées Rwandaises (Rwandan Armed Forces, FAR),[11] as well as members of the Hutu militia known as the Interahamwé. The fleeing Hutu genocidaires set up bases in UNHCR camps in North and South Kivu, from which they operated with impunity, launching attacks against Kigali's victorious Tutsi regime (Lischer 2005). Working with soldiers from the national government and other local strongmen in the east of Zaire, they also began to attack the local Tutsi population, forcing many from the community to seek shelter in neighboring Rwanda, where, according to one Congolese Tutsi leader, they appealed to the government in Kigali for support (interview with Rwasamanzi).

---

10. "Autochthonous" is a contentious word that roughly translates from the Greek as "from the soil itself" and means something close to "indigenous." In this context it is used to refer to Congolese groups that claim and are recognized as indigenous by the state and other authorities. See S. Jackson (2006) and the special issue of *African Studies Review*, vol. 49, no. 2, dedicated to the subject.

11. Up to twenty thousand fighters in Bukavu and thirty to forty thousand around Goma, according to Mahmood Mamdani (2001, 254)

The Rwandan leadership, now under the control of Paul Kagame, the for-mer leader of the victorious RPF,[12] aligned with members of the Congolese Tutsi community out of both a sense of ethnic kinship and a desire to put an end to its regional problems. Kagame encouraged the new wave of refugees to merge with the Congolese Tutsi fighters who had joined the RPF during the Rwandan war, forming a formidable force. In 1996 these militants returned to South Kivu, escalating local skirmishes into all-out combat. The Rwandan presence in the region, however, cemented the perception among the autochthonous Congo-lese groups—themselves a contentious bunch—that the Rwandophone popula-tion of Zaire had sided with the foreign invader, despite the fact that a majority of the community had remained in the Kivus throughout this difficult period (S. Jackson 2006).

The Emergence of Africa's First Continental War

Concerned with the escalating tensions to their west, Rwandan leaders invaded Zaire in 1996. Sensing an opportunity to end the constant source of trouble that Mobutu's Zaire had become, a number of leaders from neighboring countries— including Burundi, Uganda, and Angola—also entered their armies into the fray. From the beginning, then, the conflict in the D.R. Congo has been transnational in nature. Uganda, which was fighting its own set of insurgencies based in the Kivus, joined the Rwandans in supporting the new rebel organization. Mobu-tu's demise came at the hands of the Alliance des Forces Démocratiques pour la Libération du Congo (Alliance of Democratic Forces for Liberation, AFDL), a coalition of disparate anti-Mobutuist forces that included the remnants of Kabila's PRP, the Alliance Démocratique des Peuple (Democratic Alliance of the People, ADP)—a primarily Congolese Tutsi group led by Deogratias Bugera— and the Mouvement Révolutionnaire pour la Libération du Zaire (MRLZ), the Conseil National de Résistance pour la Démocratie (CNRD), and a faction of the Mai-Mai[13] (Kayunga 2000). The Rwandan government brought these factions together with deserters from the national army and local recruits to mount the most serious threat to Mobutu's existence since the Mulele rebellion. Looking

---

12. Officially, Kagame became president of Rwanda in 2000, a position he retains to this day. But from the RPF's initial victory in the war in 1994, most observers agree that he has always been the real power behind the Rwandan regime.

13. Mai Mai refers to a plethora of ethnically defined militias that (usually) claim autochthony and have operated in the country since the 1960s on all sides of the political axis. The term means "water" and refers to a belief in magical powers that protect fighters from enemy bullets.

for a Congolese veneer to legitimize the nascent insurgent army, Museveni and Kagame plucked Kabila from his comfortable life in Kampala and Dar es Salaam to lead the movement. The two neighboring countries provided the bulk of the military force to the insurgents, who marched all the way to Kinshasa from their bases in eastern Congo in less than seven months in 1996 (Dunn 2002).

Kabila's government, propped up by direct support from the Rwandan regime, was welcomed by the weary Congolese populace. The new regime even began to pay government bureaucrats and soldiers salaries after years of neglect under Mobutu (interviews with Tunda and Kahorha). In the Kivus, the AFDL was initially viewed as an efficient and disciplined force, a fact that many attributed to the influence of the Rwandan personnel within the organization (interviews with M. Ingezayo and Tunda). But Kabila eventually chafed at the perception that he was a Rwandan lackey.[14] Rwandan involvement was indeed extensive—for example, Kabila's army chief of staff was a Rwandan Tutsi officer named James Kabarebe, and Rwandans held many other high-ranking positions in the army. In fact, it was Kabila's decision to remove Kabarebe from his position and send him back to Rwanda that precipitated the second war. These internal conflicts over who would rule the newly named Democratic Republic of Congo combined with Kabila's increasingly autocratic tendencies, forcing the regime to turn to foreign backers (both state sponsors and transnational capital) for survival. In this and other ways, the Kabila regime became remarkably reminiscent of its Mobutuist predecessor (Dunn 2002).

In office, Kabila was never able to meet the needs of the Congolese citizenry. Nor was he able to satisfy his original patrons in Kigali and Kampala, who increasingly were concerned about the worsening situation along their western flanks—the motivation for their initial desire to intervene. His decision to break with Rwanda was never going to be easy, but the fact that he also began using vitriolic anti-Tutsi rhetoric and expelling Tutsi (both Rwandan and Congolese) from the national army was viewed by Kagame as purposely provocative (Dunn 2002). In May 1998, Kabila also began conducting house-to-house searches in Bukavu, which the Banyamulenge (a subset of Congolese Tutsi) viewed as a move to disarm them (Kayunga 2000). Furthermore, each of the AFDL's other constituent groups had joined the coalition for its own reasons, and Kabila consistently failed to appease these factions, even going as far as refusing to meet with the

---

14. Kagame's willingness to openly claim credit for the war, which was initially viewed as a positive step by the international community, certainly did not help. In a 1997 interview with the *Washington Post* he admitted that he was the mastermind of the war and that it was fought primarily to support Rwanda's interest. He also claimed that Kabila's involvement was intended to provide a Zairean facade for the operation (cited in Dunn 2002, 56).

other leaders (interview with Wamba dia Wamba; Kayunga 2000). After his visit to Kinshasa in early 1998, I spoke with Ernest Wamba dia Wamba, a Congolese Marxist intellectual and leader of the powerful exile community in East Africa, on the developing situation in Congo. He could barely control his disgust as he recounted Kabila's refusal to grant him an audience despite his traveling from Dar es Salaam, a complaint echoed by many other opposition figures at the time.

Kabila's numerous failures triggered a second rebellion just over a year after he came to power. Composed of a fractured assortment of rebel forces variously drawn from former members of the AFDL coalition and disgruntled Congolese soldiers and dissidents, as well as the Ugandan and Rwandan armies, many of the same individuals who once backed the AFDL now aligned with the new rebel army in the east. As one RCD colonel explained to me, "The same people who began the AFDL also began the opposition" (interview with Kaduma). Present in significant numbers in the new rebellion were Congolese Tutsi, many of whom had participated in the first war with hopes of resolving the citizenship question and who thus felt betrayed by Kabila's anti-Tutsi turn.

Unlike the first war, during which Kagame and Museveni attempted to mask their involvement by recruiting Congolese to lead the insurgency, the new rebellion was more overtly under the command of its foreign organizers (Nzongola-Ntalaja 2002, 224). The 1998 conflict began when two units of the Armée National Congolaise (Congolese National Army, ANC) in Goma and Bukavu deserted. The Rwandan government launched a massive support effort for the mutineers, hoping for another quick victory (Afoaku 2002, 115). It initially appeared that the second insurgency would be as successful as the AFDL, but Kabila had effective contingency plans, persuading the leaders of Angola and Zimbabwe to support his regime.[15] The intervention by these reputed armies produced a stalemate in the conflict that would last for eight years and for which the new insurgency, having banked on a quick victory, was not ready, devoid as it was of a coherent political leadership.

Origins of the RCD-Goma

Two weeks *after* the start of fighting in August 1998, the political wing of the anti-Kabila forces was formed in Goma, taking the title Rassemblement Congolais pour la Démocratie (Congolese Rally for Democracy, RCD) (Afoaku 2002). Initially unified under Wamba dia Wamba at the helm, the RCD, like the AFDL

---

15. On the involvement of foreign countries in the Congo war, see Clark (2002a).

before it, was composed of at least three different factions (Kayunga 2000; Majavu 2003). Wamba dia Wamba was the most prominent member of a group of academics and exiles that became involved in the political wing, most with roots in other provinces outside the Kivus (interview with Kaduma). This group received support from Museveni, who hoped to model the nascent rebellion on his own once-formidable rebel force, the National Resistance Army in Uganda. A second group was composed of former cabinet ministers and army officers from the Mobutu regime who were anxious to return to power.

Finally, a third group included leaders who participated in the AFDL but had been marginalized by Kabila: Bugera of the MRLZ; Emile Ilunga, a political activist with a long history of participating in insurgencies in the mineral-rich Katanga province; and Bizima Karaha, a powerful Munyamulenge closely tied to Kagame and the Rwandan regime.[16] Knowledgeable commentators disagree on the extent of Congolese Tutsi involvement in the rebel command, with seminal observers of Congo like Crawford Young (2006, 307) arguing that the RCD was "contaminated" by the "large Tutsi element in its leadership."[17] Others, like Simba Kayunga (2000, 5), a Congolese professor at Makerere University, argue that "[u]nlike the common perception that the rebellion was 'Tutsi' led, the leadership of RCD was drawn from a wide spectrum of the Congolese community."[18]

To accommodate the diversity of interests represented by its constituent factions and to prevent the emergence of a dominant figure—in the way that Kabila had come to dominate the AFDL—the new rebel command was organized with a consensus-based collective leadership. A complex political structure including a presidency, general assembly, political council, and an executive council was established with close to two hundred members split among the various organs. According to Kayunga (2000), this arrangement led to internal disputes among the different structures and undermined Wamba dia Wamba's command over the RCD, eventually resulting in the formation of multiple power centers within the organization. Uganda and Rwanda preferred to deal with different

16. "Munyamulenge" is the term for a single Banyamulenge (Congolese Tutsi from South Kivu).

17. Even within the Congolese Tutsi population there was no consensus on how to treat the new rebel group. Some members of the community felt that they would never be accepted in the region by other Congolese ethnic communities and looked to Rwanda to provide security. Others felt that tying the fortunes of the Congolese Rwandophone community to Rwanda would undermine their claims to belonging in the region and hence sought to distance themselves from Kigali (Romkema 2001).

18. During a conversation in his office in Kampala, Kayunga told me that he had been approached by leaders of the political wing asking him to join the RCD organization, but he declined. The presence of Wamba dia Wamba and other prominent academics in the movement could undermine the objectivity of many academic observers as their opinions are clearly shaped by their relationships to the leaders of the RCD, though I have no reason to doubt Kayunga's interpretation. As mentioned in the preface, I studied with Wamba dia Wamba and remain close to members of his family.

factions within the leadership, and this caused a split early in the life of the rebel command. Museveni supported Wamba dia Wamba's attempts to push for a political solution to the crisis in D.R. Congo up to the point of negotiating with Kabila. However, Kagame preferred a military solution based around the quick capture of Kinshasa, and he threw his support behind RCD vice presidents Moise Nyarugabo and Jean Pierre Ondekane and the former AFDL fighter and RCD minister of health, Dr. Emile Ilunga. The stalemate produced by the entry of Angola and Zimbabwe into the conflict brought the internal divisions plaguing the budding insurgency to the fore.

Although commentators viewed Wamba dia Wamba as an indigenous face for a foreign invasion, it is not so easy to dismiss his position as he had sympathizers among a segment of the RCD leadership and was also supported by the Ugandan regime. Museveni, the regional kingpin, respected Wamba's intellectual credentials and hoped that he could provide the nascent insurgency with an appropriate ideological underpinning (Tull 2004).[19] Wamba dia Wamba was acutely aware of the need for local support, and with different coauthors— including his wife, Elaine Wamba, and Jacques Depelchin (another exiled Congolese intellectual)—he released several lengthy missives outlining their approach for mobilizing popular support for the insurgency. In these documents and in a series of interviews given to different media outlets about his agenda, Wamba dia Wamba explained his views on dealing with civilians in the areas the RCD came to control: "People must be empowered so that they can participate in improving their own lives, but also making sure that the institutions which are put in place reflect their aspirations" (Ayebare 1998). He expanded on the question of governance in a 2000 interview soon after he was deposed as president of the RCD in favor of Ilunga:

> Administration is very difficult, very complicated, especially in wartime. Figuring out how to link administration to political values while you are still in the bush is a very serious matter. Recently the other faction of the RCD accused me of trying to introduce democracy into the movement. Imagine that! "Democracy will come later," they said. But we need to make sure that we aren't really preparing ourselves to be a one-party state. (Vazquez 2000, 152)

After the split in May of 1999, Wamba dia Wamba and his supporters relocated his faction of the group to Kisangani, coming to be known variously as the

---

19. Museveni and Wamba dia Wamba both also had connections to the University of Dar es Salaam and were close to Julius Nyerere, the former Tanzanian president.

RCD-Wamba, the RCD-Kisangani, and eventually, the RCD-Mouvement pour la Libération (RCD-ML).

With the RCD imploding in the east, Jean-Pierre Bemba, a millionaire businessman with connections to both former Mobutuists and the Ugandans, launched the Mouvement pour la Libération du Congo (MLC), quickly gaining control of Equateur province in the north of the country. Museveni, fearful of Kagame's increasingly central position among the powerful remnants of the original rebellion, began working with Bemba even before the crisis in the RCD leadership came to a head. Cut off from the majority of the insurgency, including the bulk of its military force, Wamba was forced to align his movement with Bemba's, a position that satisfied Museveni but closed the door for a reconciliation between the two factions of the original RCD organization, despite several attempts by key figures to bring the two sides together (Clark 2002b). In 2001 the MLC merged with the RCD-ML to form the Front de Libération du Congo (FLC). But for the rest of the conflict, the FLC had a minimal presence in the Kivus, as Bemba preferred to focus on controlling Equateur province and raising his national profile (Afoaku 2002, 119; Lemarchand 2003).

The RCD-Goma in the Second Congo War, 1999–2003

In July of 1999, representatives from the government and each of the main insurgent groups traveled to Lusaka, Zambia, to sign a ceasefire agreement. But unresolved tensions between the belligerents prevented the accords from having any consequential impact on the conflict. By this point the majority of the RCD had aligned with the Rwandans, remaining in Goma with Ilunga as the new president and Nyarugabo and Ondekane serving as his deputies (IRIN 1999). Having shed its academic wing, the renamed RCD-Goma now consisted of two elements from the original coalition: disgruntled former members of the AFDL (with substantial representation from the Banyamulenge population) as well as the former Mobutuists (Afoaku 2002). Both supported the Rwandan-backed militaristic strategy focused on a quick capture of Kinshasa. At its peak, the renamed RCD-G had a force of close to twenty thousand fighters[20] and came to control an expansive territory in the east of the country including most of North and South Kivu, the northern part of Katanga, Maniema, and a portion of Kasai Orientale (see figure 6.2) (Clark 2002b, 156). Despite the size of its territory, the

---

20. The UN Panel of Inquiry (2001a, 28) gives a slightly lower figure of twelve to fifteen thousand fighters.

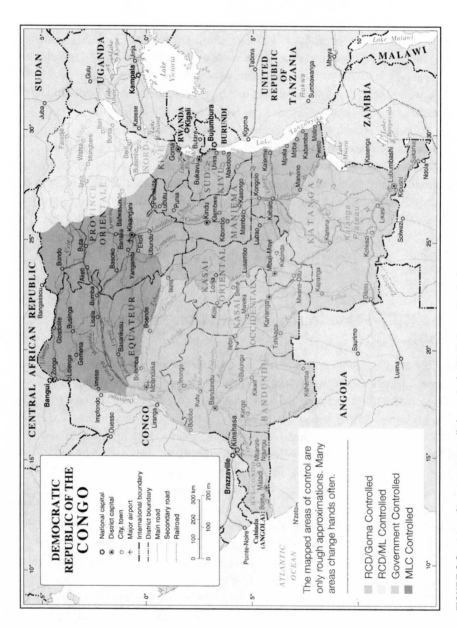

FIGURE 6.2. Map of insurgent-controlled areas in the DRC. *Source:* Dustin Ross.

organization's control of the area was never uniform, with rural areas in particular remaining outside direct control (interview with Kahorha). According to Severine Autesserre (2006, 67), the area in the east credited to the group "was in fact a mosaic of enclaves under the control of competing armed bands. The RCD-G controlled the main towns (such as Goma, Uvira, Bukavu), while the Mai Mai—now mostly allied with Kabila—the Interahamwés, Burundian rebel military groups, and other military or paramilitary groups controlled parts and pieces of the countryside in an ever changing pattern."

Despite the failure of the Lusaka accords, in February 2000 the United Nations passed Resolution 1291 authorizing a mission in Congo known as Mission de l' Organisation des Nations Unies en République Démocratique du Congo, or more commonly by its French acronym, MONUC. The initial mission was composed of slightly more than five thousand troops and was authorized to monitor the largely nonexistent ceasefire in the country, a task for which such a small force was clearly insufficient. In fact, throughout the Kivus, people referred to the UN peacekeeping force derogatorily as Monique, a play on the French pronunciation of the mission's acronym. Faced with a weak military capacity, the leaders of the mission reached out to the RCD-Goma command to shore up their precarious position in the region. However, MONUC's willingness to work with the insurgent organization led many of my informants to perceive the UN force as being a biased intervener in the war, much to its detriment (interview with Maindo).

For the rebel leadership, this early international recognition of its control of the Kivus was both a boon and a burden.[21] On the positive side, UN recognition created significant economic opportunities for the insurgents by legitimating their interactions with transnational economic networks. Having control over the exploitation of natural resources and profitable customs fees allowed the organization to establish a degree of financial independence from its Rwandan and Ugandan patrons (United Nations Panel of Inquiry 2001a). The emergence of such lucrative activities did not go unnoticed. Eventually, Rwanda and Uganda began to look at the war in Congo less as a security issue and more as a financial opportunity—as demonstrated by the violent fighting between the two erstwhile allies over the rebel-controlled city of Kisangani in 1999 and again in 2000 (Clark 2002b). Evidence of this shift was apparent as early as 1999, when the UN estimated that fully 20 percent of Rwanda's gross domestic product, or about $320 million, was derived from its commercial ventures in Congo (United Nations Panel of Inquiry 2002, 15). Less profitably—but important in other ways— the RCD began imposing taxes on the civilian population, as well as collecting

---

21. The RCD cultivated international support from the very beginning, sending high-ranking delegations to Europe to garner support for the insurgency.

various fees from charitable and commercial enterprises, processes that benefited from the international recognition.

On the negative side, international recognition further undermined the credibility of the rebel group among the majority of the local residents of the Kivus. Economic opportunities allowed the RCD to gloss over its limited capacity to govern in the east, and the insurgency did little to share its wealth with local communities. It was already viewed as a foreign creation, and its reliance on external markets, close partnerships with foreign governments, and recognition by the UN contributed to the widespread perception of the organization as more a tool of transnational interests than an indigenous representative of local concerns (Young 2002, 27). With a foreign revenue source readily available, the rebel command had little motivation to mobilize popular support through the provision of services, preferring instead to focus its resources on military engagements.

Foreign enterprises were quick to make deals with the rebel command, which laid claim to a region filled with many lucrative natural resources, including cobalt, palm oil, elephant tusks, gold, timber, and diamonds (Montague 2002; Nzongola-Ntalaja 2002, 235–40). In fact, at the peak of the war, as many as eighty-five multinational companies were profiting from the conflict in some way, many working directly with the RCD-Goma in the east, according to the UN (BBC News 2003). For example, the organization was able to extract significant financial resources during the coltan boom[22] by levying licensing fees and collecting taxes from multinationals engaged in the trade (United Nations Panel of Inquiry 2001a; International Crisis Group 2003a, 23). Insurgent leaders were known to work closely with coltan dealers in an efficient transnational network that transported the mineral from hundreds of individually dug shallow pits— many created with forced labor—through Kigali and Kampala to manufacturers in Asia and Europe. These manufacturers used the mineral to produce mobile phones for consumers across the globe (Montague 2002; Romkema and Vlassenroot 2002; United Nations Panel of Inquiry 2002). A visit in 2004 to the Karibu Hotel, a popular bar and eatery in Bunia, provided a snapshot of how these commercial networks functioned in eastern Congo as foreign merchants mixed freely with rebel commanders, local politicians, and even personnel from international agencies and transnational aid organizations.

Ilunga's control of the RCD was short-lived as his reign was plagued with even further fragmentation of the command, and in 2000 he was replaced by Adolphe Onusumba, the insurgency's former foreign affairs representative (BBC News

---

22. Coltan is short for columbite-tantalite, a metallic ore comprising niobium and tantalum. Eastern Congo is a major supplier of coltan, which is used worldwide to make capacitors for electronic equipment like mobile phones, computers, and DVD players.

2000). Finally, in 2002, Azarias Ruberwa, a Munyamulenge from the Kivus with close ties to the Rwandan government, became the leader of the organization. Also a former member of Kabila's AFDL, Ruberwa had been a professor of law in eastern Congo and in Rwanda before the war (Asuman 2006). His ascendancy completed the transformation of the RCD-Goma from a loose multiethnic coalition to an overtly Congolese Tutsi organization (interview with S. Ingezayo). By this point it was impossible for the insurgency to combat perceptions that it was little more than a lackey of the Rwandan regime under Kagame. The leadership did attempt to recruit leaders from other communities to shore up support for the coming election and to combat the widespread anti-Tutsi/Rwandan prejudice that had swept the Kivus but with little effect (interview with Maindo).

In April of 2002, soon after Ruberwa's ascendancy, an agreement was formalized in Sun City, South Africa, that called for national elections that, ideally, would lead to a unified, multiparty democratic government. A flawed document that left many contentious issues unresolved—including the difficult task of creating a unified army—the agreement did manage to bring representatives of the major combatants to agree on a framework for ending the war. The Sun City Agreement provided for a two-year transitional government to be led by Joseph Kabila that would prepare the country for elections in 2005, the first in forty years.[23] The agreement also offered government positions to leaders of the various insurgent groups; these included the post of prime minister for Bemba of the MLC and a shared vice presidency for Ruberwa, who nonetheless refused to sign the final document. Despite the signing of the accord, low-level conflict persisted throughout the eastern part of the country until 2006, when elections actually took place. While the Kivus continued to be torn by violent conflicts, life in the rest of the country was relatively unaffected, and the region was essentially abandoned in the Congolese and global consciousness to the UN force.[24]

After the Sun City Agreement was signed, the UN mandated MONUC to work with the newly created Government of National Unity, which now included the RCD-Goma, entrenching the international perception of the insurgent organization as the dominant political actor in the east (UN Security Council 2003). However, fed up by the brutality associated with an organization still perceived to be a foreign invasion, fighting continued in the east as local actors continued

---

23. In January 2001, Laurent Kabila was killed during a coup attempt that included members of his own family. His son Joseph, who had been raised largely in Tanzania, came to power ten days after his father's death and remains in office after winning a national election in 2006.

24. In early 2009, the fall of Laurent Nkunda's Tutsi army, known as the Congrès National pour la Défense du Peuple (CNDP), again focused global attention on the persistent crisis in the east. Nkunda was a commander of an army brigade of the RCD-Goma before starting his own violent movement in 2006 (Africa Confidential 2008; Stearns 2008).

to reject attempts by the RCD-Goma organization to exercise hegemony over the Kivus. The Mai-Mai, a loose collection of ethnic militias, mounted the most serious violent challenge to the insurgency's control of the region, but their presence was limited to the rural areas (Lemarchand 2003, 31). In addition, Kagame's decision to withdraw troops in accordance with the 2002 peace deal strengthened the Hutu militias, who continued to threaten the authority of RCD-Goma in rural areas even further. In the cities, rebel control was challenged most seriously by government forces, who eventually retook Bukavu from the "former" insurgents in 2004, in direct violation of the prohibitions against the use of force provided for in the Sun City Agreement. The discussion of civilian governance below takes into consideration the entire period of RCD control in the Kivus, from the conflict's beginning in 1998 to the election of 2006 when the RCD, now transformed into a national political party, fought unsuccessfully for the presidency.

The RCD-Goma Governance System

From the outbreak of hostilities in 1998, the leaders of the insurgency were ill prepared to handle the demands of establishing a governmental system over the areas they came to control. Aspirations to portray the rebel command as a government-in-waiting were hindered by the leaders' failure to comprehend the harsh political environment they confronted upon taking power in the Kivus. The ensuing stalemate forced insurgent leaders to reluctantly face up to the reality of being little more than a localized rebellion with limited territory and extremely difficult relationships with its own public (interview with Weiss). In the words of the RCD vice president Arthur Zahidi Ngoma, "We hadn't realized that we would have to set up what is more or less a government so fast, but it's an obligation now" (BBC Monitoring 1998, cited in Tull 2004, 133). After the split within the movement, these inadequacies became even more exposed as those figures who had thought the most about civilian governance went with Wamba dia Wamba and the RCD-Kisangani.

Perceptions and reality concerning the RCD-Goma diverge around the contentious subject of how the organization treated local occupants of the Kivus during the conflict. Horrendous violence has come to typify the Congolese conflicts, and rough estimates for the number of war-related deaths range between 2 and 6 million—a strikingly high number considering the relatively short duration of the conflict—though it is impossible to place an exact number on the organization's share of the dead.[25] Throughout the country, 2.3 million Congolese

---

25. This number refers not only to deaths on the battlefield but also to deaths resulting from the breakdown in political order.

were internally displaced with the two provinces of North and South Kivu that the RCD-Goma controlled, accounting for 1 million of the displaced. More than 400,000 Congolese also found refuge in neighboring countries (Autesserre 2006, 71). Although a startling indictment of the violence perpetrated by combatants, these figures also represent the culmination of a gradual process of decline and disorder that had begun much earlier. Rather than representing a fundamental disjuncture, rebel rule over the Kivus reflects a degree of continuity between the degraded preconflict state institutions and the forms of political order that emerged in the absence of the state. This is encapsulated in the remarkable work of Denis Tull (2004, 8), who spent a considerable amount of time in the region during the war:

> To some extent, the political arena is remarkably structured, not least because institutions, modalities, logics and practices dating back to the pre-war period have not been radically swept away. Rather, they reveal an astounding persistence while, at the same time, being subjected to modification and change. As such, we do not witness a radically altered or altogether novel configuration, but a rupture that intersects with elements of continuity. Violent transformation is structured by older institutions and practices that continue to shape and inform the agency of local actors.

The RCD sought to impose order over its territory through a variety of strategies, none of which succeeded. There were a number of reasons for this, largely related to the organization's reliance on external relationships. By providing the nascent insurgency easy access to weaponry and other military resources, Rwanda and Uganda undercut the need for a prolonged period of popular mobilization. Instead, pro-Rwandan forces in the leadership advocated for a quick military victory. It was assumed that challenges to insurgent rule could be contained through coercive means alone, a strategy that showed its weaknesses after the entry of foreign powers on the side of the Kinshasa government led to a stalemate in the fighting.

But reliance on Rwandan state patronage and intraregional trade networks is not the sole reason for the failure of the RCD's governance project. Once the invasion stalled, a variety of actors operating from within rebel territory directly challenged the insurgents, driven by a xenophobic hostility to the organization's perceived Rwandan taint (Longman 2002). Even genuine efforts by the insurgents to develop governance structures ran into complications as a result of the complex political landscape the group was forced to navigate. Thus, viewing the insurgency's behavior simply as warlordism is insufficient, despite the certain resemblance of its financial strategy to activities generally associated with transnational criminal gangs (Reno 1998; Young 2002). Failure to implement political order is different from promoting disorder. And while the insurgents certainly contributed to the chaos in the east, their minimalist approach to governance did comprise two discernible goals in line with the command's own agenda. First, they sought to limit violent challenges to their rule and reduce other sources of disorder within the territory they controlled. And second, they sought to co-opt preexisting administrative structures that operated in the Kivus, either by replacing local administrators with rebel sympathizers or by inducing, through coercion or material benefits, local actors to support their agenda.

The diminution of the state under Mobutu and the emergence of an alternate political order in the Kivus prior to the war required the rebel leadership to develop relationships with a constellation of distinct local political actors, including the remnants of the state, private trading networks, and civil society actors like churches, traditional authorities, and aid organizations. Initially, like the AFDL, its precursor, the RCD attempted to take charge of the preexisting bureaucratic institutions still operating in the east. Higher-ranking positions including provincial governorships were generally given to rebel loyalists. To fill the ranks, personnel were often drawn from members of the Congolese Tutsi community, hence reinforcing the perception that the insurgency was nothing more than a foreign-backed militia of the local Rwandophone community (Prunier 2001, 157). But more often, local administrative positions were left in the hands of the same bureaucrats who had manned those positions before the outbreak of the conflict as long as they did not challenge the insurgency's military agenda (Tull 2004, 134). Personnel of foreign aid organizations who had worked with both the Mobutu regime and the rebel civil administration testified that in the initial months after the invasion, the insurgents sought to reinvigorate the state institutions and use them as a basis for their own governance system, with some success (interview with Martinez).

Eventually the command recognized that these former state structures were beyond the pale and incapable of being resuscitated. They had been hollowed out many years before, serving only as sources of patronage for local elites. Resources generated through the trade in natural resources or from foreign patronage might have been productively directed toward reviving the civil administration, but their purpose was never to improve civilian livelihoods but rather to pay for military expenses or line the pockets of individuals within the rebel organization. Thus, as with the situation prior to the war, bureaucrats operating in the rebel-controlled Kivus were left to their own devices to raise revenue through extraction from the local population.[26] Recognizing the inadequacy of relying on these

---

26. The same approach was used to compensate soldiers within the RCD-Goma who did not receive paychecks but relied on extracting resources from civilians

former state institutions, the command sought to expand its governance project by working to co-opt the real sources of political order in the region.

In the Kivus, this meant reaching out to civil society actors, including the churches, NGOs engaged in human rights and developmental work, traditional authorities, and unions.[27] As discussed earlier, Mobutu's reign had created opportunities for these nonstate actors to emerge as significant players in the region's social, political, and economic life. Their centrality to the daily functioning of civilian life in the provinces was further bolstered in 1994 after the Rwandan genocide, when huge amounts of international money flowed into the region to alleviate the refugee crisis (Romkema 2001, 36).

As with most things in the Kivus, ethnicity came to play an increasingly important role in the realm of civil society after the outbreak of conflict. In South Kivu, where the Banyamulenge were a relatively small portion of the population, civil society was dominated by the so-called autochthonous ethnic communities, which vacillated between recognition of the struggle of the Banyamulenge and viewing them as interlopers in the province's politics (Romkema 2001, 36). Civil society leaders tended to resist efforts by the rebels to support the insurgent political program and openly challenged the group's control of the region despite their stated agendas to work as peace builders. Community leaders that I spoke to in Bukavu openly condemned the rebels, portraying the RCD as a tool of Tutsi domination and expressing harsh, stereotypical views about the broader Tutsi community in the region (interviews with Wakenge, Tegera, and Stauss; Longman 2002; Wolters 2004). The rebels fared better in Goma, the capital of North Kivu, where the Rwandophone community constituted a much higher percentage of the overall population than it did in Bukavu. Indeed, this favorable population composition helped the RCD administrators to integrate their governance efforts with local civil society actors who were more sympathetic to the struggle of the Congolese Hutu and Tutsi communities.

The various civil society actors in the Kivus did not limit themselves to performing discrete roles; rather, organizations often engaged in a variety of political activities. For example, while some NGOs did attempt to pursue secular and nonethnic agendas, many others explicitly affiliated with religious or tribal interests. Still, it is possible to delineate different modalities in the distinct relationships between various civil society actors and the rebel civil administration.

At the forefront of all civil society actors active in the Kivus were various religious institutions, especially the Catholic Church. The church's prominence in

---

27. Some may question considering traditional authorities as part of civil society because of their exclusionary nature, but many of the functions performed by chiefs in the African context warrant their inclusion in this section.

eastern Congo has roots in the colonial era, when it was a favored partner of the Belgian colonial regime. Under Mobutu, after the authenticité campaigns initiated in 1971, the relationship between church leaders and the central government was often contentious. But the weakness of the Congolese state allowed the church to reemerge as a powerful social and economic force in many parts of the country, including the eastern provinces. Often organized into an elaborate structure with multiple technical departments, churches filled in for the absence of state authority, especially in the neglected Kivus, providing public goods such as health, education, and other developmental services (Prunier 2001, 156). Churches from all denominations were also the most important employer in the region. According to Tull (2004, 253), each provincial office often hired hundreds or thousands of salaried employees.

Recognizing that the churches were a potential rival center of power, the rebel command initially hoped to co-opt church leaders into its governance efforts (Human Rights Watch 2000). The fact that several prominent church leaders (monsignors) in and around Goma were of Rwandophone descent gave the group some initial success and led many to question the loyalties of the various churches (Romkema 2001, 44). However, the churches were also divided.[28] And other monsignors were more supportive of autochthonous groups, including the powerful leaders of the Catholic Church in Bukavu, generally considered the "most important site of resistance [to rebel rule] in South Kivu," in the words of one aid official who worked in the region at the time. In fact, the ethnic sympathies of Christian leaders often came to the fore when they discussed their opinion of the RCD-Goma, and several prominent church leaders, including the powerful monsignor Monsengwo Pasinya of Kisangani, a leading figure of the anti-Mobutu opposition, openly attacked the insurgency in a variety of national and international forums. In early 2001 I interviewed Pasinya in a New York City hotel, where he had come seeking an audience after the assassination of the elder Kabila. With surprising vitriol, he openly expressed his overtly racialist criticisms against the Congolese Tutsi and the RCD insurgency.[29]

In 2000 Catholic leaders in Bukavu, under Monsignor Emmanuel Kataliko, organized a one-week strike against what they claimed was a foreign occupation. The strike was encouraged by foreign donors and took place in conjunction with several national and international NGOs (interview with anonymous aid

---

28. As discussed earlier, the fact that South Kivu's Rwandophone population was much smaller than North Kivu's meant that few members of South Kivu's Catholic Church had any interest in working with the RCD-Goma.

29. Monsengwo also claimed that Uganda's president was a Tutsi and part of a larger conspiracy including Rwanda's president Kagame that sought to carve out a Tutsi empire in the region.

official). Faced with a direct challenge to their authority, RCD-G leaders arrested the monsignor, whom they blamed for the strike, placing him under house arrest for seven months. Kataliko had consistently been a bane to the rebel leadership, criticizing the organization openly and widely. But the insurgents overreached when they targeted him for arrest. The Catholic Church as well as the Protestant and Kimbanguist[30] churches expanded the strike, closing schools and suspending mass (Human Rights Watch 2000). Kataliko died soon after his release, and even the Tutsi leader of the National Episcopal Conference was forced to condemn his arrest, permanently breaking the few remaining ties between the churches and the pro-Tutsi rebel leadership (Prunier 2001, 159). The command's awkward attempts to pressure religious leaders into supporting the insurgency's governance project not only failed to co-opt these institutions but also exacerbated civilian resentment for what was rightly perceived as meddling by the insurgents. In response, the organization was forced to extricate itself from interference in the affairs of the churches, thereby returning them to the position they had occupied prior to the conflict—that is, a source of social and economic stability with an antagonistic relationship to the local political regime, which now was under the control of the RCD-Goma insurgents.

The rebels had more success with their attempts at co-opting tribal authorities in the east. As discussed earlier, bami were empowered throughout Congo's history by state authorities seeking to project their dominion across the length of the country. Bami were thus habituated to accommodating a wide variety of political regimes that came to power in Kinshasa. Indeed, in regional capitals like Goma and Bukavu, they often found ways to manipulate the political authority to bring greater material benefits to their constituents. The RCD-Goma leaders adopted the Mobutuist strategy of inducing cooperation among the traditional authorities through a mix of coercion and material incentives. Bami served a number of functions for the leadership, including raising material support and recruits for the insurgent army and helping the group extend its authority into remote rural areas. They also helped collect information on other armed groups operating in the Kivus (Tull 2004, 145–47). Thus, claiming their support was an important strategy for the insurgent command. To this end, in September 2001, the organization held an inter-Kivutien dialogue with an agenda of forcing traditional leaders to recognize the Rwandophone community. During this meeting, a number of bami, both Rwandophone and from other ethnic communities, were forcibly recruited into the rebel force (interview with Rwasamanzi; Englebert 2003).

---

30. Kimbanguism is an African Christian tradition founded during the colonial period by the Congolese spiritual leader Simon Kimbangu.

In cases where the bami proved more recalcitrant, the insurgents would inter-
fere in succession disputes involving chiefs with the intention of installing more
sympathetic leaders. Unlike the church, which could always call on transnational
networks to publicize any harassment by the rebel army, traditional authorities
had only two options for refusing the organization's overtures—they could either
flee the area or resist violently. Many chose the latter option, especially those
representing autochthonous groups, often forming alliances with the Mai Mai
militias in the region to challenge rebel rule, frequently with considerable success
(Jackson 2006).

Despite the widespread belief that the RCD-Goma was a lackey of Rwandan
Tutsis, government officials in Kigali took a pragmatic approach when forming
local alliances with traditional leaders. In practice, what this meant was that leaders of the rebellion were pushed to align the organization with non-Tutsi bami if
it would bring greater rewards in the short term. Thus, despite its presumed affiliation with the Congolese Tutsi community, the insurgent command began to
solicit support from other ethnic communities, including the Congolese Hutus
as well as other autochthonous ethnic communities with histories of antagonism against the Congolese Tutsi. This vacillation by the rebel organization left
many Tutsi leaders feeling as if the insurgency, long associated with the Congolese Rwandophones, had actually done more long-term damage to the interests
of their community (Longman 2002, 132). Anecdotal accounts from the region
confirmed that before the outbreak of conflict in 1996, the Tutsi community
faced significantly less antagonism from its ethnic neighbors than it did after
Rwanda exported its ethnic crisis to the region. Toward the official end of the
conflict, the Tutsi community began to agitate against the rebel leadership. But
without support from the Rwandan authorities or from any other local political
power broker, Tutsi leaders in Congo had few options, and the community as a
whole was increasingly marginalized from participation in the social and political life of the region (interview with Rwasamanzi). In fact, when I visited Bukavu
in March of 2005, shortly after the insurgents had lost control for the last time,
people from all sectors of society approvingly referred to the town by the Swahili
phrase "mji safi" or "clean town" in reference to the expulsion of the bulk of the
Tutsi population.

The insurgency's attempts to forcibly co-opt societal actors extended to the
ethnicized realm of NGOs in the Kivus. The organization early on saw the value
of winning over personnel from the Kivus' dynamic civil society sector, hoping
to piggyback off their significant influence in the urban areas. In both North
and South Kivu, the organization relied on a familiar mix of sticks and carrots
to induce support or at the least to limit the challenge such actors could pose.
It is important to distinguish between two categories of NGOs operating in the

Kivus.[31] On one hand were the local branches of international humanitarian and relief organizations such as World Vision and Médecins Sans Frontiers (Doctors Without Borders, MSF), the presence of which escalated significantly following the migration of Rwandan Hutus to the region in 1994 (Lischer 2005). On the other hand were advocacy organizations such as the Pole Institute in Goma and Héritiers de la Justice and the Initiative Congolaise pour la Justice et la Paix in Bukavu that had engaged in peace and democracy work in the region before the outbreak of conflict and were staffed mainly by local Congolese personnel. In keeping with their respective positions vis-à-vis the debate on political neutrality, organizations that engaged in relief and development work had a more congenial relationship with the rebels than groups advocating democracy or human rights, whose personnel were often targeted for harassment (interviews with Stauss and Tegera).

Staff from relief and development organizations described their relationship with the insurgent civil administration as cordial, though they were aware of the politicized nature of their interactions and were accustomed to bribing the rebels with cash or other material items (interviews with Bulambo, Martinez, and Ulrich; United Nations Panel of Inquiry 2001b, 6).[32] Like the SPLM/A in South Sudan (as discussed in chapter 5), the insurgent command recognized the benefits of attracting relief and development organizations to their territory. For example, in a 2001 interview, Joseph Mudumbi, the RCD-G minister for territorial administration, proclaimed, "In our area, humanitarian agencies have always been free to work.... We are doing what we can to facilitate the agencies because our people need help" (Gough 2001).[33] Such organizations were expected to provide details to the rebellion about the work they intended to do so that the civil administration could regulate their behavior (Human Rights Watch 2000). Informants related to me the ways in which the insurgents sought to channel aid to communities perceived as sympathetic to the insurgent cause, granting operating permission to relief and development organizations only if they were willing to direct aid to these areas (interview with Bulambo). In a consistent

---

31. I prefer not to distinguish between 'international nongovernmental organizations and community-based organizations because it implies that the latter is a local entity while the former is international. In fact both types are often transnational in terms of their audience and funding sources. I think the relevant distinction in the case of eastern Congo is not the groups' origins but their specific purpose—whether they viewed their role as engaging solely in relief activities or in politics. Thus I would categorize a transnational organization like Human Rights Watch alongside a local organization like the Pole Institute as they both engage in documentation and advocacy work.

32. Tull (2004, 172) claims that in 2002 charities paid a 5 percent customs tax to the RCD-Goma to import equipment and medicine, as well as a vehicle license tax of $80 to $120.

33. Mudumbi also occupied other positions during his career with the RCD-Goma, including a stint as minister of foreign affairs.

fashion, the civil administration did not hesitate to place restrictions on organizations operating in areas sympathetic to the rebellion's perceived competitors, such as those under the control of various Mai Mai militias (interviews with Bayunda and Hangi). However, in order to avoid accusations of favoritism and maintain the facade that the civil administration was prodevelopment, the rebels would not restrict aid groups openly. Rather, they had a number of strategies to control aid delivery. For example, noncompliant organizations would frequently be targeted with strategic checkpoints designed to impede mobility to certain areas. Or the rebels would simply refuse to provide security to areas perceived as nonsupportive. More threateningly, the insurgency would engage in anonymous raids of aid resources that could not be traced back to rebel cadres (interview with Bulambo).

The relationship between overtly political advocacy groups and the rebellion exhibited considerably less congeniality. The leadership was acutely aware of the importance of prodemocracy and human rights organizations in shaping opinions about the RCD-Goma in the international arena (interview with Tegera). Furthermore, many advocacy groups were actively tied into transnational human rights networks that sought to document the behavior of the insurgency in ways the command accurately assessed to be detrimental to its image in international circles (Romkema 2001). Therefore, within areas clearly under its control, the organization often sought to restrict the activities of these human rights activists (interviews with Wakenge and Stauss). The insurgent command put into place travel restrictions on personnel from local advocacy groups in order to limit their interaction with colleagues in the West. This limited the fund-raising and advocacy activities of local activists, both locally and abroad (Human Rights Watch 2000). The insurgents also attempted to avoid perpetrating violence openly in urban areas under their control, preferring instead to use coercion away from the international spotlight, mostly in rural areas where human rights activists, both local and international, were less likely to go (interview with Stauss).

As with all things in the Kivus, the NGO world was divided ethnically, and certain organizations did overtly align with the rebel leadership. This was more common in North Kivu, where the demographic strength of the Rwandophone community meant that local Tutsis commonly played a role within various civil society organizations. In South Kivu, the demographic weakness of the Banyamulenge community allowed hostile civil society organizations to largely exclude the RCD-Goma from making inroads into the robust Bukavu nongovernmental world.

One prominent example of collaboration between the rebels and a local aid organization demonstrates the fluid nature of relationships between actors involved in the politics of the region. Tous pour la Paix et le Développement

(Everyone for Peace and Development, TPD) was an organization founded in Goma in October 1998, just two months after the start of the second war, by a group of Hutu and Tutsi Congolese Rwandophones from North Kivu (Mararo 2004). Initially, TPD was closely aligned with the reigning undivided insurgent organization, working on jointly defined goals in a fashion similar to that of the rebel-affiliated aid organizations in Sri Lanka or Sudan. Its original goal was to help with the resettlement of Hutu refugees to the sensitive Masisi area of eastern Congo. For this purpose, TPD was able to draw on impressive external resources, including money from the Rwandan government and international agencies including UNHCR. Under the leadership of Eugene Serufuli, a Congolese Hutu, the organization also engaged in public works projects.[34] Though these services were primarily cosmetic,[35] Serufuli often took credit for projects completed by other agencies, such as the restoration of the University of Goma with World Bank funds and actions by other, smaller aid organizations operating in the region (interview with Bulambo). Through its systematic collection of taxes, residents of North Kivu came to view the organization primarily as a revenue-generating device for the insurgent government and its Rwandan patron, despite the consistent efforts by TPD leaders to portray themselves as a comprehensive governing authority (Pole Institute 2003).

Over time, the organization did gain control over many governmental functions in Goma. This process was formalized when the RCD-Goma appointed Serufuli governor of North Kivu, fusing TPD into the administrative structure of the province. Serufuli replaced the popular governor of the province, Lionel Kanyamuhanga, a Tutsi from the region who was a consistent thorn in the side of the insurgent organization (interview with Tegera). But Serufuli was not content with even this level of responsibility and remade the organization again, this time incorporating his own personal militia; this increased his appeal to leaders of the RCD-Goma, who hoped to incorporate his troops into their own flagging military force (interviews with Kahorha and Tunda).

After the signing of the Sun City Accords in 2003, major personnel including the organization's leader, Azarias Ruberwa—now the president of the rebel-affiliated political party—shifted to Kinshasa. In the absence of the insurgent command, TPD became its own regional power, successfully usurping the RCD-Goma's authority in the region, apparently with the support of the Rwandan

---

34. Serufuli had a long history in North Kivu, having been a part of the quasi-Hutu ethnic militia Mutuelle Agricole des Virunga (MAGRIVI) that had been active during the violence in North Kivu in the early 1990s. See the history of TPD provided by Mararo (2004).

35. I witnessed this myself during my visits to Goma. In 2004, workers from TPD were actively engaged in sprucing up the town center by planting flowers.

regime (interviews with Stauss and Tegera; Pole Institute 2003; Wolters 2004). The alignment of the primarily Hutu community in North Kivu with the Tutsi regime in Kigali through the machinations of TPD is just one example of the shifts in ethnic loyalties that the conflict produced. This transition also cemented perceptions among many Tutsi in the region that their interests were no longer germane.

The Provision of Services in Eastern D.R. Congo

Considering the convoluted nature of the RCD-Goma's civilian governance efforts, it is hard to draw clear lines between the insurgency and the provision of even minimal services in the Kivus during the war. From the emergence of a second rebellion in 1998 to the official end of the war in 2002, when control of several nonstrategic public services passed back to the central government in Kinshasa (Autesserre 2006, 123), the organization did develop a civil administration divided between specific departments of education, health, social affairs, and so on. Other departments such as taxation, security, and immigration remained under rebel control even after the 2002 agreement, in much the same way that service provision in the northeast of Sri Lanka was divided between the government and the Tamil rebels. To regulate service provision in the Kivus, in 2001 the Department of Territorial Administration of the rebel authority set up provincial assemblies within areas under its control (Pole Institute 2003). The assemblies were designed to allocate funds provided from the provincial budgets, though in an interview even the president of the North Kivu assembly admitted its lack of utility.[36]

Administrators affiliated with the insurgency would often tout their initiatives or simply take credit for actions by other societal actors on television and other media under insurgent control. Journalists I spoke with in the region confirmed that they were frequently approached by the insurgency to help craft an effective message for media broadcasts (interview with Kahorha). Though most demurred, the RCD did engage in a variety of media offensives. For example, Goma Radio hosted a show produced by insurgent sympathizers called *Towards a New Congo*. And speeches by the political leadership were often broadcast on TV Goma, interspersed with popular music to attract audiences. Civilians I observed

---

36. See the interview with Faustin Buunda Ndyanabo conducted by Leopold Rutinigirwa and Onesphore Sematumba of the Pole Institute in Goma, December 2002 (Pole Institute 2003).

FIGURE 6.3. A makeshift outdoor market in Goma under RCD-Goma control, 2004.

at a local restaurant in Goma tended to pay far more attention to the gyrating hips than to the garrulous politicians.

In my description below of the security, health, and education systems, I assess the actual ways in which civilians met their basic needs in the Kivus, focusing on the relationship between a variety of nonstate service providers and the rebel governance system. In general, the RCD-Goma deserves little credit in any of these three sectors because other societal actors retained their premier position as the source of social and political order in the Kivus, despite insurgent leaders' frequent efforts to intervene in these institutions and processes.

The Security System

Upon assuming power in the Kivus, the insurgency left many of the Mobutu-era Congolese legal codes, judicial structures, and even personnel in office (interview with Kahorha). As during the preconflict period, the civil administration provided few funds for salaries for security personnel. From magistrates to prison guards, workers involved with the security system approached their official positions as sources of income by demanding bribes from the civilian population (interview with Bulambo). Thus there was a widespread feeling among civilian informants in urban areas that the security system in rebel territory was primarily a tool through which the group extracted resources from the population. Justice between civilian disputants in rebel-controlled courts was viewed to be solely a function of who could pay a higher bribe (interview with Tegera; Human Rights Watch 1999). Furthermore, unlike the insurgencies in Sri Lanka and Sudan, both of which imposed strict behavioral codes on their cadres, particularly when they interacted with noncombatants, RCD personnel rejected any disciplinary strictures, behaving with relative impunity in the region under rebel control.

The judicial system did serve an instrumental purpose for the insurgency by allowing it to control challenges to its rule by civil society actors (Human Rights Watch 1999). By detaining contentious voices through its reading of Congolese legal codes, the leadership was able to accomplish two objectives. First, by relying on detentions instead of more coercive measures, the rebellion was able to avoid international condemnation of its behavior while effectively silencing internal critics. And second, since civil society institutions in the Kivus were often the only source of paying jobs (Romkema 2001, 36), detaining workers from these institutions was a way for the organization to provide the judiciary with a steady supply of detainees capable of paying bribes to the prison authorities.

In rural areas most disputes were left to bami and other tribal leaders, though their rulings were often ignored by civilian disputants because of the war-induced breakdown of traditional authority structures. Furthermore, violence in the rural areas forced many bami to migrate to the relative security of various towns, away from the areas in which they traditionally held sway (interview with Bulambo). Despite these disruptions, North Kivu did have a multiethnic conflict resolution structure known as the *barza intercommunautaire,* which was brought together by the insurgent command in Goma in 1998. Composed of twenty-four members drawn equally from each of North Kivu's eight ethnic communities and designed to replicate a traditional village council, the barza sought to informally resolve disputes between civilians in a mutually acceptable manner. While the precise relationship between the barza and the insurgency is hard to delineate, several leaders of the barza were tied to the rebel authority and hence were viewed with some suspicion by other civil society members (Romkema 2001, 44–45). Still, according to Tull (2004, 223–24), the barza was able to resolve a significant number of disputes in the rural areas of North Kivu, especially land conflicts, which were common in the region for reasons explained earlier. Though RCD administrators did try to replicate the barza model in South Kivu, their efforts were rebuffed by local chiefs who consistently refused to work with the civil administration because of their distaste for the insurgency more generally (interview with Tegera).

In addition, several civil society actors played a role in resolving disputes within the Kivus during the conflict. Through the Commission Justice et Paix

(CJP) of Caritas, a Catholic relief organization, the church was able to use its historical position as a caretaker of the rural and other underserved populations to play an important role in providing a modicum of order during the conflict (interview with Pasinya). The CJP addressed a wide variety of conflicts including land disputes, rape, and theft through the training of local intermediaries (known as *para-juristes*) to serve as conflict mediators. If the dispute remained unresolved, the parties could request a hearing from the *conseil de sages* (council of elders), which was a committee composed of representatives from each of the local area's ethnic groups. Above this level, the *comité paroissial justice et paix* (parish committee for justice and peace) was the highest conflict mediation body within the Church (Tull 2004, 226–27). At each level, hearings were open to the public and emphasis was placed on determining individual guilt in order to prevent disputes from taking on broader ethnic overtones. Solutions were crafted on the basis of broad interpretations of Congolese law in order to avoid perceptions that the institutions were biased toward any specific community.

Local humanitarian organizations with support from the international community also played an important role in resolving interethnic disputes throughout the Kivus through both ad hoc mediation of disputes and longer-term campaigns to promote the peaceful coexistence of ethnic communities (Tull 2004, 226). Despite repeated efforts, the rebel civil administration failed to appropriate either the church or humanitarian initiatives, and they continued to function somewhat autonomously, and effectively, throughout the conflict.

The Education System

Like most rebel authorities, the RCD leadership prioritized the establishment of a policing and judicial system that could also serve as a mechanism for resource extraction.[37] Thus during the war the education and health systems were run much as they had been before the outbreak of conflict—that is, they were neglected and abandoned to the initiatives of civilians and nonstate organizations. As a point of reference, in 1990 only 2 percent of Zairean government expenditures were devoted to education and health services (Tull 2004, 217). This meant, for example, that by the 1997–98 academic year, of those children who were enrolled in school, only 15 percent attended government primary and secondary schools.[38] Fully 80 percent attended Protestant and Catholic schools, and the rest went to private institutions and other religiously affiliated schools (213). Many children, of

---

37. The LTTE land courts are one such example, discussed in chapter 4.

38. Tull (2004) points out that in 1974, government schools enrolled a significantly higher proportion of secondary school students (35.3%), but this number dropped dramatically alongside the deflation of the state.

course, were not fortunate enough to attend school. Under rebel rule, education continued to be left to the initiative of the churches and aid organizations, which survived through donations and by drawing fees from parents with adequate resources. Occasionally, groups of concerned parents even banded together in mutual aid networks to form their own informal educational systems (interviews with Bayunda, Hangi, and Maindo).

According to one school administrator who worked with the RCD-Goma education ministry, since the schools had long operated independently of the political authority, there was little interest among rebel officials in taking direct control of the educational system. The insurgents generally limited their involvement in the schools to ensuring the loyalty of school headmasters, many of who came to be viewed as rebel sympathizers. Naturally this varied dramatically between Goma and Bukavu, where civil society groups adamantly opposed any efforts by the RCD to meddle with the school system (interview with Kahorha).

Instead of suffering a dramatic reduction in capacity, as might have been expected, the educational system in eastern Congo during the war was surprisingly vibrant, increasing enrollment for the entire period between 1993 when the first skirmishes began through 2003, a fact attributed to the Congolese faith in education as a tool for personal advancement (interview with Kahorha; Tull 2004, 213). Unlike the SPLM/A—which adopted foreign curricula for its schools, overtly disavowing Khartoum's educational agenda—the RCD-Goma continued to operate Congolese schools within its territory, using the central government's curriculum in both primary and secondary education.[39] The focus of the educational system was to prepare students to take the centrally controlled final high school exams that determine access to Congolese universities. In fact, during the war, MONUC or United Nations Development Program aircraft would transport the exams to the ministry of education in Kinshasa for evaluation (interview with Kahorha; Tull 2004, 216), generally with no involvement of the rebel civil administration.

The Health System

On health issues the rebels initially appeared interested in taking a more proactive role, sending Dr. Emile Ilunga, the RCD minister of health, to Europe in October 1998 to encourage international aid organizations to set up shop in the Kivus. The strategy did see some initial success as the Belgian government, among others, sent large sums of money for humanitarian purposes to areas under insurgent

---

39. As I discuss in chapter 5, the focus for educational institutions in SPLM/A territory was to prepare students to attend schools in neighboring Kenya and Uganda. Hence the use of foreign curricula.

control (Tull 2004, 125). Upon taking control of the health ministry in the Kivus, the RCD civil administration assumed responsibility for the functioning of the ministry, which had already been limited to playing an oversight role before the conflict (interviews with Ulrich and Martinez). As with the educational system, the bulk of health services under Mobutu and Kabila were provided by nonstate actors, including the churches and international aid organizations. For example, churches provided fully 75 percent of health services in rural areas as early as 1972 (Tull 2004: 217).

The RCD Ministry of Health continued to outsource the actual provision of health services to these nonstate service providers. Insurgent administrators were content limiting their role to monitoring and supporting the health-related activities of the churches and international aid organizations. The Health Ministry eased the registration process for health NGOs, providing limited tax exemptions and helping aid groups bring personnel and medicines across the Rwandan border. In order to regulate the behavior of aid organizations operating within their territory, the insurgency relied on memorandums of understanding that formally limited the projects a specific organization could undertake. In practice, health care providers were generally allowed to select the types of programs they wanted to implement, though the ministry occasionally directed them to conduct distinct health-related campaigns or to focus their efforts in specific areas—requests that most NGOs were willing to oblige knowing too well the consequences of challenging the insurgency's edicts.

Even though the command frequently took credit for the health efforts ongoing within its territory, most health care providers accepted this as a necessary cost of doing work in rebel-controlled areas, and they rarely protested. Indeed, they embraced the greater autonomy their work offered them. Health organizations were astutely aware of the benefits they provided to the rebel organization and that this gave them more latitude than almost any other societal actor. In the words of one informant who worked with an international health organization during the war, "Health care as a commodity is always positively perceived" (interview with Ulrich).

This piecemeal approach to providing health care in the Kivus did provide some relief to civilians during the conflict. NGOs and churches, in essence, maintained a tiered health care system in which many villages had access to minimalist health posts, and urban areas were served by a mix of health centers for basic problems and hospitals for more serious concerns (interview with local medical personnel, Goma). Smaller community organizations also engaged in campaigns to promote awareness about HIV/AIDS, malaria, and other illnesses. Funds for these activities came from a mix of modest user fees, donations from religious institutions, and funds provided by the international donor community. The

conflict did open up new transnational sources of revenue for both church institutions and aid organizations that were savvy enough to tap into international
donor networks. Several churches were even able to use the influx of funds to
modernize hospitals in both Bukavu and Goma (Tull 2004, 218). Personnel
shortages were endemic to most organizations involved in health provision during the war, though the available Congolese staff operating within the system
was generally well trained, a counterintuitive outcome of their having practiced
in areas bereft of any formal health system. According to one foreign aid worker,
this remained true even when Congolese personnel were compared with those
available in neighboring countries (interview with Martinez).

According to the staff of MSF in Goma, good lines of communication characterized interactions with the insurgent Ministry of Health.[40] As one foreign
health worker told me, "The RCD was always very supportive of MSF's health
initiatives; they [the RCD civil administration] have a strong will to create a sense
of predictability" (interview with Ulrich). Generally this assessment of the rebel
leadership held throughout my conversations with people involved in the health
care sector. There was a general sense that though the insurgency devoted few
material resources to improving conditions for health care providers, it did take
seriously the task of administering the plethora of organizations dealing with
health issues within its territory. Indeed, after the signing of the Sun City Peace
agreement in 2002, new protocols required registration and other administrative
tasks to go through Kinshasa instead of Goma, a shift decried as inefficient by
several aid workers in the region. This is not to say that the insurgency put in
place a comprehensive or even coherent system to coordinate the activities of the
different groups operating in the region or that the insurgent administration was
even capable of orchestrating such a program. Rather, it is a testament to the will
of societal actors to prevent the utter collapse of the health care system in eastern
Congo, a role they had been well prepared for after the state withdrew from meeting the health needs of the population under Mobutu.

The failure of the RCD-Goma command to establish effective civilian governance resulted from its inability to adequately deal with several important factors
that affect rebel organizations more generally. There are three main reasons that I
have tried to highlight in the preceding discussion. First, from the beginning the

---

40. MSF is an international NGO that has operated in the Kivus since 1992 providing primary
and secondary care, including support for hospitals. It emphasizes its neutrality and hence is able to
work with government and rebel forces in many different conflict zones. If a minimal level of security
can be achieved, it has a policy of collaborating with the authorities that control a specific piece of
ground regardless of the politics.

leadership was riven by internal factions that had differing visions of the internal organizational strategy for the group, specifically whether they should engage in efforts to win over the local population or focus resources on building their military capacity. Second, before the war, the state had largely withdrawn from the region the insurgents came to control. Administration in eastern Congo was abandoned to multiple nonstate actors that the command failed to co-opt into its governance project despite repeated efforts. And third, the insurgents were never able to shake the perception that they were a monoethnic organization sponsored by a foreign patron. This was a particularly costly mistake because of the contentious ethnic dynamics in the region.

The split of the command and the subsequent affiliation of the RCD-Goma leaders with the Rwandan government structured its fundamental external objective, i.e., capturing Kinshasa. During the short-lived reign of Wamba dia Wamba, the undivided rebellion sought to orchestrate a broader political transformation of the Kivus, which they hoped to export to the rest of the country. However, the RCD-Goma, controlled from the outset by the more militaristic components of the original force, never developed a viable political agenda in the east, relying instead on its coercive capacity to thwart challenges to its rule (Afoaku 2002, 119). The task for any rebel group operating in the Kivus was not to replace a preexisting political authority (as in Sri Lanka) or to construct order where it had never existed before (as in Sudan). Instead, rebel leaders needed to find a way to navigate between disparate political actors that had parcellized elements of state sovereignty between them, not in a neat, cohesive manner but rather with competing modalities of control. This was a task that the Congolese rebels clearly failed to accomplish.

Furthermore, the division between the two factions of the original rebel command diluted the ability of the RCD-Goma to present itself as a multiethnic, indigenous revolution. After the split the new leaders became even more closely aligned with the agenda of the Tutsi regime in Kigali, a political sin that haunted the group till its death in the 2006 election, when the newly created RCD political party could muster only 2 percent of the vote for the former rebel leader and presidential candidate, Azarias Ruberwa. The alignment with Rwanda provided the group with economic opportunities that reduced its motivation to develop mutually beneficial relationships with local social groups. It was this failure to cultivate a local base that led to consistent challenges to rebel rule by violent actors—most prominently the Mai Mai militias—undermining the ability of the command to establish even a minimal system of governance in those areas where its rule was contested.

Nonetheless, the RCD's approach did not represent a fundamental disjuncture from previous modes of financing pursued by earlier political authorities, which also tended to engage with the Congolese citizenry through coercive modalities of rule. Indeed, the insurgency's reliance on external state patrons and transnational capital represented a remarkable degree of continuity with the Mobutu regime's revenue accumulation model and hence reinforced the same brutal and manipulative patterns of state/society relations.

7

COMPARATIVE INSURGENT GOVERNANCE

> **To the degree structures of domination can be demonstrated to operate in comparable ways, they will, other things equal, elicit reactions and patterns of resistance that are also broadly comparable.**
>
> —James Scott, *Domination and the Arts of Resistance*

In the preceding pages I put forth a framework for understanding variation in insurgent governance systems, stressing how a rebel command's interactions with a constellation of actors shape civilian administration through the interactions' influence on specific insurgent structures and governance practices. The previous three chapters illustrated aspects of the framework by examining the range of outcomes produced by the governance efforts of insurgencies in Sri Lanka, Sudan, and the Democratic Republic of Congo. Though the case studies provided observable support for several of the propositions, they do not focus directly on the causal mechanisms that link the various hypotheses to the actual governance outcomes by insurgents. Therefore, in this chapter I focus on each individual proposition, identifying the relevant mechanisms and exploring their applicability to the different case studies. Using this comparative method, I find considerable support for the framework, with some important refinements and qualifications.

One concern is whether the framework has any merit outside the three cases discussed above. It is possible that all three share unspecified similarities that are not common to other contemporary insurgencies. In order to assess the relevance of the framework for understanding cases beyond those discussed above, I also incorporate examples drawn from other recent and contemporary civil wars that had their own distinctive experiences with insurgent governance provision. Bringing in the additional cases can help reveal whether or not the three cases I selected are distinct from the broader universe of insurgent organizations developing civilian governance structures and practices. The evidence presented below corroborates my intuition that the framework does indeed travel beyond the selected cases. The analysis is obviously not designed to be comprehensive but rather serves to highlight commonalities between various contemporary rebellions by looking closely at the distinct mechanisms underlying each hypothesis. This comparative approach demonstrates that despite the deeply contextual nature of most civil wars, as the quote from James Scott above suggests, rebel organizations do face common challenges in their attempts to establish a program for civilian governance that can provide productive comparisons.

Such an approach for assessing the framework has a mix of strengths and weaknesses. On the plus side, a comparative approach is useful for understanding how the mechanisms that undergird the various hypotheses presented in chapter 3 actually function under real-world conditions. On the minus side, despite selecting cases with highly variant outcomes in regard to civilian governance, the analysis was not designed to cover the universe of rebel experiences. In order to do this, it would first be necessary to create a data set of all insurgent groups that develop governance systems or at least to ensure that the sample being discussed was truly representative, a task that remains outside the scope of this project.[1] The additional cases do provide some supplementary support, but since they were selected at random, I make no claims regarding how well they represent the broader universe of insurgent governance systems.

In the assessments that follow, I begin by clearly specifying the causal mechanisms that explain the impact of the various hypotheses on civilian governance. These mechanisms are not discrete but often are linked to each other to produce the observable effect. Nor are they limited to each individual proposition, as certain mechanisms may underline multiple hypotheses. I then draw on evidence from each of the case studies to illuminate the precise dynamics at work. Finally, I look for similar effects in other cases beyond the three under examination in this book to see whether they existed in these conflicts as well.

State Penetration: Habituation and Cooptation

H1a: If an insurgency emerges in a state with minimal penetration into society, it is less likely to develop an effective governance system than one that emerges in a state that penetrated deeply into society.

---

1. Nelson Kasfir is currently undertaking such an effort, but the results are several years away. Once the data set is completed, it will be useful to assess this framework on an independent sample of groups drawn from the Dartmouth project.

H1b: If an insurgency emerges in a state with high penetration into society, it is more likely to be able to co-opt preexisting institutions and networks into its civil administration, thereby improving governance provision.

At least three mechanisms seem to work together to provide support to these two related hypotheses. First, hypothesis 1a has to do with the ingrained political behavior of specific civilian populations regarding the political regime in power. If a "civilian expectations" mechanism does have influence on insurgent governance decisions, then we should observe evidence that (1) civilians made demands on the rebel political authority consistent with their prior relationship to the state authority and (2) the insurgent organization was concerned with civilian feedback, either through overt proclamations by the insurgents or, more directly, through efforts by the rebellion to solicit civilian input. Second, both hypotheses address the preconflict capacity of the state in areas under rebel control during the war. If a "state capacity" mechanism is operational, then we can expect to see (1) evidence of meaningful interactions between the state and civilians living in rebel-controlled areas *before* the conflict and (2) evidence that the insurgent organization sought to use these preexisting state institutions to provide civilian governance or to supplement their own efforts. Finally, hypothesis 1b is concerned with the difficulty of negotiating the broader political environment for a budding insurgent organization. If a "multiplex governance" mechanism is at work in the cases, then we should see evidence of (1) a multifarious political environment with multiple nodes of political power *before* the outbreak of conflict and (2) unsuccessful efforts by rebels to negotiate with these multiple political actors.

The civilian expectations mechanism is most clearly on display in the discussion of the LTTE. The Tamil insurgents had to address expectations from a civilian population accustomed to high levels of public welfare before the war. Civilian demands were both overt and explicit. During the initial confusion following the outbreak of conflict in 1983, a robust debate about the methods of the LTTE broke out, with many in the Tamil community contrasting the nascent insurgency with the relatively sedate politics of the nonviolent leaders of the Tamil movement. In addition, several other militant groups emerged at the same time, often led by more established activists. Many of these leaders criticized the Tigers as youthful, inexperienced, and relatively unsophisticated when it came to addressing the needs of the Tamil community (Jeyaraj 1985). Though it relied heavily on coercion to quiet dissent, the LTTE also went to great lengths to quell Tamil dissatisfaction with living conditions in rebel-controlled areas. When it came into control of a large territorial enclave after the departure of the Indian peacekeeping force, the organization established various structures designed to gather input from civilians and civil society leaders, hoping to mobilize popular will behind the insurgent program. Indeed, the civil administration originated with one such structure, the Tamil Eelam Economic Development Organization (TEEDO), which drew on the expertise of local community leaders. Pressure from civilians led the command to go as far as striking a complicated arrangement with the incumbent state to ensure the continued provision of services to denizens of its territory.

In Southern Sudan, where civilians had little meaningful prior interaction with the state bureaucracy, rebel leaders did not face demands from the civilian population till more than a decade into the insurgency. As one community leader and participant in the struggle stated simply, "To be honest, there was no pressure from the civilian population" (interview with Gideon, Sudan). Eventually, the SPLM/A did face pressure to address civilian needs largely as a result of ad hoc meetings with societal actors representing civilian interests, including religious and church leaders who vigorously decried the abhorrent conditions faced by their parishioners. This led to a process of reform initiated at the national convention in 1994, an outcome of which was the establishment of legislatures at multiple levels with the explicit purpose of culling civilian feedback. However, without the support necessary to function effectively, they remained of little relevance to civilians I spoke with in the region. It is unclear to what degree the process of governance reform was related to popular criticism and to what extent it was a response to internal organizational tensions expressed by ethnic factional leaders. Even if they were simply advancing their own personal agendas in order to bolster their appeal to the international community, these dissidents did frame their criticism of the insurgency as reflecting civilian discontent, a position that resonated with many local community leaders.

The RCD had multiple voices criticizing its rule of eastern Congo, but the organization never took seriously the task of addressing civilian criticism, preferring to rely on more coercive instruments to generate compliance. Though some members of the initial leadership did articulate the need for outreach to the inhabitants of rebel-controlled areas, the organization never developed the appropriate structures that would have made such an effort successful. Indeed, civilian resistance to rebel rule never led to a process of negotiation with the political administration concerning governance issues. Rather, it took on explicitly violent contours through the formation of ethnic militias, in a manner evoking the preconflict resistance by civilians to the incumbent political regime.

This variation in civilian pressure does seem to be accounted for by the effect of the second mechanism, state capacity. The Sri Lankan experience is also illustrative in this regard. As the discussion of the postcolonial state in Sri Lanka demonstrates, the Tamil population had been habituated to expect robust public goods provision by its interactions with an extensive state bureaucracy before the war, which provided generous social services throughout the north and east provinces in which community members were concentrated. Furthermore, when the insurgents came to power, they were able to work with the preexisting state bureaucracy, which allowed them to maintain high levels of service provision throughout the conflict. Through the complicated joint mechanism that meticulously partitioned the education and health systems between insurgent and state structures, the rebels were also able to make their governance system seem legitimate in the eyes of the civilian population. Though civilians often decried the brutality of the insurgency—particularly its brutal methods for stifling internal dissent—the LTTE governance system received widespread popular acceptance, particularly in the northern province, which was more uniformly under rebel control.

In contrast, South Sudan, having long been marginalized by the central government, had few salvageable remnants of the ineffective state bureaucracy. Local communities in the region never had much interaction with the modern Sudanese state, turning instead to traditional and religious leaders to serve authority functions. Local civil society organizations never came into being because the population had little opportunity to develop a capable and consistent challenger to state power. Thus, once the SPLM/A took over, only transnational aid organizations, churches, and traditional leaders were able to articulate a challenge to the insurgent regime, though they were generally more concerned with meeting basic needs and less with ensuring that the local population was represented in political decision making.

The Congolese political arena before the war was distinct from both the Sudanese and Sri Lankan cases. By contrast with Sudan, which lacked governmental institutions, civilian governance in D.R. Congo had been partitioned between a variety of societal actors who took over many of the tasks of the failing state bureaucracy. Rather than abandon the state altogether, many worked with state agents to maintain the veneer of governmental control despite the lack of any real investments by the authorities in Kinshasa. In this case, the third mechanism, multiplex governance, is most relevant. Upon taking control in eastern Congo, the RCD insurgents found themselves confronted by a complex political environment that they consistently failed to comprehend. Though they did manage to appropriate the remnants of the state bureaucracy, occasionally even receiving accolades for their control of these institutions, insurgent administrators were unable to develop a comprehensive civilian governance system because their efforts to incorporate other important societal actors were consistently rebuffed.

If we look to other cases to assess the validity of hypotheses 1a and 1b, there does seem to be evidence suggesting that these dynamics are not limited solely to the above three cases. Multiple rebellions operating in areas of low state penetration have struggled to develop effective governance systems, including the MLC in Congo, as well as groups such as the Communist Party of Burma (CPB) (Lintner 1990, 40–42), the Kurdish Democratic Party (KDP) in Iraq (Romano 2004, 153), and Resistência Nacional Moçambicana (RENAMO) in Mozambique (T. Young 1997, 134). This contrasts with several insurgent organizations that operated in areas of high state penetration and were able to develop an effective civilian governance capacity, including the FMLN in El Salvador and Gerakan Aceh Merdeka (GAM) in Indonesia (McClintock 1998; International Crisis Group 2001). GAM, for example, adopted an approach reminiscent of the LTTE in responding to civilian demands, allowing the state to continue providing certain services while retaining control over the security system and taxation apparatus. According to the International Crisis Group (ICG) (2001, 13), GAM allowed "state health and education programs to continue in areas under its control." At the same time, "GAM members officiate[d] over other legal and social issues and collect[ed] taxes, said to be eight per cent, on transactions such as land purchases."

Secessionism and Ethnonationalism

> **H2: If the insurgency is secessionist or ethnonationalist, it is more likely to develop an effective system of governance than groups that seek to capture power at the center.**

As with hypothesis 1, several mechanisms seem to account for the impact of this hypothesis. The proposition posits that the strategic objective of an insurgency will affect its ability and desire to address civilian needs. There are two contrary scenarios for how a "strategic objective" mechanism could unfold. First, reformist (center-seeking) insurgent leaders in charge of the allocation of resources within the organization believe that devoting resources to civilian governance is counterproductive as it diverts resources from the military objective of capturing power at the center. If this is occurring, we should observe evidence that the organization (1) does not devote financial or human resources to the civilian governance system at the outset of the rebellion as they have no intention of making any long-term claims to territory and (2) does not attempt to operate within a specific territory but rather allows military strategy and conflict dynamics to determine its areas of operation. Conversely, if the mechanism is correct, then for an organization with a secessionist agenda, we should see (1) that a particular territorial space has significance beyond its military utility and (2) that the organization devotes resources to portray itself as the "national" government among a target segment of the population.

The hypothesis also incorporates an "insurgent promises" mechanism, essentially the inverse of the civilian expectations mechanism. If this is relevant, we can expect that promises made by reformist insurgencies to improve the conditions of civilians are worded in a way to condition inhabitants of rebel territory to expect an improvement in their living conditions only *after* that organization takes power in the center. Again, conversely, we might expect to see that for a secessionist insurgency, efforts are made to condition civilians to view the insurgent organization as already constituting *the* government during the war itself.

In the Congolese war, the strategic objective mechanism certainly provides part of the explanation of the insurgency's failure to develop effective civilian governance. Leaders of the RCD and its offshoots always viewed their ultimate objective as the capture of power in Kinshasa, an outcome they expected to occur quickly as a result of their prior experiences with the AFDL insurgency. The command was so confident of a quick victory that the political wing of the organization was not even brought together until two weeks after the start of fighting. The leadership consistently framed the struggle in national terms, devoting few resources to stabilizing life in the vast areas it soon came to control. Furthermore, the RCD had little interest in retaining control over a specific area within Congo. Instead, territorial control was purely a function of military expediency, and the organization's control of various areas of eastern Congo shifted regularly, and often dramatically, as a result.

In contrast, the LTTE's governance programs were always driven by the command's desire to demonstrate its credentials for ruling its own Tamil state to both its local and diasporic populations as well as to the international community. By claiming a mandate to represent the Tamil people and framing its struggle in a secessionist manner, the insurgency went to great lengths to mimic the behavior and appearance of a traditional nation-state. For example, from its founding, the organization incorporated the term "Eelam", the name given to the wished-for Tamil homeland, demonstrating its attachment to, and desire to represent, a particular piece of territory within Sri Lanka. The insurgents also limited their military efforts to this area, only rarely venturing outside the claimed historical homeland and never attempting to control territory outside its boundaries.

The SPLM/A provides a more ambiguous example. On one side, the organization sought to create the appearance of an autonomous zone in the south of the country, prominently labeling territory under its control New Sudan and adopting its own flag, currency, and other nationalist symbols. Students in areas of South Sudan under rebel control were taught to view Garang as the president of New Sudan and the SPLM as the government. However, the appellation New Sudan could be interpreted as either the name for the territory that the organization hoped to carve out from the larger state shell or a reference to the larger goal of transforming the entire country. Garang strategically worked both positions, purposefully remaining ambiguous in order to take advantage of the loyalty secessionist movements can engender among a defined population while leaving the door open for the more ambitious political project of transforming Sudan itself. Toward this end, the organization worked to cultivate other insurgent efforts outside South Sudan, including in Darfur and the Nuba Mountains, demonstrating its willingness to expand the theater of operation outside the traditional homelands associated with SPLM/A leaders. However, the fact that the insurgency adopted a more overtly secessionist position to compete with the forces of the openly secessionist SSIM lends some support to the impact of secessionist pressures. In fact, it was only as a result of this competition that the rebel command began to initiate a process of governance reform, which led to the establishment of the Civil Administration of New Sudan in 1994.

Evidence of the second mechanism, insurgent promises, demonstrates a similar ambiguity in the Sudanese case. Reformist insurgencies generally make promises to improve civilian welfare only after victory at the center, while those with a secessionist agenda often promise to improve living conditions soon after coming into control of territory. Thus the strategic objective articulated by insurgent leaders is a signal to potential supporters regarding the timelines by which the insurgency intends to produce improvements in civilian livelihoods. Both time horizons have an impact on civilian expectations and affect the nature of the demands they are likely to make on the insurgent command. For example, on one side, Garang (1992) frequently spoke of a future multiethnic, multireligious, and democratic Sudan as the goal of the SPLM/A. In this way his promises resemble those made by many other reformist insurgencies in which the time horizon for fulfillment is always the day after victory. However, in South Sudan, civilians were also taught to view the insurgent organization as the legitimate sovereign in areas it controlled, and this approach generated more immediate expectations regarding living conditions within rebel territory.

In this way the SPLM/A resembles the LTTE under Vellupillai Prabhakharan, who went to great lengths to encourage civilians to view the organization as the official government of the northeast province. The assumption was that Tamil civilians should look to the insurgent administrators to meet their basic needs as the Sri Lankan government once had. Prabhakharan and other insurgent leaders even sought to encourage practices of civic engagement within their territory, organizing an annual Heroes Week to commemorate the fallen (Roberts 2009). In contrast, the undivided RCD under Wamba dia Wamba did produce a series of documents that laid out his vision for a transformation of the country according to democratic principles, but as with the SPLM/A, no timeline was ever produced for the fulfillment of such lofty ambitions. Once the organization was divided, the reconstituted RCD-Goma command never devoted much attention to clarifying its governing agenda, articulating few promises regarding civilian welfare, most with little if any substance. Throughout its existence, the RCD retained a steady focus on capturing power in Kinshasa, never once expecting to get bogged down in the east for the entirety of the war, as eventually happened.

Many other secessionist rebellions have exhibited a similar dynamic. In Somalia, where the Somali National Movement (SNM) began fighting in 1988, the rebellion made a successful transition to ruling what became the embryonic state of Somaliland, having put in place governance structures before the collapse of the incumbent state (Bradbury 2008). Other secessionist groups—such as the Bakonzo rebellion in Uganda, GAM, the KDP, and the Eritrean People's Liberation Front (EPLF)—also developed governance structures of impressive sophistication. Of course, not every secessionist organization will develop effective governance systems—the Moro National Liberation Front (MNLF) in the Philippines stands as one example—but secessionist and ethnonationalist groups do seem to have multiple incentives to devote attention and resources to civilian governance. On the other side, countless center-seeking groups that controlled territory—including the CPB in Burma, the NPFL in Liberia, and the RUF in Sierra Leone—struggled to develop effective governing structures within areas under their control, focusing their resources instead on the military objective of capturing the capital city.

Ideology

H3: If an insurgency chooses to implement a Maoist organizational structure, it is more likely to develop an effective governance system.

There are two general and two specific mechanisms that are likely to explain the effect of this hypothesis, all drawn from Mao's theory of guerrilla warfare. Rather than relying on hit-and-run tactics, Mao called for conventional warfare against incumbents that required the marshaling of substantial resources and the holding of territory from which to launch such attacks. He also advocated that insurgents develop effective civilian governance capabilities to win the support of inhabitants in the territories they controlled. Mao also prescribed two specific organizational strategies. First, he emphasized the need for a prolonged period of political mobilization to educate the population on the goals of the insurgency. If a "political mobilization" mechanism is valid, then we should observe (1) evidence in the organization's propaganda and public rhetoric that popular support was indeed an important organizational concern and (2) structures put in place to foster noncoercive participation with the insurgent organization. Second, Mao emphasized the importance of disciplined troops who did not behave in ways that ostracized the civilian population. If a "cadre discipline" mechanism is functioning, we should see evidence that indiscipline by rebel cadres was an important concern for the command.

These mechanisms work together to improve civilian governance outcomes. Insurgents who fight using solely hit-and-run tactics can only affect civilian livelihoods for the worse because governance remains the preserve of the incumbent. In contrast, holding territory requires the development of a security force to demonstrate insurgent control, which is, of course, an elemental building block in a broader system of governance. Ensuring troop discipline signals to the public that the organization has the ability to mediate the use of violence within its territory. Finally, devoting personnel to political mobilization is necessary to educate the public about the organization's intentions so as not to ostracize its potential base of support. But it also requires the organization to develop structures to mobilize the population—structures that can be repurposed for other governance concerns such as providing education, delivering public health messages, delivering medications, and so on.

To be clear, the official ideological proclamations of insurgent leaders are of little concern. Rather, the focus must be on the actual internal organizational strategy adopted by the leadership, as well as its ability to put that strategy into practice. All three insurgencies studied here did draw on Maoist theories of political mobilization, but they differed strikingly in their commitment and ability to implement the various components outlined above. Regarding the general mechanisms, all three did attempt to fight conventional wars, building up large armies capable of engaging in direct and sustained battles with the incumbent authority and holding territory for this purpose. In each of these territories, the insurgents also chose to develop civilian governance structures to demonstrate their control, though as we have seen, the outcomes were highly divergent.

For the RCD, the academically oriented faction under the leadership of Wamba dia Wamba went to great lengths to tout its adherence to an extended program of peasant outreach in line with the political mobilization mechanism. However, the weakness of the political wing within the command and Wamba dia Wamba's early ejection meant that the more militarist component quickly came to the fore, with little interest in engaging in the difficult task of winning popular support through mobilization efforts. Structures to generate civilian participation were never developed, a fact that demonstrated the relative lack of concern the insurgency had for popular support. Furthermore, regarding the discipline of the cadre, the insurgency had notoriously poor control over its troops, and reports of civilian abuse were widespread in areas under rebel control. RCD-Goma struggles to establish effective governance structures reflect these inadequacies.

The SPLM/A engagement with Maoist strategies emerged out of its early dependence on the Marxist Dergue regime in neighboring Ethiopia. From early on in its lifespan, the insurgency claimed a Maoist organizational strategy. But as demonstrated in the case study, the command's willingness to actually divert resources to peasant mobilization did not manifest until well into the war. The LTTE's relationship with Maoist strategies is more complex. Initially the group, like many ethnonationalist insurgents, espoused a commitment to Tamil nationalism blended with leftist politics. However, there is little evidence that it took seriously the task of mobilizing popular support. Only when it came into control of vast territories after the departure of the Indian peacekeepers do we see a corresponding increase in civilian mobilization efforts. Once in control of territory, however, both the Sri Lankan and Sudanese insurgencies did draw on one aspect of Maoist strategy, cadre discipline. In particular, both groups placed severe prohibitions on their cadres regarding the treatment of civilians so as not to ostracize the rebellions from their prospective civilian bases of support, instead favoring an approach that sought to limit and codify the behavior of their respective army personnel.

The most striking support for the efficacy of a Maoist organizational strategy is evident in the case of a right-wing insurgency that sided with the NATO alliance during the Cold War, the União Nacional para a Independência Total de Angola (UNITA). Under the coldly calculating leadership of Jonas Savimbi, UNITA engaged in effective and regular political mobilization campaigns, creating structures within the civil administration specifically for this purpose (Potgieter 2000, 258; Burke 1984). Furthermore, despite their ferociousness in battle, the organization's cadres were widely viewed as well trained and disciplined, particularly in their interactions with their primary base of support, members of the Ovimbundu community (Burke 1984). As a result, according to one observer (Radu 1990, 30), "UNITA has been most successful in establishing an effective state-within-a-state," providing "schools with a centralized curriculum, medical facilities, food production and distributions." In the Terras Libres de Angola (Free Lands of Angola), the name given to rebel-controlled territories, the organization established an impressive educational system:

> UNITA established 22 secondary schools in the areas they occupied, almost 700 primary schools, with 7,127 teachers and 224,881 students. Dozens of UNITA students were sent abroad to study at universities.…The main focus of the education programme abroad was medical, engineering, and agricultural skills, necessary to ensure

UNITA's self-reliance and development of parallel hierarchies to sustain its insurgency. (Potgieter 2000, 262).

Insurgent-controlled territory in 1987 housed eleven thousand rebels and family members, to whom the group provided educational, social, economic, and health services (Heywood 1989, 60).

Other groups that relied on Maoist organizational strategies—including the FARC in Colombia, the Communist Party of Nepal-Maoist (CPN-M), and Sendero Luminoso (SL, Shining Path) in Peru—also seem to lend support to the hypothesis. Each of these groups did develop significant civilian governance structures drawing on Maoist principals of peasant mobilization and discipline within the rebel organization.

A closer look at the case of Nepal is useful as it shows the limits of such organizational strategies, especially when insurgents operate in rural areas that were minimally incorporated into the state bureaucracy before the conflict. One observer noted that the insurgents "set up People's Courts which look into cases and [give] verdicts" by encouraging "local commanders to take judicial action" (Rajamohan 2004, 3), an assessment supported by others who have studied the organization's judicial system (Sivakumaran 2009). However, little was done to provide other public services to the rural population, which had long been marginalized by the government in Kathmandu. According to one CPN-M cadre, the party had fewer than twenty medical personnel who could function as doctors, a strikingly low number considering the size of the terrain and depth of poverty (Thapa 2005, 233). And the insurgents did little to provide education, viewing teachers as a threat to their political agenda. As reported by Somini Sengupta (2005), a journalist who visited the rebel-controlled region, "the number of children who showed up for year-end exams had dropped by nearly half [since the start of the war]." Furthermore, in one town under rebel control, "no one in the last two years had passed the national 10th-grade matriculation exam, a benchmark recognized as the completion of formal schooling."

Internal Cleavages

H4a: If an insurgency is able to form a unified political command either through subjugating competing factions or through incorporating them into a single command, it is more likely to develop an effective system of governance than an organization riven by multiple and competing poles of power.

H4b: If an insurgency fails to compensate minority factions through the design of the civil administration, a rupture is probable.

There are two related mechanisms that account for the impact of hypothesis 4a. First, a "rivals" mechanism seeks to explain the effect of competition—both for control within the organization and for control over territory by other violent groups—on civilian governance outcomes. If this mechanism is occurring, we should observe evidence that (1) such rivals articulate grievances related to civilian treatment to challenge the leadership and (2) such claims lead various political actors, including civilians, to choose between the two sides, undermining support for the original faction. Second, an "organizational capacity" mechanism addresses the impact of such rivals on the internal structure of the organization—specifically, its ability to actualize its agenda for civilian governance. If this is valid, we should see that one of two scenarios has transpired based on the response by the leadership to the rival claimants to power. First, a rival's presence forces a restructuring of the organization to better address civilian needs. If this occurs, we should see evidence that competition leads to the development of new structures designed to address civilian governance concerns. Alternatively, the presence of rivals could further undermine the capacity of the organization to address civilian governance. If this effect is unfolding, then we should see either (1) that the presence of rivals leads to disarray within the organization with direct impacts on the governance of civilians or (2) that it leads the organization to direct resources toward the military wing to subdue such challenges.

Evidence of the rivals mechanism was most evident in Sudan during the split between the various factions of the SPLM/A. The leaders of the Nuer faction under Riek Machar initially took control of huge territories away from the original organization when they split in 1991. The impact was to pressure the remaining forces under Garang's control to focus attention on the military struggle in order to regain the territory lost to both the Machar faction and the Khartoum government, which used the split between the two southern factions to bolster its military operations. Machar immediately set out to form alliances with other political actors operating throughout the south. Portraying the SPLM/A under Garang as undemocratic and unconcerned with civilian welfare, his strategy of wooing other societal actors, primarily INGOs, was initially successful, and he was able to divert significant resources away from the original insurgent organization. Equally important, Machar's demands resonated with segments of the civilian population unhappy with the rule of Garang, undercutting the ability of the original faction to generate collaboration. His verbal assaults were particularly effective with the Nuer people, many of whom had long chafed under what they perceived as Dinka domination within the southern rebellion.

However, the mainstream faction led by Garang responded to this competition seriously, and as the organizational capacity mechanism suggests, began a process to restructure the SPLM/A to better meet the needs of its civilian subjects. The split that ripped apart the organization had much to do with the failure of the leadership to adequately design structures that could rectify the perceived imbalance between the dominant ethnic community and minority communities. By building a civil administration that devolved governance decisions to the local level, the SPLM/A was able to prove to the various Southern Sudanese ethnic factions that its actions to empower the local level were more than rhetorical. Garang's response to the challenge posed by the rival SSIM caused support for Machar's organization to wither away and eventually led to a rapprochement between the two leaders.

The rivals and organizational capacity mechanisms also help account for the success of the LTTE in Sri Lanka. Early in its existence, the insurgency expended considerable efforts to brutally eliminate any rivals to its claim to be the sole representative of the Tamil movement in the northeast. By clearing the political space before gaining control of territory, the command was able to devote more attention to civilian governance issues and fewer resources to suppressing violent challengers to its rule.

The two mechanisms also help explain the eventual split that fatally weakened the LTTE organization. The reduction in fighting that followed the 2002 ceasefire brought to the fore long-dormant tensions between the eastern and northern factions. Since control over the eastern territories remained divided between the government and the insurgents, the rebel command was incapable of expanding its civil administrative capacity to the same extent it had in its northern holdings. This led to significant discontent with the overall conditions of life for civilians in the east, particularly in the aftermath of the ceasefire, when expectations for improvement in social conditions peaked. Furthermore, the command's attempt to centralize control, moving away from the relatively autonomous design that had defined the organizational structure during periods of active fighting, was poorly received by eastern commanders, who resented the northern leadership's centralizing impulses. Ultimately these events produced the debilitating split in the group's command. The eastern faction under the command of the LTTE number two, Colonel Karuna Amman, cited these inequalities in governance provision, as well as the centralization efforts, as the key motivating factors for its actions (Jeyaraj 2004).

In contrast, the RCD command faced both severe internal challenges to its control that led to multiple splits and challenges from other violent militant groups, including those led by former RCD leaders. Internal challenges undermined the ability of the organization to develop its civilian governance efforts since it was constantly concerned with putting down these inner revolts. Internal divisions within the command also tended to percolate throughout the organization, reducing the ability of the dominant faction of the RCD to implement a single political agenda and maintain organizational discipline. At the same time, external rivals sought to legitimate their existence by expressing empathy with civilian discontent. This led the RCD-Goma, the reconstituted entity, to devote more and more resources to its military wing for the purpose of suppressing such challenges.

The experiences of UNITA and Colombia's long-running FARC insurgency lend further support to the importance of a unified command. For most of their existence, both insurgencies had unified commands that consistently maintained a hierarchical organizational structure capable of implementing a specific political program in regard to civilian governance, with considerable success (Burke 1984; Arjona 2009a, 2009c). On the opposite side, consider the case of the MNLF in the Philippines. Operating in an area with a high degree of state penetration and openly professing a secessionist agenda, the budding insurgency faced potentially favorable conditions for the development of an effective civilian governance system. Instead of building on these advantages, the MNLF fell victim to infighting, and multiple factions began to compete for control of the leadership, undermining its ability to implement a coherent system of civilian governance. A split by the more conservative faction (what became the Moro Islamic Liberation Front) forced the original command to devote its attention and resources to dealing with internal squabbles. Consequently, governance efforts were abridged, and civilian welfare suffered as a result (International Crisis Group 2004, 4).

Conflict Intensity

H5: If a civil war exhibits periods of relative peace—through either a stalemate or a ceasefire—the insurgents are more likely to devote resources to the civil administration, and this results in a more effective governance system over time.

Several mechanisms also account for the effect of hypothesis 5. The primary mechanism has to do with the organization's distribution of resources during this period. If a "resource allocation" mechanism is at work, we should see an increase in resources, both material and personnel, devoted to civilian governance structures as a result of lulls in fighting. Contributing to the dynamic are two supplemental mechanisms. A "stability" mechanism addresses the impact of reduced fighting on relief and development efforts. If this mechanism is at work, during pauses in fighting, we should observe an influx of actors, both national and international, engaging in humanitarian activities in rebel-controlled areas. And finally, we see a variation of the civilian expectations mechanism; in this case, civilian populations enjoying a reprieve from the fighting are likely to make additional demands on the insurgent organization to improve governance provision. If a "peace dividends" mechanism is in effect, we should observe (1) that the civilian population or societal leaders articulate explicit demands for improvements in their material conditions and (2) that the insurgents make efforts to address these demands.

The Sri Lankan case provides evidence of all three mechanisms at work but also demonstrates the relative frailty of this proposition. After the ceasefire in 2001, the LTTE did devote a larger share of its resources to its civilian governance efforts. The civil administration was expanded, and new structures came into being as the organization sought to professionalize its efforts, with considerable success. The command devoted a large number of personnel, including many high-level commanders and experienced cadres, to staff these new institutions (interview with Puleedevan). The political space in the northeast also opened as a result of the ceasefire, and civilian voices were more willing to openly criticize the insurgency, demanding an improvement in their conditions after two decades of battle (interview with Miller). Finally, for the first time, a large number of NGOs entered Tiger territory, where they supplemented the efforts of the insurgent civil administration. The net effect of these three mechanisms was to increase the capacity of the LTTE governance system to a level never achieved before, a situation that persisted until fighting resumed in 2007.

The Sudanese rebels also devoted considerable attention to governance issues in the years following the ceasefire in 2002. For the next three years, while SPLM leaders negotiated a comprehensive peace agreement with the government in Khartoum, the organization devoted substantial resources to develop the capacity of its civil administration. For the first time the organization sought to provide more than a judiciary and police force within territory under its control. Plans were put in place to increase SPLM involvement in almost every public sector, and the organization worked to gain control over the increased number of NGOs engaging in relief and development efforts within the region (Branch and Mampilly 2005). Furthermore, the political space in South Sudan cracked open, and numerous newspapers and other media venues for expressing civilian discontent with both the government and insurgent regimes emerged.

The Congolese case does not provide much evidence for any of the three mechanisms because fighting levels generally remained high, even after the 1999

Lusaka ceasefire agreement that first brought together the major belligerents to negotiate the entrance of a UN peacekeeping force (Autesserre 2008). Even after the official end of the war in 2003—when the RCD-Goma retained control of large areas of the east, including several key towns—the organization did little to expand its governance capacity in areas under its control. Rebel leaders focused their resources on transforming the RCD into a political party, with the goal of being competitive in the national elections that eventually took place in 2006. Furthermore, the organization did little to open the political space in the Kivus, consistently resorting to coercive means to subdue any challenges to its control.

Though it does seem that periodic lulls in fighting can lead to improvements in civilian governance efforts, the overall impact of such periods is less durable than initially theorized because the expansion of insurgent administrative capacity is dependent on the political events that follow. Thus in Sudan, where the 2005 comprehensive peace agreement followed the ceasefire, the expanded civil administration went on to become the basis of the new Government of South Sudan that took control of the semiautonomous territory. This contrasts with the case of Sri Lanka, where fighting recommenced in 2007 and quickly led to a drastic reduction in the LTTE's governance capacity as more and more areas fell under the control of the government or allied militias. As ceasefires break down and violent skirmishes inevitably break out, rebel organizations readily abandon governance efforts to better deal with more immediate military concerns; this demonstrates the primacy of the military struggle in structuring the relationship between rebels and their civilian denizens. To paraphrase Mao, the military struggle must always trump civilian governance efforts. Though other insurgencies, such as the FARC in Colombia, did witness a similar aggrandizement of their civilian governance systems during periods of reduced conflict, the durability of this effect was similarly limited once fighting recommenced.

Supporters

H6: If an insurgency is able to co-opt humanitarian organizations into its governance project, then it is more likely to develop an effective system of governance.

The mechanism involved in this hypothesis has to do with the insurgent organization's efforts to co-opt various aid organizations concerned with relief and development efforts into its broader political program. If a "co-optation" mechanism is present, then we should see evidence that (1) the insurgent organization develops structures within its civil administration able to coordinate the activities of aid organizations and (2) humanitarian organizations accept direction from the insurgent administration.

In all three cases, the insurgents attempted—to varying degrees and with differing levels of success—to co-opt humanitarian actors into their civilian governance projects. The SPLM/A was the most successful in this regard, recruiting and manipulating humanitarian organizations to serve instrumental purposes in propagating rebel rule. The insurgency relied on religious aid organizations and foreign NGOs to support the welfare of the civilian population, using a variety of strategies to insert rebel political structures between aid operations and the civilian population they targeted. Most effectively, the organization used memorandums of understanding to specify precise activities and areas of operation for aid organizations seeking to work in rebel-controlled areas of South Sudan. Though resented by many, most NGOs eventually fell in line, fearful of the consequences of failing to heed the insurgency's directives. The effect was to provide the command an opportunity to lay claim to relief and development efforts without having to devote its own meager resources to civilian welfare issues.

The LTTE also attempted to co-opt foreign aid organizations into their civilian governance efforts, particularly after the ceasefire in 2002, when such organizations entered Tiger-controlled areas in large numbers. By establishing structures such as the Planning and Development Secretariat to regulate the recovery process, the organization initially received plaudits from the international community, and international agencies and foreign aid organizations willingly worked with the civil administration. This process accelerated after the tsunami of 2004. Through the co-optation of development efforts the insurgency was able to accomplish two important goals. First, it sought to expand its civilian governance efforts by funneling international aid to areas that previously had remained out of its reach. Second, it sought to delink the civil administration from its reliance on state institutions by replacing government support with international aid (Mampilly 2009). Generally these efforts did improve the quality of life for civilians in LTTE territory, at least until the outbreak of renewed fighting.

Even the RCD-Goma was able to co-opt humanitarian organizations to a degree. What little credit the insurgency deserves in meeting the needs of civilians during the war is limited to its support for the efforts of foreign aid organizations. Organizations such as Médecins Sans Frontières willingly worked with the rebel civil administration to provide much-needed health services to the affected population. In exchange, the insurgents expedited the registration process and provided limited tax exemptions to encourage aid organizations to operate in areas under their control. However, the insurgency did little to support similar humanitarian efforts orchestrated by religious institutions, as church leaders consistently rebuffed the structures developed by the organization for this purpose.

Though not generally considered humanitarian actors, traditional leaders also played an important role in meeting basic civilian needs in both Congo and Sudan, as they have done in many conflicts around the world. For this reason insurgent leaders in both cases recognized the value of co-opting traditional leaders to support the rebel program. Indeed, the leaders went to great lengths to incorporate traditional authority structures into their civilian governance efforts. In Sudan traditional leaders were expected to rally their community to contribute to the war effort by providing material support and recruits to the rebel organization. They were also given prominent roles within the SPLM judiciary, helping to adjudicate civilian disputes.

The RCD-Goma also worked to co-opt traditional leaders, with limited success. For example, the insurgency supported the development of the barza intercommunautaire, a forum for traditional leaders that played an important role in resolving disputes in North Kivu during the war, one of the few positive contributions the insurgency made to promoting social order. Attempts to incorporate traditional authorities are also evident in many other cases. RENAMO in Mozambique relied heavily on traditional authorities to govern the civilian population (Weinstein 2007, 181). And in East Timor, insurgent leaders sought to manipulate the outsize influence of traditional leaders by incorporating them into their governance programs (Kilcullen 2009, 199). Even the Taliban in Afghanistan has worked assiduously to win over the loyalty of traditional leaders by granting them positions of power within its political arm (Khapalwak 2010).

Competitors

H7: If an insurgent leadership faces challenges to its rule from local and transnational civil society actors, then it may develop a more effective system of governance under certain conditions.

Two mechanisms are relevant for understanding the impact of competitors on insurgent governance efforts. First, in regard to transnational human rights networks, an "international pressure" mechanism accounts for the impact of such networks on insurgent behavior. If this mechanism is operating, we should see (1) evidence of pressure from human rights activists or religious institutions on an insurgent group regarding civilian treatment and (2) evidence that the organization responded to such challenges without resorting to coercive means. A second mechanism, related to the co-optation mechanism described above, addresses insurgent efforts to respond to criticism from local societal actors. If a "switching sides" mechanism is valid in this context, we should observe (1) efforts by insurgents to incorporate *critical* societal actors into their broader political project and (2) that such actors willingly cooperate with insurgent efforts.

In all three cases, rebel regimes constantly faced pressure from both local and transnational actors regarding their treatment of civilians. And all three insurgencies responded to such pressure in distinct ways. Evidence of the switching sides and international pressure mechanisms are evident in both the LTTE and SPLM/A cases. For example, in both countries, religious leaders came to play a significant role in criticizing the rule of the insurgent organization. Christian priests often viewed themselves as the primary protectors of civilian welfare, openly speaking out against abuses perpetrated by insurgent cadres. In both cases, commands worked to mitigate the negative effects of such challenges, providing regular opportunities for religious leaders to present their concerns to rebel commanders. Though it would be wrong to suggest that religious leaders became uncritical boosters of either rebellion, they did take advantage of these opportunities to air their concerns.

Priests I spoke with in both countries made it very clear that while they were willing to engage with the rebel administrators, they consistently viewed their mandate to be the protectors of civilians rather than simply boosters for the insurgent cause. In the words of one Sudanese priest who lived through the worst days of the fighting, "The church could not be separated from the people. We supported them [the SPLM] only because we were in their territory" (interview with Okello). However, such a conditional endorsement of the insurgency does not escape the reality that as a result of overtures by the rebel command, religious leaders did tone down their public criticism, instead working with administrators to address civilian concerns. Collaboration was aided by the brutal counterinsurgency strategies pursued by both the Sri Lankan and Sudanese governments. These debilitating offensives generated mutual concerns between the insurgency and societal leaders regarding civilian welfare and hence common ground between the two.

In both cases, however, the decision by the insurgency to take seriously critical voices tended to fluctuate as a result of certain factors unaccounted for by the mechanism. For example, in contrast to their relative deference to religious leaders, the LTTE took a much harsher approach to intellectuals who criticized its treatment of Tamil civilians. In 1989 the organization killed Rajini Thiranagama, a leading academic at the University of Jaffna and a frequent critic of the organization through her work with the University Teachers for Human Rights (Hoole et al. 1990). The organization did try to incorporate other societal voices, including women's, into its political project. But despite accounts by pro-LTTE figures like Adele Balasingham (2001), the leader of the organization's women's wing, these structures did little to provide women an autonomous voice within the organization. Members of the women's wing were largely expected to toe the organization's line, and their numbers in the leadership were limited even though female fighters constituted approximately 30 percent of the cadre. As a reflection of their sheltered lives within the rebellion, female fighters received no exposure to various strands of global feminism and were even unaware of the presence of women in other violent movements around the world (interview with De Mel).

The Sudan case also provides evidence of the international pressure mechanism. Negative international pressure regarding civilian treatment can undermine the willingness of aid organizations, international agencies, and even MNCs to work with a specific rebel organization. Such pressure can be costly for insurgents, affecting their ability to take advantage of the financial and other resources such relationships provide. This case also illustrates the limitations of this mechanism, as it required two compounding idiosyncratic factors for this mechanism to have an impact, in this case the presence of a rival and the SPLM/A's relative dependence on transnational aid to meet civilian needs. The split between the two main ethnic factions caused a division among human rights activists, many of whom hoped the faction under Machar would be more attuned to the needs of civilians affected by the fighting. In general, though there is some evidence that local and transnational civil society actors were able to alter rebel behavior by mobilizing international pressure, the precise mechanism that brought about this transformation remains unclear. Only by looking at a much larger sample and specifying various mechanisms that could make international pressure more effective are we likely to decipher the precise dynamics at work.

In contrast, the Congolese case provides a vivid example of the failure to incorporate such competitors. Despite the significant military force the group was capable of mustering, it never developed the appropriate structures to co-opt the key societal figures that it needed to develop into a legitimate political authority. Instead, its presence was constantly challenged by an array of civil society actors including religious leaders, traditional authorities, and members of local and international NGOs, all of whom criticized the behavior of the insurgency in a variety of local and international forums. I was struck, for example, when meeting with prominent leaders of Kivutien civil society, that many were not shy in condemning the rebel organization, often leveling criticisms that targeted the insurgency's presumed Tutsi bias. In addition, the RCD-Goma faced a widespread revolt led by Christian leaders that delivered a painful blow to its ability to generate popular support among the civilian population. And traditional leaders went further, aligning with Mai Mai militias to directly challenge the organization's control of territory. The net effect of such competitors was to undermine popular support for the insurgency, directly hindering its ability to establish an effective civilian governance capacity.

The purpose of this chapter was to provide an assessment of the framework developed in chapter 3 through a comparative analysis of the three cases, with additional evidence brought in from other insurgencies around the world. Since rebel governance provision will always entail a labyrinthine set of interactions among many concerned actors, it is unlikely that a single dimension would account for the majority of the variation we witness between cases. What the chapter demonstrates is that rebel organizations face multiple comparable challenges that shape the nature of their governance projects. By adopting a systematic approach toward understanding how insurgent leaders operating in contemporary conflict zones make decisions, we can understand the impact for civilian welfare that these decisions can have.

Of course, every conflict has its own historical context and produces its own dynamics that determine the nature of the civilian/rebel relationship. Too often, however, such complexity is used as an excuse for ignoring the potential for engagement with the nonstate systems that regulate civilian lives in contemporary war zones. Examining the common motivations and challenges faced by the diverse actors involved in today's civil wars can help make sense of the commonalities that do exist between cases For those concerned with navigating this treacherous terrain, it can also provide some clarity on how best to access populations caught behind rebel lines.

8

RULES AND RESISTANCE

New Agendas for Studying Insurgency
and Governance

**When history is written as it ought to be written, it is the moderation
and long patience of the masses at which men will wonder, not their
ferocity.**

—C. L. R. James, *The Black Jacobins*

**Despite the fact that some 90 percent of all casualties today are
civilians, that more children die in war than soldiers, and that the
front lines run through average citizens' homes and livelihoods, texts
on war, museums, military novels, art, and statues all help reinforce
the idea and the ideal that war is about male soldiering.**

—Carolyn Nordstrom, *Shadows of War*

Narratives of war often spotlight the martial elements. Strategy, weaponry, soldiering, violence, and casualties constitute the basic jargon with which we discuss
civil war, privileging the bellicose over the humdrum of daily life. This is true
even in the face of evidence that the costs of war are disproportionately borne
by those with no military ties beyond living in areas where the conflict is active,
as Carolyn Nordstrom eloquently notes above. Casualty numbers, which include
more civilians than combatants, reflect this simple reality.

Indeed, studies have confirmed that "battle deaths," the number killed by military operations, including soldiers and civilians—represent only a fraction of the
total war-related deaths that conflicts commonly produce. Though the number
of dead illustrates only one facet of the impact of warfare on civilians, it is a useful measure for providing some sense of the relative distribution of suffering.
For example, as Bethany Lacina and Nils Petter Gleditsch (2005, 156) note, while
estimates of the total killed during the Congolese civil war reach over 2.5 million,
only about 6 percent, or fewer than 150,000, of these were attributable to direct combat. A further 200,000 deaths resulted from other violent actions. These
two figures combined represent less than 15% of the total mortalities caused
by the direct actions of either state or rebel forces. What accounts, then, for the

remaining 85 percent who were killed? By and large, most of those who die as a result of internal war fall victim to the broader breakdown in social and political order. As physical infrastructure and support networks collapse because of fighting, massive impairment to human health and security is the inevitable outcome. Though the exact numbers for these estimates can never be precise, the figures presented in the Congolese case are not unique. In South Sudan estimates put the number of deaths at over 2 million, mostly resulting from a conflict-induced breakdown in the food supply, with only around 50,000, or 3 percent, caused by direct combat (ibid.).

These numbers stand in stark contrast to the number of dead during the two-and-a-half-decade-long war in Sri Lanka. According to a government report, during the first fifteen years of the fighting (between 1983 and 1997), around 10,000 government soldiers were killed (Arunatilake, Jayasuriya, and Kelegama 2001, 1494). On the insurgent side, the LTTE estimated that it lost over 9,000 fighters during the same period, though the Defense Ministry put the number at closer to 22,000. The number of battle deaths as a share of total war-related deaths (estimated at close to 60,000 during this period), would equal either 32 percent using the lower estimate and 53 percent using the higher figure. Though that still leaves a horrific number of civilians dead, both the total number killed and the proportion of dead in relation to combatants are dramatically lower than in the two other cases. A portion of this discrepancy is certainly accounted for by the relative stability and effectiveness of the LTTE governance system. Though evidence from these three cases is meant only to be suggestive rather than conclusive, it does point to the importance of understanding insurgent-produced, localized political orders in preventing massive humanitarian crises.

I conclude in the following three ways. First, I consider the significance of understanding insurgent governance for political scientists and students of conflict more generally. I address how a deeper understanding of the governance dimension of insurgent behavior can increase our understanding of two processes— recruitment and use of violence—that have come to predominate in studies of insurgent behavior. Second, I assess the potential impact of incorporating a better understanding of rebel governance systems into current policy responses toward nonstate violent groups. In particular, I address the treatment of insurgent organizations within international law. I argue that an assessment of rebel governance systems can provide a more meaningful method for distinguishing between different categories of violent groups and determining under what conditions a degree of official international recognition for the organization might be warranted. And finally, I consider the transformation of the international system and its effect on the forms through which oppositional political perspectives can be expressed. To address that issue, we must first assess whether the perceived evolution of political violence is the result of a process internal to insurgency itself or whether these changes are responsive to broader structural shifts in the international system, evolving in tandem with bigger questions about the organization of the global community.

Significance of the Book

The preceding chapters put forth a framework for understanding the performance of sovereign functions by insurgent organizations. I argued that it is important to view the provision of governance as a strategic decision by rebel leaders to generate collaboration among the civilian population in pursuit of their broader military and political agenda. Not every group deems it necessary to elicit popular support, of course. And these different insurgent objectives produce variations in strategy concerning the costly decision of pursuing a comprehensive civilian governance program. In many cases, groups decide not to take territory at all, as with the Lord's Resistance Army in Uganda. Others may decide to establish base areas in neighboring countries, as the Palestine Liberation Organization did in Lebanon at one point during its war against Israel. And finally, some insurgents may choose to capture territory only to depopulate these areas once in control, as the Rwandan Patriotic Front did during the Rwandan civil war. This project says little about any of these situations.

However, since most internal wars are innately concerned with control of territory and civilian populations, many other insurgencies deem it important to capture and manage vast areas in pursuit of their strategic objectives. In these cases, generating internal consent from the civilian population is integral to fulfilling the rebel project. Therefore, in this book, I focus attention on the behavior of insurgent leaders who—either a priori or as a result of some shift in the conflict dynamics—have decided that developing a system of governance is an essential step in pursuit of their broader goals. But the decision to construct a civilian administration has little to do with the actual ability of the system to meet the needs of inhabitants for stability and other basic public services. I have argued that it is essential to understand both the internal organizational challenges insurgents face and how their relationships with a variety of actors during the conflict shape the governance outcomes that we observe. Such political actors emerge from multiple locations, operating from below, as civilians and religious and traditional leaders challenge or collaborate with insurgent control, and from above, as transnational actors increasingly intercede into civilian livelihoods in contemporary conflict zones.

Rebel Behavior

The findings in this book contribute to several ongoing academic debates. Most directly, the project engages the contemporary literature on rebel behavior, shifting focus away from ideological or economic factors commonly posited as shaping civilian/insurgent relations to an interactional approach that emphasizes the dynamic political landscape that contemporary rebel leaders must navigate. The discussion in the preceding chapters demonstrates that the political environments insurgent leaders operate within are broadly comparable while also taking into consideration the specific local contexts that shaped the observed governance outcomes. There are four broad dimensions that shape the political environment highlighted in the above discussion: (1) the history of state penetration in the region and the legacy of the different political and social institutions that emerge as a result; (2) the internal and external agendas of the insurgency and their relationship to the internal structure of the organization; (3) the broader conflict dynamics—in particular the competition for territorial control between the insurgency, the state, and rival factions; and (4) the relationship between the insurgency and societal and commercial actors, both local and transnational.

Historical factors have been largely overlooked in recent studies of internal war. In particular, understanding how political behaviors developed during the preconflict period persist during times of war is a central concern of this book (Guha 1997). Too often, analysts in the policy community and within humanitarian organizations like Human Rights Watch and Amnesty International view civilians as either passive victims of violence or accomplices to the insurgent organization. But civilians retain a number of strategies for responding to rebel rule. Whether adopting the exit option by fleeing a rebel-held territory or engaging in violent or nonviolent challenges to the insurgent political regime, civilians have considerable latitude in determining their relationship with a violent group. By using various available strategies, civilians articulate demands on the rebel political authority, often forcing leaders to address the question of governance or risk losing support from the residents of the area. A more nuanced understanding of the political possibilities available to civilians in such moments of crises must start by assessing the forms of political engagement that characterized state/society relations before the outbreak of fighting. Thus this book has sought to explain how civilian political expectations are formed by their prior relationship to the incumbent political authority and what this means for efforts by insurgents to develop governance systems.

From an organizational perspective, I examined how the different strategic agendas a rebellion may profess can shape the type of governance strategy it pursues. Developing a parallel system of governance is an essential imperative for any secessionist movement that seeks to bolster its claim for independence. This contrasts with reformist insurgents, who can delay expectations until the outcome of the war is clear. I have also examined the internal organizational approach of various insurgencies, emphasizing differing leadership styles and how they affect the ability of a command to develop an effective civilian governance system. Some rebellions are led by charismatic or ruthless leaders able to impose discipline throughout the organization. Others preside over decentralized and fractious bodies. Such differences in the organizational structure often determine the capacity of an insurgent group to handle the demands made upon it by both the civilian population and other actors operating within its areas of control. However, even the most structured or disciplined rebel commands may not be able to develop effective governance structures and practices as they face vastly differing conflict dynamics. Thus it is important to consider how the relationships between the command and other political actors affect civilian governance performance.

To this end, I focused attention on the broader conflict dynamics and their interplay with insurgent governance efforts, the third dimension mentioned above. Insurgencies operate within a competitive environment in which the incumbent state, its allies, and even unaligned militias compete with a specific rebellion for the loyalty of local communities. A basic element of counterinsurgency strategy has always been to "outgovern" the insurgents by providing more stability and better public services than the insurgency can offer (Kilcullen 2009). Incumbents and rival militias also frequently resort to violence to undermine governance efforts, with devastating effect. The more the insurgency has to respond to the military strategies of its rivals, the less it is able to devote resources to its governance system, with distinctly negative effects on civilian conditions.

Finally, not every actor operating within or around an insurgent zone of control is necessarily hostile. Though some choose to challenge rebel control, either directly or by throwing their support behind rival actors, other societal and commercial actors may collaborate with the command if it furthers their interests to do so. Insurgent leaders make realistic assessments of the role such actors can play and may alter their treatment of civilians—both positively and negatively—accordingly. For example, important political actors such as aid organizations, community-based organizations, traditional leaders, and religious institutions that claim a mandate of ensuring civilian welfare frequently have complicated relationships with insurgent organizations, choosing to collaborate with the political authority only when they believe it is in the interest of local inhabitants. More commercially minded actors also impact rebel governance efforts, either by reducing the incentive for insurgents to develop a meaningful administrative capacity or by providing revenue that insurgents may devote to their governance system.

Ultimately no single dimension described above can fully account for why some insurgents are able to develop highly effective governance systems while others do little for civilian inhabitants. Local contexts matter, and strategic decisions embraced in one war zone may produce highly divergent outcomes in another, depending on the compounding factors. The point is to recognize the complexity of insurgent governance as an object of analysis while also providing an initial framework for comprehension and comparison. My hope is that this book begins to open the door to expanding the research agenda around insurgent governance systems.

There are many questions that warrant further analysis. How does variation in governance systems affect insurgent use of violence? Does it play a role in shaping insurgent recruitment? Is there an impact on war outcomes? If so, what is it? What are the implications for those who study complex emergencies? Those concerned with public health? Educational outcomes? More broadly, can understanding insurgent governance deepen our understanding of other forms of resistance, both violent and nonviolent? In the next section I briefly consider how governance may enhance understanding of two central issues that analysts of internal war continue to debate: the use of violence by insurgents and their noncoercive recruitment practices. Again, my intent here is not to be conclusive but rather to demonstrate how a better grasp of insurgent governance systems may deepen our understanding of these two processes.

Insurgent Governance and the Recruitment of Cadres

Beyond ideological conviction or material incentives, noncoercive recruitment is also recognized as resulting from two other common pathways: the degree of control that insurgents exhibit over a specific territory and the penetration of insurgent networks within a particular area and community. Both would benefit from a better appreciation of civilian governance, as I discuss below.

Scholars have convincingly shown that the best predictor of the loyalties of a specific population has more to do with which political actor controls the territory that a community inhabits than with its preconflict political preferences. The logic is straightforward. As conflicts inevitably transform local economies, increasing poverty levels and reducing the available material goods necessary for survival (Chingono 1996; Lubkemann 2008), civilians shift their allegiance to the political actor best capable of ensuring their welfare, that is, the one in control of the territory in which they reside. As Stathis Kalyvas (2006, 111) explains, "A robust empirical observation is that the allocation of collaboration among belligerents is closely related to the distribution of control, that is, the extent to which actors are able to establish exclusive rule on a territory."

However, this argument cannot account for cases where an insurgency displays a high amount of territorial control but is unable to win the support of the local population. For example, despite the vast areas of eastern D.R. Congo under the control of the RCD-Goma, the insurgency was never able to translate its territorial gains into higher levels of popular support. This failure resulted from the insurgency's inability to improve the material conditions of denizens of its territory, which meant that few individuals voluntarily joined the insurgency's ranks. A purely militaristic explanation of control cannot account for the complicated interplay between an insurgent organization and its public. To better understand the variation in governance systems, it is necessary to examine how some groups in control of territory are able to generate civilian collaboration while others face violent and nonviolent challenges. Control is better thought of as a first-order condition that makes the production of collaboration possible, while governance provision is the necessary condition to actually bring civilians into the insurgent organization on a noncoercive basis (Kalyvas 2006, 128).

Recruitment has also been linked to the density of social relationships that connect individuals to the insurgent organization (Wickham-Crowley 1987; Viterna 2006). As one empirical study of voluntary recruitment found, "when individuals have community ties that link them to members of a fighting group, they are more likely to join" (Humphries and Weinstein 2006, 449). Jocelyn Viterna (2006, 15–17), in her study of the FMLN insurgency in El Salvador, identifies three types of social relationships that can foster participation in violent groups: family ties to the rebels, relational ties through membership in social change organizations, and experiences of living in refugee camps or repopulated communities. The relevant mechanism here is that as the number of points of contact with an insurgent organization increase, individual participation tends to swell in tandem. As a result, an increase in the density of social relations linking an organization to the society it seeks to control has an impact on the ability of the insurgency to recruit members. Governance can be viewed as the method through which insurgents seek to monopolize the social, political, and economic interrelations of a defined community. As such, it expands the scope of the insurgent interface with civilians, improving the rebellion's ability to foster voluntary participation.

INSURGENT GOVERNANCE AND THE DISTRIBUTION OF VIOLENCE

Violence in civil wars is rarely truly random. Belligerents utilize repertoires of coercive actions in pursuit of tactical objectives. How they do so has underexplored connections to governance. Inevitably, all insurgencies begin as violent entities, reliant on coercion and only minimally concerned about civilian welfare.

Even groups that begin with a professed concern for civilians have little capacity to protect or provide for them in the initial phases of the conflict. Thus in the early stages of a civil war, most rebellions look fairly similar in regard to civilian governance. However, once insurgents are in control of a territory and population, they often organize violence for particular effects geared toward ensuring compliance; in another words, the violence is tactical.

Do governance strategies have any relationship to the use of violence by insurgents? Violence in civil wars is never uniform, varying widely even between adjacent villages. Areas of stability inevitably attract a greater number of journalists, human rights activists, and aid workers who document the treatment of civilians they encounter, disseminating this information via networks that link them to the outside world (Zahar 2001). The presence of such transnational witnesses can prevent insurgents from openly mistreating civilians for fear of ruining their reputation with their carefully cultivated international audience. They will prefer to concentrate violence against civilians in areas outside the scope of such transnational networks.

Recognizing this dynamic, rebels may strategically allocate governance provision, devoting resources to improve conditions in areas they want transnational actors to visit while neglecting areas they prefer remain hidden. By drawing transnational actors to specific areas, insurgents can knowingly manipulate coverage of their behavior, presenting their best face precisely where the spotlight is brightest. At the same time, rebels may strategically neglect areas by purposefully not providing security and other public goods, rendering them inaccessible to transnational witnesses. Insurgents have successfully used such a strategy by allowing access only to areas of the map where their political authority is more generally accepted and hence less reliant on violent means (Scroggins 2004). It is no coincidence that much of the worst violence perpetrated against civilians in war zones takes place in rural villages composed of homogenous ethnic communities (Mkandawire 2002). Marginalized by locale and often other social or cultural markings, these communities tend to remain outside the glare of transnational actors, suffering the consequences accordingly.

Political Order

Analyzing insurgent governance systems also deepens our understanding of the development of political order by nonstate actors. Most analysts continue to accept the norm that the state is the sole purveyor of political order. However, as this book has shown, insurgent-controlled territories may be host to patterned configurations of social and political actors that demand the attention of scholars. Rather than looking at this phenomenon as a malicious deviation from statehood or as an existential threat to the prevailing international order, I am arguing for a perspective that recognizes multiple systems producing order within a single territory as an important contemporary reality, worthy of its own analysis. Still, the normative assumption that the state is the sole producer of political and social order is indeed a powerful one, which I hope this book brings into question.

To a limited degree, scholars have begun to analyze the alternate power systems operating co-existentially with the state system. Anthropologists in particular have highlighted the assumption of sovereign functions by a wide selection of actors including nongovernmental organizations, international agencies, corporations, religious institutions, criminal networks, and traditional authorities (Nordstrom 2004, 116; Roitman 2001). However, political scientists have generally remained impervious to these insights, failing to incorporate them into discussions of the behavior of nonstate violent actors. This is an unfortunate omission. Political scientists could bring a unique understanding of the distinct political challenges insurgents face as they attempt to provide a modicum of social and political order through the development of a governance system. Indeed, understanding of rebel governance would advance with a more extensive discussion of the relationship between insurgent rule and many other central concepts in the political science literature, including legitimacy, authority, representation, and of course, governance itself. Instead, many of these concepts are walled off, used solely in discussions of recognized state governments and treated as inapplicable to the host of concurrent systems that compete with the nation-state.

For example, though other nonstate actors such as NGOs frequently engage in order-producing activities similar to those of rebel governments, such as providing health and education, they rarely claim a *right* to govern a local community. Legitimacy for their activities is derived externally, through the interpretation of relevant international human rights principles and documents.[1] In contrast, insurgents in control of territory establish governmental systems specifically to buttress their claims to represent a targeted population. Thus I view the processes and modalities that determine rebel behavior as being similar to, though distinct from, those of other types of nonstate actors *that do not violently challenge the state authority,* even if the latter may be unconcerned with or even contemptuous of state power. In this way I draw from political scientists by acknowledging the close interrelations between insurgent and state forms of order while also relying

---

1. Private corporations that perform governance functions usually assume these duties in pursuit of profit. International agencies are beholden to the whims of the donor nations, commonly the great powers, which maintain a disproportionate influence over the workings of UN agencies, the World Bank, the International Monetary Fund, and other such agencies. In both cases, legitimacy is not derived from the local community.

on other disciplines by recognizing the kinship of insurgent politics to forms of order produced by other nonstate actors.

The discussion of rebel governance also sheds light on another important social science concern, the fixity of a particular political order. Political scientists disagree on the durability of institutions, arguing whether it is best to conceive of them as transhistorical entities or whether it makes more sense to think of them dynamically, constituted as a product of a wide variety of interactions between political actors. Anthropology tends to exaggerate the latter perspective, stressing the social nature of nonstate structures, in particular their flexibility and contingency on other actors within a system. However, rebel structures and practices are not merely ephemeral or necessarily bounded by the timeline of the conflict itself. Instead, they can have significant legacies over the postconflict dispensation, raising important questions about the inheritance bequeathed by a dying political order to the institutional matrix that arises in its place, an issue I turn to now.

Postconflict Legacies

A better comprehension of rebel governance efforts is crucial for what it may tell us about the behavior of insurgent leaders in the postconflict period and why some peace processes produce long-term solutions while others devolve into renewed fighting. Though any assessment of the legacies of rebel actions should be wary of drawing simplistic assertions about the relationship between conflict dynamics and postconflict outcomes, as Elisabeth Wood (2008, 555) notes, "sometimes the social processes of civil war leave enduring changes in their wake." Indeed, analyses have shown that local structures and practices developed during conflict, including those developed by insurgents, are likely to persist even after the culmination of fighting (Manor 2006; de Zeeuw 2008). Rebels transitioning from camouflage-wearing guerrilla fighters to suited bureaucrats are unlikely to simply abandon the governance practices developed during times of war. Naturally we are able to see these legacies only if the rebellion is successful in earning a share of state power or if it actually takes control of the government (de Zeeuw 2008). For example, the leadership of the Eritrean People's Liberation Front, which developed a highly effective governance system during the conflict, sought to retain wartime structures as the underpinning of the postconflict bureaucratic infrastructure upon coming to power (Pool 2001). The autocratic nature of the authority relationship between the rebel organization and civilians also carried over to the new regime's interactions with the citizenry as the former insurgents promoted a militarized ethos among the newly independent Eritrean population.

In the cases examined in this book, the legacy of rebel governmental practices is far more mixed, shaped primarily by the distinct ends to each of these difficult and devastating wars. None of the insurgent organizations achieved an outright victory over government forces. In Sri Lanka, LTTE leaders often called for the structures of the Atasialthurai to serve as the basis for any independent state or autonomous province the organization might have won in the north and east provinces (TamilNet 2002b, 2003). However, since the defeat of the rebellion, the government of Sri Lanka has sought to wipe the slate clean, rejecting any calls to incorporate insurgent structures or personnel into the postconflict dispensation. The government has even worked to eradicate the physical legacies of insurgent rule, going as far as tearing down physical infrastructure and memorials to dead cadres erected by the Tigers.

The wars in D.R. Congo and Sudan, however, both ended with negotiated settlements, opening up the possibility for elements of the governance system created by the two insurgent groups to endure. On one side, leaders of the RCD-Goma cared little about maintaining the failed structures and practices they had developed in eastern Congo, rushing off to Kinshasa to assume positions in the transition government at the earliest opportunity. Though a new insurgency filled with RCD personnel, the Congrès National pour la Défense du Peuple of Laurent Nkunda, did take power in areas of the Kivus, rather than embrace the failed practices of its predecessor, the organization explicitly rejected them, achieving greater success in winning popular support in the areas it came to control (Stearns 2008, 261–65). In contrast, the SPLM/A had a clear agenda for postconflict governance and sought to position its civil administration as the basis for a new postconflict political order (Branch and Mampilly 2005). However, the death of John Garang and the organization's failure to entrench its governance system during the conflict left only a weak connection between it and the newly created Government of South Sudan. Still, many of the same personnel in addition to some of the ruling structures and practices developed by the SPLM/A continue to shape everyday life in South Sudan, demonstrating the legacy of insurgent rule in at least one of my cases.

Policy Responses

Current policy approaches for dealing with areas under rebel control too often treat them as little more than *terra nullius*—territories devoid of any political or social order.[2] This assumption renders such areas virtual black holes on the

---

2. Several authors have written on the significance of the label *terra nullius* and its role in promoting and fostering the idea of a singular relationship between a territory, a people, and a government. See, for example, Sven Lindqvist (2007).

global geopolitical map, places of mystery and chaos that are impenetrable by the international community despite significant evidence to the contrary. Scholars have contributed to this dynamic by treating territorial control as being the sole prerogative of the nation-state. Rather than attempting to understand daily life in areas outside state control, political science and economic studies prefer to focus on state weakness as the object of analysis. As Ranajit Guha (1997, 3) insightfully noted in his seminal work on the subject, too often scholars have not centered civilian welfare in their analyses of civil war, instead choosing to make "the security of the state into the central problematic of peasant insurgency."

Policymakers understandably exhibit considerable reticence when engaging with violent groups, fearing that any interaction may be viewed as legitimizing an unpredictable and potentially unconstrainable political actor. This is regardless of the fact that many insurgent organizations are no more erratic than many recognized state regimes, few of which ever face sanctions on their behavior. Indeed, several approaches currently utilized in dealing with insurgents start with a normative bias that preserving the nation-state is desirable for its own sake rather than prioritizing the welfare of civilians on the ground.[3] In this section, I will address the shortcomings in the ways in which the international community has sought to engage with insurgent organizations through a variety of mechanisms. I will then consider how a better appreciation of insurgent governance systems can improve the ad hoc process of recognition that currently prevails.

Current Policy Approaches for Dealing with Insurgent Organizations

Powerful states, international organizations, and transnational activists frequently threaten to place specific insurgencies on lists of proscribed organizations. "Naming and shaming" rebel leaders may have some value, if, for example, an insurgency with a demonstrated interest in civilian governance fears the consequences of being labeled an international pariah and as a result increases its efforts to improve civilian welfare. However, the insurgent organizations most in need of shaming are generally unconcerned about their image. Furthermore, this approach can have the adverse impact of limiting the involvement of humanitarian organizations in rebel-held areas as a result of the legal restrictions that being placed on such a list can initiate. Invariably, the impact for civilians is

---

3. For example, William Zartman (1995) has called for strengthening the current state system rather than providing support to incipient challengers to the established political order, with little concern for the behavior of the governments involved.

detrimental as humanitarian actors face prosecution, the freezing of assets, and even expulsion for their activities behind insurgent lines. Despite the clear (if indirect) support aid organizations may provide to rebel groups, restricting their involvement can only cause further hardships to civilians.

Others recognize that international actors have already penetrated every contemporary conflict zone and argue for greater regulation of their interactions with rebel organizations. This would be achieved by pressuring states to cut external aid to insurgents or using sanctions and certification regimes to stem the flow of natural resources from insurgent-controlled areas. The hope is that if access to external revenues sources is restricted, war will be less detrimental for civilian populations because insurgents will be forced to rely on local communities for support and hence will be more likely to engage in activities that improve civilian welfare (Weinstein 2003, 523–26). However, as discussed in Chapter 1, the flexibility of revenue sources renders this an ineffective approach for manipulating insurgent behavior around civilian treatment. Though it might be worthwhile to pursue such restrictions for other reasons, it is too blunt a tool to have much impact on rebel behavior.

Some have suggested strengthening the International Criminal Court (ICC) as a possible improvement. The hope is that under its prosecutorial gaze, insurgent leaders will think twice before abusing the civilian population. Unfortunately, too often the use of international tribunals and courts tend to overwhelm local political dynamics initiated by civil society organizations on the ground, undermining local efforts to respond to rebel violence. Operating within the yet-to-be-proven structure of international humanitarian law, legal experts from North America and Western Europe frequently come across as more interested in promoting the merit of the latest legal contrivances than in making a genuine effort to promote civilian welfare (Branch 2004, 2007).

The above approaches share several innate weaknesses. First, they treat all violent groups as *illegal actors*. Certain groups may escape this designation on the basis of the role they play in broader geopolitical competitions. But in general, recognition or sanction of a particular organization has little or no connection to the merit of the cause or the group's treatment of civilians. More problematically, these approaches exhibit an overt bias toward incumbent governments. Current international norms resist legitimizing challengers to a recognized sovereign—despite the origins of many Third World political systems and boundaries as the arbitrary byproducts of colonial-era imperatives—for fear of eviscerating state legitimacy more generally (Herbst 2000; Nadarajah and Sriskandarajah 2005). The state bias persists even where a regime has clearly broken the boundaries of international law through massacres or extrajudicial killings, for example. Because the above approaches are based on mandates provided by nation-states, they inevitably privilege the interests of national governments over the welfare of civilians living behind rebel lines.

An even more prejudiced approach, popular among states fighting insurgencies either domestically or abroad, treats them not only as illegal but as *irrational* actors. Commonly deployed by using the "terrorist" epithet, labeling insurgents as irrational closes the door to finding a noncoercive basis for negotiation.[4] If an actor is viewed as irrational, there is generally no room for negotiation, as it is presumed that the only language that such actors understand is force.

Furthermore, tagging an insurgency as irrational allows other actors such as the incumbent government, other states, and commercial actors to operate within rebel-controlled areas with impunity. The assumption that a territorial space lacks political order because it is under the control of an irrational actor provides carte blanche to those who would seek to pursue their own political or commercial agendas—whether the dumping of toxic wastes, the illegal expropriation of natural resources, or the perpetration of hidden massacres. Indeed, the perception that such spaces lack order or a political authority that can be engaged renders them "states of denial" in which the international community can choose to not know about the questionable activities happening within (Cohen 2001).

From the Ethiopian invasion of Somalia that caused widespread death and destruction to the Sri Lankan government's targeting of Tamil civilians caught behind the front lines, prominent media sources largely preferred to accept untruths rather than interrogate what really unfolded. Indeed, both the Ethiopian and Sri Lankan governments successfully manipulated these perceptions of nonstate anarchy, denying that massacres even took place despite the plethora of evidence that managed to surface. Even the U.S. government relies on a similar stance of "plausible deniability" regarding whether a particular explosion is the handiwork of Predator drones targeting militants hiding in areas along the supposedly ungoverned Pakistani border with Afghanistan, which demonstrates that this strategy is not limited to autocratic states in the developing world (Bergen and Tiedemann 2010).

Recognition and International Law

There remains considerable scope for improvement in current international practice regarding recognition of violent groups that I believe can improve conditions for civilians in areas outside state control. Thus far, the focus of current international legal thinking, supported by the many countries battling terrorism

---

4. Think of the cliché adopted by many governments in many different times, "We do not negotiate with terrorists."

at home or abroad, is to find ways to hold violent organizations accountable for any perceived human rights violations without extending to them any of the rights available to even other types of nonstate actors, such as private corporations or nonprofit aid organizations, let alone traditional states (A. Clapham 2006; Zegveld 2002). International law as determined by the International Court of Justice in the *Nicaragua* and *Iran Hostages* judgments[5] only chooses to delineate precise mechanisms by which the behavior of nonstate violent actors can be *attributed* to their state sponsor.

This in itself is not surprising because the principles of most international laws of war regarding the treatment of violent groups are derived from broader norms regulating interstate warfare. These were generally designed to punish states for supporting violent organizations by holding them accountable for the actions of their insurgent proxies. Meanwhile, Common Article 3 of the Geneva Conventions, which extends the laws of war to internal conflicts, was drafted to hold individuals affiliated with nonstate violent groups accountable for their actions within a state but says nothing about the actual organizations that employ individual militants. Consequently, it does not grant recognition to insurgent organizations as *persons* within international law (as states are deemed), nor does it levy the same obligations and rights on insurgent organizations as on traditional states out of concern for undermining the sovereign privileges that accompany formal statehood (Somer 2006).

For example, if Hezbollah had been viewed as the legal equivalent of a state in its conflict with Israel in 2006, the concern was that its leadership and combatants would have been entitled to the same legal protections offered by the Geneva Convention to formal states (though it would have been expected to reciprocate these to Israeli soldiers as well). Despite this legal arrangement, the UN Security Council continues to make demands for *all* belligerent parties in an internal war to enforce International Humanitarian Law (IHL), with little success (Sivakumaran 2009, 497). Efforts to pressure rebels to behave in line with IHL without granting them recognition will always run into a basic contradiction, as insurgent

---

5. In the cases, officially referred to as the *United States Diplomatic and Consular Staff in Tehran (United States of America v Iran) (1979)* and the *Military and Paramilitary Activities in and against Nicaragua (Nicaragua v United States of America)* (1986), the ICJ was asked to determine whether the behavior of nonstate armed groups was the responsibility of a state government. In the former, the court was asked to determine the culpability of the Iranian government for the behavior of armed students who took over the American embassy in Teheran. The latter case concerned whether Nicaraguan support for Salvadorian rebels constituted an armed attack that justified military action by the United States in collective self-defense with the government of El Salvador. In both cases, the ICJ found that states could be held responsible but only under conditions in which the actions of militant groups were directed by a state actor. Supplying weapons and other support was not considered a sufficient condition to determine state liability.

organizations have little recourse to the same structures of international justice for activities carried out by the incumbent government that contravene relevant human rights statutes within territories under their control.

Despite these prejudices, insurgents have proven amenable to behaving according to the principles of IHL, opening the possibility for more productive methods for engaging with their governance systems if the appropriate legal approach can be developed. For example, in his analysis of insurgent legal systems, Sandesh Sivakumaran (2009, 495) shows that rebel courts have met both criteria recognized as essential for a fair trial outlined in the relevant IHL documents (Common Article 3 and Additional Protocol II of the Geneva Conventions), that is, regularly constituted courts and due process guarantees. He argues that rebel judicial systems that meet these requirements could be entitled to recognition under the current framework of IHL, though such recognition is rarely if ever forthcoming.[6]

South Africa provides one telling example of this contradiction. In 1980, Umkhonto we Sizwe (Spear of the Nation), the military wing of the African National Congress (ANC), was the first insurgent organization to explicitly agree to abide by the dictates of the Geneva Convention (Tambo 1980). But throughout its existence, it remained a proscribed organization—a position determined by the incumbent that it fought—despite widespread condemnation of the South African government during the antiapartheid struggle. The apartheid regime was supported by no less a power than the United States, a close ally, which removed Nelson Mandela and other ANC leaders from a terrorism watch list only in 2008 (Hall 2008). Indeed, since 9/11, the pendulum has swung even farther away from ever recognizing any violent group as a legitimate political actor, regardless of how it is viewed by its civilian constituency.[7] Consequently, civilians living in rebel zones of control are left to pursue justice in national courts, even in cases where it is the incumbent government that is violating their human rights.

This deference to state authorities and willful ignorance of facts on the ground have constrained the emergence of genuinely novel approaches for dealing with rebel-controlled territories. Despite widespread recognition of the importance of

---

6. The emergence of an organization such as Geneva Call with the stated mission of pressuring rebel groups to comply with international humanitarian law in exchange for recognition of their behavior by the organization is one step in the right direction. But such efforts remain few and far between and are generally limited to nonstate actors with little influence on the international humanitarian legal apparatus. Information about the organization is available at its website, http://www.genevacall.org/.

7. Venezuela's president Hugo Chavez's call for the armies of the FARC and ELN to be viewed not as terrorists but as insurgents with a political agenda—and treated accordingly—represents a rare (and decidedly nonmainstream) counterperspective to the labeling of insurgent groups as little more than irrational terrorists or mere economically driven violent actors (McDermott 2008).

negotiating with insurgent structures to access communities living behind rebel lines, geopolitical preferences continue to determine which rebellions are considered legitimate by international actors and hence worthy of engagement. Certain groups such as FALINTIL in East Timor and the PLO did achieve a degree of official international recognition, receiving observer status at the UN (despite never having full control over the territory or population they claimed to represent). However, the advantages accrued by this reluctant recognition fall far short of the significant benefits on offer to even the most despotic tyrant at the head of an internationally recognized state authority.

Ignoring or denying the existence of insurgent governments is a contravention of the legal principle of *Ex facto jus oritur,* or, that the law should arise out of facts rather than opinions. By this standard, our treatment of rebel-governed territories falls short. The consequence is that areas under rebel control are treated by international actors as devoid of partners with whom they can carry out legitimate commercial transactions or implement humanitarian and development programs on the ground. Instead, the international community continues to engage such spaces through the juridically recognized state authority—perhaps the only actor that has proven itself incapable of promoting order within them.

A more honest and effective approach would begin by acknowledging that insurgent organizations frequently come into control of vast territories and human populations and that their position as the supreme authority within that territory necessitates a structured method of recognition from international society. What are the stakes of international recognition? Any actor operating in the international arena that is not constituted through the mutual consent of the primary units of the system—i.e., states—will face considerable prejudice against its ability to function and even its ability to survive. While multiple ad hoc bilateral relationships are possible and in fact already provide a degree of recognition to rebel governments, these are heavily weighted toward the interests of specific states. As such, they make no pretensions to consider the welfare of civilians on the ground, a principle that I am hoping to interject. This can be achieved only by moving toward a more formal process of recognition.

Under an objective consideration of the organization's governance system, certain insurgencies that meet specific criteria could be deemed a distinct category of international actors, what I refer to as "counterstate sovereigns," with a defined and limited set of rights within the international system. Thinking of rebel governments as potentially constituting a discrete category of sovereign actors is an essential step, as sovereignty remains the cornerstone of international recognition. Without a degree of recognition, it is impossible for a political authority to participate meaningfully in international society, and thus its ability to wield its sovereign powers and ensure the welfare of its constituents is undermined (Philpott 1999, 575).

For the international community, creating a distinct category of sovereignty for insurgent organizations can provide a standardized framework for engagement, an opportunity to move beyond the ad hoc toward a more regularized and structured approach for dealing with order-producing actors. By recognizing that counterstate sovereigns constitute a discrete category within the international system, the international community can develop coherent policy approaches that acknowledge their distinct nature. In effect, what I am calling for is distinguishing between insurgent organizations according to their desire and ability to develop effective civilian governance systems, providing those that do a limited degree of juridical recognition, which they have always lacked within the current international order.

By questioning the nature of the political order within these spaces, we can begin the difficult process of providing standardized criteria for how rebel organizations in control of territory should be judged. Not every, or even most, insurgencies deserve recognition. But a starting point would be to recognize that in certain cases, counterstate sovereigns capable of ensuring both stability and civilian welfare can and do emerge and that they need not necessarily serve only a destabilizing role within international society. Rather than accept the view that only states produce political and economic order, granting insurgent organizations the ability to engage directly and openly with international actors is a first step toward a realistic appreciation of the role such organizations play in ensuring civilian welfare.

For such an approach to be operable, it is necessary to move away from the notion that the international community functions as a unitary actor. In reality, transnational actors, including states and private corporations, are already engaged with insurgent leaders in every conflict zone across the world. Even UN agencies, though designed to work with national governments, are not prohibited from working within rebel-controlled territories, nor are they restricted from working with violent groups more generally (L. Munro 2004, 131), as the discussion of OLS in Sudan demonstrates. The key is to intervene selectively with rebel groups, distinguishing those that may be susceptible to international influence from those unlikely to be affected and adjusting involvement accordingly. The question is not whether the international community should engage rebel political authorities but rather, how international actors can leverage their engagement to foster better conditions for civilians caught within contemporary war zones.

There are multiple advantages to thinking of certain insurgent governments as possessing a form of sovereignty. For starters, it would rationalize our current framework of international law, which as it is currently constituted cannot account for the existence of territories on the map governed by nonstate actors, an oversight with considerable political and economic consequences. International agencies, aid organizations, private corporations, and even neighboring states would benefit from being able to coordinate their activities with a legitimate authority, whether these activities are humanitarian aid projects, controlling a border between an insurgent area of control and a recognized national boundary, or conducting transnational commerce.

For example, responding to a humanitarian crisis within a rebel zone of control can pose unique challenges for aid organizations as they try to navigate barriers placed in their way by the incumbent government, the rebel political authority, and international law, as well as any restrictions placed on the rebellion by the organization's home country. Recognition would facilitate a speedier and more efficient response than the convoluted processes that currently undermine humanitarian efforts as they seek to reach populations on the ground. Or consider that goods and resources brought out of insurgent-held territory are technically neither legal nor illegal, as international law applies only to formal states and not areas under the control of insurgent organizations (Nordstrom 2001, 224). A standardized process of recognition will allow the international community to more forcefully regulate the numerous transnational commercial actors that actively operate within these territories, distinguishing between those engaged in legitimate commerce and those pursuing more nefarious objectives.

Incorporating counterstate sovereigns into the international system would also allow for a formal partitioning of sovereign responsibilities between the insurgent organization and the incumbent state or other international actors. Some may reject the idea that sovereignty is divisible, but there are examples of this dynamic already available at different levels of the international system.[8] The advantage of partitioning sovereignty in a formal manner is that it may reduce the politicization of governance as an issue during a civil war (Mampilly 2009). A formal division of responsibilities can defuse the ability of insurgents to manipulate civilian welfare to promote their cause, and it can ensure that governments do not abdicate their responsibilities to civilians in pursuit of strategic military gains. Since there is no direct pathway between developing a governance system and gaining statehood, insurgents and incumbents should be encouraged to provide for civilian welfare without linking it to the broader conflict outcome.

Offering a degree of international recognition as a positive inducement to insurgents can encourage them to develop their governance capacity while also putting pressure on other violent groups to take more seriously the task of providing

---

8. For example, most member states of the EU allow the supranational body to be supreme in trade issues while retaining supremacy over defense matters (Philpott 1999, 571).

for the welfare of civilians in territories they control. It may also be time to con-sider rebel treatment of civilians, as evidenced by their governance systems, as a precondition for participation in internationally sanctioned peace talks. While the principle of force will continue to be the primary determinant of which orga-nizations get invited to the negotiating table (Tull and Mehler 2005), letting rebel leaders know that the international community takes seriously the treatment of civilians in conflict zones can establish a new international norm that at least some insurgent leaders are likely to take seriously.

The biggest resistance to offering recognition to insurgents naturally arises from states concerned about ceding sovereign privileges to nonstate actors. Gov-ernments rightly perceive international recognition as a boost to the legitimacy of a direct challenger to the state system. A first step to ameliorate these concerns would be to demonstrate that insurgent organizations commonly appropriate aspects of sovereignty without necessarily embarking on the trajectory of state-hood. As I argue in chapter 2, it is uncertain whether rebel governments genu-inely represent an existential challenge to the state system, as some authors and political leaders tend to assume. The desire to analogize state formation to insur-gent behavior has the effect of aggrandizing the threat such actors pose, obscur-ing a clearer vision of their behavior. In fact, such nonstate sovereigns have long coexisted alongside the post-Westphalian global order, posing little real threat to the current state system.[9]

Tellingly, the ultimate aspiration for almost all rebel rulers is to either enter into the comity of nations as equal members or to be recognized as the legitimate rulers of a preexisting state authority. Most insurgent leaders do not desire to challenge the state system but actually hope to reinforce it by becoming passport-issuing members themselves. As a result, the scope for engagement with at least a subset of insurgent organizations is far greater than generally recognized and is unlikely to pose any existential challenges to the current global system.

Finally, in regard to the viability of postconflict settlements, a better grasp of rebel governance systems is essential for the process of integrating parallel authorities as a result of a peace agreement. For international mediators, incor-porating insurgent governance structures and personnel into the government bureaucracy is frequently a significant obstacle to implementing a negotiated set-tlement. Agreements that stipulate both the reintegration of rebel administrators

---

9. One need only consider the Sicilian Mafia, which, since its emergence in the late nineteenth century, has always competed directly with the Italian state in the provision of protection, long con-sidered the quintessential prerogative of the Weberian state (Gambetta 1993). However, despite the direct challenge it poses to the recognized political authority in Italy, the existence of the Mafia has never been viewed as the harbinger of a new international system of plural sovereigns.

and the seemingly contradictory imperative of rebuilding state authority generally fail to provide a blueprint, or even a sense of the best practices, for how this should occur. Indeed, international mediators often speak of being confounded about how to fulfill the competing imperatives. United Nations officials I spoke with in Goma about the reintegration of the CNDP, for example, described the process as a "laboratory," bereft of any specific model that could delineate the best way forward (interview with anonymous MONUC officials, Goma, 2009). Instead, insurgent administrators were haphazardly incorporated into the post–peace agreement political dispensation without any understanding of their purpose during the war or their capacity to perform administrative tasks. The result has been unsatisfactory to all, contributing further cracks in the already weak peace agreement.

The Future of Insurgency

One question that remains unanswered as states rush to adopt the terrorist adage in their dealings with violent domestic opposition is how the collapsing of all forms of insurgency into a singular category will shape the behavior of future rebellions. Michael Bhatia (2005, 16) notes the implications of placing all challengers to the state into a singular terrorist category:

> As a consequence, the micro-histories of many of today's conflicts become hidden. Complex local variations, motives, histories and interrelationships are consistently played down in favour of meta-narratives and grand interpretations. Each conflict is seen through whatever classificatory lens has been recently adopted to aggregate violence in the outside world.

As a result, while the embrace of terrorist rhetoric has provided governments in Russia, Colombia, and Sri Lanka the ability to crush violent domestic insurgencies, it has also relieved them of the responsibility of addressing the real grievances that underlie the origins of violent groups representing the Chechens, the Tamils, and the Colombian peasantry.

The risk, of course, is that by delegitimizing actors who may embrace political violence but who seek to model their insurgencies on the incumbent they are fighting, we fail to see what new forms of political violence oppositional groups might come to adopt instead. Indeed, the future of territorially defined insurgencies is more opaque today than at any point in the past century. Two trends in particular have contributed to this evolving dynamic. First, the rise of China is transforming the structure of the post–Cold War international system with tangible consequences for the viability of territorial insurgencies. Second, the devolution of the nation-state as the dominant form of political organization has brought into question the most effective forms of expressing violent discontent. I will briefly consider both in turn below.

The Rise of China

China's rise has unleashed a distinct set of dynamics within the global system that have significantly altered the bipolar world order of the Cold War. The Soviet Union was engaged in the construction of an alternate political and economic project to rival the dominant global system erected by the NATO powers. In practice, this meant that for would-be insurgents, aligning with one or the other superpower could provide steady access to material and financial resources in addition to potential support from neighboring allied regimes and bases from which to operate. The effect was to render the competition between insurgent and incumbent far more level, as both sides in any internal war sought to manipulate the relevant superpower to advance their military position, often with significant effect.

The convergence between the Chinese and American economic agendas and the high levels of interdependence characteristic of this relationship produce a highly divergent context for the practice of contemporary insurgency. Though sometimes thought of as rivals, the two superpowers more often than not will in fact side with the incumbent power in a civil war, thereby undermining the ability of a violent challenger to win a conventional victory. Indeed, superpower support to countries in the former Third World has taken on the tenor of competitive outbidding, with both China and the United States seeking to woo incumbent regimes rather than lining up on opposing sides. As a result, controlling territory from which to launch a rebellion is no longer an advantage for would-be insurgents because the cost of holding territory has risen. Instead, incumbents have been able to count on both military training and weaponry from both China and the United States with which to deal with domestic challengers.

Even in Sudan, a case where the U.S. government has overtly supported the SPLA in its struggle against the Chinese-supported Khartoum government, the geopolitical rivalry is not as straightforward as it might appear. Instead, many in both the Bush and Obama administrations have sought to normalize relations with Khartoum, a position increasingly likely to come into being since the death of Garang and the increased marginalization of his supporters in Washington. More typical are cases where both the Chinese and American government actively work to strengthen the incumbent, as in Sri Lanka, where they joined a motley crew of nominal rivals aligned in support of the government of Mahinda

Rajapaksa, and as they are currently doing in D.R. Congo in throwing their support behind the government of Joseph Kabila.

One exception to this trend may be Islamist insurgencies such as the Taliban in Afghanistan, rumored to be receiving weapons directly from Iran in its battle with the American-led coalition. But Iran is no Soviet Union, nor does it even come close to China at this moment in history. Indeed, the Taliban has struggled to hold territory despite seemingly favorable conditions and the desire of leaders to fight a conventional war against the government of Afghanistan. Though it remains early to confirm, its seems likely that we will witness fewer territorial insurgencies as those willing to embrace political violence calculate that the cost of holding territory outweighs the value it provides.

The Devolution of the Nation-State

Combined with the difficulty of pursuing a territorial strategy, there is a potentially larger transformation occurring with important effects on insurgent behavior that analysts have yet to fully come to terms with. In this book I have shown how the nation-state continues to structure the behavior of violent challengers to its primacy, both militarily and as a model for a distinct form of political organization. But what happens when the nation-state no longer remains the dominant form of political organization in the contemporary world? The early twentieth-century evolution of insurgent practice toward a strategy of challenging the nation-state by manipulating its forms in the ways described may no longer be as relevant in the coming century as the nation-state itself continues to come under assault by forces from an increasingly globalized world. One manifestation of the global war on terror, for example, is the recent debate about whether contemporary insurgencies have become decentralized, cellular groups that engage in clandestine and seemingly random acts of violence or whether they continue to be top-down entities, capable and desirous of challenging that nation-state on an equal footing.[10]

Philip Bobbit (2008, 98) writes about the transformation of the international legal order from one based on nation-states to one in which the dominant unit within the system will be what he refers to as the "market-state." He argues that this emerging global system will be characterized by, among other things, a denationalized constitutional order in which the well-being of the individual will take precedence over the interests of a particular nation. Bobbit also ponders whether the future of insurgency will reflect this shift. In his view, just as twentieth-century

---

10. See the vigorous debate between Bruce Hoffman (2008) and Marc Sageman (2008) based on their contradictory positions that played out in the pages of *Foreign Affairs* and elsewhere.

insurgents mimicked the form and style of the nation-state, twenty-first-century violent groups are developing techniques and strategies adopted from the market-state, specifically a decentralized, nonnational and nonterritorial structure epitomized by Al-Qaeda. The increase in terrorist activities by groups with no territorial basis is, in his view, a part of this trend. If true, such a shift portends a number of challenges for analysts of contemporary insurgencies, posing important questions on the nature of violent conflict in the future.

Though I tend to think Bobbit's assessment of the end of the nation-state may be premature, it is worth considering what his analysis means for the future of insurgency and the response of the international system. Thus far, the reaction has been to seek and destroy nonterritorial insurgents wherever they hide, even in areas outside the control of a recognized state authority. However, many of the spaces that such insurgents flock to are not ungoverned but rather are under the control of other nonstate groups that tolerate or even embrace the activities of their nonterritorial kin (Kilcullen 2009). Despite this reality, the international community, led by the preferences of powerful states, has become obsessed with managing such perceived localized disorder.

Whether the states involved are those with a weak central government—such as Afghanistan or Somalia—or those with territories outside their control—such as Pakistan or Yemen—a dominant perception of nonstate areas as spaces of terror and disorder has calcified (Rabasa et al. 2007). Media figures have consistently promoted the idea of nefarious spaces in need of taming by vigilant and concerted global action.[11] It is assumed that the lack of a clear and legitimate sovereign in control of these spaces makes them threats to the stability of the international community and that therefore they must be managed, inevitably with force.

Though the idea of recognizing rebel governments can be distasteful, the alternative is equally problematic, especially for those communities that bear the brunt of such militaristic strategies. Regardless of what is said about any of the territorial insurgencies studied here, they all keenly sought to reach out to segments of the international community and responded to incentives, either material or political, on offer. If the international community instead abdicates engaging with such actors to the whims of powerful states, heinous though violent territorial groups can be, I worry far more about their potential replacements. The sporadic bombing campaigns that seem to erupt periodically from Mumbai to Istanbul and from Madrid to Dar es Salaam, organized not by clearly defined insurgent organizations but rather by cellular groups of individuals seemingly

---

11. The recurring obsession with Somali piracy is one such example.

disconnected from a larger political whole, may end up being far more devastating and immune to analysis than any territorially defined insurgencies. By denying the existence of political order within rebel-held areas and refusing to offer a meaningful pathway to recognition based on civilian treatment, the international community is taking a position that essentially abandons large areas of the map, too often to the detriment of civilians living within.

INTERVIEW METHODOLOGY AND LIST OF INTERVIEWEES

Research for this project was conducted both during and after recent conflicts in the Democratic Republic of Congo, Sri Lanka, and Sudan. As many who have conducted such research have noted, people's recollections about prior experiences can shift dramatically between the period of actual warfare and the postconflict dispensation (Nordstrom 2004, 30). There are several problems with relying solely on postconflict interviews. First, humans have a limited capacity to recall specific historical events, particularly if those events have to do with relatively mundane issues of day-to-day livelihoods. Second, the basic human tendency to interpret historical events through present-day identities renders accounts of past events more an act of interpretation than of empirical fact (Viterna 2006, 13). And third, individuals have huge incentives to reinterpret their own behavior during periods of violence in order to cast a more benign patina over their actions.

Conducting interviews during a conflict also imposes several limitations. First, the insecurity of wartime can make interviewees justifiably reluctant to criticize political actors who may take revenge on dissident voices. Second, the insecurity of the conflict can limit the ability of the researcher to access certain populations and areas of the map, and thus the interviewee sample may be biased in favor of those living in areas of relative security.

To mitigate these weaknesses, I conducted interviews during both the conflict and postconflict periods, revisiting each location up to three times between 2004 and 2010. This allowed me to corroborate information gathered during the war and to flesh out a fuller picture of events that transpired. It also allowed me to identify key moments and situations that I could then reference to help trigger memories in the postconflict period.

The selection of interviewees was determined by my desire to speak to those closest to governance issues at the local level. Thus, while I did conduct many interviews with rebel leaders, I also sought out everyday voices, people most affected by issues of local governance in areas of insurgent control. I identified elite interview subjects on the basis of recommendations from individuals knowledgeable about the different insurgent organizations. Other interview subjects were identified on the basis of their occupations in various sectors, as well as through visits to service provision sites and recommendations from other interviewees.

During the wars, members of insurgent groups sometimes accompanied me to monitor the content of my interviews. For example, the SPLM delegated a representative to be my guide in a 2004 visit to Yei. But generally such monitoring was rare, and even when it did occur, the monitors frequently got bored with the content of my interviews once they realized that I was asking only about the civilian bureaucracy.

Where interviewees requested, I agreed to conduct interviews anonymously. I have also chosen not to include certain names, particularly the names of people engaged in work unrelated to the conflict, instead referring to them only by the types of careers they were engaged in during the conflict. Below is a comprehensive list of the individuals I spoke with during the course of my research. I have organized them according to the country of relevance, rather than the location of the interview.

Sri Lanka Interviews

Anpu, acting administrator, judicial division of the LTTE. Kilinochchi, July 2005.

P. K. Balachandran, journalist, *New Indian Express*. Colombo, January 2010.

Lawrence Christie, Tamils Rehabilitation Organization. Colombo, July 2005.

S. Damian, staff doctor, Kilinochchi Hospital. Kilinochchi, July 2005.

Neloufer De Mel, Department of English, University of Colombo. Colombo, January 2010.

Rohan Edrisinha, Legal and Constitutional Unit, Centre for Policy Alternatives. Colombo, January 2010.

Arjunan Ethirveerasingam, Tamils Rehabilitation Organization. Colombo, June 2004 and July 2005.

Nagalingam Ethirveerasingam, Tamil diaspora activist. Lancaster, CA, October 2005, and Cerritos, CA, February 2006.

Jeyanesan, principal priest, St. John's Church. Batticaloa, July 7, 2005.

Chulani Kodikara, International Center for Ethnic Studies. Colombo, January 2010.

T. Lankanesan, project director, Asian Development Bank. Colombo, June 2004.

Maran, managing director, LTTE Planning and Development Secretariat. July 2004.

Mathy, Administrative and Gender Issues, LTTE Planning and Development Secretariat. Kilinochchi, July 2005.

Jason Miller, Catholic priest. Batticaloa, July 2005.

Nagendran, local resident. Kilinochchi, July 2005.

Pararajasingham, director, Tamils Rehabilitation Organization. Colombo, July 2005, and Los Angeles, December 2005.

Gajendrakumar Ponnambalam, M.P./leader, All Ceylon Tamil Congress. Colombo, January 2010.

Seevaratnam Puleedevan (deceased), secretary general, LTTE Peace Secretariat. Kilinochchi, July 2004 and July 2005.

Murali Reddy, journalist, *The Hindu.* January 2010.

Arjun Ray, major general (ret.), Indian Army/IPKF. Bangalore, December 2006.

Pakiasothy Saravanamuttu, director, Centre for Policy Alternatives. Colombo, January 2010.

T. Sathyamourthy, deputy provincial director of health Services. Kilinochchi, July 2005.

J. Sivam, administrative officer, Tamils Rehabilitation Organization. Batticaloa, July 2005.

K. Sivananthan, GoSL Ministry of Relief, Rehabilitation and Reconciliation. Colombo, July 2005.

Dharmaretnam Sivaram (deceased), Tamil journalist and activist. Marina Del Rey, CA, December 2004.

Jeevan Thiagarajah, executive director, Consortium of Human Agencies. New York, September 2008, and Colombo, January 2010.

J. C. Weliamuna, director, Transparency International. Colombo, January 2010.

Sri Lanka: Anonymous Interviews

Auto driver. Kilinochchi, June 2004.

Diaspora members. Los Angeles, 2006–7, and Toronto, September 2009.

Local civilians. Batticaloa, Jaffna, Kalladi, Kilinochchi, and Trincomalee, June 2004 and July 2005.

Doctors and nurses. Kilinochchi, June 2005.

NGO workers. Batticaloa, Jaffna, Kilinochchi, June 2004 and July 2005.

Tamil professor, University of Colombo. Colombo, July 2005.

Teachers, secondary school. Batticaloa, July 2005.

Sudan Interviews

Akram Osman Abdo, former SPLM/A member. Cairo, July 2008.

Festus Fuli Akim, education coordinator for JRS/SRRC. Nimule, February 2004.

Isaas Alajabo, SRRC deputy director. Rumbek, August 2008.

Bakry Aljack, former SPLM/A member. Cairo, July 2008.

Louis Androga, assistant project manager, Catholic Relief Services. Yei, February 2004.

Sedonia Arkangelo, SRRC gender coordinator/SPLA soldier. Yei, March 2005.

Daniel Arop, SRRC database and monitoring officer. Nimule, February 2004.

Ajith Awan, resident education consultant, Jesuit Refugee Services. Nimule, February 2004.

Patrick Butler, former SPLM/A pilot/Norwegian People's Aid. Rumbek, August 2008.

Michael Deng. Sudan Medical Care senior medical assistant/program administrator. Yei, March 2005.

Chol Gideon, former program manager, Church Ecumenical Action, and member of parliament, Rumbek East County. Rumbek, August 2008.

Emmanuel Gumbiri, former CANS official and program manager, Pact. Juba, August 2008.

Riak Jeroboam, SPLM/A commander. Kampala, January 2004.

Jok Madut Jok, Department of History, Loyola Marymount University. Washington DC, January 2004.

Charles Matata Khamis, CDC program officer, Yei County. Yei, February 2004.

Cherry Leonardi, Department of History, Durham University. Juba, August 2008.

Morris Lokule, commissioner of Yei County. Yei, February 2004.

Zachary Lomo, director, Refugee Law Project. Kampala, February 2004.

Martin Luther, educational officer (International Aid Sweden) and county education officer. Yei, March 2005.

Geoffrey Mangwe, director, Sudan Human Rights Association. Kampala, January 2004.

Abraham Manyuat, assistant field coordinator, Catholic Relief Services. Nimule, February 2004.

Ismail Mathews Mukhtar, executive director of Yei Town. Yei, February 2004.

Constance Nako, SRRC office manager and SPLA lieutenant colonel. Yei, March 2005.

Tracey O'Heir, Jesuit Refugee Services. Nimule, February 2004.

Andrea Usman Okello, head priest, Catholic Diocese of Rumbek. Rumbek, August 2008.

Dickson Omondi, National Democratic Institute. Juba, August 2008.

Aden Raj, Jesuit Refugee Services. Kampala, February 2004 and February 2005.

Lawrence Sala, CDC officer. Yei Town, February 2004.

Sebit, former SPLA soldier. Rumbek, July 2008.

Bob Shuknecht, assistant director, Catholic Relief Services. Juba, August 2008.

Adele Sowinska, director, Catholic Relief Services. Juba, August 2008.

Selena Pita Sworo, head nurse/hospital matron. Yei, February 2005.

Samuel Taban, CRS project manager for Yei and Juba. Yei, February 2004.

Linda Thu, acting country director, Norwegian People's Aid. Juba, August 2008.

Donald Wani, assistant payam administrator. Nimule, February 2004.

Kevin White, former SPLM/A/timber transporter from Kenya. Adjumani, February 2005.

Sudan: Anonymous Interviews

ACROSS officer. Yei, February 2004.

Adult literacy trainers. Nimule, February 2004.

Aid workers with CRS and JRS. Yei and Nimule, February 2004.

Boda-boda driver. Yei Town, February 2004.

SPLM/A officer. Kampala, January 2004.

Local civilians. New Sudan, February 2004 and March 2005.

SAF representative. Kampala, January 2004.

SPLM/A soldiers. Nimule and Yei, February 2004 and March 2005.

Democratic Republic of Congo Interviews

Marcel Akpovo, Amnesty International. Kampala, February and March 2004.

Rwagasana Antoine, FDLR soldier. Goma, July 2009.

Massimo Nicoletti Altimar, Cesvi. Bunia, February 2004.

Richard Bayunda, Centre de Recerche sur l'environnement la Democratie et Droits del Homme. Goma/Gisenyi, February 2004.

Julius Njinkeng Bekong, MONUC. Via e-mail, January 2004.

Joel Bisubu, Justice Plus. Bunia, March 2004.

Horeb Bulambo, communications officer, World Vision. Goma, March 2005.

Kadume Byambo, ex-AFDL member and former RCD-G colonel. Goma, August 2009.

Olivia Caeymaex, Enough Project. Goma, July 2009.

Vit Gionni, field coordinator, MSF. Bunia, February 2004.

Sheldon Munihire Hangi, Centre de Recerche sur l'environnement la Democratie et Droits del Homme. Goma/Gisenyi, February 2004.

Aime-Francois Ilakiza, captain, FDLR. Goma, July 2009.

Madame Ingezayo, owner, Karibu Hotel. Goma, March 2005.

Nyota Ingezayo, resident. Goma, March 2005.

Simba Ingezayo, entrepreneur. Goma, March 2005.

Kaduma, ex-colonel, RCD. Goma, July 2009.

Jack Kahorha, freelance journalist. Goma, July 2009.

Simba Kayunga, Department of Political Science, Makerere University. Kampala, February 2004.

Beverly Lochard, U.S. State Department. New York, February 2001.

Marcos Lorenzana, DDRRR officer, MONUC. Bukavu, March 2005.

Christian Lukusha, Justice Plus. Bunia, March 2004.

Alphonse Maindo, former mayor of Kisangani. Los Angeles, October 2004.

Carla Martinez, head of mission, MSF Holland. Goma, March 2005.

Fred Meylan, field coordinator, MSF. Bunia, February 2004.

Monsignor Monsengwo Pasinya, archbishop of Kisangani. New York, February 2001.

Gode Mpiana, Justice Plus. Bunia, March 2004.

Samuel Muganda, political affairs officer, MONUC. Kampala, February 2005.

Patrick, hotel clerk. Goma, July 2009.

Rwasamanzi, Tutsi mwami. Goma, March 2005.

Karen Stauss, researcher, Human Rights Watch. Goma, March 2005.

Jason Stearns, DDRRR officer, MONUC. New York, October 2004.

Ayaka Suzuki, political affairs officer, MONUC. New York, October 2004.

Aloys Tegera, director, Pole Institute. Goma, July 2009.

Mattias Tunda, former RCD-G intelligence officer. Goma, July 2009.

Patrick Ulrich, deputy head of mission, MSF Holland. Goma, March 2005.

Raphael Wakenge, Initiative Congolaise pour la Justice et la Paix. Bukavu, March 2005.

Elaine Wamba. Via e-mail, January 1999.

Ernest Wamba dia Wamba, University of Dar es Salaam. Dar es Salaam, March 1998.

Herbert Weiss, senior fellow, City University of New York. Via phone, May 2006.

Democratic Republic of Congo: Anonymous Interviews

Driver with an international aid organization. Bukavu, March 2005.

International aid official. Goma, August 2009.

Journalists. Bukavu, March 2005 and August 2009.

Local civilians. Bunia, Bukavu, Goma, and Kisangani, February and March 2004, March 2005.

Local medical personnel. Goma and Bukavu, March 2005.

MONUC Official. Goma, August 2009.

NGO workers. Bukavu and Goma, February 2004, March 2005 and July 2009.

Shopkeepers. Bukavu and Goma, March 2004 and 2005.

RCD administrator. Goma, March 2005.

Other Interviews

Shameza Abdulla, Forum on Early Warning and Early Response (FEWER), program manager. Via e-mail, February 2005.

Adam Barbolet, International Alert. Via e-mail, August 2006.

References

Abdel Salam, A. H., and Alex de Waal, eds. 2001. *The Phoenix State: Civil Society and the Future of Sudan*. Trenton, NJ: Red Sea Press.

Abdullah, Ibrahim. 1998. "Bush Path to Destruction: The Origin and Character of the Revolutionary United Front/Sierra Leone." *Journal of Modern African Studies* 36 (2): 203–225.

———. 2006. "Africans Do Not Live By Bread Alone: Against Greed, Not Grievance." *Africa Review of Books* 2 (1): 12–13.

Afoaku, Osita. 2002. "Congo's Rebels: Their Origins, Motivations and Strategies." In Clark 2002a, 109–128.

Africa Confidential. 2008. "The Man Who Says No." Vol. 49 No. 23. http://www.africa-confidential.com/article-preview/id/2866/No-Title.

African Rights. 1995. *Imposing Empowerment? Aid and Civil Institutions in Southern Sudan*. London: African Rights.

———. 1997. *Food and Power in Sudan: A Critique of Humanitarianism*. London: African Rights.

Agnew, John. 1994. "The Territorial Trap: The Geographical Assumptions of International Relations Theory." *Review of International Political Economy* 1(1): 53–80.

Ahmad, Eqbal. 1982. "Revolutionary Warfare and Counterinsurgency." In *Guerrilla Strategies: An Historical Anthology from the Long March to Afghanistan*, edited by Gerard Chaliand, 241–262. Berkeley: University of California Press.

Akol, Lam. 2009. *SPLM/SPLA: Inside an African Revolution*. Khartoum: Khartoum University Printing Press.

Alier, Abel. 1990. *Southern Sudan: Too Many Agreements Dishonored*. Exeter, UK: Ithaca.

Anderson, Benedict. 1983. *Imagined Communities: Reflections on the Origin and Spread of Nationalism*. New York: Verso.

Anderson, Mary. 1999. *Do No Harm: How Aid Can Support Peace—or War*. Boulder, CO: Lynne Rienner.

———. 2001. *Reflection on the Practice of Outside Assistance: Can We Know What Good We Do*. Handbook for Conflict Transformation. Berghoff Research Center.

Anderson, Perry. 1976. "The Antinomies of Antonio Gramsci." *New Left Review* 100 (November–January): 5–80.

Arendt, Hannah. 1970. *On Violence*. New York: Harcourt Brace.

Arjona, Ana. 2009a. "Armed Groups Governance in Civil War: A Short Literature Review." Unpublished Manuscript.

———. 2009b. "One National War, Multiple Local Orders: An Inquiry into the Unit of Analysis of War and Post-War Interventions." In *Law in Peace Negotiations*, edited by Morten Bergsmo and Pablo Kalmanovitz. FICHL Publication Series. Oslo: International Peace Research Institute.

———. 2009c. "Social Orders in Warring Times: Armed Groups' Strategies and Civilian Agency in Civil War." Paper presented at the program on Order, Conflict and Violence, Yale University, February.

———. 2010. "Social Order in Civil War." PhD diss., Yale University.

Arou, K. N., and B. Yongo-Bure, eds. 1988. *North-South Relations in the Sudan since the Addis Ababa Agreement.* Khartoum: University of Khartoum.

Arunatilake, Nisha, Sisira Jayasuriya, and Saman Kelegama. 2001. "The Economic Cost of the War in Sri Lanka." *World Development* 29 (9): 1483–1500.

Asad, Talal. 2008. *On Suicide Bombing.* New York: Columbia University Press.

Asuman, Bisiika. 2006. "Who Will Be DR Congo's Next President?" *New Times,* August 13.

Atem, A. 1999. "The Current Status of the Civil Military Relations: The Case of the SPLM/A." Paper presented at the Conference on Civil Military Relations, Nairobi, April.

Autesserre, Severine. 2006. "Local Violence, International Indifference? Post-Conflict "Settlement" in the Eastern D.R. Congo (2003–2005)." PhD diss., New York University.

——. 2008. "The Trouble with Congo—How Local Disputes Fuel Regional Violence." *Foreign Affairs,* May/June, 94–110.

Ayebare, Adonia. 1998. "Interview with Dr. Wamba dia Wamba." *The Monitor,* August 26.

Ayoob, Mohammed. 1998. "Subaltern Realism: International Relations Theory Meets the Third World." In Neuman 1998, 31–54.

Badal, Raphael. K. 1994. "Political Cleavages within the Southern Sudan: An Empirical Analysis of the Re-Division Debate." In Harir and Tvedt 1994, 105–125.

Balasingham, Adele. 2001. *The Will to Freedom: An Inside View of Tamil Resistance.* London: Fairmax.

Ballentine, Karen, and Jake Sherman, eds. 2003. *The Political Economy of Armed Conflict: Beyond Greed and Grievance.* Boulder, CO: Lynne Rienner.

Bangura, Yusuf. 2000. "Strategic Policy Failure and Governance in Sierra Leone." *Journal of Modern African Studies* 38 (4): 551–577.

Barnett, Michael. 2001. "Authority, Intervention, and the Outer Limits of International Relations Theory." In Callaghy, Kassimir, and Latham 2001, 47–68.

Barnett, Michael, and Martha Finnemore. 1999. "The Politics, Power, and Pathologies of International Organizations." *International Organization* 53 (4): 699–732.

Bastian, Sunil. 2006. "Sri Lanka's International Straitjacket." *Himal South Asian,* December, 37–39.

——. 2007. *The Politics of Foreign Aid in Sri Lanka: Promoting Markets and Supporting Peace.* Colombo: International Center for Ethnic Studies.

Bates, Robert, and Dau Hsiang Lien. 1985. "A Note on Taxation and Representative Government." *Politics and Society* 14 (1): 53–70.

Bayart, Jean-Francois. 1993. *The State in Africa: The Politics of the Belly.* London: Longman.

BBC Monitoring. 1998. "Rebel-Held Territory to Be 'Showpiece,'" September 7.

BBC News. 2000. "Congolese Rebels Choose Onusumba as Leader," October 28.

BBC News. 2003. "Resource Fight in North-east Congo," March 12.

Beckett, Ian. 2001. *Modern Insurgencies and Counter-Insurgencies: Guerrillas and their Opponents since 1750.* London: Routledge.

Berdal, Mats, and David M. Malone, eds. 2000. *Greed and Grievance: Economic Agendas in Civil Wars.* Boulder, CO: Lynne Rienner.

Bergen, Peter, and Katherine Tiedemann. 2010. "No Secrets in the Sky." *New York Times,* April 26.

Bhatia, Michael. 2005. "Fighting Words: Naming Terrorists, Bandits, Rebels and other Violent Actors." *Third World Quarterly* 26 (1): 5–22.

Bierschenk, Thomas, and Jean-Pierre De Sardan. 1997. "Local Powers and a Distant State in Rural Central African Republic." *Journal of Modern African Studies* 35:441–468.

Blaney, David, and Naeem Inayatullah. 2004. *International Relations and the Problem of Difference*. New York: Routledge.

Bob, Clifford. 2006. *The Marketing of Rebellion: Insurgents, Media and International Activism*. Cambridge: Cambridge University Press.

Bobbit, Phillip. 2003. *The Shield of Achilles*. New York: Anchor.

———. 2008. *Terror and Consent: The Wars for the Twenty-first Century*. New York: Knopf.

Boone, Catherine. 1998. "'Empirical Statehood' and Reconfigurations of Political Order." In *The African State at a Critical Juncture: Between Disintegration and Reconfiguration*, edited by Leonardo Villalon and Phillip Huxtable, 129–141. Boulder, CO: Lynne Rienner.

Bose, Sumantra. 1994. *State, Nations, Sovereignty: Sri Lanka, India and the Tamil Eelam Movement*. New Delhi: Sage.

Bradbury, Mark. 2008. *Becoming Somaliland*. London: James Currey.

Branch, Adam. 2004. "International Justice, Local Injustice." *Dissent Magazine* 51:3. http://www.dissentmagazine.org/article/?article=336.

———. 2007. "The Ambiguous Politics of Global Justice: Political Violence and the Violence of Humanitarianism in Northern Uganda." PhD diss., Columbia University.

Branch, Adam, and Zachariah Mampilly. 2005. "Winning the War, but Losing the Peace? The Dilemma of SPLM/A Civil Administration and the Tasks Ahead." *Journal of Modern African Studies* 43 (1): 1–20.

Bulathsinghala, Frances. 2003a. "Tiger and Its Lair: The LTTE Quietly Builds Up Its 'State' in the Northeast." *The Week*, November 16.

———. 2003b. "Tiger Cops Learn Sinhala." *Sunday Observer*, October 12.

Bull, Hedley. 1977. *The Anarchical Society: A Study of Order in World Politics*. London: Macmillan.

Burke, Robert. 1984. *UNITA: A Case Study in Modern Insurgency*. Virginia: Marine Corps Staff and Command College.

Buzan, Barry. 1983. *People, States, and Fear: The National Security Problem in International Relations*. Chapel Hill: University of North Carolina Press.

Byman, Daniel. 2001. *Trends in Outside Support for Insurgent Movements*. Santa Monica: RAND Corp.

Cabral, Amilcar. 1966. "Presuppositions and Objectives of National Liberation in Relation to Social Structure." Speech delivered to the First Solidarity Conference of the Peoples of Africa, Asia and Latin America, Havana, January 6.

Callaghy, Thomas. 1984. *The State-Society Struggle: Zaire in Comparative Perspective*. New York: Columbia University Press.

———. 2001. "Networks and Governance in Africa: Innovation in the Debt Regime." In Callaghy, Kassimir, and Latham 2001, 115–148.

Callaghy, Thomas, Ronald Kassimir, and Robert Latham, eds. 2001. *Intervention and Transnationalism in Africa: Global Networks of Power*. Cambridge: Cambridge University Press.

Carayannis, Tatiana. 2003. "The Complex Wars of the Congo: Towards a New Analytic Approach." *Journal of Asian and African Studies* 38 (2–3): 232–255.

Castells, Manuel, Shujiro Yazawa, and Emma Kiselyova. 1996. "Insurgents against the Global Order: A Comparative Analysis of the Zapatistas in Mexico, the American Militia and Japan's Aum Shinrikyo." *Berkeley Journal of Sociology* 40:21–59.

Centeno, Miguel. 2002. *Blood and Debt: War and the Nation-State in Latin America.* Philadelphia: Penn State Press.

Chaliand, Gerard, and Arnaud Blin. 2007. *The History of Terrorism from Antiquity to Al Qaeda.* Berkeley: University of California Press.

Chalk, Peter. 2000. "Liberation Tigers of Tamil Eelam's (LTTE) International Organization and Operations—A Preliminary Analysis." Commentary No. 77, Canadian Security Intelligence Service Publications.

Chingono, Mark. 1996. *The State, Violence and Development: The Political Economy of War in Mozambique 1975–1992.* Aldershot, England: Avebury.

Clapham, Andrew. 2006. "Human Rights Obligations of Non-State Actors in Conflict Situations." *International Review of the Red Cross* 88:491–523.

Clapham, Christopher. 1996. *Africa and the International System: The Politics of State Survival.* Cambridge: Cambridge University Press.

——, ed. 1998a. *African Guerrillas.* Oxford: James Currey Ltd.

——. 1998b. "Introduction: Analysing African Insurgencies." In Clapham 1998a, 1–18.

Clark, John, ed. 2002a. *The African Stakes of the Congo War.* New York: Palgrave.

——. 2002b. "Museveni's Adventure in the Congo War: Uganda's Vietnam." In Clark 2002a, 145–168.

Cohen, Stanley. 2001. *States of Denial: Knowing about Atrocities and Suffering.* Cambridge: Blackwell Publishers.

Collier, Paul, and Anke Hoeffler. 2004. "Greed and Grievance in Civil War." *Oxford Economic Papers* 56 (4): 563–595.

Crossley, Kenn. 2004. "Why Not to State-Build New Sudan." In Kingston and Spears 2004, 135–152.

Dak, Othwonh. 1988. "Southern Regions: Decentralization or Recentralizations." In Arou and Yongo-Bure 1988.

Daly, Martin. 1993. "Broken Bridge and Empty Basket: The Political and Economic Background of the Sudanese Civil War." In Daly and Sikainga 1993.

Daly, Martin, and Ahmad Alawad Sikainga, eds. 1993. *Civil War in the Sudan.* London: British Academic Press.

Daniels, Valentine. 1997. "Suffering Nation and Alienation." In *Social Suffering,* edited by Arthur Kleinman, Veena Das, and Margaret Lock, 309–358. Oxford: Oxford University Press.

Debray, Regis. 1980. *Revolution in the Revolution? Armed Struggle and Political Struggle in Latin America.* New York: Grove.

DeClercq, Geert. 2004. "Tamil Bank Symbol of Sri Lankan Rebel Autonomy." Reuters, March 10.

DeMars, William. 1994. "Tactics of Protection: International Human Rights Organizations in the Ethiopian conflict, 1980–1986." In *Africa, Human Rights, and the Global System,* edited by Eileen McCarthy-Arnolds, 81–106. Westport, CT: Greenwood Press.

De Mel, Neloufer. 2007. *Militarizing Sri Lanka: Popular Culture, Memory and Narrative in the Armed Conflict.* Los Angeles: Sage.

Desai, Raj, and Harry Eckstein. 1990. "Insurgency: The Transformation of Peasant Rebellion." *World Politics* 42 (4): 441–465.

De Silva, Chandra. 1999. "The Role of Education in Ameliorating Political Violence in Sri Lanka." In Rotberg 1999, 109–130.

de Waal, Alex——. 1997a. *Famine Crimes: Politics and the Disaster Relief Industry in Africa.* Oxford: James Currey.

——. 1997b. "Sudan: Social Engineering, Slavery, and War." *Covert Action Quarterly* 60.

de Zeeuw, Jeroen, ed. 2008. *From Soldiers to Politicians: Transforming Rebel Movements after Civil War.* Boulder, CO: Lynne Rienner.

Dunn, Kevin. 2002. "A Survival Guide to Kinshasa: Lessons of the Father, Passed Down to the Son." In Clark 2002a, 53–74.

Englebert, Pierre. 2003. "Why Congo Persists: Globalization, Sovereignty, and the Violent Reproduction of a Weak State." Queen Elizabeth House Working Paper 95, Oxford University.

———. 2009. *Africa: Unity, Sovereignty, and Sorrow.* Boulder, CO: Lynne Rienner.

Eriksen, Stein Sundstol. 2005. "The Congo War and the Prospects for State Formation: Rwanda and Uganda Compared." *Third World Quarterly* 26 (7): 1097–1113.

Escude, Carlos. 1998. "An Introduction to Peripheral Realism and Its Implications for the Interstate System: Argentina and the Condor II Missile Project." In Neuman 1998a, 55–76.

Ethirveerasingam, Nagalingam. 1999. "An Appraisal of Education and Sports in the Northeast Province of Sri Lanka." Provincial Ministry of Education, Culture, and Sports, May.

Fanon, Frantz. 1968. *The Wretched of the Earth.* New York: Grove.

Fearon, James. 2007. "Iraq's Civil Wars." *Foreign Affairs* 86 (2): 2–15.

Fearon, James, and David Laitin. 2003. "Ethnicity, Insurgency, and Civil War." *American Political Science Review* 97 (1): 75–90.

Ferguson, James, and Akhil Gupta. 2002. "Spatializing States: Toward an Ethnography of Neoliberal Governmentality." *American Ethnologist* 29 (4): 981–1002.

Forrest, Joshua. 1998. "State Inversion and Non-State Politics." In *The African State at a Critical Juncture: Between Disintegration and Reconfiguration,* edited by Leonardo Villalon and Phillip Huxtable, 45–56. Boulder, CO: Lynne Rienner.

Foucault, Michel. 1982. "The Subject and Power." In *Michel Foucault: Beyond Structuralism and Hermeneutics,* edited by Hubert L. Dreyfus and Paul Rabinow, 208–228. Chicago: University of Chicago Press.

Friedrichs, Jörg. 2001. "The Meaning of New Medievalism." *European Journal of International Relations* 7 (4): 475–501.

Gambetta, Diego. 1993. *The Sicilian Mafia: The Business of Private Protection.* Cambridge, MA: Harvard University Press.

Garang, John. 1992. *The Call for Democracy in Sudan.* London: Kegan Paul International.

Gates, Scott. 2002. "Recruitment and Allegiance: The Microfoundations of Rebellion." *Journal of Conflict Resolution* 46 (1): 111–130.

Gerring, John. 2004. "What Is a Case Study and What Is It Good For?" *American Political Science Review* 98:341–354. New York: Cambridge University Press.

Giap, Vo Nguyen. 2004. *Fighting under Siege.* Hanoi: Gioi Publishers.

Gleditsch, Kristian. 2007. "Transnational Dimensions of Civil War." *Journal of Peace Research* 44 (3): 293–309.

Goodhand, Jonathan, and Nick Lewer. 1999. "Sri Lanka: NGOs and Peace-Building in Complex Political Emergencies." *Third World Quarterly* 20 (1): 69–87.

Gough, David. 2001. "Congo War Blamed for 2 1/2 Million Deaths." *San Francisco Chronicle,* May 5.

Gramsci, Antonio. 1992. *The Prison Notebooks.* New York: Columbia University Press.

Guevara, Ernesto. 1969. *Guerrilla Warfare.* New York: Vintage Books.

———. 1999. *The African Dream: The Diaries of the Revolutionary War in the Congo.* New York: Grove.

Guha, Ranajit. 1997. *Domination without Hegemony: History and Power in Colonial India.* Cambridge, MA: Harvard University Press.

Gunasinghe, Newton. 2004. "The Open Economy and Its Impact on Ethnic Relations in Sri Lanka." In Winslow and Woost 2004, 99–114.

Gutiérrez Sanín, Francisco. 2004. "Crime, (Counter-)Insurgency and the Privatization of Security—The case of Medellín, Colombia." *Environment and Urbanization* 16 (2): 17–30.

———. 2008. "Telling the Difference: Guerrillas and Paramilitaries in the Colombian War." *Politics & Society* 36 (3): 3–34.

Gutiérrez Sanín, Francisco, and Mauricio Barón. 2005. "Re-stating the State: Paramilitary Territorial Control and Political Order in Colombia (1978–2004)." Working paper 66, Crisis States Research Centre, London School of Economics.

Guyer, Jane. 1994. "The Spatial Dimensions of Civil Society in Africa: An Anthropologist Looks at Nigeria." In *Civil Society and the State in Africa,* edited by John Harbeson, Donald Rothchild, and Naomi Chazan, 215–230. Boulder, CO: Lynne Rienner.

Hall, Mimi. 2008. "US Has Mandela on Terrorist List." *USA Today,* April 30.

Harir, Sharif, and Terje Tvedt, eds. *Short-Cut to Decay: The Case of the Sudan.* Uppsala, Sweden: Nordiska Afrikainstitutet.

Herbst, Jeffrey. 2000. *States and Power in Africa: Comparative Lessons in Authority and Control.* Princeton: Princeton University Press.

Heritage. 1987. "Colonel Dr. John Garang Speaks to Heritage on (War and Peace in the Sudan)," November 2.

Heywood, Linda. 1989. "UNITA and Ethnic Nationalism in Angola." *Journal of Modern African Studies* 27 (1): 47–66.

Hobbes, Thomas. 1997. *Leviathan.* New York: Touchstone.

Hobsbawm, Eric. 1990. *Bandits.* London: Abacus.

Hoffman, Bruce. 2008. "The Myth of Grass-Roots Terrorism: Why Osama bin Laden Still Matters." *Foreign Affairs* 87: 133–138.

Hoole, R., D. Somasundaram, K. Sritharan, and R. Thiranagama. 1990. *The Broken Palmyra, the Tamil Crisis in Sri Lanka: An Inside Account.* Claremont, CA: Sri Lanka Studies Institute.

Horowitz, Donald. 1985. *Ethnic Groups in Conflict.* Berkeley: University of California Press.

Human Rights Watch. 1994. *Civilian Devastation: Abuses by All Parties in the War in Southern Sudan.* New York: Human Rights Watch.

———. 1999. *Casualties of War: Civilians, Rule of Law, and Democratic Freedoms.* 11 (1A) February. New York: Human Rights Watch.

———. 2000. *Eastern Congo Ravaged: Killing Civilians and Silencing Protest.* 12 (3A) May. New York: Human Rights Watch.

———. 2006. *Funding the "Final War": LTTE Intimidation and Extortion in the Tamil Diaspora.* New York: Human Rights Watch.

Humphries, Macartan, and Jeremy Weinstein. 2006. "Handling and Manhandling Civilians in War." *American Political Science Review* 100 (3): 429–447.

Idris, Amir. 2001. *Sudan's Civil War: Slavery, Race and Formational Identities.* Lewiston, NY: Edwin Mellen Press.

———. 2005. *Conflict and Politics of Identity in Sudan.* New York: Palgrave Macmillan.

International Crisis Group. 2001. "Aceh: Can Autonomy Stem the Conflict?" Asia Report 18, Jakarta/Brussels, June 27.

———. 2003. *The Kivus: The Forgotten Crucible of the Congo Conflict.* Africa Report 56, Nairobi/Brussels, January 24.

———. 2004. "Southern Philippines Backgrounder: Terrorism and the Peace Process." Asia Report 80, Singapore/Brussels, July 13.

Integrated Regional Information Networks (IRIN). 1999. "Democratic Republic of Congo: Ilunga New RCD Leader." Update no. 675 for Central and Eastern Africa, May 20.

Jackson, Paul. 2003. "Warlords as Alternative Forms of Governance." *Small Wars & Insurgencies* 14 (2): 131–150.

Jackson, Robert. 1990. *Quasi-states: Sovereignty, International Relations and the Third World.* Cambridge: Cambridge University Press.

Jackson, Stephen. 2006. "Sons of Which Soil? The Language and Politics of Autochthony in Eastern D.R. Congo." *African Studies Review* 49 (2): 95–123.

Jenne, Erin. 2003. "Sri Lanka: A Fragmented State." In Rotberg, 2003, 219–244.

Jeyaraj, D. B. S. 1985. "How Strong are the 'Boys'?" *Frontline* 2. April 5. http://www.flonnet.com/fl2701/stories/19850405080.htm.

——. 2001. "The Historical Quest to Restore Tamil Rights." *Sunday Leader.* Colombo, March 18.

——. 2004. "The Conflicts Within." *Frontline* 21 (7). http://www.hinduonnet.com/fline/fl2107/stories/20040409005201300.htm.

Johnson, Douglas. 1998. "The Sudan People's Liberation Army and the Problem of Factionalism." In Clapham 1998a, 53–72.

——. 2003. *The Root Causes of Sudan's Civil Wars.* Oxford: James Currey.

——. 2009. "Mamdani's 'Settlers,' 'Natives,' and the War on Terror." *African Affairs* 108 (433): 655–660.

Johnson, Douglas, and Gerard Prunier. 1993. "The Foundation and Expansion of the Sudan People's Liberation Army." In Daly and Sikainga 1993.

Jok, Jok M., and Sharon Hutchinson. 1999. "Sudan's Prolonged Second Civil War and the Militarization of Nuer and Dinka Ethnic Identities." *African Studies Review* 42 (2): 125–145.

Joseph, Richard. 2002. "War, State-Making, and Democracy in Africa." In *Beyond State Crisis? Postcolonial Africa and Post-Soviet Eurasia in Comparative Perspective,* edited by Mark Beissinger and Crawford Young, 241–262. Baltimore: Johns Hopkins University Press.

Kahler, Miles, and David A. Lake. 2004. "Governance in a Global Economy: Political Authority in Transition." *PS: Political Science and Politics* 37 (3): 409–414.

Kalyvas, Stathis. 2003. "The Ontology of 'Political Violence': Action and Identity in Civil Wars." *Perspectives on Politics* 1:475–494.

——. 2006. *The Logic of Violence in Civil War.* New York: Cambridge University Press.

Kamalendran, Chris. 2004. "LTTE Opens First 'Court' in East." *Sunday Times.*

Karim, Ataul. 1996. *Operation Lifeline Sudan: A Review.* Geneva: UN Department of Humanitarian Affairs.

Kasfir, Nelson. 2002. "Dilemmas of Popular Support in Guerilla War: The National Resistance Army in Uganda, 1981–1986." Paper presented to the Laboratory in Comparative Ethnic Processes 6, UCLA, November.

——. 2004. "State Formation by Guerrillas: Choosing Extensive Administrative Structures for the Rwenzururu Kingdom Government." Paper presented to the African Studies Association, San Francisco, November.

——. 2005. "Guerrillas and Civilian Participation: The National Resistance Army in Uganda, 1981–86." *The Journal of Modern African Studies* 43: 271–296.

Kassimir, Ronald. 2001. "Producing Local Politics: Governance, Representation, and Non-State Organizations in Africa." In Callaghy, Kassimir, and Latham 2001, 93–114.

Kayunga, Simba. 2000. "The Leadership Crisis within the Congolese Rally for Democracy (RCD) and Its Implications for the Peace Process in the Democratic

Republic of Congo." Paper presented at the Conference on Conflict and Peace-Making in the Great Lakes Region, Entebbe, Uganda, July 10–12.

Keen, David. 1994. *The Benefits of Famine: A Political Economy of Famine and Relief in Southwestern Sudan, 1983–1989.* Princeton: Princeton University Press.

Keethaponcalan, S. I., and Ravi Jayawardana, eds. 2009. *Sri Lanka: Perspectives on the Ceasefire Agreement of 2002.* Colombo, Sri Lanka: South Asia Peace Initiative.

Kelegama, Saman. 1999. "Economic Costs of Conflict in Sri Lanka." In Rotberg 1999, 71–88.

Keller, Edmond. 1997. "Rethinking African Regional Security." In Lake and Morgan 1997, 296–317.

Khapalwak, Ruhullah. 2010. "A Look at America's New Hope: The Afghan Tribes." *New York Times,* January 29.

Kilcullen, David. 2009. *The Accidental Guerrilla: Fighting Small Wars in the Midst of a Big One.* New York: Oxford University Press.

Kingston, Paul, and Ian Spears, eds. 2004. *States-within-States: Incipient Political Entities in the Post–Cold War Era.* New York: Palgrave.

Kohli, Atul. 2002. "State, Society and Development." In *Political Science: The State of the Discipline,* edited by Ira Katznelson and Helen Milner, 84–117. New York: Norton.

Krasner, Stephen. 1999. *Sovereignty: Organized Hypocrisy.* Princeton: Princeton University Press.

——. 2001. "Sovereignty." *Foreign Policy* 122:20–29.

Kriger, Norma. 1992. *Zimbabwe's Guerrilla War: Peasant Voices.* Cambridge: Cambridge University Press.

Kuol, Monyluak Alor. 1997. *Administration of Justice in the (SPLA/M) Liberated Areas: Court Cases in War-torn Southern Sudan.* Oxford: Refugee Studies Programme.

——. 1999. "Holding Armed Opposition Groups Accountable: The Case of the Sudan People's Liberation Movement/Army." Working paper, International Council on Human Rights Policy, Geneva.

Lacina, Bethany, and Nils Petter Gleditsch. 2005. "Monitoring Trends in Global Combat: A New Dataset of Battle Deaths." *European Journal of Population* 21(2–3): 145–166.

Lake, David. 2008. "The New American Empire?" *International Studies Perspectives* 9:281–289.

Lake, David and Patrick Morgan, eds. *Regional Orders: Building Security in a New World Order.* Pennsylvania: Pennsylvania State University Press.

Lagu, S. 1980. *Decentralization: A Necessity for the Southern Provinces of the Sudan.* Juba, Sudan: Juba University.

Lemarchand, Rene. 2003. "Democratic Republic of Congo: From Failure to Potential Reconstruction." In Rotberg 2003, 29–70.

Leonard, David, and Scott Strauss. 2003. *Africa's Stalled Development: International Causes and Cures.* Boulder, CO: Lynne Rienner.

Leonardi, Cherry. 2007. "Violence, Sacrifice and Chiefship in Central Equatoria, Southern Sudan." *Africa* 77:535–558.

Lesch, A. M. 1998. *The Sudan: Contested National Identities.* Bloomington: Indiana University Press.

Lichbach, Mark. 1995. *The Rebel's Dilemma.* Ann Arbor: University of Michigan Press.

Lindqvist, Sven. 2003. *A History of Bombing.* New York: New Press.

——. 2007. *Terra Nullius: A Journey through No One's Land.* New York: New Press.

Lintner, Bertil. 1990. *The Rise and Fall of the Communist Party of Burma (CPB).* Ithaca: Cornell Southeast Asia Program.

Lischer, Sarah. 2003. "Collateral Damage: Humanitarian Assistance as a Cause of Conflict." *International Security* 28 (1): 79–109.

——. 2005. *Dangerous Sanctuaries: Refugee Camps, Civil Wars, and the Dilemmas of Humanitarian Aid.* Ithaca: Cornell University Press.

Longman, Timothy. 2002. "The Complex Reasons for Rwanda's Engagement in Congo." In Clark 2002a, 129–144.

Lubkemann, Stephen. 2008. *Culture in Chaos: An Anthropology of the Social Condition in War.* Chicago: University of Chicago Press.

Luttwalk, Edward. 1999. "Give War a Chance." *Foreign Affairs* 78:36–44.

Majavu, Mandisi. 2003. "The Failure of an African Political Leadership: An Interview with Professor Wamba dia Wamba." *Z-Net,* July 18. http://www.zcommunica tions.org/the-failure-of-an-african-political-leadership-by-mandisi-majavu.

Malok, Elijah. 2009. *The Southern Sudan Struggle for Liberty.* Nairobi: Kenway Publications.

Mamdani, Mahmood. 1993. "Pluralism and the Right of Association." CBR Working Paper 29, Centre for Basic Research, Kampala.

——. 1996. *Citizen and Subject: Contemporary Africa and the Legacy of Late Colonialism.* Princeton: Princeton University Press.

——. 2001. *When Victims Become Killers.* Princeton: Princeton University Press.

Mampilly, Zachariah. 2007. "Stationary Bandits: Understanding Rebel Governance." PhD diss., University of California, Los Angeles.

——. 2009. "A Marriage of Inconvenience: Tsunami Aid and the Unraveling of the LTTE and the GoSL's Complex Dependency." *Civil Wars* 11 (3): 302–320.

Mann, Michael. 1986. *The Sources of Social Power: A History of Power from the Beginning to A.D. 1760.* Vol. 1. Cambridge: Cambridge University Press.

Manor, James. 2006. "Introduction: Synthesizing Case Study Findings." In *Aid That Works: Successful Development in Fragile States,* edited by James Manor, 1–36. Washington, DC: World Bank Publications.

Mao Zedong. 1961. *On Guerilla Warfare.* New York: Praeger.

Mararo, Bucyalimwe Stanislas. 2004. "Le TPD à Goma (Nord-Kivu): Mythes et réalités." In *L'Afrique des Grands Lacs: Annuaire 2003/2004,* edited by Filip Reyntjens, Paris: Harmattan.

Marten, Kimberly. 2006–7. "Warlordism in Comparative Perspective." *International Security* 31 (3): 41–73.

Mbembe, Achille. 2000. "At the Edge of the World: Boundaries, Territoriality, and Sovereignty in Africa." *Public Culture* 12 (1): 259–284.

McCalpin, Jermaine. 2002. "Historicity of a Crisis: The Origins of the Congo War." In Clark 2002a, 33–52.

McClintock, Cynthia. 1998. *Revolutionary Movements in Latin America: El Salvador's FMLN and Peru's Shining Path.* Washington, DC: US Institute of Peace Press.

McDermott, Jeremy. 2008. "Colombia's FARC Back in Spotlight." *BBC News,* February 28.

McLaughlin, Abraham. 2004. "Sudan's Refugees Wait and Hope." *Christian Science Monitor,* February 18.

Menkhaus, Ken. 2004. *Somalia: State Collapse and the Threat of Terrorism.* New York: Routledge.

——. 2007. "Governance without Government in Somalia: Spoilers, State Building, and the Politics of Coping." *International Security* 31 (3): 74–106.

Metelits, Claire. 2004. "Reformed Rebels? Democratization, Global Norms, and the Sudan People's Liberation Army." *Africa Today* 51 (1): 65–82.

Migdal, Joel. 1988. *Strong States and Weak Societies: State-Society Relations and State Capabilities in the Third World.* Princeton: Princeton University Press.

——. 2004. *Boundaries and Belonging: States and Societies in the Struggle to Shape Identities and Local Practices.* New York: Cambridge University Press.

Minear, Larry, ed. 1991. *Humanitarianism under Siege: A Critical Review of Operation Lifeline Sudan.* Trenton, NJ: Red Sea Press.

Mkandawire, Thandika. 2002. "The Terrible Toll of Post-colonial 'Rebel Groups' in Africa: Towards an Explanation of the Violence against the Peasantry." *Journal of Modern African Studies* 40 (2): 181–215.

Montague, Dena. 2002. "Stolen Goods: Coltan and Conflict in the Democratic Republic of Congo." *SAIS Review* 22:103–118.

Moore, Barrington. 1966. *Social Origins of Dictatorship and Democracy: Lord and Peasant in the Making of the Modern World.* Boston: Beacon Press.

Moore, Mick. 2004. "Revenues, State Formation, and the Quality of Governance in Developing Countries." *International Political Science Review* 25 (3): 297–319.

Mortimer, Edward. 1998. "Under What Circumstances, Should the UN Intervene Militarily in a 'Domestic' Crisis?" In *Peacemaking and Peacekeeping for the New Century,* edited by Olara Otunnu and Michael W. Doyle, 111–144. Lanham, MD: Rowman and Littlefield.

Mukarji, Apratim. 2000. *The War in Sri Lanka: Unending Conflict?* New Delhi: Har Anand Publications.

Munro, Lauchlan. 2004. "Providing Humanitarian Assistance Behind Rebel Lines: UNICEF's Easter Zaire Operation 1996–1998." In Kingston and Spears 2004, 119–134.

Munro, William. 1996. "Power, Peasants and Political Development: Reconsidering State Construction in Africa." *Comparative Studies in Society and History* 38 (1): 112–148.

Muttettuwegama, Ramani. 2001. "'But I am Both': Equality in the Context of Women Living under Parallel Legal Systems: The Problem of Sri Lanka." *Lines Magazine* (Colombo), December.

Nabulsi, Karma. 2001. "Evolving Conceptions of Civilians and Belligerents: One Hundred Years after the Hague Peace Conferences." In *Civilians in War,* edited by Simon Chesterman, 9–24. Boulder, CO: Lynne Rienner.

Nadarajah, S., and D. Sriskandarajah. 2005. "Liberation Struggle or Terrorism? The Politics of Naming the LTTE." *Third World Quarterly* 26 (1): 87–100.

Neeran. 1996. "The Civil Administration in Thamil Eelam." Unpublished manuscript, May 10.

Nest, Michael, with François Grignon and Emizet F. Kisangani, eds. 2006. *The Democratic Republic of Congo: Economic Dimensions of War and Peace.* Boulder, CO: Lynne Rienner.

Neuman, Stephanie. 1998a. *International Relations Theory and the Third World.* New York: Palgrave.

——. 1998b. "International Relations Theory and the Third World: An Oxymoron?" In Neuman 1998a, 1–30.

Newbury, Catherine. 1993. *The Cohesion of Oppression: Clientship and Ethnicity in Rwanda 1860–1960.* New York: Columbia University Press.

New York Times. 1862. "The Capture of New Orleans," April 28.

Nolan-Haley, Jacqueline. 2002. "The Intersection of Religion, Race, Class, and Ethnicity in Community Conflict." *Negotiation Journal,* October, 251–255.

Nordstrom, Carolyn. 1992. "The Dirty War: Civilian Experience of Conflict in Mozambique and Sri Lanka." In *Internal Conflict and Governance,* edited by Kumar Rupesinghe, 27–43. London: St. Martin's.

——. 2001. "Out of the Shadows." In Callaghy, Kassimir, and Latham 2001, 216–239.

——. 2004. *Shadows of War: Violence, Power, and International Profiteering in the Twenty-First Century.* Berkeley: University of California Press.

North, Douglass. 1990. *Institutions, Institutional Change and Economic Performance.* New York: Cambridge University Press.

Nzongola-Ntalaja, Georges. 2002. *The Congo from Leopold to Kabila. A People's History.* London: Zed Books.

Obi, Cyril. 2001. "Global, State, and Local Interactions: Power, Authority and Conflict in the Niger Delta Oil Communities." In Callaghy, Kassimir, and Latham 2001, 173–196.

Olson, Mancur. 1993. "Dictatorship, Democracy, and Development." *American Political Science Review* 87 (3): 567–576.

Organski, Abramo F. K., and Jacek Kugler. 1980. *The War Ledger.* Chicago: University of Chicago Press.

Ortiz, Roman. 2002. "Insurgent Strategies in the Post-Cold War: The Case of the Revolutionary Armed Forces of Colombia." *Studies in Conflict & Terrorism* 25:127–143.

O'Toole Salinas, Anne, and Brian C. D'Silva. 1999. *Evolution of a Transition Strategy and Lessons Learned: USAID Funded Activities in the West Bank of Southern Sudan, 1993 to 1999.* Washington, D.C.: USAID Office of Foreign Disaster Assistance.

Ottaway, Marina. 2003. "Rebuilding State Institutions in Collapsed States." In *State Failure, Collapse and Reconstruction,* edited by Jennifer Milliken, 245–266. New York: Blackwell.

Pandolfi, Mariella. 2003. "Transitory Identities, Mobile Sovereignties: Humanitarian-Military Technologies and their Discontents." Speech delivered at the Political Theory Workshop, UCLA, February 3.

Pegg, Scott. 1998. *International Society and the De Facto State.* Aldershot, UK: Ashgate.

Philpott, Daniel. 1999. "Westphalia, Authority, and International Society." *Political Studies* 47:566–589.

———. 2002. "The Challenge of September 11 to Secularism in International Relations." *World Politics* 55:66–95.

Pole Institute. 2003. *Democratic Republic of Congo: Peace Tomorrow?* Goma, March.

Pool, David. 2001. *From Guerrillas to Government: The Eritrean People's Liberation Front.* Oxford: James Currey.

Potgieter, Jakkie. 2000. "Taking Aid from the Devil Himself: UNITA's Support Structures." In *Angola's War Economy: The Role of Oil and Diamonds,* edited by Jakkie Cilliers and Christian Dietrich, 255–273. Pretoria, South Africa: Institute for Security Studies.

Prunier, Gérard. 1997. *The Rwanda Crisis.* New York: Columbia University Press.

———. 2001. "The Catholic Church and the Kivu Conflict." *Journal of Religion in Africa* 31:139–162.

Prunier, Gérard, and Rachel Gisselquist. 2003. "The Sudan: A Successfully Failed State." In Rotberg 2003, 101–127.

Rabasa, Angel, Steven Boraz, Peter Chalk, Kim Cragin, Theodore Karasik, Jennifer Moroney, Kevin O'Brien, and John Peters. 2007. *Ungoverned Territories: Understanding and Reducing Terrorism Risks.* Santa Monica: RAND Corp.

Radu, Michael. 1990. *The New Insurgencies: Anti-Communist Guerrillas in the Third World.* London: Transaction Publishers.

Raeymaekers, Timothy, and Koen Vlassenroot. 2004. "The Politics of Intervention and Rebellion in Ituri: The Emergence of a New Political Complex?" *African Affairs* 103:385–412.

Raeymaekers, Timothy, Ken Menkhaus, and Koen Vlassenroot. 2008. "State and Non-state Regulation in African Protracted Crises: Governance without Government?" *Afrika Focus* 21 (2): 7–21.

Rajasingham-Senanayake, Darini. 1999. "The Dangers of Devolution: The Hidden Economies of Armed Conflict." In Rotberg 1999, 57–70.

Rajamohan, P. G. 2004. "Communist Party of Nepal (Maoists)." Institute for Conflict Management, New Delhi.

Reno, William. 1995. *Corruption and State Politics in Sierra Leone.* New York: Cambridge University Press.

——. 1998. *Warlord Politics and African States.* Boulder: Lynne Rienner.

——. 2001. "How Sovereignty Matters: International Markets and the Political Economy of Local Politics in Weak States." In Callaghy, Kassimir, and Latham 2001, 197–215.

Rich, Paul, and Richard Stubbs. 1997. *The Counter-Insurgent State: Guerrilla Warfare and State Building in the Twentieth Century.* New York: St. Martin's.

Richardson, John, Jr. 2004. "Violent Conflict and the First Half Decade of Open Economy Policies in Sri Lanka: A Revisionist View." In Winslow and Woost 2004, 41–72.

Riehl, Volker. 2001. *Who Is Ruling in South Sudan? The Role of NGOs in Rebuilding Socio-political Order.* Uppsala, Sweden: Nordiska Afrikainstitutet.

Roberts, Michael. 2009. *Confrontations in Sri Lanka: Sinhalese, LTTE and Others.* Colombo, Sri Lanka: Vijitha Yapa Publications.

Roitman, Janet. 2001. "New Sovereigns: Regulatory Authority in the Chad Basin." In Callaghy, Kassimir, and Latham 2001, 240–266.

——. 2005. *Fiscal Disobedience: An Anthropology of Economic Regulation in Central Africa.* Princeton: Princeton University Press.

Rolandsen, Oystein. 2005. *Guerrilla Government: Political Changes in the Southern Sudan During the 1990's.* Uppsala, Sweden: Nordiska Afrikainstitutet.

Romano, David. 2004. "Safe Havens as Political Projects: The Case of Iraqi Kurdistan." In Kingston and Spears 2004, 153–166.

Romkema, Hans. 2001. *An Analysis of the Civil Society and Peace-Building Prospects in the North and South Kivu Provinces, Democratic Republic of Congo.* Bukavu, D.R. Congo: Life & Peace Institute.

Romkema, Hans, and Koen Vlassenroot. 2002. "The Emergence of a New Order? Resources and War in Eastern Congo." *Journal of Humanitarian Assistance,* October 28. http://jha.ac/articles/a111.htm.

Rosenau, James. 1992. "Governance, Order and Change in World Politics." In *Governance without Government: Order and Change in World Politics,* edited by James Rosenau and Ernst-Otto Czempiel, 1–29. Cambridge: Cambridge University Press.

Ross, Michael. 2004. "How Do Natural Resources Influence Civil War? Evidence from Thirteen Cases." *International Organization* 58:35–67.

Rotberg, Robert I., ed. 1999. *Creating Peace in Sri Lanka: Civil War and Reconciliation.* Washington, DC: Brookings Institution Press.

——, ed. 2003. *State Failure and State Weakness in a Time of Terror.* Washington, DC: Brookings Institution Press.

——, ed. 2004. *When States Fail: Causes and Consequences.* Princeton: Princeton University Press.

Rubongoya, Joshua. 1995. "The Bakonjo-Baamba of Uganda: A Colonial and Post Colonial Integration and Ethnocide." *Studies in Conflict and Terrorism* 18 (2): 75–92.

Sageman, Mark. 2008. "Does Osama Still Call the Shots? Debating the Containment of al Qaeda's Leadership." *Foreign Affairs* 87:163–166.

Samaranayake, Gamini. 2002. "Ethnic Conflict and Guerrilla Warfare of the Liberation Tigers of Tamil Eelam in Sri Lanka." In *Ethnicity and Polity in South Asia,* edited by Girin Phukon, New Delhi: South Asian Publishers.

Sambandan, V. S. 2003. "LTTE Chief Inaugurates Police Headquarters." *The Hindu,* September 7.

Sambanis, Nicholas. 2001. "Do Ethnic and Nonethnic Civil Wars Have the Same Causes? A Theoretical and Empirical Inquiry." *Journal of Conflict Resolution* 45 (3): 259–282.

Sanderatne, Nimal. 2000. *Economic Growth and Social Transformations: Five Lectures on Sri Lanka.* Colombo, Sri Lanka: Tamarind Publications.

Sarvananthan, Muttukrishna. 2005. *An Introduction to the Conflict Time Economy of the North and East Province.* Colombo, Sri Lanka: Point Pedro Institute.

Sassoli, Marco. 2006. "Transnational Armed Groups and International Humanitarian Law." Occasional paper 6, Program on Humanitarian Policy and Conflict Research, Harvard University.

Schatzberg, Michael G. 1988. *The Dialectics of Oppression in Zaire.* Bloomington: University of Indiana Press.

Scott, James. 1990. *Domination and the Arts of Resistance: Hidden Transcripts.* New Haven: Yale University Press.

Scroggins, Deborah. 2004. *Emma's War: Love, Betrayal and Death in the Sudan.* London: Harper Collins.

Sengupta, Somini. 2005. "Where Maoists Still Matter." *New York Times,* October 30.

Seneviratna, Anuradha. 2001. *The Lions and the Tigers: Religious and Cultural Background of the Sinhala-Tamil Relations.* Nugegoda, Sri Lanka: Sarasavi Publishers.

Shain, Yossi. 1989. *The Frontier of Loyalty: Political Exiles in the Age of the Nation-State.* Middletown, CT: Wesleyan University Press.

Shain, Yossi, and Aharon Barth. 2003. "Diasporas and International Relations Theory." *International Organization* 57 (Summer): 449–479.

Shearing, Clifford. 2006. "Reflections on the Refusal to Acknowledge Private Governments." In Wood and Dupont 2006, 11–32.

Shivji, Issa. 1996. *Intellectuals at the Hill: Essays and Talks, 1963–1993.* Dar es Salaam, Tanzania: Dar es Salaam University Press.

Silverstein, Ken. 2007. "Parties of God: The Bush Doctrine and the Rise of Islamic Democracy." *Harper's,* March, 33–44.

Sivakumaran, Sandesh. 2009. "Courts of Armed Opposition Groups: Fair Trials or Summary Justice?" *Journal of International Criminal Justice* 7: 489–513.

Sivathamby, Karthigesu. 2005. *Being Tamil and Sri Lankan.* Colombo, Sri Lanka: Aivakam.

Skaperdas, Stergios. 2002. "Warlord Competition." *Journal of Peace Research* 39 (4): 435–446.

Smith, Chris. 1999. "South Asia's Enduring War." In Rotberg 1999, 17–40.

Snodgrass, Donald. 1999. "The Economic Development of Sri Lanka: A Tale of Missed Opportunities." In Rotberg 1999, 89–108.

Somer, Jonathan. 2006. "Acts of Non-State Armed Groups and the Law Governing Armed Conflict." *ASIL Insight* 10 (21). http://www.asil.org/insights060824.cfm.

Spears, Ian S. 2003. "Reflections on Somaliland and Africa's Territorial Order." *Review of African Political Economy* 30 (95): 89–98.

Spruyt, Hendrik. 1994. *The Sovereign State and Its Competitors: An Analysis of Systems Change.* Princeton: Princeton University Press.

Stanislawski, Bartosz. 2008. "Para-States, Quasi-States, and Black Spots: Perhaps Not States, but Not 'Ungoverned Territories,' Either." *International Studies Review* 10 (2): 366–396.

Stearns, Jason. 2008. "Laurent Nkunda and the National Congress for the Defence of the People (CNDP)." *L'Afrique Des Grands Lacs,* Annuaire 2007–2008, 245–267.

Stein, Arthur A., and Steven E. Lobell. 1997. "Geostructuralism and International Politics: The End of the Cold War and the Regionalization of International Security." In Lake and Morgan 1997, 101–124.

Steinberg, Michael. 2000. "Generals, Guerrillas, Drugs, and Third World War-Making." *Geographical Review* 90 (2): 260–267.

Stiansen, Endre. 2002. *Expectations of Development: Female Perspectives on the Present and the Future in Katigiri (Southern Sudan)*. Oslo, Norway: Norwegian Support Group for Peace in the Sudan.

Stokke, Kristian. 2006. "Building the Tamil Eelam State: Emerging State Institutions and Forms of Governance in LTTE-Controlled Areas in Sri Lanka." *Third World Quarterly* 27 (6): 1021–1040.

Subramaniam, Nirupama. 2000. "Tamil Diaspora for Nothing Less than Eelam?" *The Hindu*, November 22.

Sudan Human Rights Association. 2003. *Report of the Field Assessment Visit to the Southern Sudan: 30 April–14 May 2003*, Kampala.

Sudan People's Liberation Movement. 2000. *Peace through Development*. Nairobi: Sudan People's Liberation Movement.

Sundnes, Frode. 2004. "Land of Plenty, Plenty of Land? Revival of Livelihoods and Emerging Conflicts in Yirol County, a Liberated Area of the Southern Sudan." Master's thesis, Norwegian University of Life Sciences.

Swamy, M. R. Narayan. 2002. *Tigers of Lanka*. New Delhi: Konark Publishers.

Tambiah, Stanley. 1986. *Sri Lanka: Ethnic Fratricide and the Dismantling of Democracy*. Chicago: University of Chicago Press.

——. 1996. *Leveling Crowds: Ethnonationalist Conflicts and Collective Violence in South Asia*. Berkeley: University of California Press.

Tambo, Oliver. 1980. "Statement on Signing Declaration, on Behalf of the ANC and Umkhonto We Sizwe, Adhering to the Geneva Conventions of 1949 and Protocol 1 of 1977, at the Headquarters of International Committee of the Red Cross, Geneva." ANC press release, November 28.

TamilNet. 1997. "Tamil People Flock to New LTTE Courts," September 25. http://www.tamilnet.com/art.html?catid=13&artid=7328.

——. 2002a. "LTTE Opens First Thamileelam Court in Trincomalee District," December 2. http://www.tamilnet.com/art.html?catid=13&artid=7925.

——. 2002b. "LTTE Police Stations 'Not a New Phenomenon'—Balasingham," December 3. http://www.tamilnet.com/art.html?catid=13&artid=7932.

——. 2003. "Thamil Eelam Judiciary Said a Basis for Rebuilding Northeast," October 30. http://www.tamilnet.com/art.html?catid=79&artid=10277.

Tamils Rehabilitation Organization. 2004. *Reconstruction and Rehabilitation Towards Peace-Building—Challenges, Opportunities and Engagement of Diaspora*. Report of the conference held by TRO, Colombo, Sri Lanka, June 18–19.

Taylor, Brian, and Roxana Botea. 2008. "Tilly Tally: War-Making and State-Making in the Contemporary Third World." *International Studies Review* 10 (1): 27–56.

Thapa, Manjushree. 2005. *Forget Kathmandu: An Elegy for Democracy*. London: Penguin.

Thies, Cameron, and David Sobek. 2010. "War, Economic Development, and Political Development in the Contemporary International System." *International Studies Quarterly* 54:267–287.

Tilly, Charles. 1985. "War Making and State Making as Organized Crime." In *Bringing the State Back In*, edited by Peter Evans, Dietric Rueschmeyer, and Theda Skocpol, 169–191. Cambridge: Cambridge University Press.

——. 1990. *Coercion, Capital, and the European State, AD 990–1990*. Cambridge: Basil Blackwell.

———. 2003. *The Politics of Collective Violence.* Cambridge: Cambridge University Press.

Timmons, Jeffrey. 2006. "Taxation and Credible Commitment: The Fiscal Basis of Social, Worker and Corporate Welfare in the OECD." Unpublished manuscript, UCLA.

Treasury Department. 2007. "Treasury Targets Charity Covertly Supporting Violence in Sri Lanka," November 17. http://www.ustreas.gov/press/releases/hp683.htm.

Tull, Denis. 2004. "The Reconfiguration of Political Order in Postcolonial Africa: A Case Study from North Kivu (DR Congo)." PhD diss., University of Hamburg.

Tull, Denis, and Andreas Mehler. 2005. "The Hidden Costs of Power-sharing: Reproducing Insurgent Violence in Africa." *African Affairs* 104 (416): 375–398.

Tvedt, Terje. 1994. "The Collapse of the State in Southern Sudan after the Addis Ababa Agreement: A Study of Internal Causes and the Role of the NGOs." In Harir and Tvedt 1994, 69–104.

UNORHCS (United Nations Office of the Resident and Humanitarian Coordinator for the Sudan). 2004a. "Sudan Transition and Recovery Database: Rumbek County." Version 2, 23, March.

———. 2004b. "Sudan Transition and Recovery Database: Yei County." Version 2, 6, April.

United Nations. 2003. "Sri Lanka: Assessment of Needs in the Conflict Affected Areas." Report cowritten by Asian Development Bank, United Nations, and World Bank. Colombo, Sri Lanka.

United Nations Panel of Inquiry. 2001a. *Report of the Panel of Experts on the Illegal Exploitation of Natural Resources and Other Forms of Wealth of the Democratic Republic of the Congo.* New York: United Nations.

United Nations Panel of Inquiry. 2001b. *Addendum to the Report of the Panel of Experts on the Illegal Exploitation of Natural Resources and Other Forms of Wealth of the Democratic Republic of the Congo.* New York: United Nations.

———. 2002. *Final Report of the Panel of Experts on the Illegal Exploitation of Natural Resources and Other Forms of Wealth of the Democratic Republic of the Congo.* New York: United Nations.

United Nations Security Council. 2003. "Resolution 1493," July 28.

Uyangoda, Jayadeva. 2005. "Ethnic Conflict, the State, and the Tsunami Disaster in Sri Lanka." *Inter-Asia Cultural Studies* 6 (3): 341–352.

———. 2008. *The Way We Are: Politics of Sri Lanka 2007–2008.* Colombo, Sri Lanka: Social Scientists Association.

Vazquez, Michael C. 2000. "The Guerrilla Professor: A Conversation with Ernest Wamba dia Wamba." *Transition* 10 (1): 140–159.

Vega, Luis Mercier. 1969. *Guerrillas in Latin America: The Technique of the Counter-State.* New York: Praeger.

Vinci, Anthony. 2006. "A Conceptualization of Warlords as Sovereign Non-State Actors." Paper presented at the annual meeting of the International Studies Association, San Diego.

———. 2008. "Anarchy, Failed States, and Armed Groups: Reconsidering Conventional Analysis." *International Studies Quarterly* 52 (2): 295–314.

Viterna, Jocelyn. 2006. "Pulled, Pushed, and Persuaded: Explaining Women's Mobilization into the Salvadoran Guerrilla Army." *American Journal of Sociology* 112 (1): 1–45.

Vlassenroot, Koen, and Chris Huggins. 2004. *Land, Migration, and Conflict in Eastern D.R. Congo.* Pretoria, South Africa: Institute for Security Studies.

Walzer, Michael. 2004. *Arguing about War.* New Haven: Yale University Press.

Weber, Cynthia. 1998. "Performative States." *Millennium—Journal of International Studies* 27:77–95.

Weinstein, Jeremy. 2003. "Inside Rebellion: The Political Economy of Rebel Organiza-tion." PhD diss., Harvard University.

——. 2007. *Inside Rebellion: The Politics of Insurgent Violence.* Cambridge: Cambridge University Press.

Weiss, Herbert F., and Tatiana Carayannis. 2005. "The Enduring Idea of Congo." In *Borders, Nationalism and the African State,* edited by Ricardo Laremont, 160–177. Boulder, CO: Lynne Rienner.

Welch, Claude. 1975. "Ideological Foundations of Revolution in Kwilu." *African Studies Review* 18 (2): 116–128.

Wickham-Crowley, Timothy. 1987. "The Rise (and Sometimes Fall) of Guerrilla Gov-ernments in Latin America." *Sociological Forum* 2 (3): 473–499.

Wijemanne, Adrian. 2002. "Sudan Peace Accord and Sri Lanka," July 23. http://www.tamilnation.org.

Wimmer, Andreas. 1997. "Who Owns the State? Understanding Ethnic Conflict in Post-Colonial Societies." *Nations and Nationalism* 3 (4): 631–666.

Winslow, *Deborah,* and Michael Woost, eds. 2004. *Economy, Culture, and Civil War in Sri Lanka.* Bloomington: Indiana University Press.

Wolters, Stephanie. 2004. "Continuing Instability in the Kivus: Testing the DRC Transition to the Limit." Occasional paper 94, October. Pretoria, South Africa: Institute of Security Studies.

Wondu, Steven. 2002. *The Challenges of Peace.* Washington, DC: U.S. Institute of Peace.

Wood, Elisabeth. 2000. *Forging Democracy from Below: Insurgent Transitions in South Africa and El Salvador.* New York: Cambridge University Press.

——. 2003. *Insurgent Collective Action and Civil War in El Salvador.* New York: Cam-bridge University Press.

——. 2006. "Variation in Sexual Violence during War." *Politics & Society* 34 (3): 307–341.

——. 2008. "The Social Processes of Civil War: The Wartime Transformation of Social Networks." *Annual Review of Political Science* 11:539–61.

Wood, Jennifer, and Benoit Dupont, eds. 2006. *Democracy, Society, and the Governance of Security.* Cambridge: Cambridge University Press.

Yongo-Bure, B. 1988. "The First Decade of Development in the Southern Sudan." In Arou and Yongo-Bure 1988.

——. 1993. "The Underdevelopment of the Southern Sudan since Independence." In Daly and Sikainga 1993.

Young, Crawford. 1994. *The African Colonial State in Comparative Perspective.* New Haven: Yale University Press.

——. 2002. "Contextualizing Congo Conflicts: Order and Disorder in Postcolonial Africa." In Clark 2002a, 13–32.

——. 2006. "The Heart of the African Conflict Zone: Democratization, Ethnicity, Civil Conflict, and the Great Lakes Crisis." *Annual Review of Political Science* 9:301–328.

Young, Crawford, and Thomas Turner. 1985. *The Rise and Decline of the Zairian State.* Madison: University of Wisconsin Press.

Young, Tom. 1997. "A Victim of Modernity? Explaining the War in Mozambique." In Rich and Stubbs 1997, 120–151.

Zahar, Marie-Joelle. 2001. "Protégés, Clients, Cannon Fodder: Civil-Militia Relations in Internal Conflicts." In Chesterman 2001, 43–66.

Zartman, William, ed. 1995. *Collapsed States: The Disintegration and Restoration of Legitimate Authority.* Boulder, CO: Lynne Rienner.

Zegveld, Liesbeth. 2002. *Accountability of Armed Opposition Groups in International Law.* Cambridge: Cambridge University Press.

Index

Page numbers followed by letters *f* and *t* refer to figures and tables, respectively.

CPSIA information can be obtained at www.ICGtesting.com
Printed in the USA
LVOW07s0801230615

443173LV00027B/36/P